A Smudge in Time

The unfolding of our past present and future, as was foretold by those few blessed with the true gift of prophecy

George E Moss

Gemma Books

Gemma Books
Ruyton
Charlmead
East Wittering
West Sussex
PO20 8DN
e-mail: georgemoss@onetel.net.uk

A CIP catalogue number for this book is available from the British Library.

Printed and bound in Great Britain.

ISBN 1 902320 19 0

About the author

George E Moss C.Chem., F.R.S.C. is now a retired independent forensic scientist. He has the experiences of scientific research, development and consultancy through half a century. In 1972 he set up his own practice … Commercial & Forensic Laboratories in Reading, Berkshire. The laboratories handled an incredibly varied workload at a time when it was becoming more and more fashionable for firms to contract out matters that were technical or chemical conundrums. The preparation of scientific court evidence, a growth factor in the latter decades, became an area of personal expertise; leading to casework in several of London's terrorist bombing trials.

Affirmation

As a forensic scientist I am well versed in the principle of the sworn statement, and there are many of my professional acquaintance frequenting the law courts, who know that I would not take such a matter lightly. Regarding the content of this book, there may be some readers who feel they have reason to doubt certain parts. It may therefore assist if I give my formal testimony as to its nature and its truth.

I accordingly swear that:

(1) The chapters 1-24 have all been written with reference to known facts and/or reported data.

(2) Accounts of the two clairvoyant readings are consistent with my notes taken at the time and have been checked by she who shared that experience.

(3) Every detail of the adventure described in chapter 6 is correct, except for the use of fictional names for those participating.

(4) The passages of spirit communication contained in chapters 25-29 and appendices III-VII happened exactly as described. They were witnessed by those present including myself and are as recorded on tape.

(5) The various prophecies cited are as accounted in the Holy Bible, other historic writings and as reported from Mary's visions.

(6) Chapters 30-31 describe how things *are* in the mid-21st century. They do not represent a prediction but are merely my own thoughts concerning our possible future development. The comet of 2061 however, has its precise schedule and should appear in the heavens in that year.

We can concentrate on a question and intuitively know the answer immediately, or it comes to us in wonderful "coincidental" ways through a newspaper article, a book or a comment made to us. We begin to understand that we're a part of the cosmic dance. Balance becomes an expression of energy, which we have the tools to comprehend and orchestrate ourselves: we want to for we are no longer on "automatic pilot."

Chris Griscom *Time is an Illusion*

To all those who truly seek the meaning of life and mystical writings, the illusion of time, our place in the universe, the human record to date and what the future holds.

Contents

Acknowledgements

Over the years, I have been a scientist and have subscribed to the scientific method. But in researching the material for this book, I have deliberately ignored the normal boundary markers set by 'established' science, partly because many of the important factors in life are not of that domain and partly because answers to certain key questions can only be obtained from elsewhere. In my research, I have continued to subscribe to some of the ways of the forensic scientist, valuable in piecing together the many clues and scraps of information that make up our human story. It is a sound basic principle, where forensic investigation is concerned, to look at the various pieces of circumstantial evidence, bring them together, and see if a meaningful pattern emerges. There are 'rich pickings' to be had from a wide variety of literature, for which I am humbly grateful, to so many able and distinguished authors.

I acknowledge with thanks the writings of all those authors whose works are listed in the bibliography without which, this book would simply not have been possible. Those works embrace a great many subjects: history, prehistory, anthropology, palaeontology, science, religion, spiritualism, mysticism, new age, crop circles, psychiatry, aural field energy, healing, philosophy, prophecy, art, travel, poetry and include a number of biographies. My debt to those authors is huge and my thanks sincere.

Many of the writings have been inspired and my debt is therefore not confined just to Earth plane. In fact, in order to adequately research our connection to spirit realm, I was drawn to sit in with a spirit/healing circle; a most excellent circle that had already enjoyed several decades of dedicated work. I have continued to sit regularly during the six years of working on this book. My thanks to Leslie and all concerned. As a result of this I have found myself in the privileged position of being able to seek answers to certain questions or confirm information, through spirit communication (all recorded and transcribed). In this way it has been possible to make clearer statements on such puzzling topics as: the Tunguska event, the Noah's ark story, the Nazca plateau markings of Peru, religious teachings, Earth energies, the nature of crop circles and the subtleties of time and prediction.

I am therefore deeply indebted to many information sources both in this world and the next.

And as regards the mechanics of getting data to finally assemble onto the computer and diskettes, I am indebted to David for sorting technical problems and encouraging me to press the right buttons. I am indebted to Ann, Sara, Mark, Paul and family in general, for mysteriously guiding so many helpful reference books into the library *at just the appropriate time*, for putting up with me and for assisting with proof reading. The way in which certain books for reference have just 'popped up' when needed, has in fact been quite remarkable. My thanks to Isabel and John, who had at one time, an interest in Adolf Hitler and passed me the four biographies. There was no need to search further for *that* information. And my thanks to Florence who, during the period of writing must have sent me ten books, all of which contributed handsomely and arrived during the course of appropriate sections. The final one ... *The Holographic Universe* ... took me quite by surprise and turned up half way through the final chapter. Perfect!

I would make special mention of the translation of the Holy Bible in Modern English by Ferrar Fenton. The Bible quotations that I have selected are mostly from this work. It is a translation into 20th century English direct from Hebrew, Chaldee and Greek. This has to be seen as a spectacular and dedicated work. Where appropriate, and credited in the text, I have also used the valuable Emphatic Diaglott translation of the New Testament from the Greek by Benjamin Wilson.

My thanks to Ian Forson for his interest and enthusiasm around the time that the first draft came together. His efforts in editing the work and proof reading at that critical stage are much appreciated.

And my thanks to Prospero Books of Chichester for organising publication in a professional way and for providing helpful guidance to aid completion.

The general point I would make is that I have been helped enormously in a number of ways by many, for which I am truly grateful.

Lastly but by no means least, this work includes numerous quotations, for which I have earnestly sought permission during the course of the past year. Many publishers, authors or agents have responded well and I take pleasure in thanking all those who have granted permission or have offered helpful information. Since copyright is currently deemed to endure seventy years following an author passing to spirit, it is perhaps not surprising that its whereabouts is sometimes difficult to trace. This difficulty has been exacerbated in recent years by changes in the publishing industry and by the world becoming a busier place. My applications have sometimes circled the world to no avail! A very small number of such quotations have nevertheless still been included in this work, where I have felt that such inclusion can only bring joy to all concerned. And needless to say, I shall be most pleased to hear from any I have failed to reach, following this initial short print run. And my sincere apologies to any that feel I may have transgressed in this.

Foreword

This book, by design, reads with some of the character of a novel but unlike a novel, it has not one single story line but many. These however, in some measure add up to trace the one big story, that of the human species upon this planet. During its narrative and dialogue, four major questions are addressed: Where are we from? What are we? Do we stand alone in the universe? Where are we heading? Ah ... you will say ... a philosophy! But let me quickly say this is not intended as a *stuffy scientific* work of philosophy. I subscribe to the principle that a book should be read and enjoyed, not worked at. Therefore like life, this is a collection of stories and again, like life itself, they represent truth and authenticity of setting.

Read this book and you will know yourself, your planet, some of the wonders of its past and what the future holds. You will understand the true nature of life and what we inadequately call death, what lies behind the world religions, and something of the changes that must come about as we navigate the 21st century.

Humanity has always been of a complex nature, an intimate blend of the spirit being and the material animal. It is of course the material self that is so strongly evident in today's Western World culture. While that part of our development has its justifications and admirable achievements, there are clearly deep pitfalls and dangers in becoming overly materialistic. The spirit within may well become so stifled as to be totally ignored by some, but the spark of spirit is always there, waiting to be rekindled. The rampant materialism that we have today, is a far departure from the styles of earlier world cultures. And there may be so much that we can still learn from those earlier societies, that were so much more sensitive to environment and who took such account of their inner spirituality. After all, they were our beginning ... our ancestors. We share their genes. They were *us*. Accordingly, the early chapters reach into a small sample of those early cultures.

Over a time span of two million years, as the human story began to unfold, its grand design must of necessity break into a network of different life patterns. These would have their tenuous connections, while each one would be an influence on what was to follow. Seen against the time scale of the parental solar system and the universe itself, two million years is but a brief spell. Nevertheless, this has still been ample time for humankind to develop and leave its residues upon the planet surface. The visible dross from mining, deforestation and nuclear testing will endure long into our future. Yet our brief time here is but a *'smudge'*. And in the poetic words of Gerard Manley Hopkins, our planet *'... wears man's smudge and shares man's smell... '* He understood well the way of it.

A fuller account of a magical few days in May just prior to committing this book to the computer and the inspiration of Sir George Trevelyan reciting the poem 'God's Grandeur', is given in Appendix II.

There is one further statement I would wish to make. If this book were to be written from a purely scientific and material viewpoint, it would be incomplete, would provide no answers and would give inadequate indication of our future path. In the accounts and story lines that follow, I therefore whole-heartedly embrace both the material and the non-material aspects of life, as is appropriate for the complex beings that we are. There may be a small minority of western scientists who would agree this approach; notably I would think, Carl Gustav Jung, who was one to clearly recognise and write about that non-material element of our being that activates the joys of synchronicity and guidance.

God's Grandeur

The world is charged with the grandeur of God.
It will flame out, like shining from shook foil;
It gathers to a greatness, like the ooze of oil
Crushed. Why do men then now not reck his rod?
Generations have trod, have trod, have trod;
And all is seared with trade; bleared, smeared with toil;
And wears man's smudge and shares man's smell: the soil
Is bare now, nor can foot feel, being shod.

And, for all this, nature is never spent;
There lives the dearest freshness deep down things;
And though the last lights off the black West went
Oh, morning, at the brown brink eastwards, springs -
Because the Holy Ghost over the bent
World broods with warm breast and with ah! bright wings.

Gerard Manley Hopkins 1877

Humankind now stands at the threshold of a new age. It is a time to pause and to be analytical of ourselves as well as our position. It is a time to reach within and to grow in spirit. We stand where we are, as the result of four major influences.

Firstly, there was the dawn of our being ... in the African Rift Valley, which became the fount of many tribal cultures. In those tribal communities, our oneness with nature was well observed, as was the inner voice of guidance. Those genetic codes and mental urges from times past remain, and there is much that we may still learn from reflecting on ourselves as we were then, in that wild and less complex setting.

Secondly, there has been the important matter of belief. At a glance, our belief systems have been numerous, but all are evolved from just one central source. Religion, however we choose to define it, overlaps or embraces true prophecy, 'miraculous' vision, healing, matters loosely termed as 'psychic' and inspired teachings from acclaimed masters. All such matters must be faced with due enquiry. It is fundamental to our *raison d'être* that we consider the factors which have shaped and continue to shape our spiritual selves. Likewise, it is fundamental that we recognise ourselves as the spirit beings that we are, and find our God connections.

Thirdly, the developing materialism has been such a powerful influence upon the last four centuries, not least the computer, a device that will re-shape our logic, such that fudged issues and half-truths will eventually become outmoded. Whilst much has been achieved which is admirable, it remains important that guidelines are devised to protect other values vital to our continued existence upon this planet. Material progression *must* walk hand in hand with both love and wisdom, or be short lived.

Fourthly, there is the influence of our present world condition. There is our own free will factor, and there are certain other processes which prevail; well recognised by some and not accounted as yet by many. We do not stand alone in this universe. It would be extreme self-centred arrogance to suppose otherwise. Prospects for the human race are excellent if we will but allow. Guidance is to hand. Already the first faltering step that will lead us away from nuclear oblivion has been taken. This is a special time for planet Earth and all life thereon, a time to reflect on the ways of our immediate past, in order that the path to a worthy future is more clearly seen. It is for us a time of expanding awareness, of flowering prophecies and of growing spirit. As we progress into a new millennium, a wondrous future for humankind unfolds...

PART 1

Patterns of a Tribal Dawn

> *This planet is so very young that souls who come to inhabit it, come to learn. That is what you must always remember about this Earthly planet.*
> Salumet

Earth's early cultures achieved remarkable developments, not least the *shamanic principle*, which utilises out-of-body excursion and has its strong connections with mysticism and branches of modern medicine.

Chapter I

On the Savannah

Darkness slipped away. A first flush of dawn spread wide across the far horizon. All life stood out stark black against the muted gold that now touched and crept into low grey cloud. This cloud seemed to be stretched taut across the gathering half-light, and this cloud would bring the first rains of the wet season. Even now, all life out there on the flood plain could sense the moisture in the air. No breeze. All remained still.

Sounds of the Savannah slowly mellowed out from the formless murmur of a waking world. To the left, acacias stood with twisted trunks and flattened canopies, a natural beauty of form against that golden backcloth. Much of the scene was open dry scrub with parched pale soil and grass in languid clumps, now hushed until rustled by the first breath that would come with the rains. Over there, no clumps but just an endless bristled carpet going away into the distance, reaching to where the vision blurs. Far, far beyond were the mountains that form the edge of this terrain; for this was a special place and a special time.

Out there he could see gazelle. They were a good sight. They were at some considerable distance and looked the size of ants, but he could just see ... make them out against the brightness of the sky. He had watched for some time and had taken in their mood. Quiet. No sign of disturbance. She now joined him. Her approach had been silent, but he sensed her there, at his side. 'Eyes' had seen them too. Food was needed. A gazelle would be food for several days and would provide another skin and with the rains coming...

Their language was too brief ... clipped, helped out with many gestures, but they seemed to know unvoiced ideas and the eyes helped. He *loved* her dark eyes. She had joined their group from another band of hunter-gatherers over towards the mountains, a step that had helped to establish a useful alliance. There had been expeditions and hunts when the combined numbers of the two groups had been useful. She made contact with her people from time to time when out on the plain with a *gathering* party. He, 'Bush' had always called her 'Eyes'.

The hunting party for that day would be the four fit men. They were in fine shape. Very fit, by our standards, they were tall athletes. Their names were simple, taken from the environment or from the tasks they knew.

'Rocker', was best at shaping the stone and he knew the rocks and where to find them. He could flake the stone and could always find a good cutting edge. Sometimes the children would try to copy, and theirs would fly into a dozen or more pieces, to the amusement of those watching. The knack was to strike in just the right place with just the right touch.

'Burn', was fire-maker or more accurately, fire-keeper. There had been times before a storm, when a streak of fire had come from the sky and the grass and small trees had burnt. This was a time when fire could be collected ... carefully and with respect. Glowing sticks were best. They kept the fire longer than the grass. Eyes had described, by drawing with a stick, a smoking mountain where fire could be had, but it was at too great a distance. So fire had to be kept. Enough glowing embers and a turf on top was good. And in the rains it must be kept dry. A wooden torch could be used for carrying fire, but best was a large animal skull enclosing the embers.

The keeping of fire was an important and exacting job. Meat was the better to eat if cooked. There was less sickness, and it was good next day. Fire made spear points hard. Horns too ... Horns were best for digging roots. And fire at night meant safety from the prowling beasts that hunt the plains.

'Bush' earned his name by his ways ... his way of stalking. With grass and twigs stuck in a headband, he looked so like a bush and if he kept downwind, could get in really close to unsuspecting herds. She had once asked him about Juk's name and he had explained it after some hesitation: 'Juk is good with catfish. He spears them in the lagoons over by the great lake... But he gets so pleased with a good fish and hurries out and we hear the sound of his feet... They go juk! ... juk! ... juk! ... as they draw from the mud.'

Her lips had stretched, her eyes sparkled and little noises had come from her throat. He loved her like this. She was his mate, but they lived as a group ... an effective hunter-gatherer group ... a team. There were eleven including the two little ones. They had been twelve but life cannot be taken for granted on the Savannah. There is danger and there are things not yet understood.

'Zeb' would stay in camp this day with the women and children. He had had the bad luck to lose foothold on a tumbling rock and had received a bad cut. The wound had stayed clean and the red death had not got into it. He was grateful to 'Dreams' who knew something of the mysteries of keeping life. She knew about the fleshy clumps of a plant (now called *sansevieria*) growing near the lake. Some fronds of this were gathered and twisted over the wound so the juice ran into it. Where the flesh gaped, she had skilfully inserted two thorns into the skin and had drawn them together with bark thread. It was now healing but he would feel at risk until he could again run. But his stronger thought was: 'If this skill comes from her dreaming, then it is well she dreams ... it is well.'

The two other women were 'Figgie' who always enjoys the fruit gathering. While others of a gathering party might dig for roots, pick leaves or catch lizards, Figgie would always prefer to collect fruit and invariably managed to find some. Then there was 'Starfire'... Her name was of a stranger origin. In fact, as a hunter-gatherer group, this one was blessed with a good mixture of types and talents. She had always been so named. It was night at the time of her birth, but that night the sky had lit up. A star had spread a fire across the night sky. It had lasted all that night and two more. The heavens were ablaze, so much so, the grass and trees were lit like it was a full moon and more. Long will that strange night be remembered. And so, the child whose birth was with such wondrous heavenly display was named 'Starfire'. She was seen as one who is 'special' and she seemed to have certain deep insights that they valued at times of decision-making.

Zeb was the senior in years and carried scars to show. He remembered once when light had streaked from the sky and fired the Savannah. It came with such a crack and boom it made him leap right off the ground. It fired the grass and fire had roared across the scrub and then a sudden wind. The flames had reddened and run with the wind midst angry growls and crackling. Redness of the flame struck contrast with the black smoke swirl while black char flew above trees that became beacons of sparking incandescence. Then came rain. The running fire was quenched and there was left a smoking blackened space, that hissed and wheezed as springing, darting creatures went off running, wild with fear.

He sometimes thought about that day, when helping Rocker chip stone tools at dusk. It was then in the failing light, you could see the little bright sparks that fly and if a big spark lands on a dry leaf, there is a little black mark and smell of smoke, like that day. It also seemed that the fire that spread across the Savannah was like the fire that spread from the star above, but *that* fire had stayed in the sky and had shown no anger and had remained silent. The two were not the same ...

As dawn progressed, the four set out travelling light. They carried sharply pointed wooden spears with thin shafts. Rocker carried a stone sharp-edge ... he usually did. It hung in a leather pouch. At a jogging pace, they kept a keen look out. It became a lengthy trek that took them always nearer to one of the larger lakeside lagoons.

The gazelles had moved further off, towards the water and they had to make a wide detour to avoid a noisy party of apes. The apes were best avoided. They saw from time to time several different kinds. Some kept to the trees, but the ever-shortening rainy seasons were resulting in more scrub with fewer trees. So ape parties foraged on foot more and more ... into the bushy more open parts. Some had adapted well while others had not. Some went on two feet, then loped on four, then changed again. None achieved the style and skills of these fast objective hunters. They had reasoning, developing language, use of skins and shelter, tools, weapons, fire so long as it could be kept, and the ability to travel fast as an organised party.

It was late afternoon when they moved in on their quarry. Bush got in close and disturbed the chosen one towards the other three who sprang up. A spear found its mark and the despatch was quick. Cleanly done. Just the one animal needed, so it was necessary to kill just the once. Rocker worked quickly with his prepared sharp tool. The entrails would be left to lighten the load. The scavengers would waste no time in finding them.

Their prize was now on a slender pole and they would take turns, two carrying, two scouting. The sun was well past zenith and they should move fast. Another small detour to avoid a sabre-toothed cat with kill took them amongst bushy acacias that were clouding with a profusion of small white flowers that belied their thorny character. The unfolding of the flowers was a sure sign the rains were due. Now they were in an altogether greener woodland vegetation, beside the still waters of a lagoon. The level was low and where the water had receded there were rushes, and more striking, much more striking; a wild array of podgy, slimy, glistening rounded humps ... called in today's world *stromatolites*; all anchored firmly near the water's edge. How curiously they lined the shallows! And reaching that little bit too far above the surface in quaint ungainly stance, while further out, hippos were having an afternoon soak. The hippo heads, in some mysterious way, seemed to match the mood of the odd rounded plants. The surreal nature of the scene, momentarily, had galvanised their gaze. The hippos looked, with eyes alert and ears attentive ... and then, before them, was the line of their bathing companions ... entirely faceless, yet with a similar lustre. It was an odd sight. The hunters looked, grunted amongst themselves and looked again, as the hippos stared back. Then following the brief diversion, they were again on their way.

Somewhere up ahead, was the sound of monkeys ... there! They could see their movements in the trees. Passing beneath their chatter, they soon found the arid scrub and were back on course, speeding now across dry expanses away from the water and away from the danger of flash flood. The rains would be just one more day. They knew and felt all the signs. The flood plain waited, and with the first storm, the magic would begin. First the change from muted browns to green. Then a riot of colour as little flowers peep out between the grasses and for a spell, all would be a vibrant energy, accompanied by a multitude of water sounds and the merged, buzzing whisper of insect wings. Dried-out streams would live again and tumble from the mountains, they themselves pigmented by the charge of soils they carry to the lake. Rich orange-brown. Once on the plain, more slowly, then a meandering course across a fugitive flowering fairyland cloaked in the freshness of young grass. On then as far as the eye can see, except for those far mountains that signal the western edge of the Great Rift Valley ... The African Rift Valley and cradle of humankind.

One brief stop for rest they had. That was enough. A well-chosen spot, in a clump of *salvadora* trees. They feasted upon their little fruits hidden amongst the leaves. It was dark as they found camp. Many were the sounds of pleasure at their return. A good fire glowed and this had helped guide the final stage of their return. Zeb had kept the fire, with Burn away, and the children had gathered wood with Figgie and Dreams.

Half the night they sat around the glow of the good fire, stretching their minds to try to recount the happenings of the day. There were pauses for pieces of toasted meat. There were pauses too, when charade had to take over to find expression for their thoughts, and more than once the carrying pole was picked up to demonstrate some tricky manoeuvre. An even flow of language was not easy, any more than it was the custom. Words had to be interspersed with gesture and charade and somehow, transferred thoughts seemed to play a part in their discourse. All this worked well enough. But the really difficult one was trying, with their few simple words, to describe how the stromatolites had looked.

Burn and Rocker arranged the women and children in a row, on their knees, with bottoms in the air. The hunters then put skins over their shoulders and tried to look like hippos, grunting and looking out between the bottoms. The scene was acted out, again and again, each time with some embellishment. Juk moved Figgie's bigger bottom to the middle, between the two children, while Rocker thought Starfire should tilt a little and wobble when a hippo got too near. It became a fun game and finally they all fell about laughing at their ridiculous antics.

They felt good. They had food, shelter and a reasonably safe place for the next few days; and after all, the next few days was their foreseeable future. But futures cannot be predicted with any certainty in this world. Free will and the outside chance take their account.

That night, before sleeping, Bush and Eyes stood together at a short distance from the camp, looking out into the night across the plain. A crescent moon squinted through gathering cloud and gave scarcely sufficient light to cast a shadow. The night was barely tangible and veiled in a windless silence. On nights like this, they sometimes thought of the 11-year old boy. He had been lost ... over by the lake ... at the time of the flash flood ... many moons it was, but still strong in feeling. It was not a conscious thought exactly. It was like he was in the air around them, with them, not far off. His body would, they knew, be somewhere down there, by the lake; but something of him remained with them ... in the air... They felt a certain 'shared feelings cosiness' that seemed to drift around their innermost emotion. Such was this night. A shared and cherished moment of magic ...

> *During the years of fossil hunting at lake Turkana I was aware of more than the experience of discovery; I found within myself a certainty about what I was about to learn. I felt that there, in the arid sediments around that magnificent lake, answers were to be pieced together that went beyond the questions normally asked in science. If we could understand our past, understand what shaped us, then we might gain a glimpse of our future.*
> Richard Leakey/Roger Lewin *Origins Reconsidered*
> Little, Brown and Company

Following a period of survey, the work of searching for hominid fossils to the west of Lake Turkana (in the northern part of what is now Kenya), was now well in progress. Richard Leakey's excavation team was camped by the Nariokotome riverbed. The Nariokotome is one of those rivers that is a dry bed most of the time. It comes to life with the onset of the rains and briefly continues its erosion of what was once the old flood plain. Several 'promising' sites in the area were being studied.

On 23 August 1984, Kamoya Kimeu found a small piece (1.5 X 2.0 inches) of hominid frontal. It had been well spotted on a pebbly slope near the camp. But following a further two hours of laborious soil sieving, nothing else of interest seemed to be forthcoming. The sun was high and it was very hot. The dusty sieving with many black pebbles to stare at in that heat must have been most irksome. It was Frank Brown who suggested a diversion... to see stromatolite fossils, a short drive away. The suggestion was received with a certain enthusiasm. The stromatolites certainly sounded most interesting and a brief respite from the tedious task of that moment would be most welcome.

Living stromatolites are rare in today's world. They are one of nature's oddities. They look like single entities, shaped rather like flattish puffballs and up to four feet across. But they are in fact colonies of single-celled algae and other aquatic microorganisms that build up layer upon layer. They grow in shallow water and they were much more abundant in bygone ages.

The stromatolite fossils were impressive. Richard Leakey, Alan Walker, John Harris and Frank Brown looked admiringly at them. A stunning array of those beautiful and strange curiosities, all lined up just below a ridge. Clearly this had once been a shoreline. Some had split, showing their many layers. A million or so years ago this would have been a living waterside environment. Lake Turkana had since that time contracted and this had now become dry arid, although more than a little interesting, expanse of land.

As the party returned to the campsite, there was a mood of excitement. People were shouting: 'We've found more bone! Lots of skull!' And Kamoya Kimeu sat with the assortment of *Homo erectus* fragments before him. Perseverance at the site over the three weeks that followed, and meticulous re-assembly work, were eventually to produce a nearly complete skeleton.

At the end of the excavation, an area had been cleared and it was evident that it represented the bed of what had once been a body of still shallow water. The surface was now hard. There were no ripples; therefore it was not the lake itself but a smaller body of water, possibly a lagoon. An ancient sand surface. There were indications of reeds, fish and snails on the ancient bed, all being hallmarks of a still lagoon area. The *Homo erectus* had died here in the shallow water.

In the centre of the site, there remained a small thorn tree. The tree, known to some today, as the *wait-a-bit* thorn has hooked thorns and if you snag, then you must wait, sometimes for *quite* a bit. The tree was a nuisance. Richard Leakey was working around the roots when suddenly he saw something out of the corner of his eye and stopped ... stopped and just froze for the moment ... Teeth, and half an upper jaw! The fossil skeleton finally became so complete that it was possible to establish that he was a boy (from pelvis development), that he was eleven years old (from tooth development), that he was of good upright stance and stood between five feet four inches and five feet eight. A good height for a youth of tender years.

'Turkana boy', as a fossil, was a spectacular find. 'Turkana boy', as a time traveller from somewhere in excess of 1.6 million years BC, brings us a precious picture of how we were then as *Homo erectus*. It should also be said that the best dating that we are able to place on such things, by present methods, mostly tend to fall short.

> *Everything earlier than Homo erectus was more apelike ... everything after Homo erectus was distinctly humanlike, in behaviour as well as form. The beginnings of a hunting-and-gathering way of life came with Homo erectus...*
> Richard Leakey/Roger Lewin *Origins Reconsidered*
> Little, Brown and Company

The hunter-gatherer way continued on earth, through the changing conditions of more than 1.6 million years. The changes were immense. One can only imagine inadequate theories regarding the cosmic factors that must have brought about such changes. Theories may be short lived, but facts remain. One fact was the vast glacier that periodically drove southwards. Each time, the snows and ice-front brought changing needs and at the same time was instrumental in presenting fresh possibilities to those early humans. As the ice stacked up, sea levels dropped, exposing land bridges between islands, and larger landmasses appeared. Earth's tectonic plates then strained and heaved to alter things again. Clothing, shelter and migration were all requirements for meeting the new challenges brought about by the advancing glaciers. In the fullness of time, the ice again retreated and sea levels were restored.

Discovery and invention played their part, but of course, in the beginning, certain things such as fire and fire-hardened sticks just happened. They were here long before apes or humans. They were not man-invented. Cooked meat also, just happened when unfortunate animals were unable to escape forest fires. But these happenings were observed and man learnt to make use of them.

Humankind continued with upright stance and met the challenges. In meeting those challenges, man himself changed. Language, skills, tools and the thinking all became extended. He needed a larger brain for all this and steadily, over a million or so years, he got it. There emerged, a new and wiser mankind who was named by his much, much later descendants: *Homo sapiens.* As the more lengthy process of time continued he became even wiser, and so, in recognition of this, he, modern man named this still later development of himself: *Homo sapiens sapiens.*

The species did well to improve its capacity for thought, its skills and mobility. But perhaps the wisest move ... or maybe it was inevitable ... was the move to maintain and strengthen a oneness with nature and that link with whatever it was up there that seemed to tune in ... man with it or it with man? ... Or was it just all a part of that wonderful oneness of being? The early tribal cultures did well to hold on to ... to strengthen ... that primal bonding with the creation.

Chapter II

Aborigine

The lone hunter had, all that day, travelled the songline, sensing its delicate energy as if it were a ley. It had taken him through good landscape of which he felt a bonded part. The feeling was strong. He belonged to that landscape ... a hot and dusty grassland with a scattering of trees. The aromatic eucalypts were there: coolabah, bimbil, ghost gum and scribbly gum with its flaking-off, papery, insect-scribbled bark. They came in small clumps, except for the ghost gum that so often stood alone, an object of sheer delight, with its pure white slender trunk and canopy of small glittering leaves held high. And how the glittering leafy top seemed to hold the sunlight! He had passed by a straggly clump of spike wattle. It was early in the warm season and these trees were festooned with their fluffy yellow flowers and their scent seemed to embrace such a wide expanse. The curious grass trees with huge plumate heads of bristling outgrowth, out of which rose the remains of last year's flower spikes. These had once reached skywards but had since dried in strange fixed snaking postures as if caught in the rhythm of some exotic dance.

In Earth time, these were the days when giant marsupials still roamed the Australian plains. (The giant forms of kangaroo, possum, wombat and a diprotodon were to become extinct by about 12,000 BC.) This was a time when those giant forms were becoming less common, but they were all still there on the plains. The period of the hunter was comfortably within their span, and the terrain was a good deal less arid than it is today, and of course the rabbit and white settler were entirely absent. This was a *dreamed* land that enjoyed respect and spiritual input from those who felt they were a part of that magical country and who travelled its lines of subtle Earth energy. It was as yet unsullied by harsh usage, discord or death wish.

The traveller was now on a low craggy hill from where he was able to survey the beauty of it all. His stance for meditation was the traditional stance, and he looked a fine figure of darkened bronze manhood while remaining motionless up there beside the crag. Vibrant, lustrous and naked apart from the fine film of dust that seemed to make him even more a part of that earthly grandeur. Standing with left leg straight, right knee well bent with sole of foot firmly against the left thigh and the bent knee supported by a wooden spear thrower. The wooden spear was held in the left hand against his chest, pointing skywards and roughly angled in sympathy with the thrower. The right hand hung down to root chakra; and there it was ... the meditative stance of the aborigine hunter.

The breathing settled, and in those moments when the worldly 'logic' mind is stilled, the Ancestral Realm may be accessed through that intuitive door of the subconscious. Now there was the slipping into an altered consciousness ... *tjukurrtjana* ... on the edge of Dreamtime ... ground state of being ... the space of space-time ... the Ancestral Realm. A realm where, as in our dreams, the ordinary laws of time no longer apply and where past, present and future may fold into one. He understood his origins and felt strongly the interconnectedness of all things.

The one God, the original Ancestor, the primal source of creative power had begun the genesis at the very beginning of the Dreamtime. The Great Ancestors were of his, the God's creation.

His people acknowledged a creation scene in which the Great Ancestors of the Dreamtime had *dreamed* the material world and all its life forms out of the boundless continuum and into the sharp 'reality' of the physical existence. The land was 'thought' into being, through the songs, and the subtle lines of energy that connect the mythic events of that creation. The Creative Ancestors left their energetic imprints in the landscape that they had shaped. The creation process continues. The songs continue. The songlines are walked, felt, acknowledged; that was all a part of the connectedness; the ongoingness; the oneness of being, and all this formed a part of the living. By walking the lines as he did, he felt a part of the Ancestor and a part of the continuing creation. Therefore this land was sacred.

The physical world connects with the other-world ... the Dreamtime from which it was derived. Emanations from the Dreamtime determine happenings in the physical, and the voices of the universal Dreaming were there to behold. There was ample proof that this was so. Apart from his being in the dreaming as he stood thus, there were his departed loved ones, who had many times appeared to him in his sleeping dreams, in visions and in the ritual ceremony. Earth death was no end. This was a simple fact, of which he was well aware. Life just continued in that other more nebulous realm. The two worlds were well entwined, each being a part of the other, and it was both appropriate and proper to frequent the bridge between the two and so, facilitate exchanges.

Now, as for the present happening, this was no ordinary exchange. This was not his own mental process, that was for sure ... It was indeed that inner voice, although he could scarcely believe his good fortune. But yes it was the voice within ... and she was to be with child! That was it! A spirit was now ready to enter the egg in her womb, conception could take place and they would be with child! This meant so much ... so much joy. Such wonderful news to take home to Waratah ... news of the awaiting spirit.

Normal consciousness had now returned. She was still in his thoughts... a young mother! He fingered the scar on his left upper arm. It was a pain-share scar. Two years ago she had fallen and was in pain until the bone of her arm had healed. He, as was the custom, had slashed his arm to share her pain. The sharing of the pain had established a kind of bond (what we today would call telepathy). He knew that he had only to touch the scar to open the channel, and his expression of joy would be sent to her. It would be a day or perhaps longer before his return, but at least it was possible to send her the feelings of happiness. He held the scar, lost the worldly connection, and knew that part of him had reached out. That done, he headed in the general direction of home and towards a clump of distant trees that offered the prospect of a few hours rest; necessary before the next day's exertions. The sun was now low, clouds were reaching across the sky and the air held a freshness.

The night was cool. Too cool for sleep, and warmth was needed from the rainbow fires within himself. He was sufficiently well versed in the lore to have knowledge of the coiled rainbow serpent located in the pit of his stomach, four fingers below the navel. By resting his thoughts in the position of the rainbow fires he could raise the energy from there to fill his whole being. Some might know this as the kundalini energy. Comforted by the rising warmth within, he slept soundly. Such was the way of the lone hunter. He was in tune with his landscape, conscious of the subtle energies of his etheric body and able to tap into that resource.

He awakened refreshed and was quickly on his way. The morning air was good. He found young shoots to chew and a few honeypot ants... a delicacy! Beyond the next cluster of trees, there were wallaby. His silent approach went unnoticed and the spear left the thrower with a swift accuracy that felled the one he needed. He was after all a hunter and such a kill had been his objective on this trip. Once back at camp, it would be divided between relatives according to the kinship laws, after a short period of roasting whole, as was the custom, to allow the animal's spirit to escape and return home. This respect for the spirit of the animal was rigidly kept. It was so right that its spirit should receive such acknowledgement. Then the animal body would be divided into cuts and shared.

It would be his mother-in-law who would have the best piece. And curiously, it was she whom he should not face squarely or talk about... except in a joking fashion. The kinship laws were elaborate and were fairly strictly observed. They were in place to keep the lines pure and free from any weakening effect of incest and bad breeding. To this end, mother-in-law involvement in socialising was side-stepped, but she could be referred to jokingly; yet she would receive the best cut of meat. A kind of compensation perhaps? Restraint was advocated where certain other relations were concerned ... brother, sister, daughter ... but the wife's mother received the special consideration. But would it always be necessary to speak of mothers-in-law in a joking style? For just how many millennia would it be necessary for the mother-in-law joke to persist in society?

The kinship laws were also the guidelines to what was allowed in the way of sexual freedoms. The main relationships were ongoing man-woman pairings. These were natural strong bondings and they produced children. But the system, for a number of reasons, also recognised the need for *extramarital* liaisons. These were undertaken, usually with some degree of planning and secrecy. After all, the young single men required proper instruction in sex, from the married women, and the young girls too required initiation. Youth were thus guided in these matters by the more mature of the commune and this was both the norm and the tradition. Much younger children would often imitate the love-making of their elders as a kind of sex game, well in advance of their puberty, and this was often seen as a source of entertainment.

The sexual mimicry arose partly from early instruction that the children received in aspects of hunting. Aborigine children, from a very early age, would become highly skilled in the art of tracking. Any small group of children has the ability to track animal, bird or human and often would. Although out-of-camp liaisons were usually planned with secrecy, couples frequently discovered at some stage in the proceedings, that they had been tracked to the rendezvous where they had been performing before an appreciative young audience. And *voyeuring* in this way was regarded as a kind of sport by the developing children, as a slightly embarrassing nuisance by the two adults, and as a source of great amusement by others who got to know about it.

So in this corner of humankind's past, this was the accepted way: nakedness was the norm, sex and sexuality were socially accepted and not hidden away. Some privacy was sought but was not seen as essential and little or nothing was hidden from the children. The young ones *knew* their parents in whom they had full trust. There were no closed doors, no dark dungeons of the mind ... no hang-ups about sex or clothing or the lack of it, and no frustrations due to alienation. The bonded partners did not exact a full possession of each other, or indeed the child, yet marital bondings remained strong, and parental ties were there as well. The kinship laws embraced this scheme of living and these laws were the influence in many matters. All was well providing the kinship laws were observed; and yet, there was sometimes official disregard of even this overtly permissive pattern on the occasion of the *rain dance*; that fertility ritual that was celebrated at the time of the approaching monsoon. This event seemed to exact an alternative mode of consideration. The whole aspect of sexual events within the fertility ritual was seen as different. It was not a *personal* matter. The ritual took on the character of an entirely impersonal ethos, as human energies bonded with elemental energy in celebration of the season's renewal. Humankind cohabited with nature! This was the essence of it ... and the summer rains would very soon...

He stopped abruptly. Diprotodons! They were quite harmless creatures, being herbivores, but being so big (larger than a hippo and of similar solid build) the diprotodon dung heaps were correspondingly huge, as was this one before him. He looked ahead and could see their small group in the distance. There were three. He would leave them to their quest for sufficient herbage. Times were not easy for them. Today, they had some difficulty finding enough. Soon the rains would come and again there would be plenty for all, for a time at least, until the next drought. They were of course, created by the Great Ancestors and were entitled to their place in this landscape. All were entitled to their place in this landscape: kangaroo, wallaby, wombat, koala, lace monitor, goanna, death adder, blue-tongued skink, red desert scorpion, white cockatoo, honeypot ant and all the rest. And if one species required another for food, this was by design, and this was generally dealt with economically, and so far as man was concerned, there was also that *respect* to be shown for the animal spirit. Respect for the animal and respect for its spirit had a prominence. It was a part of the bonding, the oneness of creation; and if the diprotodons were into decline, in this scheme of things, then it was because the Great Ancestors considered that they have already achieved their purpose here.

The plains had been quiet, but now a rhythmic sound drifted to him. So very faint, yet he instinctively identified it. A hunt was in preparation.

Not his own commune ... another. The larger hunts would involve perhaps twenty men or more and they would be going for one of the larger animals, perhaps kangaroo or diprotodon. One of the party would begin, by *dancing* the animal to be hunted while the others stood in a circle, slapping buttocks to a rhythm. The rhythm of the slapping was steady and continuous. It carried across the plain ... three horizons. At that distance, it came like repeated wind-flutter in dry leaves, but there was the preciseness of the beat within the sound.

Every movement and muscle of the animal would be copied in the dance. It was like its very spirit was drawn to the dancer and held by him. The dance became ecstatic. The eyes of those in the circle became quite glazed. As one dancer collapsed exhausted, another took his place. Each took a turn. A strange energy developed that was not of ordinary consciousness and this was somehow held within the circle. It was of the plain, and of the spirit animal, it was shared; shared and felt, yet remote from any thought or act. The rhythm subtly drifted a little as the charge built. This was a circle of stored energy in which they stood and slapped the rhythm, as each took in the imprint of the animal spirit. All would take a turn in the dance and it would go on for hours, well into the night. All would be ecstatic, and begin to act as one. Then eventually, one would fall, and all would fall with him in a mass of raw energy as the circle finally broke ... imploded. Such would be their preparation for the hunt. They would evoke the spirit of the animal and somehow hold it.

At first light, the hunters would begin their quest, and each would still hold that energy. It would stay with them. With it, they would match the wiles and ways of the animal, until the hunt closed. Then at the kill, its release would be felt by all. His own hunt had been altogether different ... a lone venture ... a personal effort. He had simply gone off into the plains for three days, where he had been a part of that scene and was now returning with meat.

The wallaby was a good weight, but he, Guti, was well equal to the task of carrying it. The distant rhythm faded, now somewhere behind. And beyond the next scattering of wattle, he came upon a gathering party. This was the usual mix of women, children and little ones being carried ... and there was Waratah. Her pitchi was full and all their digging sticks had been busy. They had collected a variety of roots and yams. They had visited the place of the *guruwari*, the place of the earth-rings, where its energy can be felt. Here, the rings are visualised and felt in ceremony, and yams grow in abundance. It had been a profitable forage. In fact, this was a *gatherer-hunter* society in which, typically, the greater part of the food would be 'gathered' by groups such as this, while the men, either alone or in groups, hunted a smaller proportion of the daily diet. And *there* was Kurara. She was clearly pregnant now, and as they walked along, she talked with her foetus, as was to be expected ... as was the custom.

Waratah drew in a sandy patch to show exactly where they had been. Then looking to his eyes: 'You came to me when the clouds came across the sky and the sun was sinking. You were *very* happy.'

'Ah yes, I was thinking how *you'd* look talking to yourself.'

'*What?*' Her eyes searched his, but failed to find meaning.

'Soon you will be like Kurara and will walk along talking. The voices were with me.'

She understood and her face lit ... glowed, no words being necessary.

'Tonight,' he said, 'we should leave camp and be together. Just the two of us, with the trees and the togetherness of the night ... And we will take a handful of brushwood to cover our tracks!'

She hugged his arm: 'We shall not be noticed. There are busy preparations with the rains coming. The men have been pounding the red ochre. It is already mixed with the kangaroo fat. The stilted huts at the billabong are prepared. The palm leaves are inside and soon the waters will be rising.'

'We shall need a good cover of palm leaves ourselves if the monsoon is with us tonight.'

'It is expected.'

'Then we should prepare a place; and it should be well away from those huts!'

It was such an odd time. The kinship laws with their taboos, were an intricate harness, worn the year round by social life. The rules were so keenly observed ... meticulously observed ... but not so during those few days leading up to the monsoon. It was as if the system was accepted, just so long as it had a valve that would blow, and blow well, just once in the year. (As with the Rio carnival or university rag week or even the Roman Bacchanalia.) The rules were relaxed ... well, often much more than relaxed ... sometimes overtly turned on their heads. Even mothers-in-law could find themselves confronted sexually at this time ... and in public! It was all a part of freeing the psyche ... to be as free as the spirit of nature. So that the spirit of nature could be met on equal terms, and to be on equal terms with nature was fitting for the ritual of renewal that loomed.

While Guti enjoyed being a part of nature out there on the plains, he did not exactly wish to be as *free* as nature in himself. He felt his bond with Waratah passionately and was not too keen on the idea of wild public copulation. It somehow felt right *for him* to go off on a hunt at this time; which he did; and, after all, the occasional meat supply was both needed and welcomed. While he was away, there had been no shortage of recruits for the fire dance, that frenzied dance beneath the bundle of burning sparking palm leaves, and minor events leading up to the major ritual of renewal at the actual breaking of the monsoon.

Those who would take part in the ceremony had been chosen. As always, they were the young girls who had already begun menstruating in sympathy with the rains now held by the clouds. They were chosen by their harmony with those rain-clouds; the clouds being themselves seen as a female aspect of nature. Already the thunder rolls echoed through them. Bodies had been rubbed with the red oil and now shone. They were as the *Muna Muna,* mythic daughters of the Great Mother *Kunapipi*, with long-lashed eyes, coffee-tinted skin, firm resplendent bodies, full breasts and outward-reaching nipples. As the ritual advanced, men and Muna Muna would enter the huts with the many palm fronds within. The huts were now the *Nonggaru*, the place of the ring ... the symbolic uterus of the Great Mother. They must all enter the uterus so that they may be reborn. But now their bodies bent to the dance, while a setting sun briefly beamed in beneath rumbling cloud to give their glistening bodies further hues of redness in their wild corroboree.

Waratah and Guti were in each other's arms in a small but cosy bed of dried and yielding grass. Their nest was well thatched over with the palm leaf and the spot was hidden ... well tucked away, midst scrubby bush. Theirs was the personal face of bonding that reaches heights of passion, produces children in love and fondly sees them do their growing up. Their thoughts were of each other and of a ... *the* child. Over there, by the billabong, was the ritual face of bonding, an untamed thing, which reaches far out, away from any loving caress. The ritual begat no children but joined in the charging of an ageing landscape with renewal. And so, on wind's bewitching breath, the landscape waited...

All were attuned to an uninhibited abandon as the dancers entered the nonggaru huts, where *Knaninja*, the spirit of desire was evoked. Their driven energies transformed into a kind of shared unity. Kunapipi would hold and not release them until psyches had been freed by their exchanges.

Only then could each accept rebirth. That was her way ... or so they thought ... that, they thought, was how things were.

Waratah and Guti both knew the moment the child spirit joined them. They hugged and hugged again. They had no clear visual sense of male sperm entering ovum or of matrix organising protoplasm in that initial spark-of-a-moment. Such unnecessary details, were not of their domain ... not appropriate to their time; but they knew that this was the moment of *spirit* conception and it would be this spirit that was the child. They *knew*!

A sudden wind summoned the lightning snake, nature's strident expression of the male energy. The clouds opened as they left the huts, reborn. Then as thunder roared and lightning flashed, they cavorted, squealing their orgasms amid the wet palm trees. Rains thrashed their pulsing bodies and the snake from the sky, flashed and flashed again. Within each flash, a fresh glimpsed fantasy. Wet palm fronds frolicked and partly hid from view the waving lustrous limbs. Arching backs held breasts aloft to seek and meet caress by driven scudding rains; as storm-drenched bodies gasped their small exchange with that same wind, which first had summoned the snake from cloud to seek this kiss of life. It was an elemental orgasm. This was their union with the power of nature, the energy-force that powered their land ... the elemental force that now imbued their land with vibrant vigour, was reborn.

The two in the nest were still entwined. The layered roof remained secure and allowed them to savour this time of their innermost loving.

'Welcome little one. We're pleased to have you join us,' she said, looking down.

'Lovely Waratah ... You talk to your foetus already!'

'Now we are three Guti ... and the little one should be welcomed.'

'You are right ... But will you talk to me too?'

'We are three...' She repeated in mock reproof.

'Can I talk to your foetus too, Waratah?'

'Of course.'

'Then I too welcome you little one. I will teach you to track and you can accompany your mother in the gathering parties.'

They hugged and hugged and were happy.

The ritual energies were spent. The rains thrashed down, cleansing all and activating the landscape. The girls returned to camp ... together. Later the men followed ... together. The earlier squeals of the ecstatic girls, now moulded into the squeals of marsupial rats and bird calls of the dawn, as nature, liberated from drought through ritual ebullience, again emerged triumphant. The soil was once again moist. The waters in the billabong were rising fast. Young shoots showed green tips as they awakened. A mist rose from the water and beaded an expanse of spider's webs. And the morning pigeons mellowed their calls into the moist air.

The two in their nest now slept a happy sleep and dreamed their loving dreams. In tomorrow's light, the air would have a new freshness and the plains would come alive. The kinship laws would again prevail, and they ... who now slept ... and their people, would carry and care for the seed of future generations.

Whatever laws prevailed in the ancient material landscape ... and they, the man-made laws may only make sense in part ... it is the Dreamtime that is of the essence and holds the key to creation.

Later civilisations may well continue to feel both the impersonal as well as personal sexual energies; but of course, it is the personal face of bonding, allied to procreation, and to continuity of love and life and race, that continues to hold meaning. That *is*, and has to remain so. Such issues may well become confused in later times, where our ways are sometimes 'cloaked' or hidden from children ... even become hidden from ourselves. Modern mankind may have hang-ups ... get 'screwed up' ... even seek the psychiatrist. Today's broken homes are so often, so far as the children are concerned a partial reversion to the old tribal lore. The children, as like as not, look to an assortment of friends and relatives for their upbringing. And with a good spread of attention, this can be successful. It may help some, to simply look back to those tribal times when *all* was 'overt' with a greater sharing of responsibilities. After all, that is where we are from! (Albeit, one should not *dwell* on the past with the physical mind, because that is not the *spiritual* way forward.) Often, that which is overt in modern times, is only the physical. It is the surface.

It is the non-material ... the time-space patterns of the Dreamtime, that underpin the evolving world of our visible perception. Manifestation of pattern mirrors across that boundary veil between realms, into our physical existence. All will be well if we hold to that ... give our power of thought, our belief and our respect to the Dreamtime ... and our further respect to the dependent physical landscape that is underpinned by it. Hold to that respect for landscape and indeed for *all* life!

There are those anthropologists today who look to recovery of the Dreamtime as a key factor in human survival. Some also maintain that the continuing Aboriginal way of life holds the 'seeds' for its rebirth. The potential of the Dreamtime and its influence upon creation remains always alive within us.

> *The potential of the Dreamtime is still alive within us, both physically and psychologically, and holds the promise of an astonishing awareness that stretches beyond the bounds of our five senses. No objective can be of greater significance for human survival than the recovery of the Dreaming. The Aboriginal way of life and the Aboriginal revelation hold the seeds for the rebirth of the Dreamtime in humanity.*
> Robert Lawlor *Voices of the First Day*
> Inner Traditions International, Ltd.

Chapter III

Negrito

Pangat ran along the sandy margin of the dark river, at what was rather more than a brisk pace. He felt distinctly ill at ease. Somewhere behind and following, was something that was beginning to obsess him. He did not know what, but the bad feeling he had, was certainly real and seemed somehow familiar. He must keep moving. He *must* keep ahead of whatever it was back there. The river was known to him, as was that general area of what is now known to us as the Bataan peninsular, a part of the island of Luzon in the island group known as the Philippines. Just ahead, around the next bend, the sand would give way to a mass of curling mangrove roots. There! There they were! Now he was leaping from root to root. It seemed a risk to take a quick look over the shoulder ... and ... yes! There *was* movement back along the riverbank. His pursuer was there for sure. He half ran half fell from the last twisting root. One of strength and agility, yet beginning to feel fatigue.

Now he was in amongst the trees, skilfully racing and curving between them. The tree-cover was reassuring and he would be less visible in the half-light of the forest. But he was not happy. The *hunted* feeling remained, not to be shifted. He wheeled around a dense patch laced with lianas and then he rushed and rustled across an expanse of cogon grass. Once beyond the grass, there was the cave entrance. The entrance was just as he remembered.

Now he was in the cave, panting, sweating, gasping for his next breath and risking one more darting glance behind as he entered. Horrors! Dwindis! Two dwindis coming straight across the grass, for him! Tolandian had sent them with their gnashing yellow teeth and flying manes, to get him! Hopeless! ... But the cave was long, a very long cave and up ahead, a faint light offered one last chance. He kept running ... running! And the sweat was really with him now. He kept on towards the light. Yes it was an exit but they were right behind. Hardly a run now ... it had become much more a flying scamper. There was no rhythm to it. Breaths came in long painful gasps as he reached out for it. He just *had* to reach out for the light. But as he reached out, the dwindis reached out for *him* and he felt the feared tug at the shoulder ...

'Pangat ... that was a bad dream ... and the dwindis were chasing you hard that time.' It was Ogong, the old shaman. His hand gripped the shoulder and it was his touch that had surfaced the dreamer. Ogong knew about dreams and understood. He knew about dreams, and he knew also about the dwindis. People had fears and their fears would surface in their dreams. And in their dreams, if they had offended Tolandian, the god of all that is, then he would send his devices to chase them. Those with guilt might be chased by an angry thunderstorm, or worse ... the dwindis. They were creatures of big human form with fearsome horse-like heads and big gnashing teeth. If you had guilt, then you would be chased in your dreams. Whatever was the problem, it could usually be put right, and Negritos in general, took a careful account of their dreams for this reason.

'Has your father's spirit visited you at night Pangat?'

'Oh yes, he has been in my dreams often Ogong. He says I am lazy and he is not happy.'

'It has been too long since your father died and there has been no wakai. The spirits are restless without their wakai. You really should arrange the funeral feast. Your father's spirit will then be free to go to the cave of the spirits in the mountains to the north, and Tolandian, the great god will be angry with you no more. The dwindis come in your sleep to urge you to make the proper arrangements.'

Poor Pangat looked forlorn and he was still in a sweat and he trembled. 'You are right Ogong. The Dwindis come more often and they terrify me; but my father was an important man and he will require a big wakai, and I am poor and have few friends that I can call upon. That is my problem. I just don't know what to do. It is a great worry to me.'

'We need a hunt, Pangat, to provide for the feast. What can you catch?'

'I am no good at hunting the pigs, Ogong. I have been looking for runs and I have found some fresh ones, but I need more friends to make up a hunting party. I know a place down the river where I can catch many eels, but I shall need much more than eels for a big wakai.'

The old man was pleased by his show of honest endeavour and was thoughtful. The young man had an understanding of his own shortcomings, which was to his credit. Too often those of his age were afflicted by what was termed the *ningas cogon.* If the dry and rustly cogon grass is burned, it readily catches, burning brightly for a very short time, then dies out. So often his people were like this; they would apply themselves with great enthusiasm at first, only to rapidly lose interest in the task and leave it unfinished. They lacked perseverance ... ningas cogon. This one had a likeable attitude and could be helped.

He called across to Jabon who was a powerful hunter: 'Jabon ... We should all contribute to a big wakai for Pangat's father, before the dwindis get him! Now, how would you like eels for supper? Pangat will get eels for you and your friends in return for your skills in a pig hunt. What do you say?'

'I like eels very much Ogong. If Pangat provides eels tomorrow for ten of us, then we shall all go off on a pig hunt for a wakai ... and our wives will prepare happy drinks from the coconut and the sugar cane.'

'That sounds a good bargain to me. What do you think Pangat?'

Pangat was overjoyed at the arrangement. Jabon was the *best* when it came to pig-hunts. After thanking them both for their interest in his plight, he then set off right away for the eel pools down along that very same stretch of river where he had run in his dream. This time, he knew that there would be no fears, for a fine funeral feast was now in the preparation. The idea of the preparation was firmly set in his mind and his father's spirit should be well pleased, as would be the all-powerful Tolandian.

In the week that followed, there were in fact several eel-parties. They quickly caught on as a kind of popular event. This led to many helpers, and this of course, was to lead to the most incredible wakai. In preparing for the pig-hunt, Jabon and his friends went out the day before, placing the wooden spears in good positions with little markers beside the runs. Then they held a pre-hunt dance during the evening to give power to their hunt. Next day, on the day of the hunt there was a great noise in the jungle. Parties of beaters including eager children and yapping dogs disturbed the pigs. As a frightened animal ran down a run, the trick was for the concealed hunter to raise a spear at just the right moment so that it impaled. If this failed, then there was another spear placed further down the run that could be quickly grabbed and thrown. Such was their method. It worked well enough so long as they kept hard at it.

The hunting for pigs went well. Others went for porcupine, and bamboo rats, while a small party went off separately after a kind of caraboa or water buffalo. All would be roasted on the grand occasion and all the hunters seemed to get fired with an enthusiasm to make the event *really* grand. After all, Pangat's father had been highly regarded, so much so that notaries and friends from nearby tribes must be invited to the feast. It was in part an *utang na loob* or 'debt of honour' that they should be invited.

Back at the group of nipa palm huts, women organised children in the collection of banana leaves that would serve as plates and food-wraps.

The women themselves gathered rice, vegetables and various tubers including camotes ... a well liked kind of sweet potato. Much wood was gathered. And of course, they tended the fermenting happy drinks. The popular *tuba* was prepared from coconut, equalled only by the *basi* wine made from sugar cane. They would see that there were sufficient coconut shells ... to be used as drinking cups. Carefully cut thick bamboo lengths would be their carafes. The raised mound was brushed smooth and laid with leaves, where they would kneel and sing their funeral songs.

Next day, a golden dawn sun cast the first soft rays through sleepy jungle trees and a large fire was lit. It crackled away and more branches were added until it became an orange glowing mass of hot embers on which the pigs and larger animals were eventually placed. It was crudely done. The animals were simply cooked whole. They enjoyed the flavours of meat, stomach, entrails ... all of it ... and so they cooked it all in one. The wrapped vegetables were some time later placed at the edge. Likewise, the small bamboo rats were added later. There were several poorly fed, hungry dogs wanting to snap at the cooking meat and older children had the task of keeping them away with sticks. Parties of guests arrived and talked enthusiastically to those they only got to meet infrequently. They talked of their times with the deceased Lango. There were a good many shamans amongst them, for these people took serious account of their dreams and their spirit ancestors. They talked about their dreams. One old man could transport himself great distances in dreamstate. He had an attentive group around him as he described journeys on the back of a large parrot across mountain ranges ... over strange snow-covered peaks, snow being something altogether unknown to them. In the dreams there was much learning.

A party of the women now took their place on the mound. They knelt and sang their songs. Softly at first:

'The anitos ... the spirits ... have been calling to Lango
From high in their cave of Pinatoba
From the cave high up in the high mountains
The mountains that lie far to the north
They tell him it is better with them
In the cave in the high mountains
It is now time for him to join them
And they will all be happy together
When he joins them high in the mountains...'

As they sang, they swayed to the rhythm of the song. A delightful rounded swaying that took them forward and sideways. Their bared breasts in some way took up the lilt, and became a part of the rhythm of the song. The swaying body rhythms and song were inextricably entwined. And the rhythm was aided by a gentle, soft shuffle of sound that came from bamboo drums and a Tagalog guitar. The men talked and tended the meat and fire. The children periodically struck out at the unfortunate dogs as they became more daring, and the dogs yelped. The song continued, sometimes rising above the background sounds, then falling again to blend harmoniously with the drumming, the fire-crackling, the conversation and the yelps.

The happy drinks were passed around in the bamboo tubes to re-fill the coconut halves. The talk increased. The singers were not forgotten. They took their draughts and the song became the wilder, increasing in its volume. Arms were now held high and they stretched back on heels as breasts rose high to catch the altered modulation. Now twisting forward with hands to the ground. A new lilting rhythm emerged and their song continued:

'Lango ... he will be so happy flying over the mountains
Away ... so far away, far off to the cave of Pinatoba
With friends ... but he will still be able to come and visit Pangat
Lango ... will do this in his dreams while he is sleeping
And so ... now it is time for him to come with them
The time ... for him to join his friends the anitos.'

The fermented liquor powered the conversation, which now fairly buzzed. They talked of their ailments and healing, and of visiting shamans. They talked of their hunting exploits. But what they enjoyed most of all were their feasts. So most of all, they talked of the good times they had had at feasts ... The size of the fire, how it had lasted, the singing, the dancing and most of all, they talked about the food. They enjoyed these things; but sadly, it was clear from fragments of their drifting conversation, that they had lost some of that respect for animals that some of those earlier cultures had observed ... the kindly respect for the animal and the animal spirit.

One of the more daring of the dogs let out an extra loud yelp and ran off with plaintive whining and whimpering into the jungle. This prompted one little group to discuss the best way to cook dog (which was considered amongst them to be a great delicacy):

'It should always be well clubbed to make it tender.'

'Yes but the feeding of the dog before you kill it can make a big difference.'

'It's better if it has been fed.'

'Yes, but a little before you cook it, it should be fed.'

'Ah! I know, a good feed of rice makes the stomach very tasty.'

'If you can get it to take a really big feed of rice...'

'The best dog we ever cooked had no food for two days. Then it took a big feed of rice. Then we left it for a bit. When the stomach was big, it was clubbed on the head and well beaten all over. Then it was roasted and turned several times on the fire. The juices from the rice worked so well with the meat and...'

'Yes, yes! ... I was there ... The meat was yum ... so tasty! And the roast was well done to make sure the rice was getting hot inside. The best dog and best rice too! That was the best ever, and the feasting lasted all night. There was still food for eating when the birds were singing to start the dawn, but we were finding it difficult to take more by then.'

'All the bellies were as big as they could be and nearly bursting! We tried to dance but it was difficult. Just a very gentle dancing, and then we were able to eat some more...'

'All the meats were good but the dog with rice was best of all.'

'Some could not walk home on account of the size of their belly! I shall always remember that time...'

The sun was now sinking fast beyond the trees. They rose up darkly umbrous against the flushed rubescence of the sky. The orange of the fire-glow now took over the scene for itself. It gently invaded the immediate scene and stretched out to touch the darkening huts and vegetation. An orange-lit scene warmly enclosed by the dark tree shapes at the jungle's edge. There was a cry from over by the fire and a fresh buzz of excitement.

The meat of *this* feast was ready! There had been tasty bits passed around already but now the pig, caraboa and porcupine were all considered done and so were removed from the fire and torn apart. Everyone converged on the fire area and were coming away with haunches, ribs, pieces of belly on sticks, gristly bits, bloody bits, charred bits and fatty bits. They enjoyed it all. Much less talking now ... much chewing, gesturing, grunts of satisfaction and slurping. Little rivers of blood and fat trickled down from the corners of their mouths. It was a good and plentiful feast. They seemed to enjoy the gristly bits just as much as the rest, while 'the rest' was everything, apart from bone, and even some of that got opened up for its sticky hot marrow. At last the dogs got lucky and were given pieces of bone that they took off and gnawed.

They returned again and again to collect more; some portions were chewed off the bone, some were spiked on sticks and some were better heaped onto banana leaf. Another team of singers took over and well-wishing songs for Lango continued. The first singers were acclaimed and had certainly earned their supper. Ripples of conversation began again to float through the gathering as well-worked mouths took a little break from chewing. Pangat was well pleased with the wakai. It was better than he ever could have imagined.

At last, he had made so many friends, both while the wakai was in its budding and during the stage of its wild and happy flowering. And he felt charged with an energy that to him was previously unknown. He had a newness of life. He had arrived! He knew ... the voice within now told him so ... his father's spirit was well pleased and Tolandian himself had smiled on this grand occasion ... for grand occasion it truly was. All these people were so happy ... and he Pangat was linked to that happiness. He shared their love and being. This was the energy charge that now invaded ... *per*vaded his whole psyche. He enjoined the cosmic dance. In his quieter moment, he felt so drawn to Ogong for his Shaman's wisdom in opening that door which had contained his fears and the dream-demons that went out with them. No looking back after this day. No looking back!

In so many ways they were an endearing people. But they had lost some of the respect for wild animals that their ancestors once had. They had become cruel to their dogs, which was a pity. With lack of respect and cruelty, go guilt and fear. They all walk hand-in-hand and conjure up the demons of the dreamstate. These people however, took account of their dreams and of those demons of that dreamstate ... all a part of their growing up. And they recognised the one god ... the all-powerful Tolandian. To some he was known as Bathala, but of course the name in the mind of a community is of little importance; the mind-image of the one universal essence is sufficient and complete.

The Negritos had been the first to come across the land bridges to these islands from Asia. Much later, *on this very same soil*, others would arrive who would do far worse. There would be headhunters. What terrifying demons of the subconscious would *they* contrive for themselves? What nights of relentless stark horror would for them prevail? But then, at least it can be said that the headhunting was always a limited small-scale aggression. The men did it ... against men. Women and children were excluded from the head taking. Happily, this chivalrous code was strictly observed where the women and the young were concerned, which was a blessing. Unfortunately, there was no such chivalrous code to be seen in the still much later 'modern warfare'.

What was to follow in the wake of these deviations from a good morality was indeed far worse. First came the lack of respect, then a cruelty, then head taking, and finally the horrific mass and serial killings of 20th century warfare ... the battlefield terrors and their aftermath. And all was to transpire on the very same ground, on this island of Luzon, in the Philippine group.

> *All the primitive psychologists I had met in the jungle seemed to say that, with the aid of his fellows, a man can travel back to find what, inside him, is destroying his life in the present ... If he acts destructively towards a dream character, he is opposing and trying to destroy a troublesome fragment of himself, but if he acts in some way toward human beings, he is attempting to destroy what is equal to himself ... any destructive social policy to some extent turns him against his own centre.*
>
> Kilton Stewart *Pygmies and Dream Giants*
>
> The Scientific Book Club

. . . .

The more recent dreadful events that were to transpire in this same place were set in motion on 7 December 1941 Hawaiian time, (or 8 December Pacific time). Sunday morning church bells suddenly became drowned out by cannon-fire, screaming bombs, the noise of aircraft formations and many explosions; the most massive of which was the blowing of the battleship *USS Arizona's* forward magazines. The *Oklahoma* capsized, the *California* and *West Virginia* were sunk at moorings, and every other battleship received heavy damage, except for the *Pennsylvania,* which was in dry dock. The raid on Pearl Harbour by 359 Japanese carrier-based aircraft began America's war with Japan in the Pacific. As the first Nakijima 'Kate' flew across the motionless *Nevada* on Battleship Row and settled in its torpedo run, Fuchida had his radio operator signal: *'Tora! Tora! Tora!'* (Tiger! Tiger! Tiger!), the prearranged code to let Admiral Nagumo know that Pearl Harbour had been taken completely by surprise. A simple alarm message was broadcast from the control tower at Ford Island: 'AIR RAID PEARL HARBOUR, THIS IS NOT A DRILL'. The message was relayed and that is how President Franklin D Roosevelt at the White House and the American people got to hear of it. And within just a few hours of the attack on Pearl Harbour, the Philippines were surprised by an air raid, Hong Kong was surprised by an air raid and Malaya was surprised by military landings.

> *A declaration of war by Japan could not be reconciled with reason ... Sometimes they (governments) take mad decisions, or one set of people get control who compel all others to obey and aid them in folly ... Madness is however an affliction which in war carries with it the advantage of SURPRISE.*
>
> Winston Churchill *The Second World War*
>
> Reproduced with permission of Curtis Brown Ltd, London, on behalf of the Estate of Sir Winston S. Churchill. Copyright Winston S. Churchill.

The Pearl Harbour raid left 2,403 dead, 18 warships smashed beyond repair, 188 aircraft totally destroyed on the ground and casualties and repair work that would keep dedicated work teams occupied for many months. It was a damaging surprise attack that created havoc, but a crucial factor in the Pacific war was that the aircraft carriers of the United States Navy were not in harbour at the time of the attack. They remained safely at some distance and strategic; but Japan had dealt an extravagant blow and was for some time able to hold on to the military advantage. America fared badly until June 1942 and the battle of Midway. In that sea battle, Japan lost aircraft carriers, sea supremacy and carrier-based air supremacy. But until the battle of Midway, American forces continued to be sadly and sorely troubled; and none more so than those on the Bataan peninsular.

Within a few hours of the attack on Pearl Harbour, Japanese aircraft appeared over the Philippines. They bombed Davao City, Tuguegarao, Baguio, Iba, Tarlac and Clark Air Base. At Clark Air Base, the entire complement of U.S. aircraft was wiped out.

Island after island fell to the conquering Imperial forces; and the battle finally reached Bataan. On the night of 11 March 1942, General Douglas MacArthur had left his HQ on Corregidor and made his dash by PT boat south to Mindanao and then by B-17 Flying Fortress, on to Australia. There he made his solemn pledge: *'I came through and I shall return.'*

Now American and Filipino 'Western' culture ethics confronted the very different cultural ethics of the Japanese soldier. *His* training was coloured by that harshly hostile Bushido warrior discipline of the Samurai:

-to be captured means that you not only disgrace yourself, but your parents and family will never be able to hold up their heads ... Hence, death before dishonour. And there were so many Japanese soldiers who saw prisoners merely as disgraced inferior beings deserving no respect of their captors. This was a way of the Samurai. And this feudal warrior code from the 12th century still reached out into the 20th with grim effect.

General Homma Masaharu's forces had taken the northern peninsular. His troops, like the Fil-Am, were now weary, short on rations and hampered by malaria. His push to the south was faltering. But Tokyo wanted quick results and so assigned a fresh division under General Hattori, 15,000 men, 140 artillery pieces and 80 bomber aircraft for the final assault. It was enough. The Japanese blockade of shipping was effective and the less fortunate Fil-Am troops had no such reinforcement. The rumours of mile-long convoys to fulfil their urgent need never materialised.

Through Good Friday, the army chaplains went about their business giving field communion to the defending troops ... both Filipino and American. They were kept busy. The Philippine Islands have the Christian faith and 83% of population are Catholic. It was on that evening, the bombardment reached its full ferocity. Then the aircraft went to work, returning again and again with their bomb loads. Like many others, Bob and Max could only run from their positions ... to escape the burning jungle. When the jungle has had so much ill treatment that it is aflame, then the simplest animal instinct says: 'Get out or burn!' And you get out. That's how it was.

An organised chaos reigned within the inferno:

'Get back! Get back!'

'Keep it moving! Into the smoke ... That's it!'

'Half a mile ... Past the burn. We hold there!'

'Get yer butt over this way! C'mon move it!'

'Dammit! How d'y'expect anyone to ...?'

'Got any better ideas smartass? ... Just *do* it ... Go man ... go!'

'Hell! We got another flare...'

Shouts and confused commands came thick and fast through the smoke and heat. Just how many times did they fall back? That was impossible to say. It all became just a blur. Death was all around. Hughie, a good friend had bought it somewhere in that blur.

The final position held was far to the south, somewhere near Cabcaben. Major General Edward King, the commander in the field could see the hopelessness of the predicament. Comparatively, his men were poorly equipped, technically unsupported and weak from battle fatigue and near starvation. He made what he considered to be the only possible logical decision ... to surrender. So with the bombardment and the bombing still in progress, any residual dumps of fuel and ammunition were blown. Such was the orgy of destruction. As if the planet itself believed in the principle: *give back what you receive* ... an earthquake then enjoined the turmoil. The din was unrestrained. The air was thick with smoke, flame, dust, rocks, flesh ... The flying debris sank craft in the harbour. Those few who fled by small boat and managed to get across to Corregidor, found the scene they had left just too difficult to describe. Truce flags went out at 0600 hours on the 9th of April and at 0900 hours Major General King formally surrendered.

Logistics next played the key role. It had been the estimate of General Homma's HQ that 25,000 prisoners would require transportation and they would all have their personal rations. But estimates can sometimes run wild. The living facts that emerged from the chaos were: nearer 73,000 prisoners ... 62,000 Filipino and 11,000 American ... all weak and starved with *no* food, water or medicine. In the absence of transport for these numbers, the decision was made to force-march 75 miles from Mariveles in the south to Camp O'Donnell in Capas, Tarlac.

Many Japanese observed the old Bushido code. Some were more enlightened. Some even sufficiently compassionate to quietly share their own small ration with their prisoners. But the majority, were attuned to harshness and brutality. General Homma was of mature years, an old campaigner who had earned and learned respect. He did not approve brutality and conducted his own affairs with a more rounded discipline; but General Homma Masaharu, old campaigner and the conqueror of the Philippines, was not there with the marching column to impose his personal authority.

Staff officer Lieutenant Colonel Tsuji *was* there and in charge of the column at the start, and he set the disciplinary style in his own demonstrative way. Drawing a pistol, he announced: 'This is the way to treat bastards like this!' He then shot one prisoner dead. That was how it began. There were plenty that followed his example and readily executed those who fell exhausted in the march. Many were beaten or bayonetted. Such were the days of the 'Death March'. Some Filipino captives were set upon with exceptional brutality. Savagery flared into mindless massacre at one location leaving 300 butchered by the bayonet.

Bob and Max were in no shape to survive the march and make it to the camp. Any fleeting thoughts of optimism were born of unrealistic hoped-for fantasy.

'If they'd had food...'

'If the damned dysentery hadn't...'

'If just *some* transport had appeared and helped them halfway...'

'But no way, in this heat, in this damned jungle ... and with these aching, blistered, smarting festering feet...'

Earlier they had seen Mitsubishi 'Betties' flying south.

'More tetchy Betties,' Max had said.

'Off to plague those guys on Corregidor ... Sods!'

That had been hours ago. Now they were well weakened and just about done in. No longer was there any awareness of aircraft. No longer was there awareness of guards, or of the column around them. They just continued together. They were buddies. At least they were able to hold onto that. They locked arms and leaned together, staggered on and faced their destiny. A kind of rough tranquillity was enveloping them ... at least, that material world of painful influence was being steadily but surely shut out from the physical consciousness. It just whittled away. And then the end-moment came. Both fell, with arms still locked, at the track edge. Completely spent ... scarcely aware. Seeing the rifle butt descend. A grunt of effort coalesced from somewhere in a mist. Feeling impact ... a dull, distasteful, thudding impact. And then a kind of black emptiness...

But it did not end with the black emptiness. A strange thing next began to happen ... to both of them. Awareness was returning. But something was different ... several things in fact. They were not on the ground for a start. Up a tree beside the track perhaps? Maybe, but hovering weightless or just floating. Yes, that was more like it ... *floating*. They were aware of no discomfort from heat ... that had all gone. The pain had completely disappeared! No weakness. No need of strength. No fear and no bad feelings. In fact what now prevailed, was a feeling of well being! Such a feeling was from a far flung distant past that had been altogether forgotten in the last few days. A wonderful ... wonderful relaxed wholeness. Was this a dream? No! *There* was the column! It still staggered along down there. 'Down there!' ... Yes, they were somehow above it. It was there, just as it had been, still moving on. And there ... there were two bodies ... motionless, with heads crushed and bleeding ... their own bodies! They turned to each other ... amazed. Then both thought of him in that same instant.

'Hughie! Dear old Hughie! Hughie was *right*!' It had been his favourite conversation piece ... but only with close friends with whom he could confide and who would take him seriously ... the spirit circle he used to sit with back home. Oh, for sure, he got ridicule from a good many over it and that is why he was so selective. 'Spookman', they called him, and sometimes the roughnecks were downright unflattering with their 'Screwy-Hughie'. He had been just plain Hughie to them and a damn good friend ... one of the best. Hughie had talked of the spirit living on after death and how the so-called primitives had recognised this and how they had communed with spirit ancestors. He actually talked on one occasion of out-of-body-experience and all that stuff. 'And ... and ... Hughie, bless him ... Hughie was bloody right! He was just so bloody right!'

Looking down, there was ... still was ... a living hell down there. One big tough-looking guy, looking every inch like some range-rider from a western movie, grit his teeth and wept as he passed by their corpses. But here *they* were floating so gently away from all that. They seemed to be travelling along a tube ... a great tube of light that seemed to hold for them a feeling of love, which felt so very, very good. The blissful love and the light were increasing as they progressed. What a wonderful feeling! The scene below was now fading. 'What was it Hughie had said about ... about ... meeting old friends who had already taken this road? What a really excellent friend Hughie had been ... was ... *is* ... Bloody wonderful!'

And as for the blissful quality of that love that now embraced them! Why, it was just beyond anything in their Earth-life experience. They could see no figure ... yet someone was there. Someone was right there with them. They were being loved ... enclosed, enwrapped, embraced in the most caring and knowing ... *love*. Now all they could see was that wonderful light around them, but there was much more here than just the brilliance.

Their 'Light Escort' continued to enfold them, for it was *she* who had met them and it was *she* who was seeing to their passage from this world to the next. It was *she*, from realms beyond ... It was *she*, a loving spirit of pure energy and life essence who now enfolded and caressed their real selves from the harshness of the material reality. Reality? But *this* was now their reality ... *this* ... while the rest ... seemed so much more like a dream ... and yet, a rather special dream ... a dream of much learning and friendship from which they would not entirely detach. How they loved the embrace of their 'light escort'! And how their invisible friend loved to be with them! She felt so richly rewarded by their glad acceptance of her loving care.

. . . .

There are those who would say that the fighting retreat from the Philippines, was an important episode in World War II, during which the Japanese advance was slowed down and their military strength reduced. And without this, Australia and New Zealand would have been taken. They may be right.

As to the 'Bataan Death March'. This was just one of many despicable episodes that happened as a part of 20th century warfare. It was probably the bloodiest event ever to be enacted upon that jungle-clad peninsular. Of the 73,000 who set out, more than 17,000 of the Fil-Am troops fell and did not make it. It was a bloody and horrendous trail and deaths were to continue at the prison camp. The world can only hope that such tragedies as this will never again befall humanity. The world can hope, not only for the sake of those who suffer, but also for the sake and souls of those who commit atrocity.

> *The worst war in our country was the Second World War (1941-1945). It was also the worst war in the world.*
> Dr Sonia M Zaide *Philippine History and Government*
> All-Nations Publishing Co. Inc, Quezon City, Philippines.

Chapter IV

Xavante

The stars above the treetops just hung there and they sparkled so sharply with a more than crystal clarity. During the day, there were many golden flowers to be seen along the riverbank. Now, night enclosed the scene and the noises of the night infiltrated all that lay beneath the starlight. This part of the riverbank hummed with a symphony of sound from a myriad insects. But the *pium*, that small biting fly, that could be such a great nuisance in some locations, was absent from this part of the *Mato Grosso* ... the denser forest, tucked in between what is now called Bolivia and the Amazon basin. This was a domain ... an Eden of luscious tranquillity. A hanging branch slopped lazily up and down in the water, powered by the current. It was the background breath of this place. Other less continuous sounds came out of the darkness ... a screech owl ... the night monkeys ... and from over by the village, the occasional gentle, melodic singing as it drifted on the air.

The young men of the village, not yet fully adult, had their own hut at one end of the crescent of palm-thatched dwellings. At intervals through the night, they would venture out as a party and sing their songs around the huts of the families. The custom was a comfort to those who slept or who drifted in and out of sleep. They were well used to its reassurance. The songs said that all was well and that this was a happy village of good spirit; and one could rest assured that no jaguar was prowling this night. The songs were a contribution to the community. A muted and melodious night watch. The singing was their gift. Their stamping rhythm and their combined voices were symbolic of the harmony that they all sought in their lives. It was good that the youth of the village were able to make such contribution to the community of which they were so much a part.

This night, the singing was especially well done. You can tell when the energy runs high, when the psyche is aglow. They were in such good space. Tomorrow would be the day of the log run! It would, as always, be an occasion of great joy and celebration. The log run! The two palm logs would be cut in the forest early in the day, each quite a heavy log, but such that one man or woman could shoulder it and run a few paces with it. Two logs, for the two teams. In one sense it was a relay with each team member taking a turn with the log as often as exchange was necessary.

The two teams would run and the logs would change shoulders many times. But this was *not* a race. It was a celebration, pure and simple; uncomplicated by the need for winners or for losers, or indeed for any particular need to excel. This was a time before the emergence of competitive sports ... a kind of forerunner of the race.

Joto and his party moved off early to a point near the river, where they found a worthy palm with suitable trunk. They worked most of the morning, trimming two logs. Over to the right, was the white sandy beach where a jaguar would sometimes sun itself. Now, it was a family of otters who played by the water's edge. They were unconcerned. One log was heavier than the other but that was of no consequence. Why should they be equal? They were both neat and well trimmed and that was what mattered. They would serve the purpose well. Two of them carried the logs across to the track where the run would begin, springing a little and testing the feel and balance as they went. They used the trick of cushioning the weight against the muscle, as was the way. No rough spots. They felt fine. All was prepared.

The sun was high and it was approaching midday when the merry group from the village arrived, their bodies gaily-decorated in red and black. It was the most perfect place from which to begin the run. Passion flowers, bright yellow oncidium orchids and many tiny cyclamen-coloured flowers of a bromeliad were resplendent about them. All this against a backcloth of dark leafed buriti palms. At the start of the run, there were such loud enthusiastic cries that a band of startled japims flew into the air displaying their fine yellow plumage and a heron rose gracefully from the river bank. It was the prettiest of starts.

Para and Doido, the first log carriers, were side by side for almost fifty yards. Those eager for exchange, ran at their heels, while others raced and twirled amongst the trees beside the track, flailing arms and youthfully shouting encouragement. They all shared in being just so alive. Then, under the assai palms, Doido exchanged his *heavier* log. He was fairly puffed and had begun to stagger. Para managed another twenty paces before he too exchanged. As each new shoulder came along, the pace picked up afresh, then steadied. At half a mile, it was of course the heavier-log-team that was fading and despite the most heroic efforts, the gap continued to widen. That was the place of the catasetum orchids with their huge seed pods, and it was one of the seed pods that got under a foot and the heavy log nearly fell but another fresh-footed one was there at just the right moment to hold on and keep it going. It was a neat recovery that delighted the supporters. They kept a commentary going for the team up front. They were quick to take account of the position and made a tactical move.

Three of the more muscular men of the lead team dropped back and took a turn with the heavier log, to help them catch up! Whoops of delight came from the supporters. This was just what was needed. This manoeuvre might just result in the teams entering the village together for a good finish! Although this was in no way a race, there was much beauty of form in keeping the runners tightly together as the climax approached. But the front team, with three less to take a turn was now tiring fast and they were actually overtaken near the village entrance. There was huge excitement. Now it was Doido's team that was being encouraged to catch up. And in her enthusiasm, Maloca, one of the women at the village entrance lent a shoulder and managed twenty paces that reduced the arrears to a chorus of most gleeful encouragement. But now Ritimi who had been the one to so nearly fall with the heavy log, but now being fully recovered, switched teams and took the final run with the lighter log. The two logs were thrown down before the village elders at *exactly* the same instant. What a finish! The cheers and jubilation were such that the speeches had to wait. So many wanted to make speeches but it was just not possible for quite ten minutes.

When the noise had abated, there was much to be said. This was one of the finest runs that many could remember. It had been so very pretty at the start, with all the flowers on the ground and through the trees, and the birds in the sky. It had begun from extreme beauty. Then the logs ... both fine and of good shape ... had exerted their influence on the two teams. The one had been that much more difficult to carry than the other. But the two teams had compensated for this, choosing just the right moments for the one to help the other. The near fall, which had been entirely due to a seedpod (which was fully entitled to be there in the jungle), had been saved most elegantly. In this, man and jungle, had demonstrated a mutual compatibility. If a small problem arises out of the nature of the jungle, then it can be overcome. It was a part of the harmony with nature that they sought.

All through the speeches, children ran around in joy and took turns at dancing on the logs.

This had never been a race. It was never intended that it should be so. The logs were of the jungle. The extensive jungle was the world, with all its mysteries and all its wondrous provision. The logs were run to the centre of the village, the centre of their culture. The run and their sweat formed a nexus, their connection between jungle and village. There was a mutual respect between the two, and a great joy that was clearly evident in the mood of the occasion. It was a celebration and an affirmation of their harmony with nature. The run was the symbolic connection and demonstration of the oneness. The effort made them a part of it, and the 'dead heat' finish was a part of the oneness that they sought in their lives.

The occasion of the log run had such a rapturous quality with such deepness of expression and confrontation of purpose; and by comparison, with our present, the notion of a mere race in today's world, pales into insignificance. These Xavante did not care to recognise winners and losers amongst themselves. Their society had balance, a sense of connectedness, respect for environment and spirituality. We can learn from them.

Perhaps in the modern world, the spirit of the log run has not been entirely lost. There are some that might agree that more than a shadow of its residue can still be felt and appreciated in a well-played and *drawn* cricket test match, played at Lord's ... or played on some similar big city ground. In the drawn game, there are no victors or vanquished ... nothing is destroyed ... nothing lost. There is immense pleasure for the spectator in seeing the excellence and expertise of the various individuals, which in the overall, may neatly balance. There is also the pleasure in observing tactics and the bringing together of team effort. In the game, the wood of the forest is a central focus, as were the logs to the Xavante. The flying leather might also be seen as of the forest and symbolic of its wildlife.

These tokens of the forest are brought *from* the environs, to the field within the civilised metropolis, where the balanced game is played out beneath the sky, with all its character and prettiness, and to be talked about at some considerable length. Happily, the prettiness of birds in the modern game remains evident. There are always pigeons on the ground at Lord's, and cameramen and commentators dally with their antics from time to time. It is a joining together of natural world and metropolis, celebrated as an appreciation by all, midst a balance of skills. This scenario remains central to all good cricket. And so long as there remains the possibility of the balancing of skills that may result in the drawn game or series, then cricket will retain its magic ... an *old* celebratory meeting-with-nature magic that reaches back to distant tribal perceptions.

On Monday 24 June 1996 at Lord's, the second test match in a series between England and India was concluded. It was an exciting, balanced, drawn game. Just ten years into the period of Earth's transition (discussed quite fully in later pages), the game itself seemed to symbolise a balanced meeting of East and West, and seemed to be possessed of an additional beauty. The pigeons were there on the field, and at one point a cameraman picked out a particular one in close-up, exceedingly pretty and perched upon a balcony. Its iridescent feathers shone and quivered in the sunlight. And this was also the test match in which, after many years' service to the game, the well-loved umpire 'Dickie' Bird retired. This truly was a match to be remembered.

[Modern one-day cricket matches, on the other hand, appear to be deliberately designed to produce winners and losers. Skills have been eroded by induced haste and the game is entirely different. It is a form of the game in which the concepts of balance and prettiness are deliberately thrown to the winds. This variant therefore lacks the 'magic' that is central to the traditional game, and its celebratory character is sadly not evident.]

Chapter V

Tunguska

He still remembered well the time of the high fever. It had been for him, both a fearful time and a blessing. That had been twenty years ago but the memory of it always came back on occasions such as this. The typhus had weakened his material being and his consciousness had kind of drifted in and out. Several days it was that he lay in that state. Then it was his spirit being that had taken flight. That is how he now thought of it. The real self, the self that was consciousness, was somewhere up above and able to look down. There below, was the familiar hot fever-ridden body, beneath the skins in the corner of the hut. It was motionless as in sleep, yet *he* ... the conscious he ... was awake ... fully aware. There came a flood of thoughts, and the ability to reason was with his conscious self. He could see and was able to hover ... move a little. The far corner of the room would afford a better view. He began to drift there. Then whoosh! Suddenly back in the familiar body, with the fever and all its familiar feelings.

That had been the first time out-of-body, and in a sense, it had been his initiation as a shaman. Once the shift of the spirit had been achieved, it could be made to happen again and again, and this was the opening door to his shamanism. The door opened for him onto another world. There were adventures to be had in the 'away' state, in that other-world. And his coming and going, and his communing with beings of a superior knowledge could help those of his people, who were in need of the healing, who were available to the freshly freed spirit. The freeing of the spirit body was not that easy and not without its difficulties. A certain 'persuasion' was required. Ongoing drumming was the traditional aid used by his fellow Tungus shamans from earlier times. The sound, the rhythm, the fatigue and the repetition, all helped to ease the spirit away from its material, structured house ... the body. This was the way, here in this beautiful and desolate place. But this was not the only part of our planet to find and develop the shamanic principle.

It happened elsewhere in the tribal past, though the methods varied from region to region. Often, illness, a fall or an accident played a part in the initiation but not always. Then the slip from this world into the next could be encouraged, sometimes by an ecstatic dance, sometimes with the aid of certain potent plants or prepared extracts; but in these parts, it was the dancing and the drumming that had become the favoured mode. The beating of the drum was most important. This was Siberia, and it was the Tungus in this part of Siberia who named the 'Shaman' so. Much later, those came who would study and compare these things. They would take the Tungusic word and apply it to all those healers who could travel between the worlds; whether they lived and practised their art in Siberia, the Americas, Europe, the Philippines, or wherever in this wide world. All such between-worlds travellers and healers would thenceforth be known as shamans.

This then, in a location sense was the heart of it all, the Siberian Taiga, a snowy, forested land where the howl of a wolf could often be heard at nightfall; a place of some considerable renown and a place of strange energy. A strange energy was certainly there at the time of the 'Tunguska event'. That event was to come at a much later date, in the year 1908. It happened on the morning of 30th June. Deep beneath the surface of the planet, the contortions of the magma and the attendant energies are not at all well understood even today; still less how those energies connect with atmospheric charge distribution. Curiously enough, there was just one man at this time, on the other side of the planet, who sought the secrets of vibrational energies and of very high-energy electric charge. He was Nikola Tesla. Perhaps he would have been more capable than anyone else, of arriving at an understanding of the strange event that transpired.

It was morning. The sun was up, rising early in midsummer in the northern latitudes. Farmer Semenov sat in his porch at Vanavara, just forty miles to the south of what he was about to see:

A towering brilliant blue fireball filled a large part of the sky! One minute clear sky, the next ... a bright, brilliant, blue mass of fire. He turned away from the sting of its heat. How that heat stung the skin! His shirt felt hot to the touch. What could it possibly be?

There was time for him to check that no fires had started as the result of such a heat. He called across to his friend who shouted back that of course he had seen it. Who could fail to ... Then it was the shock wave of the explosion that struck. Farmer Semenov was thrown to the ground. Momentarily unconscious, he became aware as he recovered, of the ground shaking and of shattered windows. In his friend Kosalopov's house, a door flew off the stove. The ground shook over a wide area. The driver of the Trans-Siberian express stopped his train as a precaution against being shaken off the rails. Seismic disturbance was recorded throughout

Europe. Atmospheric shock waves went twice around the world, and in England, readers wrote to The Times newspaper about the brightness of the night skies that followed.

The explosion flattened or stripped hundreds of square miles of forest. Yet subsequent expeditions to the area found little ... no craters and no debris. They found nothing but the effects resulting from a massive atmospheric explosion. It did not seem to be the result a comet or some heavenly body impact. The evidence just pointed to a wild release of energy with its explosion centre high in the atmosphere above the forests of Tunguska. This untamed and only sparsely peopled domain was, it would appear, destined to be a place of strange happenings.

And even now, long before the 'event', this traveller felt an unmistakable strangeness in the air. But he was not alone, being accompanied by his assistant, at his side carrying the pack of things that they would need. The precious drum, he carried himself. The wolves were busy this night, but they were not hostile. Hostility to humans is not a part of their nature. They shared the frozen birch woods with those who were travelling. Their howls seemed to combine in making a musical cloak for the dusk. It was a drifting harmonic song that came and went on the night air. It seemed to make the night less bleak ... less chilling. The encampment now lay just ahead. The travellers had arrived.

Within the skin tent, a small fire flickered, enough to make the shadows dance. She with the sickness lay with rugs within the tent. Those concerned, sat at the tent sides and talked amongst themselves. The floor had been swept. The painted animal spirit-images, bears and deer, were placed on four sides about the fire. The shaman sat and swayed a little to a silent rhythm. At his signal, the assistant opened the pack and produced the ritual robe, breastplate, skin footwear and the antler helmet. He was helped into these and the assistant carefully warmed the drum over the fire to stretch it tight, before presenting. He struck with the stick against the side of the drum. At this signal all conversation stopped. The ritual was under way. A hiss escaped into the silence as the fire was damped. All was still in the darkness. A little starlight found its way in through the smoke vent.

A gentle drumming began and the shaman now swayed to an audible rhythm. In a voice rich with devotion and inner feeling, he sang his song to the animal spirits:

'... Deer of the Earth, bears of the Earth
Come speak with me, come speak
Fly before me. Point out my path

Fulfil all that I ask of you
Fulfil your tasks well...'

Those present joined him in chorus. The shaman continued drumming and singing softly. He called upon spirit helpers to assist in his fight against the disease, as he continued to sway slowly to the pulse of the drum. Now he addressed in turn each spirit being that would assist:

'... Bear of great strength come join me.
Noble deer, with the proud high antlers
I need your speed and guile,
And height and sight of the great eagle
Come join with me, come join me now...'

The drum ceased to pulse and became a roll. The roll finally tailed off. Then dark silence. Out of that silence came the snorting and stamping of beasts and a whirring of wings, and with the wing beats came bird cries. The shaman received the spirit helpers into himself. More warming of the drum and again it rolled and rolled. More animal spirits came and they were finally all gathered to this one place, where he held them to do his bidding.

A time for orders now. Some spirits to watch this tent, others to watch over pathways and the party to stay with him would of course include the noble reindeer spirit, his animal-double, for it would be he who would travel the tree to the lower realm. The shaman's song became wild as his double made the leap between worlds. The sounds of other spirits interspersed the song with shrieks, snorts, screams and wild wind whispers. Words and sounds came faster and faster. Drum rolls became thunder amidst all. The shaman was ecstatic betwixt thunder peals. All sounds fused save the drum, which moaned while its charged thunderous rolls echoed away to distant realms. Vibration ran rife through the tent. All trembled together. Even the poles that held the structure hummed a resonance. His helper's outstretched hands received the vibrant drum as it flew through the air. The shaman's arched form grabbed leather thongs that hung from one pole. He danced a whirling dance amid the thongs before falling pale and motionless onto the rug that had been spread in readiness.

Out-of-body now and in the world of spirit, as his assistant fanned just a little life into the fire again. He bent close to the lifeless material body of his master, whispering that he should not leave it too long before return. He feared for his safety. No response. His material body was now no more than a shell, devoid of any conscious spark. Still no response. Again he turned to the fire to fan it into life. It flared a little. Shadows danced their dance about the skin walls. He bent low and put his ear close now and sighed relief.

A hint of colour began to return ... and a breath. A whisper of spirit sounds came from the quivering lips. The sounds strengthened. Once again the assistant warmed the drum as flames flared well and again lit the scene. He gently tapped out a slow rhythm, entreating the shaman's animal-double spirit to follow the track, listen for the drum and to watch for the light of the fire. These should help guide him back. A blink. A murmur. The shaman's voice came softly at first but gathering strength. Now he cried out. The drum beat louder. He was upon his feet dancing in ecstasy, though briefly this time, and now more slowly. He had returned. The journey was done. He hung onto the thongs and swaying gently, gave instructions for the healing that he had received. The woman with the sickness, stirring, looked out from beneath her rugs.

One of those present lit a pipe and handed it to him. He sat and puffed and now was grounded.

It was similar in earlier times, in the days of the Ice Age hunters. The animal spirits were depicted on the cave walls as at Lascaux and Alta Mira. In the cave of Les Trois-Frères in Southern France, a shaman wearing antlers and skin was carefully painted into the scene. In Siberia, the shaman rituals continued much the same on into the twentieth century.

These were the first healers, the first practitioners of medicine in a variety of forms and early devotees to a religious observance of spirit connection. It was their purpose to seek to alter their own consciousness in order to access spirit connection and thus obtain 'higher knowledge' and power. Such knowledge and energy could then be used to heal and help those of their people who were in need. The shamanic principle issues from love and the desire to help others.

. . . .

10 February 1994: I first got to hear of Patricia when Ann, my wife, visited her. Patricia has the gifts of healing and of clairvoyance. During that visit, she had indicated to Ann that I was at home working on something and had a date in mind: 23 August.

They had chatted at some point during the evening, about that date and what its possible implication might be. Since it lies close to her birthday, she wondered if I might perhaps be planning a treat. Well that would have been nice but unfortunately it was not quite like that in this instance. But Patricia had been correct; the 23rd of August was indeed in my mind at that precise time, and for a very specific purpose. The fact was I had begun the writing of this book, and had just got to that point in the first chapter, when Kamoya Kimeu had found a fossil. I accordingly typed in '23 August 1984' as the date of the find! And of course, I was intrigued that a total stranger should, have picked up such a chance detail of my thought process, some 15 miles away. Well, anyway, I felt that I should meet this lady for myself ... and so, booked a reading with her.

Patricia opened the door to me. A lovely welcoming face with the high cheekbones and colourings that suggested a touch of Spanish. I later learned that a distant ancestor had been with the Spanish armada and was shipwrecked off the Irish coast. He had settled in Ireland where the family prospered and the Celtic and Spanish ancestry clearly went well together. Little was said at the outset because she prefers not to complicate things with prior knowledge; beginning the proceedings with a clean slate as it were. So while husband Miklos, whose parents had come to England at the time of the Hungarian uprising, tucked up the children in bed, Patricia and I sat across the small table. She, between worlds and me, with my mind open and a notepad ready.

On account of my reading and experiences I was not in need of any 'evidence' of other-world connection. Nevertheless I was to get plenty! The session seemed to be beginning with a body scan and healing. But let me first say a word about my health. I was fit apart from having twisted my left knee. This had left me with a condition known as *bursitis*. It was puffy and had a feeling of pressure. I had sought medical advice and had learned that an elastic support may help. But it had been as it was now for three weeks. No pain, no limp; just a swelling and feeling of pressure (even without the elastic support).

'Beginning at the top...' Words began to flow from Patricia with breaks, as if she were listening and talking at the same time. She was saying that I had an intense fear stuck in my memory from a past event ... a cold damp fear in a military situation. That surprised me at first, but later I remembered something long since forgotten. It could be just one thing ... 1953: my first parachute jump in training with the Parachute Regiment through thick cloud with zero visibility (and with no reserve 'chute in those days). It

must have made a deep impression because now that I think about it, my memory of actual passage through the cloud and from the cloud-base would appear to have been blanked out.

She went on: *'You have good hearing ... psychic hearing that is.'*

Then she got straight to the knee: *'Right ... no, the left knee ... I get mixed up between right and left with people sitting opposite. The left knee has had an injury. You are getting healing now...'* [And the swelling just went over the following few hours and it has been fine ever since].

'I am seeing an old man with a staff and wearing a hood and a cloak. It is autumn. The leaves have fallen from the trees. He has a dog running beside him ... He has a youthful step. He has wisdom with numerology ... ... He is telling me that he often sits with you in a room full of books. He is describing the room ... Big open fireplace ... as you enter, the fire is to the right, also the dog [That would be Emma our elderly collie], *a small table and a single shelf of books over the window opposite. There is something about a secret passage ... beside the fire. There is something in the same wall as the fire. It is not as it appears.'*

[The room described is the room that we have made into a library. I use it for my writing. It has many shelves but just the one above the window. I was aware of a 15-inch-deep cavity beside the fireplace, filled with builder's rubble. I have since cleared out five barrow loads. It is a hideaway but hardly big enough to be called a standard 'priest hole', but a hideaway nonetheless. At one time it would have had a concealed entrance from the upper part of the library wall, where the bricks are of a later type. The house is 17th century and predates the civil war. The wall is indeed *'not as it appears'*.]

'He says he has been helping you for a very long time ... in the gaining of knowledge. He is telling me he is from ... Russia! ... He's saying something ... Varof ... Varda ... I can't catch the full word. It's foreign. I can't quite catch what he's saying ... it's in Russian ... Siberia! He's from Siberia!'

'Your mother was protective of you and found it difficult to talk to you ... [Being protective of one who wanted to be adventurous and was not too good at it, couldn't have been easy.] ... *Elizabeth ... sat by this fire many times. You can look into a fire and see things.'*

Then followed some names from the 1930s and my childhood: *'Jacobs'* ... They had owned the garage 300 yards away down on the main road and many times I had walked down the lane to the garage to get the 'wireless accumulator' charged. [They had mains electricity at the garage, which isolated farmhouses, did not have in those days]. There was a description of a lady dressed in Victorian style with a frilled headpiece and a 'pinny' apron. [That would be Mrs. Finch next door. She had been in service.] And then 'James' I just could not place. [But I had Mrs. Finch's old family bible back home in the library. The answer was written inside the cover. It was her husband who was James. I, as a small boy of the '30s, only ever knew him as Mr. Finch and she always called him by a pet name: 'Googy'. He would have departed this life when I was about seven but I recall him well as a kindly gentleman and he made me my first rabbit hutch. That was James.]

Then it was my spirit guide again with his message: *'Creative energy is to be used.'*

Next, Patricia was describing the Siberian scene to me: *'The night sky is very beautiful with a bright moon. And the wolves ... Their sound is like they are in tune ... almost like singing. Your guide, wrapped in his cloak, shares an awareness with them. He stoops to light a fire ... He likes to have a small fire.*

He is signing off now ... with a poem! ... Arkanu ... It's in Siberian, I can't understand it ... Ah! He's translating:

'Supreme is the world
Energy is the darkness
Dawn is the light
That always awakens us
Hungry are the wolves
Helpless are the sinners
Pretty are the maidens
Who work with the spinners.'

He's giving his name ... He's spelling it for me ... 'Ashenak Fervos'.'

It had been a truly wonderful evening, and we all enjoyed a good chat over a pot of herb tea in conclusion. There were just two more significant items to record:

Patricia had looked a little surprised and coy at the end of the session as she said: 'He blew me a kiss ... like this.' I could not help thinking his gesture went with the last two lines of the poem ... Patricia was the maiden working with the spinning energy chakras to make a bridge between the worlds. This evening, *she* had been the pretty maiden working with the spinners.

Then there was the business of *Varof* ... *Varda* or something like it that Patricia could not quite catch. I had dismissed it as something too unspecific to put meaning to, until I re-read my notes; that was *after* having written in the previous pages of the 'Tunguska event', and the trading station of *Vanavara*. That was it! ... Vanavara! It was already included in the chapter!

I must have been somehow guided to that place and idea at the time of writing, without being consciously aware of the guidance. But then, as I now know, I am not alone when working in this room on this book.

. . . .

There are many kinds of between-worlds travellers. The shamans had and have their various ways. Today's gifted ones, as Patricia, may simply and quietly sit across the table and bridge between worlds in semi-trance. In Britain, our tradition and our landscape are heavily impregnated with reminders of the older between-worlds exchanges.

It is the goddess Rhiannon with her white horse who flies from the wave crests, who has been such an influence in this realm. It is a white mare she rides. The white mare of Rhiannon is the white mare emblazoned on the chalk hills of Southern England. It is she who, by tradition, rides her white mare, the *night mare* between the worlds in our dream-state. Sometimes the journey is frightening and if you have awakened in the night in a sweat, then perhaps you have run with Rhiannon's white mare. And perhaps your dream was not just of the 'ordinary' kind. In children's terms, she is the fine lady who rides a white horse to Banbury Cross. She is the between-worlds nightrider. And especially at Beltane when the portals in the hollow hills and in the sacred mounds, between this world and that other-world are said to be more fully opened.

She is not just the night-rider of our dreams who knows the pathways to the portals. Beltane is the spring festival and she is the Springtime Goddess. On May Day, the maypoles are danced in celebration of the new energy that she brings. And lovers leap the Beltane fire to seal their pact to travel with the goddess in love.

Chapter VI

Palenque

'I am Chan-Bahlum ... *Snake-Jaguar* ... of the Dynasty of Palenque, in this time of our wondrous Golden Age. I acceded the throne in the year 9.12.11.12.10 counting from the zero time of our calendar, as we traverse its 8,000-year cycle. I speak of the year of 9 baktuns, 12 katuns, 11 tuns, 12 uinals and 10 kin.'

[Or in the terms of that less precise form of calendar to which we are accustomed today, Chan-Bahlum acceded in the year AD 684. And that zero time when the Mayan calendar began, corresponds to 13 August 3114 BC.]

'My accession followed the death of my illustrious father Pacal ... *Shield* ... or 'Pacal the Great', as he was known to our people. He was in his 80th year. He was indeed a great, perhaps the greatest of the Golden Age rulers. He took office from his mother, the Lady Zac-Kuk and while she still lived for a further 25 years, she and my father shared the power. I am thus directly descended of the Lady Zac-Kuk and am proud to continue her line in this ... Golden Age of Inspiration.

The power and the influence remained very much with the Lady Zac-Kuk while she still lived. Pacal was the nominal ruler, and so, it was several years after her departure to Xibalba, that he was able to dedicate his first temple ... the temple Olvidado, which stands on the western ridge of our wonderful city. But what a temple! In this, Pacal set the grand style of large interior volume and the superior natural lighting that has since been our standard. There followed the temple of The Count and extensions to the Palace ... our exquisite and now extensive Palace. But then ... then that wonder-of-wonders ... our finest structure the Temple of the Inscriptions. Standing there, such an elegant pyramid with its nine terraces, at the very foot of our sacred mountain. A well chosen site. While in his 70s, Pacal organised the most skilled of masons and sculptors to work the limestone, and then the finest of scribes and artists to write the records and to beautify. Such dedication! Palenque's dynastic statement has been cut and truly recorded in the stonework of this special place for the benefit of future generations, for of course we know that time is a great wheel and the past returns to us. Past and future turn together on the wheel of time and so, such records should surely be.

It is of course the deep vault of this temple that is now the resting-place of our dear departed Pacal. He merely rests. Death is a dream from which we all awaken. His spirit is journeying and of that, we are reminded by the unsurpassable crafting of the sarcophagus; and of the entire delicate inscription throughout the temple, this is surely the most inspired. There he is surrounded by the six prior generations, of which his mother and father Lady Zac-Kuk and Kan-Bahlum-Mo have pride of place. Pacal at the centre, is the seventh generation in this genealogy. He is seen to fall. Pacal descends the Wacah Chan ... the World tree. That is his journey. It is the journey that we all must take when it is time. The tree is the path that connects material world and other-world. At its summit is the celestial bird and guiding influence in life. In its branches is the serpent ... a two-headed serpent, symbolic of the duality. It is the sceptre of authority carried by rulers and it is also the serpent of the vision ... the *vision serpent* that opens the door into the other-world ... to the domain of Xibalba.

It is the king himself who personifies the Wacah Chan in flesh, and it is his act of blood letting that awakens the vision serpent of the trance. At the foot of the tree is Maw of Xibalba. Maw is the symbolic monster of the other-world. Maw's great mouth is the living entrance to that realm. Maw lives, as does that other realm at no great distance. The souls of the dead pass freely. The living too, may in part, take that journey, through activation of the vision serpent, but of course their paths quickly return.

Following the necessary rituals of Pacal's burial and my accession, it became my responsibility to complete Pacal's great temple. When that was done, my masons and craftsmen built the 'Group of the Cross'. That is, the Temple of the Cross, the Temple of the Foliated Cross and the Temple of the Sun. Much of Palenque's dynastic history would be written into these, each with its pib na ... that inner room symbolic of an underground building and with other-world connection. It is the 'mountain's heart' approached through the holy portal of the 'living' hollow hill. Each temple has its holy portal into the central pib na. The temples are built in their 'triadic' form. They are the three pathways to Xibalba and three large doorways in the front wall lead to a majestic antechamber before the inner holy portal is confronted.

My father's funeral stays so fresh in memory. Our people had gathered and we were becoming weaker in the material self from the fasting preparation. Following Pacal's entombment, it was at last the time for public blood letting for my brother Kan-Xul and myself. Many followed our example and the many blood-reddened papers were all brought to the high terrace, to the braziers fashioned in the form of the great Ancestral Twins. The shamans, who stood by, watched intently for the onset of trance. They judged the moment. The blood and flesh of trees, that is the copal, rubber and wood, were thrown onto the braziers with the well-blooded papers and the sacrifice of our blood was consumed. As the pillar of dark smoke rose and swirled, the conch trumpets sounded and their earthy tone echoed from the hills. Away somewhere out in the jungle, a howler monkey responded. Then as the sky reddened with the steady sinking of evening sun, this was the moment of the spirit ancestors. They enjoined Pacal and took him on his way, as he floated and fell on his downward journey within the Wacah Chan to Xibalba.

The Sun Temple, though of a lesser grandeur than Pacal's great masterpiece, is nonetheless a temple of immense beauty and grace. Episodes of Palenque's dynastic events have been tenderly inscribed on its pillars and plaques, not least the details of my own accession. That event was well timed. I was 48 years old at that time. The proceedings began on 1st January 684, just 123 days after the death of my dear father. As it was on the occasion of his funeral, there was a great gathering of the people. There followed the fasting and later the blood letting, to bring forth the vision serpent. Through the vision serpent I was then able to commune with the spirit being of Pacal. This took place in the pib na, where such communions are made, once the vision serpent has been awakened. The accession rites were just ten days into their progress. Pacal confronted me and bestowed his kingship upon me. I then received the heavy, feathered head-dress and stood before the people as Ahau of Ahauob ... Lord of Lords.

The proceedings drew finally to a close as our well-observed Evening Star; the planet Venus reached the furthest point in her heavenly path. Her path across the heavens, that is ... where she dances with the sun as Morning Star and Evening Star. And as our Evening Star began her return from that furthest point, so too did our new realm begin its course. The trusty regulator of our calendar marked well the Earthly event of my accession. As their king, I have served my people well and have held their trust and respect, while Venus continues to shine forth her subtle radiance upon us.

Such is my statement regarding our more formal matters. I would also speak to you concerning 'knowledge', which may on occasions have a curious manner of growth. As with all civilisations upon this planet, ours has its attendant accumulated facts and logic. But I have to point out that not all things to which we have been privy, have come from the fount of our own inspiration. There have been prior great civilisations ... and these in their time have achieved much. Ultimately, for whatever reason, they have met with their demise. But not before some of their ways have been passed on ... and so we have our past links.

Evidence of one remote connection is that ancient city on the river that you call Rio Grande. The present name of that city now describes it well, since the intervening years have taken their toll. 'Lubantum' ... *the place of the fallen stones* ... is a place that predates Palenque and all architecture that is truly Mayan.

It was only a short time after its discovery by your Western World that Lubantum yielded the 'crystal skull'. This treasured and beautiful artefact has often been a focal point in our deeper ceremonies. It is remarkable in that it has been fashioned from pure rock crystal in the most perfect manner. The process of its manufacture always remained unknown to Mayan technology; just as it is unknown to your scientists and to your own technologies of much later times. The crystal skull predates all that was ever Mayan.

I have already stated that the Great Cycle of time into which our own age was born, began on your calendar date: 13 August 3114 BC. It will last for the span of exactly thirteen bactuns; that is just 1,872,000 days. You will see that your own time still lies within that same Great Cycle. The Fourth Cycle of Existence is indeed something that our two cultures have in common. We share a place in time, and it is appropriate that we pass on knowledge as yet unknown to you; just as helpful criteria and artefacts were conveyed to us by great ones who had taken their different path.

Some of your scientists already take account of what you term *astrogenetics*, and are well familiar with the changing and periodic output of our host sun. Those few are aware of ... not only the dependence of all Earth life upon sun energy, but equally upon the changing qualities of life that must follow in the wake of the engulfing solar wind that flows from our host. Our calendar does not arise from any scant or fanciful pursuit. It runs in tandem with those periodicities within our sun that is in so many ways, our master.

Your scientists are well familiar with the outwardly visible sunspot cycle that lies close to a full cycle time of 11 years. There are other determining revolutions within the great engine of the sun, of much, much longer duration, and our time-keeping systems endeavour to embrace these. In our preserved document that you now call the *Dresden Codex*, we give details of our shared Great Cycle in time and we account the special number: 1,366,560. Counting from our beginning, this represents the period in days to the time of solar magnetic field reversal. This was that period which you account as 7th century AD. The resulting altered fields and solar radiations felt in these latitudes, were a heavy burden upon Mayan life. That period came as ordained and as calculated, and our decline was to follow.

Concerning that other number ... the Great Cycle number, which defines the Fourth Cycle of Existence, you will see that it closes on AD 22 December 2012, and a new age then begins. There will be difficult changes upon Earth at this time ... not in this instance from any solar magnetic field reversal, but resulting from other factors within the cosmic balance.

It is true that this period is conveniently described as thirteen bactuns ... using our more formal counting system. The same number of days, however, emerges from our more cosmic and prophetic calendar, that has contained within itself the units of the 365-day *haab* and the 260-day *tzolkin* ... or *sacred year*. And 52 *haab* make up one *calendar round*. In these units, the period of 1,872,000 days may be expressed equally as 100 X (one calendar round less one tzolkin) or as 7,200 tzolkin. The significance of the latter unit may not be directly apparent, but I can assure you it has a subtlety. It may help to know that the more ponderous Mars takes almost exactly three times as long to complete his orbit compared to our beloved Venus. This relates to Earth in that the alignment *Mars - Earth - Sun* occurs once every 3 X 260 days. The numbers: 365 and 52 will already be familiar to you. All are factors that enmesh in the wheels of cosmic pattern.

Mode of expression of the number 1,872,000 matters not. The point that I would make is this ... The prophetic number is derived of the cosmic patterns themselves, and notwithstanding extraordinary intervention by Kukulcan, remains immutable. It follows further that your scientists might do well to consider the forthcoming changes that concern our planetary system, with a view to easing Earth's population as kindly as possible into the new conditions that are to prevail in the new and most wonderful Fifth Cycle of Existence.

Long after I have taken my own journey to Xibalba and perhaps long after our Mayan peoples have departed this life, the Temple of the Sun and many of our temples will remain here in this hallowed place. They carry the message of our people, of our earth and spirit connection. My message to the future ... to those who may visit this place is this:

'These blocks of stone are much, much more. They have been hewn from a carefully chosen quarry. They carry the history of our culture and account our spiritual focus. This place has an 'energy' that we have implanted here. Feel it and know us. It is Mayan to observe the Trinity of God-Nature-Humanity. The three must remain in harmony. Our one all-powerful God is Kukulcan. He is known by other names ... as Quetzalcoatl in Nahua territories. Within his Earthly domain he has lesser gods as helpers. The Sun God and the Rain God do his bidding. And 'Rainbow' is their child. It is Mayan to revere colour, for the child of these lesser gods is simply and precisely this and nothing more. Therefore enjoy knowing colour! Know this place. Be refreshed by it for your further journeys in life, and disport yourselves well before you too are met and gently guided between worlds through the Wacah Chan."

Palenque Ancient Site. Block plan of main structures.

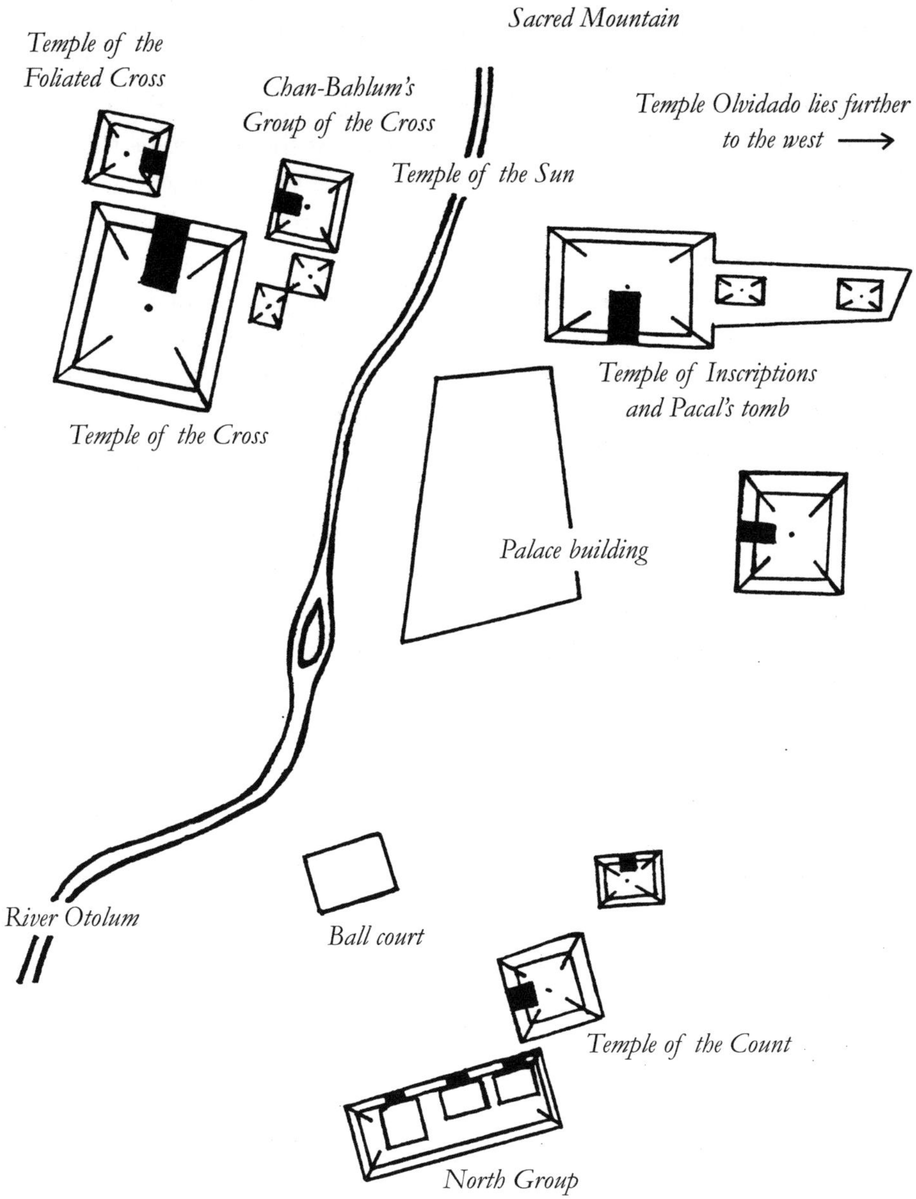

Summer of 1989: As John Slater drove along the A2 towards Dover, he was enjoying the Kent countryside and keeping a watchful eye for the 'Whitfield' sign. The road was unfamiliar. He rarely headed in this direction. Some years back, he had become a godparent to young Andrew and now it was that same young Andrew who was having a formal Confirmation. It was this occasion, which now brought him to these parts. So this was not exactly an *ordinary* day for John Slater who, in keeping with his work, mostly enjoyed scientific pursuits. Nevertheless, it should also be said that despite the scientific treadmill that earned him a salary, he was generally observant and open at least, to all things new. In fact you might say he was not really your average scientist at all. At home, he got involved in the usual family conversations and he sometimes got quite carried away with his fanciful notions; this to the extent that he had, within the family, acquired the nickname *Toad*. (This was after the flamboyant *Toad* of Toad Hall). He noticed things. He had noticed that life, for him, lacked any expectation of smooth flow. There were times when he experienced bunches of odd little *coincidences* and these often preceded what were to become especially interesting periods. He had come to think of it as like being 'tipped off' by someone 'up there' that things would be on the move again.

Something was now coming up ahead ... He could just make out the distant sign as W-H-I-T-F- ... when wham! ... *'Whitfield'* came over the car radio. That was incredible! The radio had somehow linked with his reading of the road sign! A little flush of energy ran through him and he just knew that something good was brewing, and this time, the coincidence was indeed to herald one of those special *chains* of events. It was a straightforward enough Confirmation ceremony and young Andrew was clearly happy at his school.

Things then began to happen fast. On returning home, Ruth brought him up to date with the news of the day. 'Still no news of Alex...'

The two boys were both quite bright and adventurous. They had completed university degrees, earned a little money, and had gone off to México to 'travel' for six months and possibly to tread in the footsteps of *Don Juan* about whom they had read a pile of books. They travelled together at first, then on individual paths, with a general plan to meet up before returning home. A friend, Jack, the local landscape gardener, had been round.

'An aralia tree? I don't know that one.'

'He got some from an exhibition, so they're cheap,' Ruth explained.

'Oh ... right!'

'It might go nicely by the pond. He says they're different.'

'Different! Well, let's see.' John looked it up in the book, planted the aralia tree and it did indeed look nice by the pond. It seemed a perfectly ordinary event at the time. But the idea of it being *different* remained with him.

Next came the chance meeting with a clairvoyant healer. Neither had met anyone remotely like him before ... an oddball. He was an over-the-top and larger-than-life character, but with obvious and remarkable talents. One very close to Ruth, had died some five years earlier and she had never quite regained her old sparkle. Jim the clairvoyant had been quick to recognise the retained grief and triggered its removal! She again sparkled! He earned a deep-felt gratitude for this.

He had a capability to help and heal. Wherever he went, he seemed to set people on fresh paths in life or leave them confronting old ghosts that they had thought safely tucked away in impregnable closets. His counsel delighted some, while others ranted and rebelled at his unorthodox ways ... just could not hack his crude directness. He would move on, leaving behind a cloud of dust and debris, and a scattering of new ideas. He was that sort of a guy. Life is important, therefore *no holds barred* ... seemed to be the name of his game. He was a passing ship who came into their lives, had significant exchange, then departed come what may. There were inevitably a good many that would have preferred to remain in their own carefully-constructed little backwaters of easy living ... and why not?

John's hobby was the further expansion of space-time theory. Albert Einstein was his hero. But John firmly held the view that space, far from being mere *emptiness*, was a realm that contained within its fabric, a wealth of important properties. Einstein had demonstrated the inhomogeniety of space and had formulated brilliantly his mass-energy equivalence: $E = mc^2$, but he had not gone on to establish the connection of the equation with space per se. Further study of this area, should open a Pandora's box ... should eventually lead the way to an understanding of non-matter and then to exceeding the speed of light! These ideas steered his thinking, and of course, the development of such knowledge would be essential before any serious space travel could be at all possible, since the more interesting parts of the universe lie many, many light-years distant. Slow conventional rocketry would not get very far in a lifetime. He had worked out a thing or two. Well, John had the idea of putting Jim to the test by asking a question about his own pet theory (Only he and God would know about it). Jim had looked up with hand on forehead for a moment, then delivered the *correct* answer in the terms of his theory. Good heavens! ... Then he really *was* clairvoyant, or could read minds, or could access knowledge from somewhere ... just like that! But that was not all. Jim had *then* delivered the punch line: 'Look, if you get to visit México, and you get the opportunity of a magic mushroom trip, you really should take it ... because it'll give you a heightened perception and that may help you to expand your theory and get it right!'

'Well,' replied John 'That's not an approach I would normally have considered at all; not for one moment, but since it is you who suggest it, I'll think about it.'

'Right.' And the single word reply was made the more emphatic with his characteristic chin-thrust-forward nod.

'Good heavens!' thought John. 'He knows the answer to a question on an unpublished theory that is stuck ... tucked away inside my head!'

It was Chris who phoned from Mérida, Yucatán, to say: 'Look, while we're here, why don't you come out for a holiday? We could show you all the good non-tourist spots. Take a couple of days to think about it and I'll phone again.'

Two days later, Chris was surprised to learn from his dad that his rather less adventurous parents had already booked airline tickets: 'Wow! So when are you coming?'

'Next week.'

'Wow! You didn't waste much time!'

'Well, the old Mayan civilisation was always one that interested me quite a lot. They were a fine people. I've read several books over the years.'

'I've bought a copy of their sacred book ... the Popol Vuh.'

'Well done! I read it when I was eighteen. An interesting work!'

'Then we'll visit some Mayan sites. Where are you flying to?'

'Mérida. The flight gets in at 1700 hours.'

'Mérida! Great! I'll meet you at the airport. Heard from Alex yet?'

'No.'

'Never mind. Perhaps he'll phone in the week. You never know. Gotta go now. Cheers.'

'Bye Chris. See you soon...'

It was July. It would be hot. No need for a lot of clothing. They could travel light. They would be travelling on long distance buses. One zip-up bag each with a shoulder strap should do nicely. There was really little to do, and it all just happened so quickly.

Somewhere over the Atlantic in a wide-body jet, John slept for a spell. He awakened knowing he had had one of those *special* dreams. He knew the special ones. They were always in colour and on waking, he had a feeling about them that he could not explain. He thought about this one. Perhaps this time, his subconscious had been trying to fathom the mysterious Jim. How could he heal and delight some yet enrage others, the way he did? Of his healing there was no doubt, and of his clairvoyant gift there was no doubt. He knew that well enough and anyway, he had been able to put it to the test! That side of him certainly appeared both genuine and remarkable.

In his dream, Jim had been dressed in white in a hospital room, and John's daughter Kate had been caring for him. Kate! Why Kate? In the dream, the scene had then changed. Now Jim was an odd-shaped, bright blue and gold 'creature'; a bit like a ring-doughnut with knobs! He knew it was still Jim ... it's funny how in dreams you just *know* things without having them spelled out. He seemed to have *metamorphosed*! So John thought: *Is my subconscious trying to tell me that Jim's psychic self is currently undergoing some kind of a change?* It did not make a lot of sense at the time. [But several weeks later, he told Kate of the dream. She was appreciative that some dreams are special and Kate was able to see aura colours to a useful degree. And she said right away: 'I am sure his aura colours are blue and gold, as the colours of your dream.' She had a book: 'Human Energy Systems', by Jack Schwartz. They looked up the chapter on aura input rays and found listed on page 33, characteristics for the second ray (azure blue and golden yellow). They read that second-ray people who emphasise the golden yellow tend to be clairvoyants and that they are especially sensitive to paraconscious sources of information. And if they utilise the blue more than the gold, then they may well become teachers, religious reformers or healers. John had flipped when they read it. It was clear that Jim fitted the category of a 'second-ray-person'. The author lists and describes the other ray-types, but it was only the blue-gold type described in these terms. As Jim was a clairvoyant healer who was sensitive to paraconscious knowledge, the description fitted perfectly. The blue and gold would be in a state of balance, possibly a shifting balance, and the dream made surprisingly good sense. But then, he *knew* it had been a special dream; and somehow he just *knew* that, in his dreamstate, he had accessed information from somewhere beyond that little door in his subconscious; at least, that is how he thought of it. To his credit, although of the scientific genre, he readily acknowledged that there are things in this life that lie well beyond the conventional or ordinary scientific understanding.]

Chris greeted them at Mérida. There was still no news of Alex, but never mind, even without meeting up with Alex; this would still be a great adventure. Not a holiday ... *an adventure.* They booked in at the comfortable Hotel Margarita for a last night of civilised luxury. Their family room had clean beds, a ceiling fan and the usual en suite facilities with shower. Perfect for the reunion and for planning the next stage of the adventure.

Ruth had many questions of course concerning welfare: 'Have you kept fit? You're looking thinner but you've got a good healthy glow. When did you last see Alex? Are you coping with the language? ... And has the money lasted?' There had been so many questions.

Eventually John had said: 'What do you know about magic mushrooms, Chris?'

Chris was amazed ... fairly bowled over to be in receipt of such a question, straight out of the blue like that. 'Well! Well ... you see ... Well, good heavens! The fact is ... we've been to this place where they grow ... and people seem to know about them. In fact, I've had them on my mind as a topic of interest, but I just could not think how I might broach the subject with you ... I mean ... it's drugs dammit! You uphold the 'establishment' and what it stands for ... well, you know what I mean.'

'Ah ... and you thought I was too much of a stuffed shirt to be able to talk magic mushrooms to?'

'Yes. That's it! That's right! Travellers talk about such things. That's cool. That's accepted. But that's travellers for you. Travellers are travellers ... a law unto themselves ... a set on their own ... outside ... not part of 'establishment'.'

'Well, it's a funny old world ... all a part of life's rich pattern.' The three of them would be moving across country tomorrow, and in a sense, at least for the next two weeks, they would all be travellers. Later, John had talked of the clairvoyant healer who had suggested that John partake of some mushrooms to help him sort out his theory.

'I don't believe it! *You* met a clairvoyant healer! Alex and I met a clairvoyant healer ... a German woman who speaks very good English and Spanish, in San Cristóbal. A *very* interesting lady.'

'Another coincidence. They just keep coming,' went on John. 'Like this other guy ... an acquaintance, that dropped by. We got talking, and would you believe, he had a copy of a scientific paper ... which is a homeopathic proving of *Psilocybe caerulesens Murray, variety Mazatecorum,* by a doctor from México? That's the magic mushroom from this part of the world!'

'Well that's quite something! It's like it's all meant to be. Like it's all meant to fit together like a kind of fortuitous jigsaw puzzle. 'Magic mushroom' is at least pronounceable; but what did you call it?'

'Ah. Well, it's a *Psilocybe* mushroom, that's the part that matters, and hence the active principal is *psilocybin.*' (He had become *Toad* again, just for the moment.) 'Chemically, the psilocybins are based on a substituted indole group and so should be reasonably compatible with the body chemistry, so long as one doesn't overdo it or make a habit. Unlike LSD, which contains a *naphthalene* nucleus ... Oh horrors! ... That would be such seriously bad news. One hell of a disaster area ... that! Naphthalene ... you know ... moth-balls! The naphthalene nucleus as like as not means it doesn't clear from the body *at all* well. You don't have to be a chemist to understand that. You wouldn't get me trying *that* stuff! No way! No chance!' There was a look of mild reproof from Ruth and he quickly remembered he was on holiday and not in a chemistry laboratory.

'It really is an outside chance that you should have come by a paper on the *Méxican* mushroom, in *England*, just like that, and so timely,' ventured Chris.

'Well, this is a wonderful world ... a rapidly changing world it seems, and it just is, well, so ... sparky at the moment. Sparky! That's the word. So much seems to be happening ... and connecting.'

'Then shall we head for Palenque? It's one of the best Mayan sites, with mushroom fields nearby. How about a relaxed day tomorrow, then we take the afternoon bus and travel through the evening and overnight? We go across Yucatán, over the border and into Chiapas state.'

'That sounds perfect. You seem to know your way around.'

'Well that's as it should be. I'm your tour guide!'

Next day, they purchased the essentials of two more hammocks, straw hats, a box of matches, a candle and a small glass. Then there was the enjoyment of Mexican food. There were spicy *huevos rancheros, tortillas* and the most wonderful fruit salads. And superior versions of ice lollies consisting simply of frozen crushed fruit on a stick ... oversized sweet corn vended from a ten-gallon can of boiling water on the street corner, anointed with relish and served in a paper wrap ... kept them well-fed and interested through the day. Then it was time for boarding the bus.

The modern Palenque is a small town, big enough to have its bus station, small hotels and cosy restaurants. And like all towns in this part of the world, it has its street vendors who add a colourful dimension to its commerce. The Combi taxis did regular runs, taking visitors the ten kilometres to *Las ruinas* and the nearby jungle campsite, where travellers may sling their hammocks in open shelters beneath a thatched roof. That night, the three chatted in their hammocks and watched the fireflies endlessly spiking the darkness with their silent brightness, just out there before the trees that were the jungle's edge. Below, on the ground, the candle burned in the small glass, giving out its soft light. Their conversation ebbed. It became quiet. Outside, apart from the fireflies, the night was embracing all in shadowy sleep. Dark shapes softened and began to merge. Thoughts emptied away. That was the moment the large black toad chose to move out from the darker shadow. John remained awake and watched in silence, moving only his eyes. What happened in the next few minutes remained engraved in his memory with crystal clarity. The toad squatted three inches from the candle flame, staring at it for what seemed like ten seconds. It then moved round a quadrant clockwise and again took up its stance for ten seconds. Twice more it moved round the glass, so that it had attended the flame from all four quadrants. It then retired to the shadows. But it was not finished; it returned again to the glass. The 'toad ballet' was repeated as before, exactly the same in every detail. It then finally departed into the night and was gone.

John savoured his thoughts before yielding to sleep. He was *Toad*. By some strange synchronistic fusion, the little 'ballet' had been for *his* benefit and for his alone. There was no doubt of that. The others were asleep. Only he had remained awake. He did not pretend to understand what had transpired, but just listened to what his inner voice was saying. The toad had come from the jungle and had seemed to contemplate the living flame *twice* before departing. Tomorrow, at first light, they would walk in the fields and look for the local mushroom. Then, like the jungle toad, he *'Toad'*, would be conducting his own experiment, to contemplate he knew not exactly what. His experiment, he would have considered irrational a year ago ... perhaps bizarre or even foolhardy, but a chain of events had put him on this course, in such a way that any senses of logic and conformity were somehow not offended.

At sunrise, all was still as they walked along tracks between fences. Here the jungle had been pushed back and it was now pasture. Long-horned cattle with droopy ears grazed in some of the fields. After walking about a mile, they came to a gateway leading to a large grassy area with scattered trees that had been recommended for their quest (by travellers who know about such things). But here, John stopped in his tracks and stared in momentary disbelief. There, in front of him at the entrance to the field, was a tree, its form unmistakable. It was unquestionably an *aralia* tree, just like the one he had planted back home only a week earlier! The coincidence of it somehow made him feel comfortable and nicely 'on course'.

But there were not many mushrooms to be had at this time. (Their appearance generally followed the rain pattern, so that they were not always plentiful. Local collectors would take this factor into account. They would store them, and trade in times of scarcity.)

Chris explained: 'There are those who collect in the plentiful times and preserve them in a little honey. They will sell us some to add to our few. But we should separate when we walk back. I am much more likely to be approached on my own, because I look every inch a *traveller* while you ... '

John understood. The plan was agreed. Chris went on ahead, while Ruth and John followed some 200 yards behind. It happened as anticipated. A vendor appeared, seemingly from nowhere with honey pot in hand and radiating a broad friendly smile from beneath a well-worn straw hat. But it was not the 'traveller' up ahead who was approached. It was John, who flushed with pleasure and thought ... well, it's fitting really, it is after all *my* project. But then again, he knew that Chris was into the mandatory haggling of these parts and had some idea of the value of things. So, putting his limited few words of Spanish together, John managed to convey that the *amigo* up ahead had funds and they should meet at a place up there by the river where they would do a deal. It was only a short while later, by a little waterfall at the edge of the jungle, that the deal was transacted.

Now they were equipped for the grand experiment but there was no rush. The time and place should be chosen with care. After all, this was a once-in-a-lifetime happening. There was no urgency ... no need for haste. This afternoon they would view the Mayan temples of Palenque, and what a magnificent spectacle! There! ... was the Palace with its intricately worked reliefs. There! ... was the Temple of the Inscriptions at the foot of the sacred mountain, and over there ... towards the jungle's edge, was the Group of the Cross and the superbly beautiful Sun Temple. They marvelled at its inscriptions and just enjoyed being there.

A stream runs through the site and into the jungle where the rocky terrain slopes steeply down towards the modern road. A difficult path follows the stream. At a point perhaps 500 yards from the site, it reaches a small scarp and plunges into a crystal clear natural pool. Having followed the path through the trees, the three were steamy from their exertions and so bathed in this delightful pool enclosed by smooth rocks, with the jungle trees just beyond.

Wonderfully refreshed, they then walked on to the campsite, collected their few things and took the combi taxi into town. A restaurant meal would be the next move and they could plan the evening's activities. It was during this meal that Ruth was suddenly rather poorly, becoming pale and faint. They sat her on the floor with head between knees, as the kindly proprietor nudged a local doctor who just happened to be sitting across the room. He asked two questions and knew exactly what was wrong. He had seen it many times before with visitors to México: 'Caffeine withdrawal! That is all. Visitors from the West are so used to their cups of tea at regular intervals and their bodies are so used to the regular intake. But when in México, they so much enjoy the fruits and the fruit juices that tea and coffee are forgotten. *Sudden* caffeine withdrawal causes the nausea and fainting. The remedy is simple - a cup of black coffee. I would recommend a cup each day and you should have no problem.'

He was right. Ruth was instantly recovered and they were most grateful to the doctor for his knowledge, and to the understanding proprietor. Although Ruth was perfectly recovered, the little upset influenced their planning; and they felt it prudent to book a family room at the small hotel across the street for the night. The general plan that evolved was that Ruth should be tucked up in bed at the hotel and be with their things. Chris and John would return to the Mayan site after sunset to conduct their mushroom experiment.

Chris had said: 'Such an experiment should be conducted in a magnificent setting, and there is none more magnificent than this.'

John the scientist had said: 'With the two of us taking part, we can compare notes during the course of whatever transpires. That should make it interesting and will help to validate the details.'

They took the jungle path beside the stream and could just make out their way in the darkness. It was easier once they reached the site. But it looked different by starlight. The temples suddenly loomed large and shadowy but they managed to find the Sun Temple. They were always somehow drawn to that one. The night was warm and they chose to sit on the topmost step before the three openings that lead to the antechamber and to the pib na.

There was some discussion as to the reasonable dosage of the little fungi. Chris had been informed that twelve was about right and so took twelve. John considered that he was sensitive to medicaments in general, which he rarely took and he was also cautious by nature, and so took six. This, he fancied, amounted to a half dose. Nothing happened for twenty minutes or so, except for a slight queasiness in the stomach. Then it began.

Was it less dark now, or were they just being fanciful? The condition of the night had not altered. The skies had been clear at the start and remained so. John felt that the stars were perhaps a little brighter. Was it his imagination? He raised his hands towards the stars and noticed the translucent yellowish light around the fingers. It was only when he lowered his hands and continued to stare at them, that he noticed beyond ... the new appearance of the temple stonework. It was a major source of the extra light that was all about them!

What a picture! Exquisite! The face of every piece ... every block of worked stone glowed with a bluish-violet hue. Not all exactly the same. Some stones seemed whiter and some more towards the violet. The entire site was being illuminated by the stones! And getting brighter! Every mortar course between the stones remained black and devoid of any light output whatsoever. The total effect was stunningly beautiful ... as a work of art by a 'master' in light! He, John the scientist, had seen glowing shades like these before ... in the laboratory ... strongly fluorescent materials under an ultraviolet lamp. The effect, he considered, would be akin to ultraviolet fluorescence. He moved across to Chris to see how he was faring. Chris was fascinated by the fireflies. They were brighter. Both agreed they were *very* bright and they would appear to be sparking in time to other things ... a kind of synchronous connectedness with nearby sounds and movement. That was all very fascinating ... and it was quickly established that they were both seeing the same effects.

They walked together along a ledge that ran around the temple. Despite the night, they walked in perfect safety because the stones were so brightly illuminating their path. They could each clearly see every stone from one corner of the pyramid structure to the next. This said something positive: The light was no hallucination ... no illusion. The light of the stones was *real* light that they were utilising to see their way. The light *was* real! Just as real and useful as switching on a torch, but infinitely ... infinitely more beautiful. The reality of it was an important deduction. Chris enjoyed the beauty of it all. John was being the scientific analyst and he now understood what was happening. They were both sensitive to more wavelengths than the ones to which they were ordinarily accustomed. Both were seeing beyond the normal visible spectrum band of wavelengths and their vision was without doubt extended well into the ultraviolet! These stones were special. He guessed that they absorbed the sun energy during the day, and re-emitted energy as an ultraviolet radiation at night. This, of course, would only be seen by those who, for whatever reason, were sensitive to the ultraviolet. To the vast majority the special light would remain invisible. How privileged they were, to be observing things that are normally there but remain quite invisible to modern humankind!

On the ground, there lay a large slab of rough hewn stone. It was an illuminated patchwork of blue-violet shades, with here and there a patch of black. It had the appearance of a glowing carpet of extreme beauty. [On returning to the site next day, it became clear that the black patches were zones of moist dirt that had collected in some of the little hollows. Only the bare stone had glowed in the bright shades. Clearly only the uncovered clean stone could absorb energy and re-emit.]

Walking at ground level, they chanced to look up at flowers growing on a ledge above. They looked odd ... like wheels with spokes ... and large, but much of the wheel was transparent and stars could be seen *through* it. The idea of transparent flowers seemed strange. The flowers were like none that they had seen before. [Next day, it became clear to them that the flowers were in fact daisies, the 'spokes' being the petals and the transparent part would be the encompassing flower energy field.] It was becoming clear that in the conditions of the experiment, they were able to see both the energy fields of flowers and the energy field surrounding their human bodies (prana aura), both of which can be photographed in a laboratory, in the special conditions of Kirlian photography. But the two of them, this night, were privileged to observe these things direct through their heightened perception status.

They were content to wander in their newly found wonderland with no thought of time. It took as long as it took. Eventually they made the decision to leave the site by the jungle path, reached the road and walked the ten kilometres back to the hotel. They talked over the night's work as they walked. The experience had lasted five hours. They walked at a cracking pace and in no way lacked energy following the episode. Ruth was pleased to see their return, and listened to their account of it all.

Next day, they revisited the site for their further checking; then moved on, taking the evening bus south to San Cristóbal ... a beautiful town at a higher altitude, cooler and less humid. The town has many splendid buildings. They could relax in cooler air and enjoy this place for a few days. As they walked along a street, Chris gestured to a small poster: 'That's the clairvoyant lady we met. I heard that she has moved on down to

Guatemala.' But of course, on rounding the corner, they came face-to-face with her. The chain of coincidence continued. The conversation lasted less than ten minutes but it was so free and unrestrained that it seemed longer:

She being German, and they having seen several Albert Einstein publications in bookshops in the town, John indicated that he much admired his work, and added: 'I think Einstein was much more than just a scientist.'

She replied: 'Yes. I know just what you mean. I can tell you ... he continues to do good work in spirit realm.'

'We feel this is a special time. We keep getting these little coincidences.' John said how he had planted an aralia tree back in England, then found he was looking at one in Palenque.

'Yes, they grow here. I have one as a potted plant back home.'

They met with two other friends whom Chris had made in his earlier travels. Travellers seem to be like that ... they just keep bumping into each other in foreign parts. After enjoying the town for two days they were making fresh plans. Chris made the decision to stay on in San Cristóbal for the next month, until the expiry of his visa. Then he would return to England. Ruth and John *had* thought of going on down to Guatemala and they already had the visas in preparation for that, but it was not to be. Both had an irrational yet compelling desire to return to Palenque. The inner voice seemed to be saying: *'It is important to get back to Palenque ... now!'* So they went with their feelings, bade their farewells to Chris and boarded the bus that would take them the 90 miles or so back to Palenque.

Alighting in the familiar street, they headed for a shop to purchase soap but just before they reached it, a slim young man stepped from a café with amused grin and inquired: 'Are you looking for somewhere to eat...?'

It was Alex! By this time their senses were becoming just a little confused. Should they register surprise, or should they now be regarding one more coincidence in this chain of coincidences, as a natural and regular occurrence? Surprise still came easily enough, but they quickly got around to explaining to Alex just how they were becoming accustomed to such happenings. They all hugged in delighted amazement. They learned that Alex had been travelling in *four* Central American countries, and was now on his way through to Yucatán, and was only stuck here in Palenque on account of having to wait twenty-four hours for the next bus. Hearing this, they were even more amazed at their good fortune. But it had now become clear why it was they had been guided back here at this time; and they had been so right to follow the guiding influence of the inner voice.

There was so much to talk about. They went over every detail of the past week's events and of course, there would have to be a repeat of the mushroom experiment. John had stated that any experiment of significance should as a matter of principle be replicated to check that results are consistent; also, he felt a certain obligation to see how he would respond to the regular 'full dose' of the little fungi. Furthermore, although the night at the temple had been so wonderful, John had not ventured to contemplate the philosophical issues that had been his foremost interest at the outset. There had been just so much to wonder at, that had deserved his more immediate attention. After some discussion, it was decided that John and Alex this time, would obtain a further supply of the mushrooms, and conduct a second experiment at night, at the now familiar Sun Temple. This would satisfy John's feeling that such an experiment should be checked by duplication.

It was a very similar result with some variations. One would not necessarily expect the effect to be exactly the same each time. If the perception is heightened by the psilocybin, then the result may well depend on the initial perception of the individual concerned, and the mood at the time of the experiment. In the second experiment, the brightness of the stones and the energy fields were seen exactly as they had appeared before. This, for John, was clearly a repeatable result. This time, he also made a conscious effort to meditate on atoms and the primary particles and he sat within the temple near the entrance to the pib na for this. After a short time, it began to seem to him that, in a sense, he was *within* the stonework that surrounded him. At least, he was much more attuned to it, and midst many sounds. All was in resonance. As a scientist, he well understood the theories of vibrational resonance of particulate matter, and how it all comes down to a system of energies in motion, but in his meditation, he sensed himself to be in amongst all that vibrant energy of movement. It occurred to him that it was rather like being in a huge engineering works; but although the power was substantial, the physical matter was *in*substantial. The *power* of the energy around him was *all.* Another, more individual sound attracted his attention. Somewhere within the stone temple, there was a water drip, slow and rhythmic. Putting his ear to the wall, he found it consisted of individual musical notes and he could discern each and every one. He listened for a time, quite spellbound. The sound seemed to have a certain crystal character. Each note had such a sharpness, yet the notes combined to make the water drip sound when his ear was no longer pressed to the wall.

He moved outside under the twinkling bright stars. Such wonderful stars they were. Out here it appeared just as it had on that previous occasion. What a place of such incredible beauty! Almost as if each shaped stone were translucent plastic with a lamp inside! He wondered if the Mayans had access to psychic sight, either through the conditions of their lifestyle and attunement, or via their ceremonial conditioning. If so, then the choice of this particular limestone to facilitate this wonderful effect may well have been deliberate. [It was. He was later to receive confirmation of this.] Quite literally then, there was more to this site than ordinarily meets the eye. Alex was seated to one side of the temple entrance. John sat on the topmost step looking to the heavens ... just gazing amongst the brightness and clarity of the stars ... when the thought came into his head. Such a powerful thought it was, against his rational line of thinking. It just *zapped* in from somewhere up there, as if generated from above:

'It's alright to tinker with the mechanics of the universe ... to try to figure things out ... as did Newton, as did Einstein ... It's a kind of appreciation, a kind of homage ... BUT ... the ... most ... important ... thing ... in all the universe ... is ... LOVE.'

John suddenly felt very small yet filled with an excitement. The statement somehow carried with it the power of a special dream. It brought the experiment to a conclusion in a most majestic way! He told Alex what had transpired. He had said: 'Well ... you just can't knock that. Love ... attraction ... affinity ... God ... The energy of the creative principle ... All the same really. Love has to be the most important thing.'

In the final analysis, love is all. It had been another incredible night, and a satisfactory conclusion to an incredible period. They had drifted, barely in touch with that other more opaque, more starkly stated reality. And somewhere out there in the jungle of that other reality, beyond where they could see and somehow softened by the night air; there came the sound of a howler monkey.

It transpired that there were the *two* experiments in heightened awareness that were conducted at the Sun Temple, just as there had been *two* occasions when the toad had come out from the shadows to seemingly contemplate the candle flame. The 'toad ballet' now seemed to fit and take on its full meaning. It made sense. And John Slater felt that he too had now come out of the shadows ... the shadows of his own metaphoric jungle. What had happened at this enchanting Mayan site was now burned into his memory forever. It had been a special time. It was a time for learning, and life paths would change or get on course as the result. He would read and think more on the nature of auras, subtle energies, energy fields ... and *love* as *the power* in the universe. He would toy with the intangible and let his creative instincts run their free course. There had to be so much more to this universe than just its known physical laws and its hardware. Physical laws were for a physical world, but what of that other world beyond the physical? There had to be so much more that lay beyond the bounds of his lifetime of 'old' contemporary science.

He would not encounter the mushrooms again. There was no need. Their further use would be quite pointless. A 'consciousness' had beckoned and it had been right to follow, and the experiment had yielded its rich reward.

The holiday continued for the three of them. They travelled into Yucatán and to the Mayan site at Uxmal. That was interesting enough. But the great adventure and the set of 'coincidences' that marked its course, was now ended. The conclusion of it was marked by what John continued to think of as 'that cosmic message', received on the topmost step of the Palenque Sun Temple. What more majestic place could there have been for such a happening? They felt so privileged. It had been a magical time, a time to marvel at and a time to reflect upon, and a time to talk about guardedly, just to those who might be able to take such things on board. Many would not. Perhaps the world is changing. Perhaps, given more time, many would become more receptive to such things ... to such a rank unorthodoxy.

> *We cannot open the Maya portals to the Other-world with excavation alone, no matter how careful and how extensive. For the portals are places in the mind and in the heart. We, as pilgrims from another time and reality, must approach the ruined entrances to the past with humility and attention to what the Maya, ancient and modern, can teach us through their words as well as their deeds.*
>
> Linda Schele and David Freidel *A Forest of Kings*
>
>

. . . .

[The so-called magic mushroom had of course for many centuries been known and respected by the Maya. The altered consciousness that it confers was and is utilised by shamans to obtain knowledge for use in healing. There are the *veladas* or sacred mushroom evening ceremonies. These were outlawed by the Spanish Inquisition following the fall of Montezuma and for the last four centuries such ceremonies have been conducted covertly. María Sabina (1894-1985) was during much of her lifetime, a revered practitioner and guide to proper use of the mushroom. And it must be stated that an important part of Mayan tradition is that the mushrooms should only be taken under guidance (either spiritual or Earthly) and for proper reason.]

There have always been cosmic messages. Humankind has always had the choice to listen to the inner voice and be 'in touch', or to blaze his own trail regardless. He has from his earliest times been primarily a spirit being; living his life or playing a role, in a material body of the material world; for such is the nature of this aspect of creation. Over the millennia, we have struggled for ways of expressing this, but always there are some that are so much more perceptive of how we are than others.

The Australian Aborigine would say that we are created out of the 'Dreamtime'. A late 20th century scientist would use different language. He might for example state: *All is materialised out of space-time ... as quark-patterns that equate to the resonances that arise from S-matrix theory.* Neither is likely to understand the other, but they really say the same thing. The languages differ, as do the archetypal pillars. But dreams, quark-patterns and thought, all have their associated vibrational energies, and are not so very different when we get down to basics. When the ascetic says: *'Love' is the all-important thing in this universe, and its related 'thought' the most powerful thing,* then we might care to express the 'creation' as: *thinking things into existence* ... Or to put it even more simply: *'In the beginning was the Word'.*

> *Then came the word ... Tepeu and Gucumatz talked together. They talked then, discussing and deliberating; they agreed, they united their words and their thoughts ... it became clear to them that when dawn would break, man must appear.*
> Popol Vuh *Sacred Book of the Ancient Quiché Maya*
> Adrian Recinos, trans/edited Delia Goetz and Sylvanus G Morley, University of Oklahoma Press.

PART 2

Belief and the Gift of Prophecy

I am EVER-LIVING; - for that is My Name,
And My power to others I never will give;
Or My Glory to Idols.
Past events have arrived; now the future I tell,
Before its arrival to you I announce!

Isaiah, Book II, 42, 8-9

Selected historic factors are described here. Greek and Roman influences, the development of formal religion, Mary's visions, ancient writings, the prophetic works of St. John, Nostradamus and others have all underpinned and affected the present pattern of 'belief' in the West. More current matters that include spirit communication, healing energies and the continuing work of teaching masters are accounted in Part 4. We must always remember that we are first and foremost beings of spirit, so that what we term 'belief' is always closely linked to a belief in ourselves.

Because they sought it not as from faith, but as if from rituals; they stumbled at the stumbling-stone, as it is written:
SEE, I PLACE A STUMBLING-STONE IN ZION, AND A DIFFICULT ROCK;
BUT THE BELIEVER ON IT SHALL NOT BE ASHAMED.

The Epistle of Paul the Apostle to the Romans, 9, 32-33

Chapter VII

The Greek Connection

The beautiful and youthful Persephone was in a lush meadow. She danced across the meadow gathering flowers: roses, lilies, crocuses, violets, hyacinths and narcissus. Pluto, lord of the underworld saw her beauty and appeared before her in his golden car. He took her for his bride and queen and conveyed her to the other-world that was his domain.

Her mother, the Goddess Demeter, was in much sorrow and sought the beautiful Persephone across the physical Earth. Eventually, she learned of her fate. She withdrew from the realm of the gods and took up residence at Eleusis where she appeared as an old woman sitting beside the 'Maiden's Well'. It was her vow to not return to Olympus and to not allow the corn to grow until her lost daughter was returned. In vain the oxen tilled the land but the Rarian plains remained bare. All the land remained barren and devoid of grain.

Mankind would have perished and the gods would have been denied receipt of their sacrifices, had not Almighty Zeus weighed the situation and commanded Pluto to restore his bride to Demeter of the Golden Tresses, her mother. But first Pluto gave the beautiful Persephone a pomegranate seed to eat. This would ensure that she return to him. Zeus commanded that Persephone should stay two thirds of each year with her mother and then return to the other-world of Pluto each September.

Demeter was overjoyed to receive her lost one and fondly they embraced. The Lady of the Golden Tresses then showed the sprouting cornfields to all the principalities and to King Celeus himself, and all the Earth was heavy with leaves and blossoms. Demeter and Persephone then departed to rejoin the gods on Olympus.

And so each spring, Demeter of the Golden Tresses, the Corn Goddess, fills the land with good harvest that fulfils the daily bread of mankind, and each September, the beautiful Persephone returns to the other-world.

Such in essence, was the story conveyed in the Hymn to Demeter that Homer left for us in the 7th century BC; perhaps the oldest known literary work. Demeter is clearly the Corn Goddess and is close to the Earth Mother. She is the sustainer of mankind for whom she is the source of the daily bread. Daughter Persephone is the Goddess of the 'Mysteries', who travels between worlds. And Eleusis is the centre for the Festive Rites of spring and autumn that celebrate those mysteries; the death in autumn and rebirth in spring making the ear of corn the key symbol of the immortality aspect of life. It would appear then, that the two worlds are entwined from our earliest literary works.

It was now September and the time of the Autumn Festival. Each year, the rites had been conducted with little change, from a time long, long before the days of the lyrical and literary Homer, and had now continued for some 300 years since that literary one's departure from this life.

Now it was that Xenophon left the outskirts of Athens as part of the rearguard of a lengthy procession. What a procession this was! There were so many thousands! As was the custom, new initiates had been prepared earlier in the year, during the course of the less elaborate Spring Rites. Now, this was the occasion that marked the autumn equinox, the festive time that follows harvest. The sacred icons held in the temple of Eleusinon, had been paraded the ten stades (11.5 miles) from Athens to Eleusis. Now it was the thousands of initiates to the 'Mysteries' who steadily and with good heart, marched the sacred route. Mostly they proceeded in solemn procession, but at night, perhaps not always with the same due solemnity that had prevailed during the day. Perhaps it was the dancing shadows from the torches that helped to moderate the mood. Perhaps it was in part the privacy of the stealthily encroaching dusk.

Shadows lengthened into night and it was time for Xenophon to light his torch. Those at the head had left Athens quite early in the morning to walk the dusty road, past the many white tombs, monuments and yielding olive trees in a gentle sunlight. The tail end, leaving the city in late evening would have good need of their torches and would not arrive till morning. The road was different at night. The flares of the torches gave shifting folds of colour to the white robes of the walkers. The shadow and fleeting colour seemed to have a jaunty essence of its own. At times, the procession was solemn, but often there were little ebbs of good-hearted conversation and jesting banter, especially at night. All was very much alive and as they passed the occasional tomb along the route, long shadows stabbed out and danced as if its occupant was joyful and was of a mind to come out and join the throng. Coming abreast of another tomb on the right, Xenophon was suddenly quite taken aback. The shadows leaped most oddly as a white and muted, soft-hued shape appeared above it, and the torches cast their furtive shapes and shadows. His heart fairly fluttered. Then he saw with obvious relief that it was his friend Eudemos playing a prank. The festival had its serious central theme, but cloaked in the night, the occasional little diversion was always a possibility. That would be human nature.

The majority of those in procession were ordinary people. There were skilled artisans and scribes, together with ones well respected who were held in the very highest esteem. There ... just up ahead was *Aristotle* himself! Even the great Aristotle was an initiate of the 'mysteries'! He had written and taught at the Academy and Plato ... the most excellent Plato, hailed Aristotle as *the* intellect of the school! And here he was ... on the road with the rest of us!

'Eudemos ... I'm well pleased he did not see you jumping up on that tomb. I don't know what 'is intelligence would 'ave thought of that.'

'Oh, he would have refuted the idea of a tomb-ghost right away. Mark my word. He's written a lengthy paper on *sophistical refutations* you know.'

'Really Eudemos?'

'Something about some things being genuine, while others seem to be but are not ... *a certain likeness between the genuine and the sham* ... Oh yes, with all his reasoning, I'm sure he'd spot the sham ghost right away.'

'You're so well read Eudemos. I'm impressed.'

'Well I can't understand *all* his work, but little bits here and there you know...'

'Well, all I've really read is some of 'is sea biology. Now there's my interest. That's a subject I can enjoy. He studied a lot of that over on Lesbos, of course. And 'e got lucky when 'e was in those parts. Cor ... yes! Zeus knows just how things went 'is way out there in those parts!'

'Really?'

'Well it was Assos really, in Troiad. Four of them went out to Assos and set up the Academy there. And 'e 'ad 'ermias as a pupil.'

'Now let's see, Hermias was...'

'Hermias? 'e was only the *governor* of the *colony*! Aristotle gets to be a real friend. Then marries 'is adopted daugh'er ... she was alright too ... I mean really *alright*! Then 'e spends the two years on Lesbos ... doing the sea biology mostly. Then after that, Hermias gets 'im the job tutorin' young Alexander in Macedonia. He eventually comes back to Athens of course. But 'e did well out there in the colony, did *really* well ... fell on 'is feet you might say ... The nice thing about teaching an' writin' books an' all that, you know ... it passes on, one to another and lasts forever. Y'know what I mean?'

'Xenophon, now it is *you* who impress *me.* You really are quite the philosopher. And I see *exactly* what you mean. Now take that great temple down the coast from Assos ... at Ephesos, the one Herostratos destroyed...'

'That lovely temple of Artemis ... The one that ... what was 'is name? ... *Chersiphron* built. Took him quite some time.'

'That's it! That's it *exactly*! It took all that time to build ... Such beauty, such dedication to art, such splendour ... and some mindless helmet-head comes along and smashes it ... just like that! You can't smash knowledge. It's for keeps. It has the true immortality. It's of the soul, which befits its immortality. Would you agree Xenophon?'

'Brilliant Eudemos! An elegantly constructed point my good friend. It also demonstrates well the true honesty of 'ard work and effort in *creating* something, against the childish ease with which the 'elmet-'eads of this world, without any brain or sophistication, can come along and destroy ... just destroy. I mean, to create, you must put your mind to it ... *mind*! But destruction needs no mind at all ... just the 'ard 'elmet with an absence of any ... any ... with nuffink inside ... and yet, there 'as to be a soul. Perhaps it gets some'ow switched-off.'

The night passed well, with odd little bouts of chatter and periods of trudging silence, and always, the dancing shadows. Then, as if in deliberate Homeric style, Dawn came to them and spread her rosy fingers from between the low hills edging the plain; and now Eleusis was before them. They would bathe in the sea and in the mineral springs. There were cleansing rituals and three days of fasting. They would gather within and around the great Hall of Initiation ... *the Telesterion*. There were many ceremonial aspects to the celebration of the Mysteries. There was the rite of 'Carrying things not to be mentioned'. These were the sexual symbols, the stone penises and the stone wombs. These were symbols of rebirth and continuity of being, all a part of the mystery and its celebration. But there was also the nature connection. The death and rebirth of humankind was inextricably entwined with death and rebirth of the corn; and the corn was of Demeter, she with the golden tresses that waved so like the corn itself. In communion they would share the unleavened cakes bearing the motif that was the head of Demeter.

The time came to gather in and about the great hall. In addition to the partaking of the cakes, a special draught has been prepared, to aid their seeing of the goddess. The *Ergot fungus,* that frequents the rye and various grasses, can alter consciousness sufficiently in such matters. The draught was prepared from this with all due care. The draught, together with the fasting, was the best device to raise the consciousness here in Eleusis and had stood the test of time. When all had partaken and all were prepared, the central part of the ceremony could begin. The initiating priest and the priestess of Demeter, dramatised the symbolic joining, this in deep shadow. Perhaps the initiates perceived more than was physically available to their eyes. It was the power of the Goddess that they sought and now, in conditioned state, they sought, not with eyes, but with their inner being. The Goddess herself was not of the fabric of this world but of the other.

The ritual ran its course and the priest reappeared from shadow, the symbol of death and rebirth: the ear of ripened corn was held high for all to see. This is what had been awaited. The Corn Goddess had given birth to her child. The fertile plains of Thria about Eleusis would again be blessed with plentiful harvest. 'The Mighty One has brought forth the Mighty!' saith the priest.

The names of the two enacting the Eleusian rite would not be uttered during their remaining lives. To endorse this formality, the names would be inscribed on tablets and cast into the Gulf of Salamis. And in the words of Aristotle himself: *'Those who are being initiated are not to learn anything but to experience something and be put into a certain condition.'*

The ways of spirit and psyche are sometimes unclear, as with the land when enshrouded in a mist. In the Homeric phrasing, it was the *flashing-eyed Athene* who would scatter the mist and make the land visible. And on one such occasion it was the *long-suffering Odysseus* who was so overcome by the sight once again of his dear land that he: *'kissed the earth, the giver of grain; and deeply moved he spoke to his own mighty spirit...'*

[In celebration of Communion, in Christian churches today, there are striking similarities when compared to the Eleusian Rite of old; not only in the sharing of bread and wine, but the term 'mystery' still remains in relation to death and renewal. A (1999) Eucharist service sheet reads:

> *'Let us proclaim the mystery of faith,*
> *Dying you destroyed our death;*
> *Rising you restored our life ...'*].

Chapter VIII

Ephesos

It was September 1993, about the time of year in the distant past that the 'Mysteries' would have been celebrated, when three of us took a holiday, travelling by car down the west coast of Turkey. During the period of economic recession that overshadowed much of Europe in that year, our son Mark had been teaching English at a school near Istanbul. Ann and I were able to join him when the summer term ended. In the gentle September sunshine of Northern Turkey, we set out from Silivri and travelled the north shore of the Sea of Marmara. This brought us to that narrow stretch of water once called the Hellespont where Xerxes and his army had crossed in ancient times, with some difficulty. We now crossed with considerable ease, taking advantage of the modern ferry and I am sure the 15-year old Volkswagen was grateful for the lift.

Heading south, our first objective: Troy. We were approaching the Troy of Homer, of Priam, of Helen, of Heinrich Schliemann. The world had laughed when he had begun excavations in 1870, but the mound of Hissarlik had yielded the legend, and Troy lived again. *'Looking out from Hissarlik, one can see Ida, from whose summit Jupiter looked down on the city of Troy.'* ... Schliemann's own words. As of old, one can still look out across the plain from the city and think great thoughts. Before us, lay Schliemann's first trench that found city walls. It remains open, kept just as it was, in his honour, as if it were yesterday.

It was Priam's fairest daughter Cassandra who had the 'natural' gift of prophecy ... given to her by the god. In ancient times, priestesses of the oracles were trained, and used their various aids to raise perception, but with Cassandra, it was the natural true gift of seeing into the future. It was she who foretold the fall of Troy and it was she who would be taken from the temple altar and ravished by Ajax. As in the case of Schliemann's bold venture, they ... humanity ... had laughed at such audacity. Her prophecy was simply not believed. It was unwisely unheeded. But, regardless of their disbelief, as was foretold, Troy fell.

The main route runs on south from Troy to Ayvaçik. We took the small mountain road from here to Assos, winding around foothills and passing through villages unsullied by modern times. As the little road wound higher, soon we had dreamy views of the island of Lesbos across a burnished sea.

We had heard of the sunset at Assos. It was now late afternoon and we felt an urgency to get to the distant mountain peak up ahead before that beautiful golden ball dropped out of sight. Time was running out. The road became more difficult by the minute. We reached the small village ... a few more turns ... gradients ... gradients upon gradients. Then we had just made it! Quickly parking the car, we hurried along the path to the summit. Breathtaking! The ancient columns of the temple to Athene were superbly silhouetted against the golden ball, now just three minutes before it would hit the horizon. It was time to set the camera.

There was Lesbos across the Gulf of Edremit. The sun met the horizon and just hung there for a few seconds. Athene looked on. This was the moment ... a time of beauty and a place of power.

Across there, more than two millennia ago, Aristotle had worked. There ... just below, in the ancient township, he had taught and had helped to set up a colonial Academy. Now we were treading where that teacher once trod. Later, St. Paul too, had travelled this coast.

A little below the temple is the ancient village, and the first habitation we came upon was a rather special *paynsian* and restaurant run by a lovely lady, who spoke Turkish and French, and her husband. The food and wine were excellent. Hospitality flowed, while music: Vivaldi, Bach, Enya ... danced between grape bunches that hung amiably from the vine-roof, before it filtered through the leaves and was lost to the night air.

Although replete and well rested, there remained the feeling that we still had not quite had enough of this wonderful place. We therefore walked back up the path to enjoy Athene's temple under the moon and stars. But, looking back, there was the vine-roof, now below us. The muted music wafted through the leaves and out across a timeless expanse of starlit stillness. We remained at the temple for an hour or so, rapt in its magic. A cat joined us who sat on the acropolis, equally transfixed.

In the morning, it was a traditional Turkish café breakfast down in the village: boiled egg, black olives, cucumber, tomato, feta cheese, rose jam, fresh baked bread and coffee. We watched goats walking down the street, probably just as they had since ancient times. Wonderful! But before leaving, we could not resist just one more peep in at that restaurant of the night before. Hospitality still flowed and we were plied with glasses of tea. Now the sunlight spilled in through those vine leaves, scattering bright pools of dappled gold across the stone floor. This really was a very lovely place. Aristotle surely must have fallen on his feet here in Assos...

There were other places of beauty further down the coast, punctuated here and there by an amazing amphitheatre, but Assos remained in our memories as a very special place. Then came Efes, or Ephesos, or Ephesus, with so much history. If I had to suggest a collective noun for historic sites, it would be an 'efes' of sites.

The site of the old Ionian town is linked to a prophecy of the Delphi Oracle. The story is that a settlement was founded peacefully in the 11th century BC, on what was then a small island away from the older township. The settlement outgrew the island and its ruler Androkles consulted the priestesses of Delphi as to the next move.

At the Delphi Oracle, the priestesses were able to inhale the volcanic fume that issued from a rock cleft, this to help them into trance. It was their aid to seeking that other consciousness away from the material self that would enable them to witness scenes of the future. A strange prophecy ensued: *'The site of the new town will be shown you by a fish; follow the wild boar.'* Despite the apparent fanciful or unlikely nature of the prophecy, it transpired that fishermen were seated one day, by a fire cooking a meal. A fish first leapt onto a hot stone, then into red embers. Then instantly flipped again, such that red embers scattered into nearby brushwood. This brushwood then ignited, and the spreading fire disturbed a wild boar. The boar was chased and killed at the foot of the Mount of the Nightingale. This mount became the site of the Greek Ephesos. It later became a Roman town and capital of the Roman Provinces in Asia. Being substantially destroyed by an earthquake in AD 17, it was then rebuilt Roman-style. Today the visitor may see a multiple past relating to Roman Ephesus, Greek Ephesos and Selçuk, a derived name for an ancient township on which stands the remains of the Temple of Artemis (Diana), acclaimed as one of the seven wonders of the ancient world. (That was after its rebuilding, for which Alexander the Great was responsible, and he of course, had had the benefit of Aristotle's excellent tuition.)

Artemis herself, in the likeness of Cybele the Great Mother, continues to proudly stand, in the beautifully laid out Selçuk museum. She surveys the world, resplendent with her three rows of breasts, for she symbolises the Great Mother and sustainer, on whom the whole world depends for all sustenance.

Schematic View of Ancient Efes, Turkey

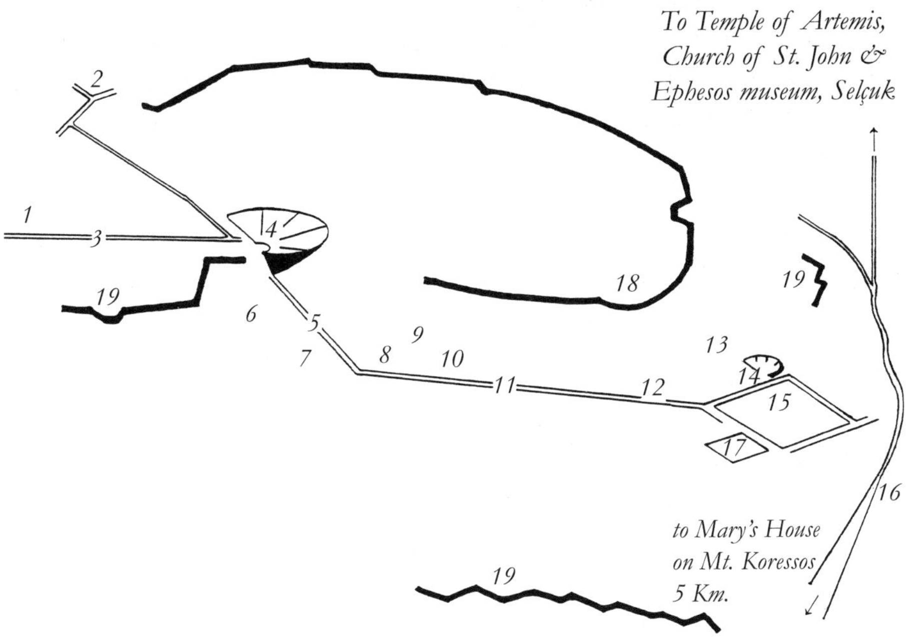

1. *Church of Virgin Mary (Theotokos) ... Council of 431.*
2. *The Stadium ... dating from Hellenistic times.*
3. *Arcadian Way ... Harbour Street.*
4. *Grand Amphitheatre, seating 24,500 ... Place of St. Paul's confrontation.*
5. *The Marble Road.*
6. *The Agora ... The commercial market place.*
7. *The Celsus Library.*
8. *The public toilets.*
9. *The Scholastikia Baths.*
10. *Temple of Hadrian ... Friezes depict legendary origin of the site.*
11. *Curetes Street ... Priest/Priestess Street.*
12. *Heracles Gate.*
13. *Prytaneum ... The town hall.*
14. *The Odeum, seating 1,500 ... Used for city meetings and concerts.*
15. *State Agora ... Used for state and religious meetings.*
16. *Tomb of St. Luke.*
17. *Museum of Inscriptions.*
18. *Old Byzantine walls.*
19. *Old Hellenistic walls.*

Before Artemis, religion centred on the Great Mother ... the Earth Goddess ... Gaia. She was gentle, in keeping with her feminine nature. It would seem so natural that a mother figure should oversee all the nature spirits of the planet; and of course, the earlier cultures were all so *in tune* with nature and the nature spirits. She was Mother Nature personified. In time, as humankind developed and thought further on how things should be, six goddesses were devised who were close to the Mother. Some would point out that the six goddesses also represent major aspects found in humanity. The people of our society are of wildly differing types and if we look around (in the arts, politics, science or amongst relatives), one can readily relate the six goddess aspects within character, in either pure or blended form. In fact, to find just a single aspect, would be rare indeed:

Demeter ... She is very much the mother, looks after her children and she loves her family; just as her aspect, the Corn Goddess loves her daughter and is so overjoyed at her return.

Athena ... In our society, this is the career woman. She probably gets her degree and does a post-graduate course as like as not; then goes into business or becomes a lawyer. She may well have a 'city' style of energy.

Hera ... Love of power. She may well have begun as predominantly Athena but then a career in politics or in the military becomes a must for this one. She loves the position of power. This type would have no time for humility and is unlikely to be seen in the company of those of a 'Persephone' disposition.

Persephone ... This is the psychic one and between-worlds traveller. She would happily attend a mind-body-spirit festival. One of this persona may be clairvoyant and is likely to embrace whole-heartedly a 'New Age' lifestyle.

Aphrodite ... She loves nice things and is an exhibitionist. She is artistic; may be in films, singing or painting, and may flaunt her body and good looks. She might well have affairs and regularly appear in glossy magazines and the newspapers.

Artemis ... This one is a country lover and nature lover. She appreciates animals and has a dislike of towns. A country cottage is for her. In today's society, she would be a disciple of the 'green' philosophy.

The Artemis of Ephesos was very much a hybrid Artemis who had much of the older Earth Mother with her. It would be she, Artemis of Ephesos, who would make the last stand for the Goddess religion against the new principally male-orientated Christian religion. Once Artemis was toppled, then the new Christian religion, albeit with subsequent modification, would sweep across Europe and on to the Americas.

In the early part of the 1st century, the peoples of the East were blessed with the teachings and the healing work, of Jesus the Christ. Following the crucifixion, there were those who were close and who would keep the faith, and who would travel away from the Holy Land, to Ephesus to reside in or around that township:

Mary, mother of Jesus: Her house may be seen just out of town, on the top of a pine-clad mountain. The house and its location were rediscovered as the result of two expeditions in 1881 and 1891. These were made on account of the visions of the stigmatised German nun: Sister Anna Catherina Emmerich. She wrote of the nature of the house and its location, with a spring of fresh water available, despite being on the top of a mountain. The details were found by the expeditions, to be just as she had described from her visions. It has been established that the foundations of the house date from the 1st century. It is a wonderfully tranquil place midst the fragrance of the pine trees.

Mary Magdalene: She, like Mary the mother, had stood beneath the cross; and on the Easter morning that followed, Jesus had said to her, *'Woman, why do you, weep? What do you seek?'*

She, thinking it was the gardener, said to Him: 'Sir, if you have removed Him from here, tell me where You have placed Him, and I will take Him away.'

Jesus addressed her: 'Mary!'

Turning round, she exclaimed in Hebrew, 'Rabboni!' which means 'Master!'

Jesus said to her, 'Touch Me not, because I have not as yet ascended to the Father. Go to My brothers, however, and tell them, 'I go up to My Father and your Father; and My God and your God!''

*Mary the Magdalene came reporting to the disciples: 'I have seen the Lord,' and what He had said to her.' John **20**, 15-18*

Mary then came to Ephesus with Mary the mother and John. Mary Magdalene would eventually end her days in Ephesus. Her burial place and sarcophagus were located in 1952, near the Cave of the Seven Sleepers, a place of curious legend, respected by both Moslem and Christian.

Saint John: As he stood beneath the cross together with the others, Jesus had said: *'Mother, see your son!' He then said to the disciple: 'See, that is your mother!' And from that hour the disciple took her into his own home.' John **19**, 27.*

Apart from a period of exile on the island of Patmos, John spent most of his remaining life in and around Ephesus. His tomb is on a hill by Selçuk and two basilicas have since been built over it. The earlier name for Selçuk was Ayasoluk meaning 'Divine Theologian', this in honour of John and his work. The name remained until invasion by the Selçuk Turks.

Saint Luke: St. Luke travelled widely and was a frequent visitor to Ephesus in the 1st century, when the town became a cradle of Christianity. His tomb also is here.

Saint Paul: St. Paul's birthplace was at Tarsus, down on the Turkish south coast. Both Paul and John preached and healed in Ephesus, with positive results; but the conversion from the goddess religion to the Christian faith was not a steady process. There were times of difficulty and there was the time of the riot, when feelings ran so high that St. Paul was eventually obliged to leave the town.

It was Demetrius, a silversmith who made silver shrines for Artemis, who voiced discontent and excited others in the trade. Discontent grew into a large and ugly scene:

'You know, men, that our wealth depends upon this trade; and you see and hear that not only in Ephesus, but indeed almost throughout the whole of Asia-Minor, this Paul has persuaded a great crowd to secede, saying, 'that they are not gods that are made by hand.' And further than that, there is danger not only that this trade of ours should come into disrepute; but also that the temple of the great goddess Artemis will be considered nothing, and that her magnificence will be swept away, which all Asia and the civilised world worship.' Acts ***19****, 26-27.*

'Fired with fury on hearing this, they shouted out, exclaiming: 'Great Artemis of the Ephesians!' And the whole city being roused to riot, the crowd rushed in a mass to the theatre, dragging with them Gaius and Aristarchus, of Macedonia, assistants of Paul.' Acts ***19****, 28-29.*

'When Paul, however, was anxious to go into the mob, the disciples would not allow him. Several also of the leading men among the Asiatics who were friends to him, sent advising him not to present himself in the theatre. Some therefore shouted one thing, some another; for the meeting was in an uproar; and the greater part of the people did not even know for what purpose they had assembled. Then some of the Judeans from the crowd, seizing Alexander, thrust him forward. But when Alexander advanced, stretching out his hand to defend himself before the mob, recognising that he was a Jew, all of them began with one voice, for about two hours, to shout, 'Great Artemis of the Ephesians!'' Acts ***19****, 30-34.*

It was the mayor who was finally able to reduce the noise of the crowd. He persuaded that any complaint that Demetrius and his artisans might have should be put through the proper channels, and after all, the men dragged before the crowd were *neither temple-robbers nor libellers* of the Goddess. The mayor dismissed the meeting and the confrontation abated.

But Paul's image in the town remained problematical and he felt it best to leave Ephesus. So he called his disciples together and took leave of them. He travelled north to Troy. Sailing from there, he made his first journey into Europe with the teaching, taking the word into Macedonia. He taught there for a time, then returning to Asia Minor, he stayed at Assos; from there travelling by boat down the coast, past Ephesus and via Syria, on to Jerusalem. A return to Jerusalem had now become his calling.

There were many that advised against such a course. It had become a city hostile to *the sons of the light.* But his desire took him there, and it was not long before difficulties were encountered. He was set upon by a mob. He was in effect, rescued from the mob by the military and made a prisoner. The situation at first appeared bleak.

Down on the south coast of Asia Minor, is a stretch of fourteen navigable miles of the river Cydnus leading to the city of Tarsus. It would be up this waterway that Cleopatra would sail one day, with all the extravagance of her 'Aphrodite' countenance, to meet Anthony. But for now, suffice to say that Tarsus is a city of the most excellent repute and capital of the Roman province of Cilicia. And it was the birthplace of he who was to become known as St. Paul.

The prisoner taken from the mob by the military was suddenly found to be of Roman birth. It followed that there were certain privileges that must be accorded to him on account of that Roman birth:

'... those who were about to torture him immediately stood back; and the Commandant himself was also terrified on discovering that he was a Roman; and because he had ordered him to be bound.' Acts ***22****, 29.*

The punishment for binding or flogging a Roman citizen was death, unless it was by order of the Emperor himself or his Lieutenant, following trial. Therefore, although a prisoner, Paul commanded a degree of respect on account of his Roman citizenship. This led to his eventual shipment to Rome, where he continued to spread the word into Europe.

Following the crucifixion of Jesus the Christ, the cradle of Christianity had then, transferred to Ephesus. Here, the new faith met Artemis in the head-on confrontation. In the 1st century, Artemis was the embodiment of the 'Goddess' religion. The confrontation became a turning point. If the new religion was known locally as the Cult of the Virgin Mary, then this was understandable. If the 'Cult of Artemis' changed to the 'Cult of the Virgin Mary' then a feminine aspect of the religion was maintained, which made the transition easier in Ephesus. Thus, Mary played an important role in the transition. A Christian following was established in Ephesus, from where Paul and others were able to go forth into Europe.

Since Mary's time on Earth, she has 'appeared' in vision on a number of occasions in Ephesus and elsewhere. The series of visions, at Fatima in Portugal 1917, may well have been special. The town of Fatima is named after Mohammed's daughter and the major religion of Turkey is Moslem. It seems appropriate then, that the two religions should themselves be linked through the visions of Mary at Fatima.

> *'O Mary! Verily hath God chosen thee, and purified thee, and chosen thee above the women of the worlds!'*
>
> *The Koran, Sura III, 37.*

> *'O Mary! Be devout towards thy Lord, and prostrate thyself, and bow down with those who bow.'*
>
> *The Koran, Sura III, 38.*

> *'O Mary! Verily God announceth to thee the Word from Him: His name shall be, Messiah Jesus the son of Mary, illustrious in this world, and in the next, and one of those who have near access to God ...'*
>
> *The Koran, Sura III, 40.*

Today, holidays along the West Coast of Turkey may be strange. Time can play tricks. One can go in and out of time warp and only occasionally be jerked back to the present. The strangest of synchronicities may arise. It was on our last day in Ephesus. The Selçuk museum is so nicely laid out, with decorous peafowl walking about its gardens. Within one of its rooms, Mark took a photograph of me beside a bust of Socrates. Socrates and I seemed to be enjoying each other's company! The photos were printed when we returned to Silivri. Ann said: 'In fact he *does* look a bit like Socrates.' It had seemed a casual enough remark at the time.

The next day we flew home. On the following day, I found Assos was still in my mind and I opened an old 1860 edition of Chambers' Encyclopædia that we had on the bookshelves, looking for *'Assos'*. There was no entry, but my quest had left the book open at page 494 ... *'Association of ideas'*. In fact, the whole of the two pages 494 and 495 were devoted to that single entry, but my eye fell upon just the one word: *'Socrates'*. Intrigued, I could not resist reading the full line: *'very peculiar face, which reminds me of the bust of Socrates.'*

. . . .

While Ephesus was so important for the Christian religion in the 1st century; millennia before that, one of the earliest of the bible stories was enacted in the eastern part of that same country. The Noah's Ark story has its true origin. The flood happened, and the boat was built *three hundred cubits long, fifty cubits wide, and thirty cubits deep* just as described in Genesis. But the story is much more ancient than is the formal Christian religion. That is why the same story occurs as part of the Epic of Gilgamesh and in the myth of Atrahasis, in Early Sumerian, in Hittite, in Hurrian and in Elamite writings. The happening pre-dates Homer, Moses and the Sumerian scribes.

During 1978, four earthquakes occurred in the region of Mahser Dagi, *the Doomsday Mountain*, some 17 miles to the south of Ararat. The fourth quake of the series occurred at 10.57 local time on 25 November. First, the sky turned silver and people went out into the streets to look at the strange effect. (There were very few casualties when the quake came for this very reason ... They were out in the streets.) The quake was not only curious in relation to the sky colour. On the side of the mountain, something moved. A boat-shaped structure, already made visible from an earlier quake back in 1948, now rose further out of the ground. The main substance of it, through whatever processes have been at work across the millennia, is now clay-like, but its shape remains unmistakably that of a boat with protruding deck-support timbers. By some strange logic, it has risen adjacent to the village of Nasar *the place of the sacrifice* on the slope of Mahser *the Doomsday Mountain.*

It was David Fasold who researched place-names, carried out field investigation, produced radar scans of sub-surface timbers and identified iron pinning. His book: 'The Discovery of Noah's Ark' describes it all most elegantly. There is evidence for the hull of the craft having been a massive bound-reed-structure, well coated with a cementitious mixture. The Atatürk University of Erzurum began core-drilling operations in 1988. An approach sign below the site now reads: NU'HUN GEMISI (Noah's Ark). The sign was placed there by the Turkish Minister of Culture. Tourist maps recognise and name the site together with various other places of interest. There is no doubt that this treasure *is* Noah's Ark. There is scientific evidence, 'channelled' evidence and, as with Schliemann's Troy, details-of-the-'legend' evidence. I am surprised that this joyful re-emergence has not created more excitement in the West, for the ark it certainly is. (We should dismiss the fictional addition to the story, about animals going in two-by-two. Ancient accounts do tend to become 'embroidered' with untruths.) But a boat was built of the size stated, the deluge came, and the unmistakable and scientifically tested residue of the craft is now half way up a mountain a little to the south of Ararat. It is here that it once settled in mud; became covered and then part damaged by earth movement. While submerged it would appear to have been protected. The craft has now emerged, perhaps as a sign for our time.

> *'To those for whom a devotion to truth and understanding bring a spark of life … welcome aboard the mother ship of mankind, built to bridge two worlds, which rode upon that cataclysm of old and bore us to our new beginnings.'*
> David Fasold *Preface, The Discovery of Noah's Ark*
> Sidgwick & Jackson Limited.

Chapter IX

The Visions and Mary's Message

Jesus the Christ and Mary continue to influence today's world. The visions of Mary, and visions associated with Mary that have been reported, have been numerous. Sister Anna had experienced the visions of Mary's house at Ephesus and those visions indicated the place and led to its discovery. Soon after that, the visions *at* the house began, the first recorded one being in 1902. They may well of course have occurred earlier at the location, but I do not know of any record. Now, in the 20th century, such things are often better accounted. Where there are such visions, holy springs often appear and one usually finds a regular incidence of healing taking place. A testimony to the healing is often the build-up of discarded limb braces, crutches and votive offerings. Such is the status quo at Mary's house *Meryem Ana.*

In 1955, George B Quatman, an American businessman, visited Ephesus. He had heard that the tomb of St. John was in a sad state of repair and wished to see for himself. He also wanted to visit Mary's home. The tomb was just as he had feared. He was saddened at the poor state of the once magnificent basilica of St. John; also of the Church of St. Mary. And although Mary's house had been tastefully restored and lovingly attended by a devoted Christian group, it was little known and not the pilgrimage centre that it deserved to be. One evening, he stood on a hotel balcony in nearby Izmir and looked out towards the house. This was the time that Mary appeared to *him*. She was larger than life and above the distant hillside. She was moving, but stopped three times. Each time that she stopped, he received a mental image of a sacred shrine: first Mary's home, then Mary's church, then the Basilica of St. John. He was inspired to act and this led to the foundation of The American Society of Ephesus, which has since carried out a wonderful amount of restoration work at the Ephesus shrines.

The better known reported visions of Mary have been world-wide and often revealed to children. They have a variety of reported form and seem to be associated with a healing energy. I should say at this stage, that perhaps I use the term *vision* in a broader sense than may be strictly correct. In the strict meaning of the word, visions are experienced in dream or trance state; in which case, the experience would be limited to one or a small group, as for example, her appearances to small groups of children. Apparitions in the sky, seen by the many or seen by a crowd, as was the case at Fatima, would be in the strict sense, *materialisation* and not a vision. It is my belief that Mary appears as vision, or as a materialisation, or even both, whichever may be fitting for her purpose at the time. The examples of her appearances that follow span the last 150 years:

18 September 1846: On a quiet hillside at La Salette, in the French Alps, two children, Melanie Calvat and Maximin Giraud were tending cows. Mary appeared to them as a radiant woman weeping over a dried-up stream-bed. She talked with the children. She spoke of famine, saying that the potato crop and the grape harvest would fail. By the time others visited the spot, the stream was flowing, and the water was found to heal. Antoinette Bollenat of Avallon was close to death and had not moved from her bed for a week. She had spoonfuls of the water from a bottle and recovered full health. As to the prophecy, the potato crop had already failed in Ireland in that year. Potato crops in France also were to fail, and philoxera destroyed many vineyards.

11 February 1858: Young Bernadette Soubirous of Lourdes, a Pyrenean town of South West France, was favoured with a series of 18 visions. On the first occasion, she appeared at a grotto out of a glow, above a rose bush. She appeared as a beautiful girl dressed in white and did not give a name. She was referred to as *Aquero*, which, in the local dialect means: 'that one'. It was during the course of the 9th vision and before a crowd, that Mary instructed Bernadette to scrabble in the muddy ground before her. A spring became apparent to the general amazement of those present. The spring continues to this day, producing the water that has the reputation to heal. In 1976, Delizia Ciroli, a Sicilian girl, made the pilgrimage and was cured. She had been given three months to live on account of cancer. Her healing is 'officially' accepted as the 65th miracle to have occurred from visits to the shrine and prayer; although of course, there are many more accounts of 'unofficial' healing. Lourdes, is a place of the vision *and* the holy spring; it therefore has the healing tradition, although of course, the majority of the millions who travel to Lourdes each year, go as pilgrims to the shrine; just to be there.

During the course of the 13th vision, *Aquero* instructed Bernadette to convey to the priest that the people were to come to the grotto in procession, and a chapel was to be built. But Father Peyramale was sceptical. He wanted the *Aquero* to give her name *and* to work a 'proving' miracle. The police threatened to imprison Bernadette for causing public disorder.

But, in these matters, it is always the devotion of the people that is the determining factor, not official negativity.

It was during the 16th vision that Mary smiled in reply to Bernadette's question as to her identity. When asked a fourth time, she replied: *'Que soy era Immaculada Councepciou.'* (I am the Immaculate Conception). The 14-year-old did not understand the phrase that she carefully repeated to Father Peyramale; but Father Peyremale understood, and he was visibly both shocked and convinced. Easter Wednesday was the day of the 17th vision. Bernadette cupped her hands around the stem of a candle. While she was entranced, the flame burnt down and was at her fingers ... to the consternation of those nearby. But Dr. Dozous, who was paying close attention, warned them to leave her and he timed the period of flame contact as ten minutes. His later inspection showed that her fingers were unaffected by the flame.

There was to be one more vision on 16 July. Bernadette had been out of town and the sceptical authorities had barricaded the grotto. She, an aunt and two friends walked the far bank of the river until opposite. Some were there already with lighted candles. She was hooded as she knelt, and was not recognised, and so once again, Bernadette experienced the vision of the beautiful Mary; saying afterwards that the vision seemed just as near as when she had been across the river and at the grotto.

21 August 1879: It would have been a materialisation, described as consisting of Mary, St. John and St. Joseph as an altar tableau seen on the gable end of the church of Knock, County Mayo, Republic of Ireland. The tableau remained for 2½ hours and was seen by a group of approximately 20 people who gathered.

30 August - 15 September 1880: A vision of Mary was seen at Llanthony Abbey, Capel-y-Fin, Wales. Four boys saw Mary with a halo in the abbey grounds, on the evening of 30 August. She vanished into a bush. She was again seen on 4 September. This followed the singing of 'Ave Maria' at the abbey. She appeared in light in that same bush. On 15 September, it was again four people who saw. This time it was a *light event* that seemed to link with the singing of Ave Maria. The heavens and the mountain are described as breaking out in circles of light. The light coalesced into a brief but detailed vision of Mary.

13 May 1917: The Fatima appearances were clearly special. Three children, Lucia dos Santos, Francisco Marto and sister Jacinta were tending the family sheep near Fatima, Portugal. The place was a large depression called Cova da Iria. They were 'prepared' by three visits from an angel.

On the 13th, there was a flash of lightning in a clear blue sky and Mary then appeared to the children. She was as a beautiful young woman and Lucia talked with her. Mary said that she had come from heaven and would come again on the 13th of every month for six months. Mary appeared each month and crowds gathered, but each time, it was the children who were able to see her. She was visible only to the children.

On 13th June, she told the children to say the rosary every day, for peace and an end to the Great War. Mary promised to take Jacinta and Francisco to heaven quite soon, but Lucia must stay. Lucia asked Mary to work a miracle to convince others. It was not surprising that she asked, since her mother was beating her for telling lies, and Francisco was being rebuked by his teacher at school and bullied by boys. On 13th August, the children were abducted to the city jail at Ourém where they were questioned in a most insensitive fashion. There seemed to be no understanding and little respect. But there were convicts at the jail who comforted them, and who kneeling, said the Rosary with them. A friend, Maria Carreira, *was* at the Cova, where the crowd heard a thunderclap and all were coloured with rainbow colours.

On 13th September, many were gathered and, according to their personal vibrations, different people saw different things. Some saw the rain of flowers. Some tried to catch them with umbrellas, but they just disappeared. Some saw the floating luminous globe, others, a star. Mary said to Lucia: *'In October, I will work a miracle to make everybody believe.'*

At the final vision of 13th October, a crowd estimated as in excess of 50,000 people had gathered. It was raining. Mary did not appear at her usual time. A priest told the children they were deluded. Lucia insisted on waiting. At 1 p.m., she said to Jacinta: *'Kneel down. The lady's coming. I can see the light.'* Mary spoke to the children, saying that she was the lady of the Rosary and that they should say the Rosary every day. The war is coming to an end and the soldiers will soon be home.

The rain had stopped. The children then saw visions in the sky, of Mary, Jesus and St. Joseph. Many in the crowd saw what was taken to be the sun, through a rift in the clouds. But it was as a glazed wheel of mother of pearl, and it emitted rays of various colours. It whirled around! Some described it as a pinwheel, spinning and throwing out blue, white and green light. Then it seemed to dive out of the sky and come menacingly close, giving out an amethyst coloured light, then yellow. This time it was the crowd who observed these things ... and the newspaper reporters. The more unswerving newspapers reported: *'a mysterious solar occurrence'*;

the more imaginative reported on: *'the dancing sun'*. The initial crowd reaction was ... fear and panic! Then the attitude changed to one of devotion, as befits a sacred encounter.

The happening is now remembered as *'the dance of the sun'* ... That is the description that held fast in memory. Some saw the sun dance from as far away as 50 kilometres while there were others in the crowd who even so, saw nothing. Many accounts of healing were reported.

At this time, three prophecies were given to the children, about which there seems to have been some small degree of confusion as regards their reported natures. The first however, seems to concern the miserable 'hell' that must be confronted by unrepentant souls who continue to refuse the good path. The second prophecy dovetailed so intricately into the tapestry of the mid-century, indicating that unless the world alter its ways, there would be a *Second World War* ... (not as a cosmic reprisal of course, but as a natural outcome of our own design). Furthermore, there would then be a portent taking the form of a *great unknown light* that would illumine the night skies. That light would be the signal for outbreak of war, and this signal would happen within the span of the *next* Pontificate.

Pope Pius was to die in the year 1939. It transpired that, on the evening of 25 January 1938, the skies over Western Europe assumed a strange light. The news media made their various reports of the *unknown phenomenon*, and in some parts it would appear that night-shift workers had no need of electric lamps. In the Berlin Reich Chancellery at this time, there was already a file containing the top-secret plans for the invasion of Austria. That followed in the March ... a first step towards the war that officially began in 1939. Such were the details of the first two prophecies.

The next was accompanied by a special instruction that was to be followed. The third prophecy was sealed in an envelope and entrusted to the Vatican with instructions to open in 1960. It is understood that Pope John XXIII read the prophecy in that year and decided that it should not be revealed to the world. It is my understanding that Cardinal Ratzinger, has also read it and has since said (1984): *'To publish 'The Third Secret' would mean exposing the Church to the danger of sensationalism, to its contents being exploited.'*

There is then, a certain air of mystery that lingers with the third prophecy. But, strange as it may appear, a clue as to its nature may be seen in the writings of St. Malachy, who lived in Ireland through the first half of the twelfth century. He was a healer and a mystic and at the same time upheld the church religion, being Archbishop of Armagh for a period of five years. It is known that he accurately foretold the time and place of his own death ... All Souls' Day, November 1148, Clairvaux, France.

It was eight years earlier that Bishop Malachy and his party of Irish monks had approached Rome in conclusion of a lengthy pilgrimage. They climbed Janiculum Hill at the edge of the city and it was on the hill overlooking the object of their pilgrimage that they spent the night. But the night was disturbed as a voice spoke out. The bishop was in trance and it was the one within who spoke. A candle was lit and a scribe moved close. As the voice spoke, the scribe recorded. Firstly *'Rome'*. Then at intervals spread through the night, a series of Latin phrases were written down. By dawn there were 111 phrases. When the bishop returned from trance, he was able to explain that he had been shown in vision all popes who would take office, from the then current Innocent II to the end. Each was depicted (sometimes in a roundabout fashion) by a brief but meaningful phrase.

Some of the phrase meanings are smart indeed. Pius III, who held office for 26 days in 1503, was listed as *De Parvo Homine* ... from a small man. Being a nephew of Pius II, he had legitimately adopted his family name of Piccolomini ... literally 'little man'! Pius X (1903 - 1914) is described as *Ignis ardens* ... burning fire. His period in office embraces the Tunguska fireball event of 1908 as well as the spectacular display of Halley's comet in 1910 (described later). A happening in Vienna, also of that year (accounted in chapter XX), contributed strongly to the Jewish holocaust of World War II, and then World War I began shortly before his death. It was certainly a fiery time in regard to world events.

It has been claimed, however, that the papal list is a forgery in the sense that it was contrived in the 16th century. That may be so ... who can tell? And yet, the Popes of more modern times still seem to fit the list quite well in terms of their description!

Pope John XXIII (1958 - 1963), who is known to have read (but chose not to reveal) the third prophecy of Fatima; his description is *Pastor et Nauta* ... pastor/shepherd and sailor. Prior to the papacy, he was patriarch of Venice with its long and famed maritime history. Hence, 'sailor' would appear a suitable fit, and he was very much a shepherd. It is reported that, at his coronation mass he made clear his desire to be above all things a good shepherd, and this was to become the hallmark of his pontificate. He also chose two most fitting symbols for the badge of the Ecumenical Council of 1962 ... a cross and a ship.

There followed Paul VI (1963 - 1978) ... *Flos Florum* ... flower of flowers. His coat of arms had three fleurs-de-lis. [In legend, a blue banner with three gold fleurs-de-lis was derived of heavenly origin, being delivered to King Clovis by an angel. The three flowers held a Trinity connotation.] Paul was not of robust health. He was of the mind ... an intense thinker; it might be said, an intellectual flower of the three flowers.

John Paul I (1978) ... *De Medietate Lunae* ... of mid or half moon was born Albino Luciani meaning 'white light'. It was a shock to the world when at the age of 65 (young for a pope) he died of heart failure after only 33 days in office. His plans had included an examination of the Vatican's finances and investigation of accusations of Mafia connection. There were grounds for considering that the death may have had suspicious connotations, albeit unproven. Suspicion lingered for a time as other possibly related untimely deaths followed. What is certain however, is that a *half moon* was in the heavens that night, illuminating the Earth with its own *white light.*

There followed John Paul II, a younger Pope and the first non-Italian to be elected since Hadrian VI (just a little after the time of *De Parvo Homine*). Pope John Paul's identifying phrase ... *De Labore Solis* ... from the sun labour/work. In the list, this is one of the more roundabout connections. He came from Krakow, Poland; as did Copernicus (also of the time of *De Parvo Homine*), and it was he who laboured concerning the sun. Copernicus had worked for years on the theory of the sun being at the centre of the solar system; and he worked midst huge controversy between his science and the Church. John Paul was from ... that place of the labour concerning the sun. It had been a deeply significant clash with the developing science and now, John Paul was a significant pontiff who would, for more than two decades, prepare his flock for the new millennium, despite an attempt on his life.

On 13 May 1981, a gunman in St. Peter's Square fired three shots into his body. The day was the 64th anniversary of the first appearance of Mary at Fatima. John Paul recovered and later visited his assassin in jail where they prayed together. It seems clear from his book *Crossing the Threshold of Hope*, that the experience and the synchronicity of it has strengthened his thoughts concerning the Fatima prophecies. He recognises continuity in regard to the sightings of La Salette, Lourdes and Fatima.

In the list of St. Malachy, there then follow: *Gloria Olivae* ... glorious olive ... a good name for a Pontiff to have during the period of transition in which it is so absolutely vital for us to learn the ways of peace. There may also be a connection to that time on the Mount of Olives when the disciples asked Jesus to tell them about the destruction of the temple and '... *the completion of this age.*'

Then comes *Petrus Romanus* ... Peter the Roman. He has the distinction of being the last in the list ... the final end-of-line Pontiff. It is also a part of the prophecy that *the seven-hilled city will be destroyed.* The prophesied destruction of Rome is likely of course to be symbolic. The Christian Church of today has for the most part evolved from the early Roman Empire's presentation of the faith. It would appear to signify the end of a system. 'The Roman' may well be a suitable description for he who is the last to represent that system. It may be an indication of course, that in a better world of peace and raised consciousness, the old form of religious bastion simply no longer has any place. St. Malachy's prophecies do not have a strong following today. They are seen as dubious. But the terminal nature of the Papal list might just connect with that sealed third prophecy of Fatima. Its timing has an element of convergence with the changing times, and such a connection might well be seen to explain the ongoing secrecy that those in Papal office have seen fit to observe.

Consistent with Mary's promise, Francisco and Jacinta departed this life early. They both contracted Spanish flu in October 1918. Francisco died in the April of 1919. Jacinta followed in the February of 1920. They had both become very spiritually aware. Mary came to Lucia on further occasions. In the visit of June 1929 she instructed her to pray that Russia would be consecrated to the immaculate heart.

[There was a 'leak' about the third prophecy in the 15th October 1963 issue of the German magazine *Neues Europa.* It was an overview relating to the letter. The overview stated that the third secret would meet strong resistance and that Mary was pleased that the miracle of the 'Prodigy of the Sun' was accepted by so many. There will be much death because of mistakes and insensitivity from those who do not care about God's Earth. And for the Church, the time of its greatest trial is to come. Pope John Paul has since declared the leak to be authentic. Following his recovery from attempted assassination, he has visited Sister Lucia and has prayed in the cathedral that now marks the location of the Fatima visions.]

<u>29 November 1932:</u> In Beauraing, Belgium, Mary is said to have revealed herself to five children on 33 occasions during the period 29 November to January 1933. Crowds gathered but it was once again just the children who saw her. They appeared to be entranced at the time of the visions.

2 July 1961: Garabandal is a small village in a valley in the north west of Spain. The *calleja* is a sunken path leading up to a clump of pine trees on a hill just out of the village. It was here that the four children, Conchita, Jacinta, Mari Lolí and Mari Cruz were playing, when the Archangel Michael appeared before them, as a young boy. He appeared several times to prepare them. Then on 1st July, he said that Mary would be with them the next day, the Feast of the Visitation. There were priests and doctors in the accompanying crowd. The girls were on their knees in trance for a long period. They reported afterwards that they had the impression of being surrounded in light. Mary came to them again and again. She was to appear to them around 2,000 times over a period of four years. Her messages made it clear that she feared for the world and we were in need of mending our ways. The cup (of indiscretions?) was filling, and with no change in our ways, it would surely overflow so that our own contrived misfortunes would be upon us.

Many healings took place and the children were well observed closely by various professional people. They described them as being in ecstatic trance, and unaware of any intrusion by those observing. They on occasions fell backwards, sometimes in unison. They received messages: warnings for the world and voiced concerns.

One reported prophetic message was given as follows: *'Firstly, there will be a warning of which everyone on Earth will become aware. Next, a miracle will happen at Garabandal. One of the girls, Conchita, will give eight days warning of this event. As the result of this miracle, the USSR will convert to Christianity and a permanent supernatural sign will be established.'*

During the visions, Mary appeared with two angels, one either side. She is described as having a white dress, blue cape and crowned with a crown of golden stars.

Others have since had experiences at Garabandal. An English woman in May 1974 had a sky-vision part of which was a map. Russia was black and Europe white. A black smoke poured out of Russia and into Eastern Europe. At this stage, she had difficulty in breathing. All Europe became affected except Spain and Portugal. That was how it was described.

24 June 1981: Thirty miles to the west of Mostar in Yugoslavia, is the village of Medjugorje. It was near here on the slopes of the Crnica Mountains, that three girls and a boy were to see Mary. Mirjana, Ivanka, Vicka and Ivan, all ran home scared the first time. The next day, three returned, but again fled. On 26 June, six children returned together with a crowd of 5,000. Many in the crowd saw three rays of light and knew the

event to be of a special nature. The six children, the original four plus Marija and Jakov saw Mary and listened to her. She said: *'I want to be among you to convert and reconcile.'* She was with her crown of stars and she repeated over and over: *'Peace. Peace. Be reconciled.'* People flocked to what had become known as 'The Hill of Apparitions'. Mary appeared weekly. There were healings. There was a 'sun-dance' seen by many. *'MIR'* (peace), was manifest in white light over the mountain and could be seen by all in Medjugorje. Friar Jozo Zovko took spiritual charge of the children.

The authorities stepped in. There was a negative media campaign and transport restrictions in the area. No religious meetings were allowed in the church. Psychiatrists examined the six children. In August, the Friar was arrested by secret police and his church despoiled. Other churches were locked and cut off by roadblocks. But regardless of such bureaucratic malpractice the pilgrimages continued. The number is estimated as in excess of ten millions over nine years. As the Marxist State policies lessened, the regime became more tolerant and Friar Jozo was released in 1988.

Secret apocalyptic prophecies were given to the children, to be made known when the time is judged to be right by our Lady of the Visions. One concerns a permanent, indestructible and beautiful sign to be on the hillside ... to convince the unbelieving. (The supernatural sign as spoken of at Garabandal?) The world, she says, is going through a period of unparalleled darkness, and no one can be true Catholic who does not respect the other religions. Too many of the area were mocking Moslem and Serb Christian. Miracles and healings continued. Some have said that their Rosaries have turned to gold. And the visions continued.

In 1991, black orbs appeared in the sky. Then followed the sound of gunfire across the hills, as Serbian military advanced through Croat and Bosnian posts. Mostar and Medjugorje were targeted. Medjugorje was cut off. But the rockets and mortar bombs seemed to have little effect, with many of the shells failing to go off. Many mortars fell short. A rocket attack killed a cow that was made into soup. A captured Serbian pilot had said his bomb-sight became obscured by a strange light. The church remained intact, and mass was celebrated every day in the basement of the priest's house. Mary had said that Medjugorje would continue as an oasis of peace. In 1992, Friar Jozo had an audience with Pope John Paul II, who gave strong words of encouragement: *'Look after Medjugorje, save Medjugorje.'*

On Sunday 24 October 1996, BBC1 TV Everyman programme reported the Medjugorje happenings. It seems that Mary continues to visit, and despite proximity of war zone, to date 22 million visitors to the shrine from many countries have been accounted.

26 April 1987: It was one year after the Chernobyl disaster that she appeared at Hriushiw in the Ukraine, over a derelict chapel. She appeared to Marina, a young peasant girl, who called her mother Myroslawa and sister Halia. They prayed; crowds came; and *all* were able to see Mary. And it is reported that Mary had much to say '... *forgive the nations who have harmed you ... Don't forget those who died in the disaster at Chernobyl, which was a sign to the whole world ... I have come purposely to thank the Ukrainian people because, during the last 70 years, it has suffered most for the Church of Christ ... the Ukraine will be an independent state ... The Ukrainians must become apostles of Christ among the peoples of Russia (USSR). If there is not a return to Christianity in Russia, then there will be a Third World War.*' On 13th May, the anniversary of Fatima, I understand Mary's outline appeared on TV screens! The crowds came; on foot, by car, by someone else's car, by the busload; half a million was the estimate.

The authorities reacted. Troops surrounded the chapel. A tree was felled across the road. Pravda (Truth) described the apparitions as the work of extremists aiming to wreck perestroika. But KGB personnel who were *there*, knelt and crossed themselves on seeing.

The people made their choice. They came to this shrine, and continued to come. The people were also told that the third secret of Fatima would be revealed to them if they remained loyal to the Pope.

As time advanced, changes then occurred and the Soviet Union was no longer in its old form. Who would have guessed that such a change was possible without great upheaval? But then, perhaps we under-estimate the extent of influence that comes to us from beyond our material realm.

Is there any kind of confirmation or corroboration of the details embraced by Mary's visions? The answer to that question is most definitely affirmative. In recent decades, both Jesus and Mary have spoken *through* others and their teaching/messages have been written down and subsequently published. (One is not always free to quote sources. It can be a difficult area.) In such work, which I have on my library shelves, Mary confirms her own appearances at Lourdes, Fatima and Garabandal and describes the latter as a sequel to Fatima. The Garabandal visions are clearly regarded as of paramount importance by those in spirit. Jesus confirms their authenticity ... that Mary indeed appeared to the children, likewise Mary's message; also that Garabandal is in sequel to Fatima. He also refers to Mary's crown of stars. The connective pattern that runs through the communications received by others and written down by them may add cogency for those who still remain uncomfortable about such matters.

The point has been made and re-made that Garabandal is to be regarded as a sequel to Fatima. At Fatima, Mary stated that the world must alter its ways or there would be a second world war. The world did not alter its ways and so war prevailed. All knew from that time on and into the Cold War period that a third world war would mean nuclear oblivion. Next, at Garabandal, she indicated that there would be a warning *of which everyone on Earth will be aware.* I believe that Chernobyl was that warning and certainly the whole world was aware of that event as well as its implications. Then, at Hriushiw, Mary indicated that Chernobyl had indeed been a sign to the whole world.

One may debate the pros and cons of each of the above communications in isolation. Quite so. It is to be observed however, that they all knit together with our history of this century, in a rational sequence without violation, in a mode of prediction or explanation. And this is a quality consistent with truth.

There have been other visions; but I believe those recounted sufficiently demonstrate a connected quality. There are, in a number of instances, the connections of healing, spring water, children in trance, series appearances, world events and so on. It is my own view that such *connective patterns* go a long way to establishing credibility. It is with such connective patterns, that the whole set of happenings then begins to feel comfortable.

The particular messages of Garabandal and of Hriushiw would appear to concern Russia's 'belief' aspirations. Since those reported happenings, we have all witnessed huge and dramatic changes within the USSR. Under the cloak of cold-war-communism, the Soviet Union was nominally atheist. This was however, in some measure a political front. Religious aspiration concerns the *hearts of the people* and not the directive of government, but the latter may at times be a heavy influence.

On 1 May 1948, 'Illustrated' magazine devoted its pages to the Soviet Union and its peoples. Its authors were photographer Robert Capa and novelist John Steinbeck, who was at one time, also a war columnist. In that delightfully informative issue, it was reported that he, John Steinbeck, found no evidence of active anti-religious propaganda and the militant atheism of post-revolutionary years had mellowed into tolerance. He goes on to describe old churches as being filled with worshippers of every generation due to a religious revival brought about by the war! And whilst the crowded cathedrals and parish churches are filled with magnificent choral singing. He also refers to the friendly greetings used: *'May God go with you!'* and *'May you be blessed!'*

When I visited Moscow in 1987, it contained 48 *worshipping* churches and had an active 'Soviet Peace Committee'. Photographs were available of the 1986 peace march through Moscow. (We in the West were well aware of our own CND peace demonstrations in London and in other towns and capitals; but we remained uninformed of parallel events in Moscow and Leningrad ... and of the sale of Russian anti-missile badges in Moscow!) Such things demonstrate the will of the people, and the fragility of uninspired governing regime. The people would raise their consciousness regardless of political front, and clearly there were fundamental changes already well under way in the mid-80s, that would continue to develop towards their eventual fruition.

It would appear that Mary's prophecy concerning the USSR is now blooming with obvious marked changes. (And Mary is not the only one to have given us such messages about those particular changes.)

Chapter X

Apocalypse

Off the coast of Ephesus, is the island of Patmos. It was during his sojourn on this island, that St. John experienced the visions that led to his writing of the Apocalypse or 'Revelation', as the last book of the Holy Bible is often called. That was in the year AD 96-97.

> *'And I went to the angel, telling him to give me the little scroll. And he says to me 'Take, and eat it, and it will make Thy belly bitter, but in thy mouth it will be sweet as Honey.'*
>
> *And I took the little scroll from the Hand of the Angel, and did eat it; and it was in my mouth sweet as Honey; and when I ate it my belly was embittered.*
>
> *And they say to me, 'Thou must prophesy again concerning peoples, and concerning Nations, and Languages, and many Kings."*
>
> *Apocalypse* ***10****, 9-11.*

The small scroll containing a potion of berries would have been in keeping with tradition, as one means of raising consciousness to aid prophecy, as was practised in some oracles. The prophet Ezekiel clearly used a similar procedure 700 years earlier *('... and it was as sweet as honey to my mouth!' Ezekiel* ***3****, 3)*. Such is the nature of prophecy. The very few, like Cassandra, had the full natural gift. Some who also already have the gift may usefully be able to raise consciousness still further, especially with divine guidance and with the good unselfish purpose. It seems to have been John's much deeper and very special *beyond physical Earth*, vision that was achieved in this way.

[Before proceeding further, I should point out that this aspect of the art of prophecy, bears no relationship whatsoever to the wanton misuse of mind-altering drugs for kicks and self-indulgence that came to be a problem in the latter 20th century. This later practice would likely be extremely damaging. Whatever development of mind or spirit is already in situ, would be exaggerated or distorted, possibly with fearful consequence. There are also toxic or non-clearing effects of certain ill-conceived synthetic chemicals, that a sadly misguided minority, seem bent on making or marketing. None of these later considerations apply here.]

St. John was a true visionary who sought the future prospects for mankind. His motive was seeking and serving, and in no way self-indulgent.

In his vision, he conversed with the Spirit who identifies as *The First and the Last* and as *The Word of God* i.e. the ultimate, the 'Word' ... the same 'Word', that was in the beginning. The spirit of John enters the door in heaven (just as St. Paul, during the course of *his* vision, was able to enter a door in the 'third heaven'). John sees the setting-free of the four horsemen that would be a part of our history:

- The first, with bow and crown, on a white horse is 'Conquest'.
- The second, wielding a sword and on a red horse, is 'War'.
- The third, with scales and high prices, on a black horse, is 'Famine'.
- The fourth, on a pale horse, is 'Death'. He has authority to kill with the sword, with famine and by other means.

This part of the prophecy is of course starkly and accurately symbolic of the two millennia that would follow his vision. There has been the blood spilt in conquest, as nations fought to establish empires under their particular 'crown'. The Mongol hordes under Genghis Khan, who careered across Asia and Europe carrying the bow, in particular exemplify the first horseman; but of course the weaponry and the means of conveyance are basically unimportant where symbolism is concerned.

Tragically, even the Church lost its way, failed to understand Christianity, and joined forces with the horseman 'Conquest'. The conquest practised by the Church took several forms. There were the nine bloody Crusades spanning the 11th to 13th centuries. Pope Innocent III, had persecuted and killed some ½ million Albigensians in the 13th century, for their different belief. (The name arises because the first attack was directed at the district of Albegeois in Southern France.) They believed that material possessions and social life are evil. They were ascetics. When Beziers was stormed, *all* were murdered ... in excess of 20,000 so-called heretics and Catholics alike!

The Inquisition was a court set up by the Roman Catholic Church to seek out and punish those of contrary belief. The punishment was sometimes death by burning. It was active in much of Europe in the 12th to 15th centuries. The Spanish Inquisition was a later tribunal, active from 1483 until 1834. The Italian philosopher Giodarno Bruno in the year 1600, saw the universe as extensive, and God relating to its entirety. He was burned at the stake for his (perfectly accurate) reasoning. The Church also had its links with the bloody and plundering conquest of the Americas; but of course, in all these things, the Church did *not* represent the true religion, with *love* at the centre of all things, neither was it following the teachings of Jesus. Instead, it was sadly devising a dogma and punishment syndrome entirely of its own making, quite alien to the God within. The political aspect of the Church thus became a shameful travesty and tragedy for the Western culture.

The greed for land possession next manifested as war. Those who lived in the 20th century know much of that horseman. The two world wars of the 20th century might well be viewed as a climax where that particular horseman has been concerned. Only towards the end of the century were there signs of his being contained. This came partly through peace-meditation by enlightened ones, partly through help from other realms, partly through peace campaigning, partly through the realisation that the manipulation of super-weapons is really beyond our realistic control and partly through rational thinking on the matter of cost and resources. All have played their part.

Those who have lived in the 20th century also know the third horseman. The famines of the African and Indian continents are only *too* well known. It has to be said that in general, there has always been a sufficiently plentiful availability of food for the world's population. The potential at least exists. Unfortunately, certain governments of the final decades, and those in support, have seemed more preoccupied with local conflict and arms supplies than with the food needs of their people; and neither have arms suppliers and other mercenaries been blameless in the tragedies that have followed. It is to the credit of some that they have helped out during those times of starvation and suffering. Another aspect of famine concerns those responsible for the plundering of fertile land and forests, resulting in their conversion to wastelands. Famines in various ways, are largely of our own making and that horseman still rides.

The fourth horseman is 'Death', the collector of corpses. He is concerned with the different aspects of death that we deal out to ourselves. There are those who fall by the symbolic sword in battle. There are those who perish through our contrived or ignored famines. There are those who die by the diseases that we bring upon ourselves: this through bad diet, overdoing the tobacco or the alcohol, or by overloading our psyche with stress and negative thoughts. In diet, Jesus himself extolled the virtue of raw food; this teaching being included in *The Essene Gospel of Peace, Book 1* from those texts known as *The Dead Sea Scrolls*. Raw food has a vibrant energy that our bodies thrive on; nothing to do with molecules or calories per gramme, and this is sadly not always realised.

The fourth horseman, according to John, is also concerned with those killed by wild animals. I cannot help thinking that the vehicles we drive on our roads have largely taken over from the prowling wild beast in that domain of death.

The symbolism of John's four horsemen of the Apocalypse, in today's world, and looking back over the two millennia since the Patmos visions, would seem to make much sense; but what of that other Apocalypse? What of St. Paul's vision? The account of *his* vision was not included in the Holy Bible anthology, but turned up as a bound papyrus book in a sealed jar, near the village of Nag Hamâdi in Upper Egypt. It was found, together with a number of other writings, which include a work by Peter. Peter describes a vision in which he sees hostile priests trying to stone himself and Jesus to death. (Symbolic of how the mediaeval church would later be treating the *Word* perhaps?) He also makes a statement indicating that what he has seen, will be presented to others who are of another race and another age. How very true! The contents of the sealed jar did not again see the light of day until its discovery in 1945! Before that date, there was no knowledge that St. Paul ever wrote an Apocalypse. In fact, it was not until 1977 that the first extensive translation of the writings became available.

While John's vision was a glimpse into the future across a considerable expanse of time, and a statement of traumatic events that we were to construct for ourselves, Paul's vision was of a rather different nature. His vision is a description of what happens when we leave this world and go on to the next ... the *other-world.*

In Paul's vision, he meets and talks with the Holy Spirit. The Spirit shows him what happens at the time of death. He is escorted through a series of 'heavens' or spirit realms, beginning at the 'third heaven'. The Spirit explains to him that there is a being, whose task it is to implant souls into fresh bodies for the purpose of reincarnation. The reincarnation procedure is for those souls who will benefit from more Earth life to further their learning and development. Reincarnation is not for those souls who are ready to traverse the higher heavens; for those souls, reincarnation is to be avoided.

On reaching the 'fourth heaven', his guide encourages Paul to look down. There, far below, on the mountain of Jericho, he can see the physical body that he has left behind. There ... is the lifeless material body; while here, in the fourth heaven, was his living spirit. It was while in this fourth heaven that he witnessed a soul in judgement. It faced the guilt of envy, of anger and of murder, and was sent down to where a body had been prepared for its reincarnation. (In cosmic law, there always remains the chance to progress, from whatever level. In Christian terms, there is always forgiveness and the chance to make amends.)

Passing on to the 'fifth heaven', he sees his fellow apostles, and there are angels scourging souls and going about their business of judgement. Paul is still accompanied by the Holy Spirit as he sees the gates of the sixth realm open before him. A light is shining down upon him from the seventh and the toll-collector ushers him through the gates. He is confronted by a shining 'light being' in white robe, who questions where he is going. Paul talks with him and offers a Gnostic sign that he remembers.

As the eighth heaven opens, he enters and embraces the twelve disciples. Together they ascend to the ninth heaven. On entering the tenth heaven, he is transformed.

It is clear from the writings, that Paul is describing in vision, his passage through ten spirit realms, as might well be fitting for one of such spiritual advancement; and he describes how souls who still have much to learn, are reincarnated for a further physical life. The spirit is imperishable. Paul's Apocalypse is doubtless consistent with the Holy Bible in its earlier form; that is, prior to the early Councils of the Eastern Roman Empire. Under the auspices of certain Emperors, references to past lives and reincarnation would have been removed, and various doctrines condemned. Despite this treatment of the scriptures however, there still remain certain interesting and relating phrases in the Bible:

> *'And they shall walk with me in white; because they are worthy.*
> *The one overcoming this, shall thus be clothed in white garments ...*
> *The one overcoming, I will make him a pillar in the temple of my God,*
> *and he shall never go out more ...*
> *The one overcoming, I will give to him to sit down with me in my throne,*
> *as also I overcame, and sat down with my father in his throne.*
> *(Let him who has an ear, hear what the spirit says to the congregations.)'*
> *Apocalypse* ***3****, 4, 5, 12, 21, 22.*

It is clear that, in these verses, the Holy Spirit is speaking to John, for the benefit of the congregations. What is it that is being overcome? It is the lower spirit realms and the need for reincarnation that are being overcome. The one overcoming, will be a pillar of the temple and shall not return to lower realms or Earth, *(he shall never go out more)*. He will share ... be at one ... with God the Father and the Holy Spirit. The Bible passage makes perfect sense in the light of Paul's Apocalypse. The passage likewise compares wonderfully with various other inspired works, such as that delightful dialogue between Paramahansa Yogananda and his departed Master Yukteswar:

> *"When a soul finally gets out of the three jars of bodily delusions," Master continued, "it becomes one with the Infinite without any loss of individuality. Christ had won this final freedom even before he was born as Jesus...The undeveloped man must undergo countless earthly and astral and causal incarnations in order to emerge from his three bodies. A master who achieves this final freedom, may elect to return to earth as a prophet to bring other human beings back to God, or like myself he may choose to reside in the astral cosmos..."'*
>
> Paramahansa Yogananda *Autobiography of a Yogi*
> Self-Realization Fellowship, Los Angeles, 1998

And the following teaching of Jesus:

> *'Jesus said: Blessed are the solitary and elect, for you shall find the Kingdom; because you come from it, (and) you shall go there again. Jesus said: If they say to you: 'From where have you originated?' say to them: 'We have come from the Light ..."*
>
> *The Gospel According to Thomas.* Nag Hamâdi papyrus. Trans A Guillaumont, H-Ch Puech, G Quispel, W Till and Yassah 'Abd Al Masïh. E J Brill.

I believe the meaning of *the Light* and *the Kingdom* to be: that more distant realm in spirit of higher vibration. Having chosen to return to Earth as a teacher and prophet, and having fulfilled his purpose of showing others the way to God, his Earthly body was then crucified. The following passage from *The Koran* relates:

> *"Verily we have slain the Messiah, Jesus the son of Mary, an Apostle of God.' Yet they slew him not, and they crucified him not, but they had only his likeness. And they who differed about him were in doubt concerning him: No sure knowledge had they about him, but followed only an opinion, and they did not really slay him, but God took him up to Himself.'*
>
> *The Koran, Sura IV, 156*

Such events may be perceived from a material/biological viewpoint or from a spiritual stance. And as we become more spiritually aware, then the spirit self becomes more clearly evident, whilst the physical reality takes second place. Both have their importance of course and have their complex connections. The connection between our physical reality and spirit may be clearly seen in John's Apocalypse. It required one as spiritually advanced as John to be able to commune with angelic and Christ spirit under guidance and to prophesy events of our physical domain.

Much of John's Apocalypse may appear mystical and symbolic and, at first at least, beyond understanding. The 'third angel', however produces a sign that might just connect with our times in a sharply definable way:

> *'... and a great star, burning like a lamp, fell from Heaven, and it fell on the third of the rivers, and on the fountains of the waters. And the name of the star is called Wormwood; and the third of the waters became Wormwood; and many of the men died because of the bitterness of the waters.'*
>
> *Apocalypse* ***8***, *10, 11*

The energy that powers the stars is of course nuclear. A nuclear process is what makes a star a star. On Earth, a nuclear reactor contains a slowed-down and very much smaller 'star' process i.e. a star but much smaller and slowed down. (*Burning like a lamp* ... could be a way of describing its slowed-down aspect.) Just what is the significance of the word 'Wormwood'? It has a precise significance. The Ukrainian word: *'Chernobyl'*, identifies with a particular kind of plant. It is the 'mugwort', a common enough member of the Artemisia species. But if one then refers to an English dictionary, it becomes clear that 'mugwort' is an alternative name for 'wormwood'. Chernobyl therefore means Wormwood. At the time of the Chernobyl disaster, river waters and springs were contaminated and many people were affected or died as the result. Contamination spread through much of the Northern Hemisphere. It prevailed in much of Europe. The fall-out affected reindeer herds in the extreme north, and in respect of high pastures in the British Isles, protective measures to safeguard milk production and the sheep trade were very necessary. These controls remained in place for a full decade. There was the sky-vision at Garabandal, in which the smoke poured out of Russia and into all Europe except Spain and Portugal. The vision foretold the event twelve years before it happened. Mary later confirmed that Chernobyl had been a sign to the whole world.

The connections of the Ukraine disaster, the sky-vision of 1974, the Mary visions and message, and the star named *'Chernobyl'* of St. John's Apocalypse, are not mere coincidence. They are parts of an orchestrated phrasing within a time matrix, which seems extensive and disjointed, only to our Earth-bound minds. Such a sequence of connected events cannot be dismissed lightly.

. . . .

Remarkable though the ancient prophets and seers were, there is one who came much nearer to *our* time, whose gift is without question, the true gift. But before confronting the work of that one, it is well that we first consider, if we are able, a little more of the nature of time.

On Earth, we are acutely conscious of the linear passage of time. We base our measurements of time upon the motions of our planet and the moon; and the units of years, months, days and hours, suit the running of our lives quite well. This construct is of our own fabrication. But for matters relating to the vastness of that small fraction of the universe that we are able to observe, the linear character of time has to go. Our scientists must have it that space-time is *curved*, and I would think it is the *time* element of space-time that actually induces the curvature. Spatial volume may be defined readily enough in terms of its linear dimensions; although it may be that we must observe space-time as a universal package that cannot in universal terms, be dismembered. (There is reference to this detail in later pages.)

On Earth, we have past and future. (The present is really no more than an imaginary division between the two, amounting to less than one nanosecond, in the scientific terminology.) We live at a thin divide between past and future, and what we call 'present', is just a transient quirk of our awareness. If we communicate with spirit realm, it soon becomes clear that time is viewed differently in those planes. What we on Earth would call past and future, are seen as 'one' in that other-world. Something that Jesus said, at first glance may appear as a riddle, but the reader may agree that in fact it compares with this notion:

> *'The disciples said to Jesus: Tell us how our end will be. Jesus said: Have you then discovered the beginning so that you enquire about the end? For where the beginning is, there shall be the end. Blessed is he who shall stand at the beginning, and he shall know the end and he shall not taste death.'*
>
> *The Gospel According to Thomas.* Nag Hamâdi papyrus. Trans A Guillaumont, H-Ch Puech, G Quispel, W Till and Yassah 'Abd Al Masïh. E J Brill.

He who stands where beginning and end ... past and future ... are perceived as one, will have spiritually advanced beyond the need for further Earthly reincarnation, and so will not taste death.

Similarly, the one in spirit who spoke to John on Patmos, said:

> *'I am the First and the Last, and the Living ... and I became dead: yet behold, I am living in the eternities of the eternities ... and possess the keys of Death and of the spirit-land.'*
>
> *Revelation* ***1****, 17, 18.*

One might also say that the past has clarity, while the future that is seen by a seer will have just a hint of indistinctness, on account of free-will-factor. It is as if we on Earth, are on a great circle of time, and can see a little of the circle ahead, and a little behind. But if we are spirit, then we are away from that circle, and can see the whole of it. It is more than a little interesting that the Mayan peoples believed in the circular nature of time and that today's scientists need the curvature of space-time, in order to further their theorising.

The true seer or prophet is able to slip into *trance*, and *see* in the way of the spirit. The truly gifted one Nostradamus, would go into trance, and would see the future of mankind laid out before him as history. It would of course be his spirit self that is seeing. Such is the nature of time and space, and such was the nature of his gift.

. . . .

Note: Certain of the Bible quotations of the above chapter are from *The Emphatic Diaglott* of the New Testament, a word-for-word translation from Vatican Manuscript No. 1209, directly from the Greek. Published by the International Bible Students Association and Watch Tower Bible and Tract Society, New York. (1942). (This translation emphasises word precision as opposed to phrasing.)

The 'orthodox' canon of 27 books, Old Testament and New Testament was formally recognised in the year AD 397 at the Third Council of Carthage in North Africa. It was deemed that from that date, nothing could be added or removed from the canon. (This means of protection relates to the complete Holy Bible in general usage and not to the *original* Torah, a translation of which appears as the first five books of the Old Testament. Tradition has it that the Torah has been kept in original Hebrew form in the Holy of Holies within the synagogue from its very beginning, without alteration. The significance of this detail will become apparent in chapter 29.)

1. The Mayan Temple of Inscriptions, Palenque. Resplendent at the foot of the Sacred Mountain. Resting place of Pacal the Great. (Chapter VI.)

2. The Temple of the Sun. One of the Group of the Cross at Palenque. Its *pib na*, that portal to the other-world, lies within. (Chapter VI.)

3. Pacal's accession. Pacal receives the feathered head-dress from his mother the Lady Zak-Kuk, whilst seated on the jaguar throne. Palace tablet, west gallery. (Chapter VI.)

4. Constantine the Great. A bronze statue now stands beside York Minster, unveiled 25th July 1998. It was close by that Constantine was proclaimed Augustus following the death of his father. Under his influence Christianity would become a state religion. (Chapter XIII.)

5. Church of *Aya Sofya* (Turkish) or *Sancta Sophia* (Latin), meaning Church of Holy Wisdom. Justinian's masterpiece, and seen as the greatest church of Christendom for almost a full millennium. Today it still remains one of the world's finest architectural works. (Chapter XIV.)

6. The grand amphitheatre, Ephesus. Its tiered rows of seating could accommodate 24,500. It was here that Paul confronted Demetrius as the crowd shouted: *'Great is Artemis of the Ephesians!'* (Chapter VIII.)

7. Within Mary's house on Mount Koressos. Discovered for the Western World in 1881 following the visions of Sister Anna Catharina Emmerich. (Chapter VIII.)

8. Silbury Hill. Europe's largest ancient earthwork, viewed from across the River Kennet. Avebury Ring lies beyond. (Chapter XXIII.)

9. A part of Avebury Ring. Its stones dwarf those who walk by. The encircling ditch was once much deeper. To the right may be seen one stone of the megalithic avenue and a party of sheep who maintain the grass. (Chapter XXIII.)

Chapter XI

Nostradamus: Prophête Suprème

Those who require an absolute proof of the truth of prophecy, or those who prefer the stance of disbelief, will say: '90% of what he says can be applied to a number of different things, and so his work can be dismissed.' They would be perfectly correct as regards the first part of that statement. But the same would be true of almost any set of prophecies that span two thousand years or so, irrespective of their accuracy. What are we able to say of the other 10%? There, within the 10%, are some much more specific happenings, and that is where proof of prophecy, is to be found. How do the sceptics account for the precision of year-dates that are given, and how do they account for his plucking of actual key names from history? If proof is to be sought, then seek within the 10% of work that is of a more specific nature; within those verses which, due to their particular content, cannot conform to any 'generalised' category.

The Prophecies of Nostradamus span more than two millennia, and were first published in two parts, in the years 1555 and 1568. (History has yet to catch up with many of his predictions, and a full appraisal will only be possible following another 1,800 years!) He also wrote an epistle to his king, Henry II of France dated 1558. The times in which he lived were much troubled. The Inquisition was active and the work of prophecy could so easily have been construed as heresy; in which event, both he and his work would have been curtailed. Nostradamus therefore exercised caution. He took care to jumble his predictive verses into a fairly random order, and made anagrams of certain key words. He used capitals for some words of special or double meaning, and sometimes omitted century or millennium digits from his dates. This made him appear to be not quite such an expert, less of a mystic, perhaps more one who amuses; yet still enabling those of sufficient insight, to understand his works. As a result of this planned subterfuge, there are many of his predictions that require careful study; but there still remain a number of verses requiring little or no effort in regard to their analysis. Any would-be sceptics might do well to look first at these.

Amongst his really specific predictions, he gives '1792' as the date of the new calendar of the French revolution. He gives '666' as the date of the Great Fire of London, connecting it with the Great Plague. (He sees both the fire and the plague as retributions for the wrongful execution of King Charles I. There are several verses relating to the execution, and Nostradamus uses the connecting phrase *'blood of the just man'*, in reference to Charles). He gives the date of the break-up of the Soviet Union as 1991 (by a simple deduction, detailed later). All perfectly accurate precision dating, relating to highly specific events of major significance.

He *named* the French chemist 'Pasteur', and said he would be celebrated as if he were a lesser god. He was indeed thus acclaimed, and the seer described him as discoverer of *'the lost thing, hidden for many centuries'*. He, of course, discovered bacteria, and made the connections between micro-organisms, disease and putrefaction. Pasteur was very much revered for his work, which saved many lives; also industries. He is still much revered, to the extent that his name appears on every carton of 'Pasteurised milk'. The seer named 'Hister' (clearly meaning Hitler, whose family name has varied a little in its spelling over the years). In the same verse, 'Hister' is described as *'the child of Germany who observes no law'*, leaving no doubt as to his identity. Nostradamus names 'Montgaulfier' (now spelled Montgolfier), in connection with military spotting *'through a hole'*. The Montgolfier brothers first flew a hot air balloon in 1783 and a balloon was used by the military for spotting at the battle of Fleurus, 1794. They will always be remembered as the brothers who pioneered flight in the Western culture. These three highly significant names from history would seem especially worthy of the seer's attention.

Where prophecy is concerned, such specific dates and specific names, cannot be explained away as a matter of mere chance. There is much, much more that, with a little analysis, is both convincing and amazing in the predictions of Nostradamus. But what of the man? Surely no ordinary mortal could make such an impression on future generations? He was in fact born Michel de Nostredame, 1503 in St. Rémy de Provençe; and so, just like Hitler and the Montgolfiers, his name also has undergone some small degree of change.

So often, dealings with the spirit realms go hand in hand with the healing profession, and with a caring nature. The seer began very much as the healer, studying medicine at Montpelier University; obtaining a degree and licence to practice medicine in 1525. It was the time of the plague in Southern France and there was much work for him, travelling Provençe and healing the sick. His good reputation was well deserved. By repute, he was kindly to the suffering and generous to the poor, and skilful in his work. After four years as the travelling physician, he returned to Montpelier and completed his doctorate, remaining there teaching for a further year before again resuming a wandering lifestyle. The healer was happier on the move, away from the strictures and structures of Montpelier. There were his own cures and treatments that he had developed, and he did not approve of the 'establishment' practice of blood-letting. When the Inquisition became interested in his chance remarks or his *other interests*, then it was no great problem to simply move on to new pastures. Mobility was a safeguard in these times of persecution.

As a healer, Nostradamus was successful. But no healer is perfect. It was 1537 when the tragedy struck. Agen had become his home town, where he had finally settled and now lived with a wife and two children. But when the plague spread to Agen, he was unable to save his own family. All perished, together with his reputation, and the inquiries of the Inquisition again came close, from a chance remark he had made. There was nothing remaining to keep him in Agen, and so, once again he travelled.

Aix was grievously stricken with the plague. It had followed on from the flooding. Most doctors and those who could travel had left the town. He went to Aix, and was to stay there throughout the epidemic, easing the suffering for many and helping those in need as best he could. Many were saved, as the result of employing a policy of clean air and unpolluted water. His famous rose pills contained herbal antiseptics combined with the perfume and *energy* of a very high proportion of rose petals. (I suspect that he would have known the value of the flower energy in the pill; especially since he saw to it they were picked fresh, early morning, with the dew still on them. Perhaps his recipe was inspired from that other realm.) In conclusion to this episode of the healer's life, the authorities of this, the capital city of Provençe, showed their great respect by voting him a pension for life.

The work completed in Aix, he moved on to Salon, which he found to be a charming town, and settled there. Apart from travelling to Lyons in answer to that city's plea for assistance with a pestilence, he was to remain in Salon for the remainder of his life. That life was to change. He married a rich widow, raised a family, made cosmetic preparations; and lived in a house with a top room. That top room was made into a study and it became a most important place. That study was to become a place of vision and of prophecy, a private and a secret place.

He would sit at night, alone, before a brass tripod supporting a glass bowl of water. Sitting upon a wooden stool, with a wand held in his hand, he would use it to sprinkle a little of the water onto the hem of his robe and onto his feet. He would then sit and lose the focus of consciousness, somewhere within that misty cloud within the bowl; and then, when time no longer seemed to flow, he would discover that the spirit was again with him. The substance of his vision then formed, and he heard the voice, now close. (The technique was as of old. He was guided by the voice within and inspired by the mystic books of his reading. The technique was borrowed from certain of the ancient Greek oracles, as practised more than a thousand years earlier. Much, much earlier still, the Aborigine Bushman adopted a stance in which wooden spear-thrower and leg replaced stool, and spear replaced wand; and the spirit was *found*, in the expanse and the quiet of the bush.) But this was 16th century Salon and here, in this time and place, in the quiet of the secret study at the top of the house, it suited him and the spirit well.

By the summer of 1558, the first volume of his prophecies had already been published, and the work had been well received ... and without it having been deemed heretical! There were of course, some that did not approve, but this was to be expected. He was relieved, and even saw fit to write a lengthy epistle to his king: Henry II of France, dated 27 June 1558. It is a blessing that the author of the prophecies wrote this letter, because in it, he discusses a number of the more important predictions.

One very specific year date is addressed: *'1792 ... everyone will think it a renovation of the age.'** The 234 years eventually passed until it became the year of the prophecy. At this time, the French Revolution was in full flower. The year named, the year 1792, saw the mob invade the Tuileries, the French Republic proclaimed, and the new revolutionary calendar was installed. This was a *renovation of the age* indeed! The Revolution was such a suitable candidate for Nostradamus' short list of the more important prophecies; and so he had written to his king about it!

The words of the seer are so remarkably succinct where the major revolutions of history are concerned. A revolution of the 20th century also appears on his short list; one that has ripened and scattered its seeds of influence so widely in our own times... *'There shall be in the month of October, a great revolution made, such that everybody will think that the earth has lost its natural motion ... accompanied with the procreation of the New Babylon, a miserable prostitute large with the abomination of the first holocaust. And this shall last only seventy three years and seven months.'**

There is only one that is generally referred to as the 'October Revolution'. The October Revolution of 1917 followed unsatisfactory times in Russia with much in the way of political intrigue, bad government and Jewish suppression. The latter included government-induced 'pogroms' ... the name given to the rounding-up of selected people and their organised bloody massacre. In the wake of October 1917, the Imperial family was murdered and the church disestablished. The regime that would follow was so very different to what had gone before, and this would last just: *seventy three years and seven months.* This period of time then, according to the prophecy, should represent the period of communist rule, up to the dissolution of the Soviet Union, and the replacement of communism by a new political system.

It was 23 October 1917, when the Bolshevik Central Committee voted for armed revolution. It was 7 November when the Bolshevik overthrew the old government in Petrograd, and appointed Vladimir Lenin as Chief Commissar and Leon Trotsky as Commissar for Foreign Affairs in the new order. The communist regime would then run from *7 November 1917.* It was *13 June 1991* when Boris Yeltsin, in free elections, was voted first President of Russia. The official communist candidates fared poorly in the polls. Yeltsin's promises to his electorate included: a democratic multi-party system of politics. The Communist regime based on Lenin had lasted *seventy-three years and seven months* almost to the day! (And Henry Roberts' translation of 1947 also very comfortably predates the fruition date of the prophecy.)

World War II with its holocaust and its various chapters of disaster, happened within this well-predicted time frame, and according to the prophecy, the first holocaust was then (1917), already into its gestation period. World War II would be such a poignant episode in the future history of the planet, that the seer would devote a number of his verses to that event. He would also mention this period in the letter to his king. The war, which would affect almost the whole of Europe as well as other more distant lands, would indeed be worthy of his prophetic quatrains. He could see it all ... the strangest of weaponry. How should he describe those weapons? How *could* he describe them? Great beasts of iron rampaging across the battlefield? Fierce fighting machines in the air ... in the air like swarms of gnats! And other swarming craft in the seas, swarming together like they were destructive locusts ... marine locusts! How to describe such strangeness of the much later times? But it was there! It was all there in the mists of the vision, and with the sanction of the God, the spirit would guide.

There were those at the close of the 20th century who claimed he foretold the end of the world in 1999. Nonsense! He clearly states that his prophecies continue until the year 3797.

> *... if I should relate what shall happen hereafter, those of the present Reign, Sect, Religion and Faith, would find it so disagreeing with their fancies, that they would condemn that which future ages shall find and know to be true.*
>
> *... I have made Books of Prophesies, each one containing a hundred Astronomical Stanzas, which I have joined obscurely, and are perpetual prophecies from this year to the year 3797 ...*
>
> From the Preface to the First Edition of
> *The Centuries, Salon 1 March 1555*.*

* Henry C Roberts translation from 1672 Edition of The True Prophecies, Published as 'The Complete Prophecies of Nostradamus', by Henry C Roberts (1947). Revised: Lee Roberts Amsterdam, Harvey Amsterdam, (1984), HarperCollins Publishers Ltd.

Chapter XII

Antichrist and World War II

(A view of the war according to certain quatrains and as it was likely to have been seen by the seer.)

As future nightmares gather in the mist
And horrors cloud the Nostradamus view.
That 'hell' defies account in 'old Provençe'
As belching metal beasts blitz World War II.
G E Moss *(1995)*

The Second World War was an event of great magnitude, taking many by surprise, half-expected by some, and foreseen by the few. It must go down as a most important and influential episode in the history of our times. Stories from that period have accordingly been told and retold, on film and in books and in song, and those stories continue. In addition, the entire epic seems to have been known to the one in the house at Salon, nearly 400 years earlier. In general, it is the important events that tend to be foretold by those few who have the sight. Furthermore, if one of such rare ability should choose to select and review his *major* prophecies in the form of a 'short list', then it may be taken that those events included in the list are truly, undeniably paramount and eminently worthy of our further consideration.

Nostradamus followed and respected the true Christian ethic; that central core of 'true' faith that can never be held responsible for the Inquisition and other madness of wild irrational misinterpretation. He therefore saw those leaders who war against the collective nominally Christian countries, as being against the teachings of Jesus the Christ, and named them 'Antichrist'. He explains that Attila would have been the first of those leaders. Attila ... 'Scourge of God', some called him ... was a crushing destroyer of the 5th century. Attila devastated all countries from the Black Sea to the Mediterranean, ruining many beautiful cities. Then he turned to the West, fighting huge battles in France and Italy. Venice was founded by people that had been driven from the inland cities by that first Antichrist. When Adolf Hitler rose to power against the nominally Christian nations of the West and against the Jewish peoples, it became clear that here was the 'Second Antichrist' of the prediction.

In his epistle to King Henry, Nostradamus says something of the Second Antichrist and the duration of that leader's reign. The seer gives a set of dates of which, as was his frequent bent, the century digits have been omitted: *' ... in 45 and others to 41, 42 and 47. And in that time and those countries the infernal power shall rise against the church of Jesus Christ. This shall be the second Antichrist, which shall persecute the said church and its true vicar by the means of the power of temporal kings, who through their ignorance shall be seduced by tongues more sharp than any sword in the hands of a madman.*

The said reign of Antichrist shall not last but till the ending of him who was born of Age, and the other in the city of Plancus (Lyons), accompanied by the elect of Modena...' *

These were the words of Nostradamus. The seer of Salon singles out '45' as the most important date of the set of dates. If we assume that the time referred to is the mid-20th century, then the whole passage makes a great deal of sense. The year 1945 was certainly the most important single year: the end of the war, and the death of Adolf Hitler ... *'him who was born of Age'*. 'Age' has been given a capital for emphasis, probably meaning the age and time of *'the infernal power'*. The other factors marking the end of the reign would be the death of Benito Mussolini of Northern Italy (of which *Modena* is indicative) and the end of the 'French Resistance' that organisation being centred on Lyons. These changes were seen as marking the end of the reign of Antichrist.

The remaining dates of the set could possibly relate to the demise of other key members of the Third Reich:

1941: Rudolf Hess (Deputy Leader) flew to Scotland and was interned.

1942: Reinhard Heydrich (Head of Gestapo) was assassinated.

1947: The eleven executions and the suicide of Hermann Goering that followed the Nuremberg Tribunal in fact occurred in 1946. The one execution of 1947 was that of ex-president Tiso of Slovakia. But the seer's expression *'to ... 47'* might well be seen as embracing those events of the year leading up to but not including '47. That would firmly include the Nuremberg Tribunal, that poignant formality that concluded the war and finally drew the curtain on it all.

According to the prophecy then, the infernal power was to rise up against the church of Jesus Christ. In fact, it rose up against most European countries, Britain (and Commonwealth) and the United States, all of which had become nominally Christian countries. The USSR, not nominally

Christian, but nevertheless with a very considerable Russian Orthodox Church following, also formed a major part of the Western Alliance. The Russian church had been disestablished by the state. But many people held to their belief, and many fine churches and cathedrals were to remain. The infernal power warred against the people of the Western Alliance, and there were those people who were especially hunted and persecuted during the years of conflict, and they were those of the Jewish descent.

Both leading up to and during the period of war, Adolf Hitler delivered the most powerful and persuasive speeches. Propaganda was rife. The power of his persuasion was a vital factor in the early days of the Third Reich. Heads of state at that time were *'seduced by tongues more sharp than any sword in the hands of a madman'*. The seer's choice of word might just carry a double meaning. A measure of madness can make speeches that much more powerful. Either way, the tongue was sharper than the sword; and the following of the Nazi party became huge.

The further details of World War II may be gleaned today from the history books, but such books can sometimes be a little dull and wordy. Alternatively, one might refer to translations of *Les Propheties de M. Michel de Nostradamus* printed in the year 1568, in that same city of Lyons that was later to become a centre for the French Resistance. (The connections are sometimes strange.)

Wars do not just happen. They are made. They have their roots in past thoughts, past deeds, past events. The seeds may go back a long way, to remote happenings long since forgotten. A year of great significance, well known to Nostradamus, was 1649. At least, it is clear that he knew of the imprisonment of Charles I of England in the *'fortress near the Thames'* and of his execution: *'the Parliament of London will put their king to death'*. Curiously, the following quatrain connects with that year of the execution and with the 20th century war.

III.57

Sept fois changer verrez gent Britannique	*Seven times you will see the British nation change, dyed in blood for two hundred and ninety years. Not at all free through German support, Aries fears for the protectorate of Poland.*
Tainz en sang en deux cents nonante an:	
Franch non point par appuy Germanique,	
Aries doubte son pole Bastarnien.	

Considering 1939 as the year concluding the period, with its *'fears for ... Poland'* at that time, then the verse makes sense. In 1939, Britain and Poland signed the treaty of mutual assistance. Germany then invaded Poland, and Britain and France declared war on Germany ... all in the same year. Subtracting the 290 years from 1939 brings us to 1649, the year of the death of King Charles and the declaration of England as a Commonwealth. It is clear from other quatrains, that Nostradamus considered the two dates as being of special importance and he is clearly spanning them in this quatrain with the 290 years of bloody conflicts. During those 290 years, the British nation warred with seven different adversaries. The countries concerned were the Netherlands, France, Spain, the American Colonies, South Africa, the Crimea; also Germany et al in World War I.

Across the years, Britain has not been free from German support, when one considers her connections through monarchy, trade and politics. Where *'Aries'* is concerned, I am tempted to take this, in this particular instance, as an oblique reference to the Nazi view of the *Aryan* race. Within the regime, *Aryan* was a word improperly used to describe non-Jewish Germans.

V.85
Par les Sueves & lieux circonvoisins,
Seront en guerre pour cause des nuees:
Gamp marins locustes & cousins,
Du Leman fautes seront bien desnuees.

Through the Swiss and surrounding areas they will war because of the clouds. A swarm of marine locusts and gnats, the faults of Geneva will be laid quite bare.

Geneva is the key word in this quatrain. At the conclusion of World War I, the League of Nations was created with its headquarters at Geneva. The tragedy was that the dubious Treaty of Versailles largely disregarded the terms of the Armistice. The terms had been agreed for the ending of the war, but the treaty had cheated on those agreed terms, thus creating unreasonable tension from the outset. (The seer must have felt the importance of the failure of the League and in fact has devoted more than one quatrain to it.) Members of the League were required to respect each other's territorial independence; also to recognise the need for disarmament. The United States refused to participate. The guidelines were broken. Numbers of warships and fighter aircraft built up ... *'marine locusts and gnats'* ...he aptly calls them. It was the *'clouds'* of these that obscured the good path and significantly added to the breakdown of the League and to war. An aggressive leader would merely hasten a situation that already ripened fast.

III. 35

Du plus profond de l'Occident d'Europe
De pauvres gens un jeune enfant naistra:
Qui par sa langue seduira grande troupe,
Son bruit au regne d'Orient plus croistra.

In the deepest part of Western Europe a child will be born of poor family, who by his speech will entice many peoples. His reputation will grow even greater in the Kingdom of the East.

Adolf Hitler was born in Braunau, on the river Inn that forms the border between Austria and Bavaria. In Mein Kampf, he describes his family as poor, although other sources say middle class. He was to develop his political thinking such that he became a most powerful and persuasive orator. His speeches were to *'entice many people'*. In the early stages of the war, his *'reputation'* grew, as one for crushing assailed countries. That reputation was to *'grow even greater in the Kingdom of the East'* ... Russia. The Soviet people lost in excess of 20-million dead during the course of World War II, a loss that far exceeded any suffered by other nations.

IX.90

Un capitaine de la grand Germanie
Se viendra rendre par simulé secours
Un roi des roi aide de Pannonie,
Que sa revolte fera de sang grand cours.

A captain of the greater Germany will come to deliver false help, king of kings; to support Hungary; His war will cause a great shedding of blood.

Hungary left the League of Nations in 1939 and was then 'taken over' by the Third Reich, otherwise the Grossen Deutchland ... *'the Greater Germany'*. In the early months of the war, it was the Third Reich policy to take over neighbouring countries to 'help' them, but it was a *'false help'* that was delivered. The title, *'king of kings'* is of course indicative of the all-powerful position of the Führer of the Third Reich at that time.

V.94

Translatera en la grand Germanie, *Brabant & Flandres, Gand, Bruges & Bolongne,* *La traifue fainte, le grand duc d'Armenie,* *Assaillira Vienne & la Coloigne.*	*He will change into the Greater Germany, Brabant and Flanders, Ghent, Bruges and Boulogne. The truce feigned, the great Duke of Armenia will assault Vienna and Cologne.*

In the early stages of the war, Brabant, Flanders, Ghent, Bruges and Boulogne all fell to the Third Reich. The truce with the Duke of Armenia relates quite well to the short duration pact that existed between Germany and Russia at the start of the war. Russia then joined the Western Alliance. The final line of the quatrain is difficult, but may relate to the final stage of the European conflict when Soviet forces assaulted from the East, as her Allies assaulted from the West.

II.24

Bestes farouches de faim fleuves tranner, *Plus part du champ encontrepart Hister sera.* *En caige de fer le grand fera treisner,* *Quand rien enfant de Germain observera.*	*Beasts wild with hunger will cross the rivers, the greater part of the battlefield will be against Hitler. He will drag the leader in a cage of iron, when the child of Germany observes no law.*

In Europe, the greater part of the confrontation was against Hitler's German forces, as opposed to Mussolini and his Italian forces. So the greater conflict was with *'Hitler ... the child of Germany'* who *'observes no law'*. The verse is quite specific. The *'beasts wild with hunger'* are likely to be the amphibian fighting craft designed for taking the war across rivers. Those *'in a cage of iron'* may well be a reference to the mechanisation of the Panzer divisions ... the Panzer kampfwagen ... the armoured tank, of which the Panzer mark IV, the Panther and the Tiger were effective weaponry. Each tank commander and crew were of course *'dragged'* in a *'cage of iron'*, powered and steered by the winding caterpillar tracks.

IV.68

En lieu bien proche non esloigné de Venus,	*At a nearby place not far from Venus, the two greatest ones of Asia and Africa will be said to have come from the Rhine and Hitler; cries and tears at Malta and the ligurian coast.*
Les deux plus grans de l'Asie & d'Affrique	
Du Rhin & Hister qu'on dira sont venus,	
Cris, pleurs à Malte & costé lingustique.	

It is a frequent practice of Nostradamus to corrupt, shorten or present as anagram, certain key words, to render the predictions easily accessible only to those who are worthy. It is clear from more general study, that 'Venice' often gets corrupted to 'Venus'. *'Not far from'* Venice is the Brenner Pass, where the Axis leaders sometimes met. This would be the time of the Tripartite Pact between Germany, Italy and Japan. The greatest one of Asia, referred to, would have been the Japanese leader: Emperor Hirohito (whose political power was usually exercised through representatives, in this instance Prince Konoye), and the greatest one of Africa at that time was Benito Mussolini. (North Africa was becoming very much an Italian preserve and 'Il Duce' claimed it as such.) The actual signing of the pact occurred in Berlin, but the agreement was eventually sealed shortly after at a Brenner Pass meeting.

> *A week later, another meeting between the Führer and Il Duce on the Brenner Pass appeared to confirm the solidarity of the Axis partnership.*
> Alan Bullock *Hitler A Study in Tyranny.* Penguin Books.

These were the circumstances in which Hitler and Mussolini (whose army was heavily dispersed across North Africa at the time) met concerning the Tripartite Pact.

This event took place at the time of the Malta blockade, the bombing of Genoa and the bombardment from the sea, of the Ligurian coast of Italy.

V.11

Mer par solaires seure ne passera, *Ceux de Venus tiendront toute l'Affrique:* *Leur regne plus Saterne n'occupera,* *Et changera la part Asiatique.*	*Those of the sun will not cross the sea in safety, the people of Venus will hold the whole of Africa. Then Saturn occupies their kingdom no longer and the part of Asia will change.*

This quatrain nicely follows the substance of the previous one. Japan in the East, is the Land of the Rising Sun, and the Japanese take the sun as their country's emblem. Following the attack on Pearl Harbour by carrier-based planes, 7 December 1941, the Japanese Navy would *'not cross the sea in safety'*. Furthermore, a few months later, following the battle of Midway in which they lost aircraft carriers, their ships were to become increasingly at risk. And the people of Venice ... the Italians ... *'will hold the whole of* (North) *Africa'*. This was very much the status quo during 1942.

Then *'Saturn'*, the father figure of the Roman mythology, left their kingdom. Saturn was the central figure of the Roman 'Saturnalia' ... that period of license when the normal restraints of law and order were cast aside. *'Saturn occupies their kingdom no longer'* would seem a neat and Roman/ Italian way of saying that they 'tired of the fight' and pulled out of the war. Italy was ready to return to normal law and order, having had enough of *'the child of Germany'* who *'observes no law'*, and so, Italy capitulated. That is exactly what happened.

The last line of the prophecy could relate to the change of occupancy of Russia as forces of the Third Reich advanced on Moscow and Leningrad. The *'change'* would have been intensified by the 'scorched earth' policy practised by the Russian army in retreat.

V.51

La gent de Dace, d'Angleterre & Polonne *Et de Boesme feront nouvelle lingue:* *Pour passer outre d'Hercules la colonne,* *Barcins, Tyrrens dresser cruelle brique.*	*The people of Dacia, England and Poland and Czechoslovakia will form a new alliance. In order to pass beyond the straits of Gibraltar the Spanish and the Italians will hatch a cruel plot.*

New political arrangements during 1940 included: recognition of the Czechoslovak National Committee in London as the provisional government, and agreements with the Polish government and the Free French. The present Romania, of which Dacia is a part, declared war on Germany in 1944.

The plot referred to would concern the meeting between Hitler and Franco, the Spanish Dictator, on 23 October 1940. It was Hitler who proposed the plot: a treaty by which Spain would join forces with Hitler in the January of 1941. Gibraltar would be taken by a special force on 10 January and would be assigned to Spain. This arrangement would facilitate the easy passage of German and Italian shipping in and out of the Mediterranean. The code name was to be Operation Felix, but for various reasons, Operation Felix was abandoned. Franco had been vague and evasive in a discussion that had lasted nine hours. Hitler was exasperated, and declared to Mussolini afterwards that he would have three or four teeth taken out rather than go through that lot again. For once, the persuasive Führer did not get his way.

V.29

La liberté ne sera recouvree, *L'occupera noir fier vilain inique:* *Quand la matiere du pont sera ouvree,* *D'Hister, Venise fasché la republique.*	*Liberty will not be regained; it will be occupied by a black, proud, villainous and unjust man. When the matter of the Pope is opened by Hitler, the Republic of Venice will be vexed.*

This quatrain mostly concerns the fortunes of Italy and brings the Pope into the politico-religious arena. The time is the mid-1930s. Mussolini was at this time Dictator of the Republic of Italy and aligned with Hitler's Reich. As the result of Mussolini and this alignment, Italy was to lose her independence, and *'liberty will not be regained'*, at least, not until the regime again changes. Mussolini rose to power as a 'Black Shirt' or 'Fascist'. Hence, *'black'* is the leading adjective used to describe Il Duce.

In Germany, the National Socialist German Worker's Party had gained such irrational power with Hitler as Reich Chancellor, that all other political parties were banned and the punishment for attempting to form a new party was penal servitude. A Catholic-orientated party no longer existed. The situation of there being no longer any such party representation in Germany was accepted by the Vatican. The formal acceptance was the subject of a Concordat (agreement between church and state), concluded with Hitler's government. Italy, a Catholic country, was now aligned with Germany, and understandably, was *vexed* by the Vatican's Concordat.

VI.49

De la partie de Mammer grand Pontife,
Subjugera les confins du Danube:
Chasser les croix par fer raffe ne riffe,
Capitfz, or, bagues plus de cent mille rubes.

The great Pontiff by the warlike party who will subjugate the borders of the Danube. The cross pursued by hook or by crook; captives, gold, jewels, more than one hundred thousand rubies.

This quatrain connects with the previous one. *'The great Pontiff* (stands) *by the warlike party'*, or at least, objections are not raised, implying tacit approval of German activities by the Pope. After all, Italy being a Catholic country and partner of the Third Reich, is party to the Concordat! At the start of the war, the Third Reich subjugated *'the borders of the Danube'*; that is, Austria, Hungary, Czechoslovakia and Yugoslavia.

The subject of the verse is the Papal relationship to the Third Reich. *'The cross pursued by* (the) *hook'* is the swastika and emblem of the Third Reich; while *'the cross pursued by ...* (the) *crook'* would represent he of high office in the church; symbolised by the pastoral staff pursuing the cross of the Christian faith. A phrase of great subtlety. The Vatican should have renounced both the policies leading to the war and its atrocities;

both of which were, of course, in flagrant disregard of the central core of Christian ethic. It did neither.

The last line illustrates the spoils of war taken from *'captives'*. It may highlight the plundering of valuables from Jews in the death camps and elsewhere, which extended beyond ordinary plunder. This seems the likely meaning, since it would also be consistent with the religious tone of the quatrain.

VI.18

Par les phisiques le grand Roy delaissé, *Par sort non art de l'Ebrieu est en vie,* *Lui & son genre au regne hault poussé.* *Grace donnee à gent qui Christ envie.*	*The great king deserted by the physicians lives through chance not the skill of the Jew. He and his people placed high in the realm, pardon given to the race which denies Christ.*

This quatrain is one of rather special significance. It contains two very important issues. The post war evidence that has come to light, is consistent with Hitler ... *'the great king'* ... having contracted the venereal disease syphilis, from a Jewish prostitute in Vienna in 1910. The evidence is also consistent with his *not* having received medical treatment in the early stages of the disease. Hitler did military service during World War I. Following a gas attack on 13 October 1918, in the latter days of that war he spent 29 days in the psychiatric ward of Pasewalk hospital. He was treated as a much-respected soldier because, in the course of duties as messenger, he had won two Iron Crosses, one first class and one second class.

Dr. Viktor Kruckmann of the Pasewalk hospital, reported that Hitler was suffering from *hysterical blindness*. His statement indicated that his condition was not due to the gas but instead related to a nervous complaint frequently arising from tertiary stage syphilis. He advised that he be examined for signs of syphilis and treated accordingly. He accurately stated that the loss of sight was not permanent. Later, in the 1930s, Helmut Spiethoff, a venereologist was appointed to Hitler's contingent of medical advisors ... and still later, Dr. Theodore Morell, who was known to be conversant in the treatment of venereal disease was appointed by the Führer as his personal physician.

It is in the nature of the disease that its progression will affect the whole body including the brain, if the micro-organism is not eradicated in the early stages. Such was the state of the art at that time. The evidence is that it did indeed affect the whole body including the brain; in which event, any inclination towards megalomania would be exaggerated.

Prior to 1910, during the first decade of the century, scientists had battled with the cause of syphilis. The spirochaete, *Treponema pallida* was found to be the causal agent, and it was found that mercurial preparations could be successfully used for treatment, *if administered at a sufficiently early stage.* There were a number of scientists who contributed noble effort to this work. Curiously, judging by their names, this corner of research may have become something of a Jewish preserve. The names in the literature of the time include Schaudinn, Hoffmann, Sobernheim, Tomasczewski, Spitzer and Goldhorn.

In those critical early stages of the disease, the evidence is that the Führer was without *'the physicians'*, and so he lived *'through chance, not the* (medical) *skill of the Jew'.* He and his senior officers were to become immensely powerful in the Third Reich... *'He and his people* (were) *placed high in the realm'.* His following yielded to the power and the persuasion. His following aided the *'great king'* in his work. But they are forgiven. *'pardon* (is) *given to the race'* ...

There are then, two major issues that are the subject matter of this quatrain. They are:

(1) The medical condition that was the reason for the exaggerated veil of megalomania, that became the more evident as the war progressed.

(2) The pardon ... that comes from beyond Earth plane ... to those who had been swept along by the powerful persuasion of Hitler, who was to become increasingly more unbalanced as the war progressed.

There are other quatrains that also relate to this important period of our history, but I believe that the twelve verses cited plus the reference from the Nostradamus epistle give an interesting perspective on the war, without further construction. They represent major aspects, including the causal criteria. The war was a potent period of our history, from which we *must* learn.

Another potent period was that which began much earlier ... the period of the developing religions ... or more specifically ... that time when the spiritual message, as received through the teachings of Jesus, was being so unfortunately distorted and clouded. It began in the days of the early Roman Empire, and this matter we should confront without delay, and unravel. And let us also observe that those much earlier times, whilst affecting the world, also had their impact upon the Nostradamus view. Some major and highly significant events seen in trance, he perceived in terms of Christ and Antichrist, in accord with his worldly conditioning.

Notes: I am very much indebted to the work of recognised translators/authors and their publishers in respect of all Nostradamus quotations in this chapter. The set of twelve complete quatrains:

The epistle extract marked * is from:

THE COMPLETE PROPHECIES OF NOSTRADAMUS by Henry C Roberts, 1947. Revised edition Lee Roberts Amsterdam and Harvey Amsterdam, HarperCollins Publishers Limited, 1984.

I have deliberately used translations by recognised experts in this field, both as a mark of respect for their authority; also in order to rule out any possible bias in favour of what would otherwise be entirely my own elaboration.

Chapter XIII

The Roman Influence

It was a sad day in the capital town of this, the most northerly province of the Diocese of Britain. History had repeated itself. It was just ninety-five years earlier that Severus had died here, in the legion headquarters at York. He had led the punitive campaign, restoring and re-garrisoning the wall of Hadrian. He had accomplished his work and then had died here. Now it was Constantius Chlorus, *the pale one*. He too had accomplished his task. The final battle had been won, the wall was well manned, and he had then returned to York, and today 25 July AD 306, he had drawn his last breath.

Nevertheless, it had been a good campaign, and he had enjoyed success with both family and career. He had lived through changing and challenging times. Diocletian had seen fit to divide the extensive Empire into four parts, each being headed by its own Augustus. Constantius Chlorus had had a brilliant military career and had become Augustus ruling that part of the Empire comprising Spain, Gaul and Britain. He was concerned with its military matters. There was the Vicar or Vicarius who saw to the civil concerns of the Diocese. It was Diocletion who had created these terms and this structure for the Empire. The division between civil and military structures was designed by him to reduce the power of military commanders. This he achieved, but of course, at the expense of giving power to the Vicars.

Constantius had on this British campaign, been joined by his son Constantine, a circumstance that had pleased them both. They had crossed the Channel together and they had fought together. Constantine had already proved himself in eastern campaigns. In Britain, he had earned the respect of the cohorts who manned the forts along the wall, and equally, of the legionary force further south. He and his father had made the Diocese safe from the Picts in the north and from the west-coast raiders. Forts to the south had also been established to guard against raids from Saxons and Franks. The Diocese made safe; it would seem that that chapter was now closed, and sealed by the death of Constantius. In that same day, the German Prince Crocus and troops of the command hailed the energetic and well-liked young Constantine as their new Augustus. Such was their respect for him. But the Emperor Galerius restricted him to the lesser rank of Caesar. It was Constantine's feeling that the lesser rank would do well enough. There was no particular urgency for his climb to power within the Empire.

These were indeed changing times. He shared the awareness of his father in that observation. The days of Jupiter and the old gods were numbered. The Christians had been despised and persecuted. Some had aspired to martyrdom. They had somehow surmounted all this. They had a persistent unity, and that unity was a quality that the Empire needed. Already, the sect had reached Britain. There were groups in the eastern part of Wales, at Isca Silurum and Venta Silurum. There still remained occasional talk of a certain Joseph of Arimathea who had in earlier times been down in the southwest, where he had lived on the Glass Isle in the wet marshes; more talk of him than Arviragus. It is there that the Christian is said to have planted the Holy Thorn that flowers at Christmas, and the first Christian church of Britain built there at the base of the Tor.

> *Arimathean Joseph, journeying brought*
> *To Glastonbury, where the winter thorn*
> *Blossoms at Christmas, mindful of our Lord.*
> *... ... ... From our old books I know*
> *That Joseph came of old to Glastonbury*
> *And there the heathen Prince, Arviragus,*
> *Gave him an isle of marsh whereon to build;*
> *And there he built with wattles from the marsh*
> *A little lonely church in days of yore ...*
> Alfred Tennyson *The Holy Grail*

The Christians had made their mark here in the Diocese of Britain. There was no doubt of that. They had been suppressed in Hadrian's day. Hadrian himself had Christian shrines levelled in Jerusalem and had raised temples there, to Roman gods. That had been the way of things in the Empire's past. Now the feelings were moderating and Constantine would be gaining power and would tip the balance away from the gods of Rome. His path to power would be via battles and diplomacy. In the six years Constantine was Caesar, Roman Britain prospered in peace. But there was discord among the Augusti of the Empire. This led to several battles, and to the decisive battle of Milvian Bridge.

It was Maxentius who made the decision to march on both Constantine and Licenius, an intention that was openly declared. But it was in fact

Constantine who marched his troops across the Alps and into Northern Italy. Towns capitulated to his forces and Modena surrendered. The Flaminian Way now lay before him, the road to Rome. While on this road, Constantine had a religious experience. He had prayed, and sought *his father's god* ... asking who he was. Then later, he and his army saw a cross of light in the sky, above the sun, and the words: CONQUER BY THIS. Later, again in a dream, while encamped not far from the Milvian Bridge, he was instructed to mark the sign of God on the shields of his troops. The sign given consisted of two letters combined together as a single sign; the letters being *chi* and *rho*, the first two 'Greek' letters of 'Christ'. Accordingly, he combined 'X' and 'P' together, and that monogram was marked on every shield. (That is the origin of what has since become a well-known Christian symbol).

The stone-built narrow bridge across the swiftly flowing Tiber stands between the Flaminian Way and the city of Rome. Maxentius knew of Constantine's approach, but Licinius did not enjoin the marching force. Observing this, Maxentius therefore anticipated a great victory to himself, he being left with the numerical advantage. He would advance to meet Constantine's smaller army. To accelerate his advance, he had constructed a pontoon bridge, so that his army could stream across two bridges simultaneously. The resulting victory would enhance and befit his forthcoming anniversary of five years rule.

The strategy chosen by Constantine, however, was first to make his headquarters at the Saxa Rubra, the red cliffs a few miles to the north of the bridge. He stationed his troops on the plateau, above the turbulent waters of the Tiber, where they would be out of sight from the plain below and from the Flaminian Way. He could create an element of surprise from this deployment. Maxentius made the decision to leave the city and meet the opposing force in open country. His army crossed the plain and reached the slopes below the Saxa Rubra. All was quiet. Constantine allowed the approaching troops to weary themselves a little negotiating the lower slopes, while his own troops with their 'chi-rho'-adorned battle shields continued to rest.

When the moment was right, he unleashed his men down the slope and at Maxentius' troops, who were caught in disarray. They were soon in retreat across the plain. Many died by the sword. They re-crossed the bridges that were crowded. The pontoon bridge was in chaos. It collapsed. Hundreds were drowned in the fast flowing waters. They crushed across the narrow stone bridge. Some were trampled and more were drowned.

Maxentius was routed; his body recovered from the waters. And the severed head was carried before Constantine's army as it marched into Rome.

Constantine had been unsupported by Licinius; he had ignored the advice of his military advisers, and had risked all. But all the details of the strategy had gone in his favour. He took no credit for this himself, having seen the cross in the sky and having dreamt the dream. He was convinced the god of the Christians had been with him in battle, and had been *for* him ... and this experience would colour his diplomacy in the coming years. The battle of Milvian Bridge must go down as one of the most significant battles in the history of the Western culture. It gave Constantine dominion over the entire western half of the Roman Empire, extending from Hadrian's wall to the Adriatic. This was a major step in his becoming Emperor of the Empire in all its completeness, both East and West. *The Christian belief would become enmeshed in this Empire and it would become converted into a state-religion.* The Milvian stone bridge was also to be the *metaphoric bridge* that led from the pagan 'Gods and Goddesses' religion of ancient Rome, to the state-religion version of Christianity.

In 313, the year that followed Milvian Bridge, Constantine and Licinius produced the Edict of Milan granting religious tolerance to all, whether pagan or Christian. All confiscated Christian property would be restored. Other legislative milestones that followed were to include:

319: Prohibition of the murder of slaves.
320: Prohibition of the ill treatment of prisoners.
321: Sunday proclaimed as the day of rest.

In Constantine's eyes, the religion of the Christians would help to keep the Empire together as a single unit. His policy would be to encourage the belief and to bind religious and state legislation together. The Christians had a oneness and a resilience that the Empire needed, and he would knit the two together, to the advantage of the Empire. As he saw it, his Empire must have that 'oneness' and now he could see just how to achieve it. It would not be easy, but he was determined.

Family bonding situations, in the days of the Empire, were often complicated by early liaisons followed by later more formal marriages; often the latter being for convenience of State. The first wife of Constantius had been Helena, originally an innkeeper's daughter from Bithynia, a district in the north of Asia Minor. She was the true mother of Constantine. Minerva was Constantine's first wife and mother of their son Crispus. Constantine later formally married Fausta, who bore him a son, also named Constantine. It was to be Helena who would next make a significant and worthy move, an active and a progressive lady for her years, and one who was to become very much admired.

At the age of 72, in the year 323, Helena embarked on a pilgrimage to the Holy Land. The object of her pilgrimage was to seek out relics of the crucifixion. It had been the Emperor Hadrian who had levelled the hill of Golgotha in connection with the building of a Venus sanctuary. Helena had some difficulty because the site of the crucifixion was now beneath the temple to Venus. But she located the three crosses from that time and identified the cross of Christ from its trilingual inscription, and from a healing property that it is understood, still remained with it. She was given the cross of Christ (which was subsequently lost in the muddle of the crusades). She also located and was given the 'Holy Stairs' that Jesus walked, on his way to Pilate in the praetorium (now preserved in Rome). Then Constantine had become sole Emperor of the entire Roman Empire (East and West) from the year 324. One of his early decisions was to bestow upon his mother Helena the title of Empress in recognition of her remarkable achievements in the Holy Land.

During his period of office, Constantine was to have Christian churches built in Rome, Jerusalem ... and Constantinople, the city that he established as the new capital for the Empire. Rome and Constantinople remained its two foremost cities; but the Christian following developed faster in the East than in the West, and his heart was really with the East. The Empire was steadily becoming more Christianised and more united. This at first appeared splendid, but new major problems now centred upon 'religious controversy'. Learned men were debating the nature of the relationship between Jesus and God with such seriousness, that the matter was becoming the new focal centre of the Christian religion! Just when it seemed that 'belief' had bonded the Empire, and was continuing to unite the Empire further; people began to support the various protagonists in the argument, creating a real danger of fresh radical division right at its heart!

Arius of Alexandria was a man of immense learning. He was presbyter of Alexandria and had been a disciple of St. Lucian of Antioch who had been martyred in the days of the persecutions. Arius preached that Jesus was not co-equal and of the same eternal value as God the Father. He asserted, that Jesus had been created by God, as his instrument to be the salvation of the world; created at one specific time, and therefore not having the same eternal value. Jesus was more man than divine. This view was not acceptable to the church hierarchy. It followed that, in the year 320, the same year in which prisoner's rights became protected, Arius was excommunicated as an heretic; his teaching nevertheless spread, and he had much support in Caesarea and in Syria. His cause was pursued by two Bishops, both named Eusebius. A request to Alexander, Bishop of Alexandria, for his reinstatement was refused and rioting resulted. Despite various diplomatic efforts, the situation steadily worsened.

It was on account of this worsening situation, that Constantine decided to convene a Council of the Church, in the Imperial palace at Nicaea, in Bithynia. He himself would preside and the proceedings were to extend over the period 20 May - 19 June, 325. He as president, was an imposing figure, in a glittering bejewelled robe and seated upon a golden chair. More than 300 bishops attended. These were mostly from the East, with a mere handful from the West. Three figures who played key roles were: Arius who spoke well and clearly, Athanasius, a young deacon still only in his late twenties, who argued the case eloquently against Arius; and Constantine himself, who was determined that the Council should reach a satisfactory conclusion.

The eloquent Athanasius had come along with the more elderly Alexander, primate of Alexandria. Athanasius had been with St. Antony and for a time, had favoured the ascetic life. He had a keen logic and a way with words. His reasoning was that the Godhead must be comprised of three: Father, Son and Holy Ghost. A 'Trinity'. During the discussions, in order to clarify and endorse Athanasius' meaning, Constantine himself introduced a new word, to indicate: *of one substance.* Father, Son and Holy Ghost were three in one, and of 'one substance'. The reasoning of the young Athanasius, was finally overwhelmingly supported by the bishops. Some were eventually swayed only reluctantly, including both the Bishops Eusebius. Bishop Eusebius of Caesarea was by repute a delightful character of moderate views, in fact, one of the more rational of those in attendance. Eusebius maintained that the all-important thing is the truth that ... *God so loves the world that he gave his only begotten Son, that whosoever believeth on him should not perish.* The promise concerns he that *believeth on him* ... and not he who works out the intricacies of precisely how he was generated from God the Father. *That* was an irrelevance.

The writings of Arius were finally condemned and burned. He was exiled as an heretic. At the conclusion of the Council just two bishops: Theonas of Marmarica and Secundus of Ptolemais heroically stood by and held their support of Arius. They understood well the position they were placing themselves in, and they too were exiled. Furthermore, anyone convicted of possessing and concealing Arian writings would risk capital punishment.

Constantine was well pleased with the outcome. It had been a triumph for his presidency, his assertive skills, and his statesmanship. The matter appeared settled. The religion and the state were welding together as he had hoped. He organised a grand banquet ... *a vicennalia*, to celebrate twenty years of his rule, and he pressed the remaining bishops to stay on and attend; and the occasion would also be in their honour. It was a grand and dazzling affair and each guest received a gift from the Emperor's own hands on leaving. It was a magnificent conclusion. Constantine's Council had furthermore, forged a first real link between eastern and western churches.

This was the beginning of a special prominence in regard to the 'Trinity' of this new state religion, and thus began the 'Nicene Creed'; and continuing into the twentieth century, service books still included what was entitled: *The Creed of Saint Athanasius*. The Nicene Creed of the Christian prayer book was born of Nicaea, while Emperor Constantine presided. And those who thought differently were sent into exile.

> *The Creed of St. Athanasius*
> *... And the Catholick Faith is this: That we worship one God in Trinity, and Trinity in Unity;*
> *Neither confounding the Persons; nor dividing the Substance.*
> *For there is one Person of the Father, another of the Son, and another of the Holy Ghost.*
> *But the Godhead of the Father, of the Son, and of the Holy Ghost, is all one: the Glory equal, the Majesty co-eternal.*
> *Such as the Father is, such is the Son; and such is the Holy Ghost.*
> *The Father uncreate, the Son uncreate; and the Holy Ghost uncreate.*
> *The Father incomprehensible, the Son incomprehensible; and the Holy Ghost incomprehensible.*
> *The Father eternal, the Son eternal; and the Holy Ghost eternal.*
> *And yet they are not three eternals; but one eternal. ...*
>
> *The Book of Common Prayer,* Eyre and Spottiswoode

But despite all that had transpired with its long-term consequences, the general situation in the Roman Empire, was very far from perfect. Rome was displeased that the Emperor should have gone against tradition and held his vicennalia in the East and not in the West. But he reasoned that their displeasure could easily be assuaged. He would travel to Rome and have another celebration in that city. It was a few months after the Council of Nicaea that he set out, and a number of his family travelled with him. It should have been a pleasant enough excursion for them all, but it was not to be. On the way, relations for some reason soured beyond any imaginable bound, with disastrous results. His son Crispus and Licinius, stepson of half sister Constantia, were suddenly arrested and removed from the party; then put to death. His wife Fausta was next. She was murdered in a bath house. He then continued his journey, having had half his family dispatched! Assertive skills can sometimes be overdone. How can such behaviour equate to his presiding over the first Church Council of the Empire?

Neither did the views of the main protagonists of the Council of Niceae, meet with universal acclaim. The events in their lives in the years that followed, illustrate the discord with a vivid clarity:

326 - Alexander of Alexandria died and Athanasius was elected to the primacy.

328 - The Emperor released Arius from exile but Athanasius refused to restore Arius to communion.

335 - Athanasius was brought before the Synod of Tyre on several charges and was deposed from his office.

336 - Athanasius' sentence was confirmed by a Jerusalem synod. He was banished to Treves. Arius travelled to Constantinople, where he presented his Emperor with a confession of faith; whereupon Bishop Alexander of Constantinople received instruction to administer to Arius, Holy Communion on the following Sunday. That following Sunday, his friends escorted him as a guard of honour to the temple, but he suddenly excused himself to go to the toilet. He next became unconscious, and died of a haemorrhage. Some said he was poisoned. Others said God had answered the prayers of Alexander.

338 - A new Emperor, Constantius restored Athanasius to the primacy of Alexandria.

341 - A Council of 90 Arian bishops condemned Athanasius, at Antioch. Next, 100 Orthodox bishops in Alexandria protested against this. A further Council of 300 bishops at Sardis was in favour of Athanasius.

349 - Athanasius resumed office in Alexandria.

353 - Athanasius was condemned by the Council of Arles.

355 - The decision was confirmed by a Council of Milan. He escaped from a company of soldiers and for some time lived in hiding in a remote part of the Egyptian desert.

361 - He resumed office yet again when Julian became Emperor, he being more tolerant in regard to religious matters, but following further controversy, he fled; this time, to the Theban desert.

363 - Athanasius took office for a short time, but he was expelled again by the supporters of the Arian view, and took refuge for several months in his father's tomb. He was next restored to office as the result of petitions, where he remained until his death in 373.

There remained those who followed the Athanasius teaching as well as those who favoured the Arius view. During the course of the next 200 years, it was deemed necessary to hold several more Church Councils:

<u>381 - 2nd Ecumenical Church Council: Constantinople:</u> This was attended by 150 bishops in the church of St. Irene. The Council formally condemned the Arian 'heresy'. Arians were forbidden to congregate in cities and all churches were required to conform to the orthodox teaching. The See of Constantinople would henceforth rate second in the Christian world, only to Rome.

<u>431 - 3rd Ecumenical Church Council: Ephesus:</u> This council concerned the teachings of Nestorius, a Syrian who had become Bishop of Constantinople. The Council convened in the Church of the Theotokos *(Mother of God)* and 198 attended. Nestorius' teaching was elaborated from a sermon of Anastasius, Bishop of Rome: *that Mary was the Mother of Jesus, but she could not be the Mother of God, since then the Divine would have to be born of a woman.* (The name of the church for this Council would appear to have been well chosen!) This led to the reasoning that Jesus had both human and divine natures, which was deemed to be unacceptable teaching. Nestorius was deposed, was confined to a monastery for four years, but did not change his views, and was exiled to an Egyptian oasis. He died in exile. The cult of Nestorianism was to continue in Persia and Syria, spreading to Kurdistan and parts of India, but the cult continued to be suppressed within the Empire.

<u>451 - 4th Ecumenical Church Council: Chalcedon:</u> The Roman Empire had for the past two decades, been paying a yearly tribute in gold to Attila the Hun. This is strange when one considers that Attila was generally known at that time as 'The Scourge of God'. So the Empire that was developing dogma in the new state-religion modification of Christianity, and was so engrossed in the precise nature of the Christ; was at the same

time paying annual tribute to *the scourge of God*, whom Nostradamus later named as *the First Antichrist*!

It is to the credit of the new Emperor to emerge in the East, Marcian, that one of his first decisions in office was to refuse Attila the tribute. There was much relief in Constantinople, as the army of the Huns continued in its plan of marching to the West. They marched on Italy and Gaul, leaving the Eastern Empire safe from reprisal. It was safe from attack, but not free from the ongoing religious wrangling. That remained. Despite strong disciplinary measures, there was *still* persistent disagreement as to the precise relationships within the now formalised 'Trinity'. Eutyches was the next to offend. He taught that in Jesus, there were two natures, the human and the divine; but the human nature was absorbed in the divine, so that just the one nature was presented. This brought objections and led to the Council of Chalcedon attended by 650 bishops. The teaching was declared to be an heresy. Eutyches was condemned and degraded. It was declared that the two natures of Jesus are united without any conversion of substance. The two natures would be united unconfusedly and inseparably as perfect God and perfect man. But the Eutychian sect were to continue in Armenian, Ethiopian and Coptic churches; and the Eutychians later became known as Jacobites following a revival by Jacob Baradæus, Bishop of Edessa.

An overall pattern was developing. As the Messianic religion of Christianity was being adapted, adulterated and distorted to become the state-religion of the Roman Empire, it was being adjusted with expansion of devised dogma. Many found the changes to be unpalatable. They were either killed or exiled, a process contrary to the fundamental principles of the original teaching. A number of splinter groups were understandably breaking away from the deviating religion. These established their own separate cults beyond the borders of the Empire. But within the Empire, the same old self-inflicted difficulties remained, reaching a peak period of difficulty in the reign of the Emperor Justinian.

[At the time of Constantine's death, there remained one noteworthy piece of unfinished business. He had made a gift to Rome of the Laterno obelisk. Being more than 100 feet high and weighing in excess of 400 tons, it was the largest of thirteen obelisks to be transported from Egypt to Rome. Quarried nearly two millennia earlier at the direction of Tuthmosis III, it had stood at Karnak, with the great temple there. At the time of Constantine's death, it had been removed and transported as far as Alexandria,

where it awaited shipment. It remained thus for the next twenty years. Then Constantius II, son of Constantine completed its transportation.

The huge Laterno obelisk was a symbol to the world. It represented, so far as the Empire was concerned, the removal of the religious centre of the world from Egypt to Rome. Being a pagan solar cult object, it also symbolised a fusion of the ancient and the new religion. In the new Christian religion, there were many parallels with both ancient Egypt as well as the 'mysteries' celebrated in ancient Greece. The obelisk that now stands in the piazza of San Giovanni is a potent symbol of the fusion between ancient religion and the new … between the old belief system respecting the sun as source of life energies and the new Christianity now centred on Rome.

On 25th July 1998, a bronze statue of Constantine was unveiled adjacent to York Minster. It is near the place where he was proclaimed Augustus following the death of Constantius. A plaque acknowledges that he established the religious foundations of Western Christendom. The statue is inscribed: 'CONSTANTINE BY THIS SIGN CONQUER'.]

Chapter XIV

Almost Beyond Belief

He watched with pleasure as well as with an inner thoughtfulness as young Martin approached. The older man and the youth often met and talked. They were uncle and nephew, mentor and pupil, in a relationship both of fondness and of mutual trust. Today he noticed that the boy looked somewhat troubled. The brow was furrowed and he looked without seeing. It was a distant mood.

'Martin! How nice to see you this sunny morning,' he challenged.

'Ah! Uncle Paulus! How are you today?'

'Less agitated in the mind than you, my boy, if I am not mistaken. What ails you?'

'Oh, nothing really Uncle. Well, I was just thinking, I would like to understand this metropolis of ours ... the people ... I mean *really* understand what is in their minds. The Emperor is an impressive leader and has built great buildings, and yet there is something that disturbs ... a fear. Uncle, you can feel the fear in people! The wonderful Christian Church of Sancta Sophia is huge and magnificent ... a truly great work. It contains 'The Cross' that Helena brought from the Holy Land, the swaddling clothes of Jesus and the table of The Last Supper. Such a masterpiece it is, and a tribute to the religion. Yet there are those who would furtively say that it is a troubled and sad monument to many dead souls, and these people who say this have so much hidden sadness within them. I am confused. It would ease my mind if I could understand these things.'

Paulus took a long look at the youth. 'You are a sensitive boy and you feel the souls of the people about you. This is good ... a gift. And you are quite right. There are both chords and discords within our city, if I may put it like that. Perhaps the time has come when we should talk more deeply on such matters. It is good to fully understand but you must use discretion and keep certain things to yourself. We must all learn things a step at a time. There are those who are not yet ready for full truth and there can be danger in being too outspoken. Those with a fuller knowledge must have the maturity to be discerning with it. All is not always as seen at the surface, but we should not talk about such things here. Perhaps if we take a lunch pack and walk into the country? Yes, that would be best for today. We shall do that.'

Martin eagerly walked ahead. The day held promise. 'So is this a good spot uncle? Look! We could sit over there on the rocks beneath the overhanging tree ... and there are figs!'

'That will indeed suit nicely, my boy. So often the difficulty in making a study of our own history is, knowing where best to begin. But perhaps if we begin in this instance, with the early lives of our Emperor Justinian and of the late Empress Theodora, it should suit our purpose quite well.

Now, the Emperor was born a Thracian named Petrus Sabbatius. He took the name of Justinian after his Uncle Justin, who formally adopted him as a son. He was indebted to Justin for his education and early career guidance ... and Justin saw to it that he became an officer in one of the palace regiments ... the *Scholae* no less! Then he took the road to power via the rank of Patrician and the post of Count of Domestics. The Empress Theodora, however, began life as the daughter of a bear keeper and a circus acrobat. She did some turns on stage herself, at the Hippodrome, in burlesque, and like a number of others of that profession, she at quite an early age, took up tarting and ...'

'What! She ... a tart!'

'Yes my boy, and a much-sought-after tart at that. The Empress has come a long way. Now you see the need for being circumspect. It would not do to talk about these matters in the street. Be guarded. Knowledge without circumspection is dangerous. I think you are now old enough and wise enough to be entrusted with the true and uncloaked knowledge that I propose to give to you. But I must firstly impress upon you the need to take care or you will soon find yourself on an execution list, and I too I shouldn't wonder. Now this is really most important.'

'I thank you for your trust uncle and I do understand. Your instruction is as ever ... most clear.'

'Good, then we shall proceed...'

'Are there going to be lots of embarrassing details uncle?'

'You may indeed find some parts embarrassing my boy but this is an historical study. Be objective in your study and the feeling of embarrassment becomes an irrelevance.'

'Yes! I understand that. So now tell me about the Empress. Why was she a tart?'

'Well I suppose, she was of that kind of a disposition, and you see, her mother and her sisters were all on the stage. One might say that women of the stage often seek the dual profession and boost their incomes through the various avenues of prostitution. But with Theodora, it was more than that. She actually flaunted herself and revelled in it, enjoying nudity even more than ... than Aphrodite herself! And she craved the sexual pleasures. Good heavens! She would go off to a banquet with a party of ten, throw off her clothes and do it with them all ... and still she would be looking for more! She would just abandon herself to whatever fantasy presented itself ... and in public as like as not!'

'Coo! ... er ... Well! ... I would think ... hardly becoming for an Empress!'

'Quite so my boy, but of course there was no thought of her ever becoming so elevated when all this was happening, and one simply could just not imagine ... Well, dear me ... and even on stage it was: she had this act with hungry geese. She would lie spread-eagled while the slaves sprinkled her body with barley grains. The geese would then be released, and would just poke about and gobble up the barley! And by Jupiter! The crowd ... the crowd would just go wild and were altogether beyond any rational sensibility. She ... the only emotion she would show in conclusion, was her pleasure in seeing their exuberant ribaldry. That's the way she used to be!'

'And how about *you* uncle? Did *you* enjoy the entertainment? ... or?'

'Cheeky young fellow! She was not for the likes of *me* you understand. But I've met a good many who got to see her ... and they were quite carried away in telling me about it!'

'But about the *history* uncle ... Is this likely to ever get into the history books? I mean, if people dare not talk about it now, then...'

'Ah! There is one ... Procopius ... yes, Procopius. I think that he will write about it ... when the time is right. That time has not yet arrived, but the time will come, and he will then set scribe to scroll. Yes, it will be recorded and those of future generations who read, should know of these things.'

'Did she ever get pregnant ... living that sort of a life?'

'A fair question. She did indeed, and managed to abort each time.'

'Each time! Unbelievable! Then how did such a woman, from that beginning, ever manage to become Empress of the Empire?'

'Well, of course, there came a time when Theodora began to look around for something better, and she still had her very good looks. Yes, for all her lusting and fooling around, she had and kept a vivacious beauty ... and a certain cleverness. She could mimic, she could persuade and she could face up to people with boldness. Perhaps that came from her time on the stage; but then there was the period of being mistress to a well-to-do civil servant, who travelled to North Africa. It is possible that some measure of decorum was developed through his influence. One cannot fault her ability to learn in any way. The relationship came to an end, however, when they quarrelled, and she worked her passage back.'

'How did she do that, uncle?'

'Well, how do you *think*, my boy?'

'Of course. Then she was still at it?'

'You could put it like that ... Yes, she was still at it. But only as far as Alexandria.'

At this point Martin just hooted: '... And does that make it alright if ... if ... if it was only as far as Alexandria?'

'Didn't mean it like that my boy. But ... Hmm! Yes! That *is* rather amusing. But the fact is that she was *at it* as you put it as far as Alexandria. Then, in that city, Theodora met up with some churchmen and they clearly had quite an influence upon her. I think she even discovered a spiritual aspect to her life. Anyway, when she finally got back to Constantinople, there was a marked difference in her bearing. The wild carefree lusting attitude had left her. Now, in her thirties, she was every bit as attractive as she had ever been, and it was now that Justinian noticed her. Their paths crossed and ... they enjoyed each other's company. Politically, they both favoured the 'Blue' party. There was a passionate reason for her preference. When still a child, her father had died, and her stepfather would have been without work, had it not been for the intervention of the Blues ... and her political leaning was sealed from that moment. Conversely, the Green party she despised because it had refused to help. Justinian became absolutely captivated by this vivacious good-looking woman who even shared in his political persuasion. That was just four years before he became Emperor. He had already developed the knack of getting what he wanted, and apart from the Empire, he wanted Theodora. He got both.'

'Wasn't her past something of a problem uncle?'

'It was indeed my boy. The law specifically forbade the marriage of those of rank to actresses and tarts and the like; so on becoming Emperor, he simply changed that detail of the law so that he was able to marry her. Like I say, he has this way of getting what he wants by whatever means ... and if the law doesn't suit, then it has to be changed! Furthermore, with her acting talent, she was able to act the part of Empress quite well; possibly better than most, and she enjoyed it.'

'Yes, I follow ... You have explained it most convincingly uncle. It still seems such a big step from ... well ... that wayward, or at least, questionable background ... to the stately Empress of our recent times.'

'Yes my boy. I agree. You should consider that despite her dubious past, she had developed this quite powerful persona which enabled her to play ... shall we say ... a significant role, as Empress. Theodora has certainly been an influence in affairs of state and often took a tougher line than Justinian ever would himself. My impression is that there was a certain detached hardness, which may well relate to the more rugged side of her earthy past. She could certainly be devious.

It was ... let me see ... back in the year 536 when Pope Agapitus died. She made a secret pact with Vigilius. He most unwisely and later to his chagrin, had become her *confidant.* Their pact was: that *she* would secure the papacy for *him*, if *he* would disavow the Church Council of Chalcedon and reinstate her friend the Patriarch Anthimus, whom Agapitus had previously had deposed. As a part of that pact, Vigilius had received quite handsome gifts. He agreed, but of course he played a most dangerous game and waded into deep waters where he was well beyond his depth.'

'So that's how he came to be Pope? That is terrible!'

'Yes my boy. Most unbecoming for one aspiring to be leader of the Empire's religion; that he should *plot* his way to the papacy!'

At this point, their attention was diverted as a small lizard moved across a dusty patch before them. Anyway, it was a good time to break for refreshment. In his unexpurgated history lesson, for that is what it was, Paulus had reached that stage in the story when the destinies of the Roman Empire and of Christianity in its state-religion form, were delicately poised. A critical point in the evolution of human affairs; a crucial, direction-dictating point, to which more import was attached than even the wise and communicative Paulus realised. It was such a critical point and yet, those at the helm at this time would be seen to be secret plotters, murderers and beings who, shall we say, display evidence of spiritual under-nourishment.

They took a little time to settle again after the break. The idea ... that tarting was quite satisfactory providing it went only as far as Alexandria ... was really a very funny notion, and they shared several chuckles before getting back to more serious matters.

'What do you know about taxes my boy? I suppose you just see them for what they are with little thought as to logic, justice or injustice?'

'Well, I hear many complaints uncle.'

'Yes quite so. The taxes are a good deal higher now than in the past. There are reasons. The wars and the plague years have reduced the population from what it was. But substantial funds are needed for the army, for road building, for churches and the state buildings; and of course the Emperor's building program has certainly been most ambitious. High taxation means discontent and resistance to the process of collecting it. In my opinion, inexcusably harsh methods of collection have been used. That very much concerns John of Cappadocia. Justinian appointed John of Cappadocia as Praetorian Prefect, a rough, hard, coarsely mannered individual, albeit a keen and able administrator. He introduced a good many new taxes and used imprisonment, flogging and torture where necessary to get them. His methods were just too harsh, and he remained in ignorance of any compassionate sentiment. He earned the titles of 'drunkard', 'lecher' and 'the most hated man in the Empire'. If you owed taxes within his region, then your daughters were not safe from his lustful attentions!'

'Yes, I have heard mention of that one. It is said that the Province of Lydia has neither wealth nor undefiled daughters, on his account.'

'You heard correctly my boy, and to think that that man professes to be a Christian! I will name one other who also came to be much hated: Tribonian.'

'Tribonian who revised the law, who produced the new Codex?'

'The same. Quaestor of the Sacred Palace, the highest position in the administration of the law. In many ways a most able man ... one of considerable learning, and of excellent manners, and wielding great charm. Doubtless Justinian chose him for those better qualities. He was a fast working and accomplished individual, who achieved much in streamlining the legal system. Although himself nominally a pagan, he was given the task of adapting the law to be compatible with the Christian teachings.'

'Then why hated? He sounds wonderful, with such a list of qualities ... and compared to John...'

'Greed, my boy. Corrupted by greed. Sold justice like it was a marketable commodity. He repealed laws and proposed new ones to suit the customers who bought his favours. There were many that lost their cases who should by rights have won them. The Gods of Rome and the God of the Christians were all on their side, but Tribonian ... he was not! Others won their cases when they should never have. The legal process was misused and simply could not be trusted. All due to this larger-than-life lawyer who cheated to get rich. As the result he was hated, and his law lost respect. It was all such a pity because he had a real talent.'

'Uncle Paulus, you are rather dwelling upon negative issues and I don't yet see where it is leading; but knowing your way, I don't doubt for one moment that you are about to make some purposeful point.'

'Ah! Yes my boy, but we are not quite ready yet. That is enough about taxes and badly used law. These matters are tedious but important, because they have created so much dissatisfaction and anger in the people. When these feelings of dissatisfaction and anger become sufficiently powerful, then that is when a society may become unstable. In this condition, it may only require one isolated event to trigger a crowd reaction. If that happens, then you have a potentially dangerous situation.'

'Are you telling me that this city became *unstable* then?'

'I'm afraid so my boy. And another thing ... rather unwisely I feel, Justinian had taken measures to reduce the power of both political parties ... the Blues *and* the Greens. The people were both resentful and restless; and so it was that on 10 January 532, at the conclusion of the chariot races in the Hippodrome, the crowd became agitated and violent. The Emperor responded by sending in troops who arrested seven main offenders. These were all sentenced to death. Five were executed; but two were found to still have the breath of life when they were cut down. A group of monks took them off, cared for them and gave them sanctuary in a monastery. The authorities placed armed guards on that monastery in an attempt to starve them out. This move provoked street demonstrations against the authorities.'

'And does this new development connect in some way with the Blues and Greens, Uncle?'

'Ah! Yes it does indeed, my boy. You see, as chance would have it, one of the survivors happened to be a Blue, and the other a Green. The event stood out like a symbol. It had the effect of *uniting* both parties. They now came together, as one, opposed to bad administration. Just three days later, when Justinian signalled the games to start in the Hippodrome, he found that the crowd was not divided into two opposing factions in support of the races any more; instead, it was wholly united against *him*! The races began, but they failed to grasp the attention of the people. They were simply no longer interested, and so they were quickly abandoned. There was disorder. There was uproar!

In wrath, the crowd stampeded from the Hippodrome. In a frenzied furore they made for the palace of the Prefect. They killed guards, released prisoners and fired the building. This was just a start. Buildings were fired all over the city. Some of the Empire's finest architecture was lost: the

Praetorian Prefecture, the Senate House, the Church of Sancta Irene and the Church of Sancta Sophia, to name a few. There was no escape from the smell of smoke or the sounds of rebellion. The rampagers returned to the Hippodrome. They demanded the immediate dismissal of John of Cappadocia *and* of Tribonian; and Justinian agreed to their demands without further ado. He faced them, offering full amnesty if they'd take themselves home and put an end to the violence. But that was not to be. They were next calling for a new Emperor!'

'So that would have been after ... only five years of his reign?'

'That's right my boy. Five years.'

'And did the people have a new Emperor in mind at this time?'

'They did indeed ... poor old Hypatius. He had no political aspirations at all, poor fellow. In fact, he tried to hide away from it all. Of course, he had long since retired from a lengthy and hard military career ... he had served on many fronts ... and was by this time an old man. The crowd had a liking for him and focused upon the idea of Hypatius for Emperor. They managed to find him and then carried him, shoulder high, into the Hippodrome, where he was symbolically crowned with a golden necklace.'

'But he never actually became Emperor did he uncle?'

'No. But he came very close. Justinian had given up; had made plans to flee the capital. But that was not to be either. Poor Hypatius! It was never *his* idea anyway, that he should ever aspire to be Emperor.'

'So what happened, and why *poor* Hypatius?'

'Well, to put it bluntly, my boy; the Empress Theodora ... took command of the situation. She had always possessed strength and determination, and was opposed to fleeing, would quell the riot, and would not endure the indignity of backing off from such a confrontation. Now ... it fitted her purpose, that the Empire's two finest generals were at the palace at this time: Belisarius, a forthright campaigner fresh returned from the Persian front, and Mundus, who happened to have a force of mercenaries to hand. At her bidding, they made a plan. While Belisarius and Mundus gathered their men and marched on the Hippodrome, Narses, Commander of the Imperial Bodyguard, stationed *his* men at the exits to cut down all that tried to escape. All those souls in the Hippodrome were then slaughtered ... just slaughtered. All! Shouts changed to cries. Cries changed to moans. Finally soldiers finished the dying ones and took their valuables, as moans and gasps gave way to silence. Amid all this, the smell of smoke was masked by the smell of blood and butchery ... the blood and butchery of 30,000 bodies. That was the count. That was the price. No quarter was given. All rioters perished ... all 30,000 of them. Such a gloom hung over a once majestic city.'

Martin was pale and silent for a spell. 'Then *that's* how it was.'

'Justinian later rebuilt the church of Sancta Sophia ... the huge, splendid building that you see today. It is indeed a masterpiece ... a greater and more accomplished work than before ... and a major centre ... *the* centre ... for the religion. Not just a fine building, but containing as it does, the table of the 'Last Supper', the swaddling clothes, 'The Cross' recovered by Helena, and the chains of St. Peter; it is surely a worthy centre for the Christian faith. But the dreadful killing that preceded the erection of such an edifice ... That is why some say it is a sad monument to a great many dead ... and since that day when so many were cut down, there has been a shadow of fear cast across this city. That is what you feel my boy. The people are accepting of Justinian's authority, but at a price. They are now ruled without riot, but they are weighed down by the great sadness of that shadow and their hearts are tempered by its fear.'

'And what of Hypatius?'

'Justinian knew that the old soldier had no political aspiration of his own will and would have acted accordingly, but again it was the Empress who took the tough line. She pointed out that he might just once again become a focus for the people's discontent and therefore he should die ... now. She could be so much the architect of harsh decision, that one. Next day, Hypatius was executed; along with his brother Pompeius, and their bodies were given to the sea.'

'Now I understand ... Thank you for telling me these things uncle.'

'You cannot understand our society without knowing such details Martin. But I say to you: keep these things very much to yourself. Look over your shoulder. Be circumspect.'

'I shall do as you say uncle. But that was not the end of the Tax Collector or of Tribonian, was it?'

'Indeed not my boy. After only a few weeks, they were both reinstated. There was some improvement in how they went about their work. There was much rebuilding to be done, so taxes had to remain high: not so impossibly high as they had been before. Justinian wisely saw to it that much more care was taken in these matters. Things became more settled. We established peace with Persia. That was a blessing. The Emperor was preoccupied for a number of years with constructing and re-constructing public buildings, for which he had a passion and of which he may be justly proud; and with restoring the Empire's far boundaries ... Then a further problem arose.

You recall I mentioned Pope Vigilius earlier, and left that matter as a loose end? As we have a little more time, perhaps we should now deal with that further problem which concerns *him*. That will then leave things neat and tidy. Is that all right with you my boy?'

'Perfectly uncle. What about Pope Vigilius?'

'Well firstly, you recall his pact with Theodora to disavow the Council of Chalcedon? Chalcedon advocated the 'Orthodox' faith, with Jesus having two natures: the human and the divine. This dogma is staunchly followed both in Rome and the West. We have always been rather more divided in the East. A great many take the view that Jesus *is* God and therefore of solely divine nature. It also followed from the widespread preaching of 'Baradaeus the Ragged', that the latter concept was increasing in the East.'

'Yes uncle. I would have thought the teachings of the religion to be much more important than the biological construction of its prophet!'

'Well ... Yes my boy. A touch crudely put, if I may say so; but you have it. It would be much more satisfactory if there were not such clouded issues being contested so laboriously by so many. Anyway, eventually there came a time when the Emperor felt the need to make a bold pronouncement in an attempt to unite all factions. He did not wish to risk the indignity of taking sides in any dispute, and so he settled for a public condemnation of the older teachings of Nestorius. That should be a safe move, he thought ... safe from repercussions. Now you will recall the Nestorians believed in a distinctly *human* nature for the nature of Jesus and they, now a half-forgotten sect, met rejection at the Council of Ephesus more than a century ago. More specifically ... at this present time ... Justinian condemned writings that became known as: 'The Three Chapters' ... Their authors being: Theodore of Mopsuestia (Nestorius's teacher), Theodoret of Cyrrhus and Ibas of Edessa.'

'This all seems very complicated uncle ...'

'I agree my boy ... but so important. Bear with me. You see ... he thought he was perfectly safe in taking this stance and not exactly taking sides you understand, but in fact it infuriated the Western Church in the extreme. After all, the writings of Theodoret and Ibas had already been pronounced entirely satisfactory at the Council of Chalcedon. It was a mess. The church was split and furious! Pope Vigilius, in Rome, would not join in condemning the Chapters. Justinian retreated ... went silent on the matter for more than a year, not wishing to rock the boat further. But then a tactical situation arose. Totila's army was marching on Rome, and a siege situation looked like developing. Justinian arranged for a military detachment to seize Vigilius and sail him on a boat, up the Tiber and away from Rome. This was done agreeably and so the Pope eventually arrived at this city.'

'Ah! That could be a problem in view of the secret pact he had made with the Empress and failed to fulfil?'

'It might well have been my boy. But the Empress seemed to be losing some of her fire in her latter days, or perhaps there were just more pressing issues at that moment. She was ageing. In any event, Vigilius found himself ... shall we say ... welcomed but in a hot seat; although on coming to Constantinople, he actually was so bold as to exert his authority! He actually had the audacity to sentence the Patriarch and his bishops who supported Justinian's condemnation of the Chapters to four months of excommunication! But then later, he changed his stance and agreed to *support* Justinian's view. In the following year, 548, Vigilius formally published his Judicatum, which anathematised ... that is, politely *cursed* ... the Chapters, which extolled the humanity of Jesus. But he, at the same time, declared his support for the findings of the Council of Chalcedon.'

'So the Pope would now be seen as something of an hypocrite?'

'Well ... almost. He at least was seen as a renegade, and it is not good that a Pope should be seen to turn about as he had done. Across Europe, he now became reviled, and the African bishops went so far as to excommunicate him. The Pope ... excommunicated! Next, another matter was to cast its shadow. The death of Theodora ... and coming as it did at this time, it was really a matter of some considerable import. You see, the fear that you feel in the people, Martin, was even stronger when the Empress was alive. The Emperor himself has through religious and military policies, measured out death to so many, many thousands of unfortunates; but it was Theodora who was seen as the more overtly direct dealer in sudden death; as at the time of the city riots. The fear was always bound more strongly to her than to Justinian. When she died, it was as if ... as if ... the 'brakes of suppression' ... were to a degree at least, being lifted from the people's real feelings.

Against mounting opposition, Vigilius again turned about and revoked his own Judicatum. He was now clearly opposed to the Emperor's stance. Justinian then published a document setting out his own views as to the basis of Christianity, and again condemning the Chapters. Vigilius objected, maintaining that the Emperor was at variance with the Council of

Chalcedon. He obtained the support of those bishops who were in the city, but as the matter came to a head, he fled to take refuge in the Church of St. Peter and St. Paul.

The refuge may have had a spiritual strength, but as for its material strength ... that failed. Vigilius clung to the columns of the high altar, as the Imperial Guard burst in with drawn swords and advanced upon him. They seized him and pulled. He held on with a resolute determination, as the columns ... they buckled and the high altar collapsed with a huge crash. A spirited crowd then gathered and protested at such a violation within the church. The military became uncomfortable and withdrew in some considerable embarrassment. The Emperor later sent his regrets.'

'Ah! This time a crowd protest was effective!'

'Yes Martin. Their protest was without violence and the ageing Justinian without his Theodora now had less fire. But the Pope and the Emperor continued to play their political games. Vigilius saw fit to flee once more, this time from a position of virtual house arrest. He went across the Bosphorus to Chalcedon and the Church of St. Euphemia ... a symbolic retreat. It was the seat of the last Ecumenical Church Council. He was able to distance himself from the Emperor, and these were the tactics that led to the Emperor's next move. He made preparation in this city, for the Fifth Ecumenical Church Council in the Church of Sancta Sophia. That was just five years ago, my boy, in the May of 553.'

'Ah! Yes, uncle. I know something of this. The *tactics* continued, because the Pope chose to stay away!'

'That's right, and neither did Justinian attend; but he sent a letter that was read to the assembly, reminding all that he had cursed the Chapters! The assembly, was very much an eastern affair. There were just two bishops from the West, nine from Africa and 157 from the Eastern Empire. After a week of sitting, the Council received from Vigilius a document that he called his *Constitutum*, upholding two of the three chapters and setting out his reasons for considering that any further debate of the Chapters should be condemned. In addition, just two weeks later, he felt sufficiently bold to send a copy to the Emperor.'

'Ah! And the Emperor was very angry!'

'Yes my boy, and there was a particular reason why he was now confidently able to *show* his anger. Narses, commanding the army in the West had fought a brilliant campaign and news of the defeat of the Goths and liberation of Italy had just arrived ... and to think that old Narses was even then well into his eighties! What a man! As a result, the Emperor now had the unwavering support of the grateful citizens of Rome. He now felt empowered to act exactly as he wished ... and as you so rightly say Martin, he was *angry*!

Any semblance of tact no longer being required, Justinian sent to the Council three documents:

(1) Vigilius' secret document of 547 anathematising the Chapters.

(2) His written oath of 550 swearing to work for their condemnation.

(3) A decree to the effect that the Pope should be excommunicated.

Following this, the Council continued to sit until 2 June. It anathematised and removed from circulation many selected writings pertaining to the religion, including those of Theodore and Theodoret. Ibas escaped personal condemnation on account of a clerical error. What had been thought of as his work, had it seems, been written by another. Anyway, that is how the story goes. Pope Vigilius was now fully excommunicated by the Council ... albeit *until he repent*.'

'And he lives, uncle?'

'Ah! I am warmed by your interest in the humanitarian aspect to life's concerns, my boy, but I am afraid he came to a sad end. He was a broken man; banished to a small island in the Sea of Marmara. With failing health and suffering agonies from kidney stones, he repented ... retracted his principles and was allowed to return to Rome. He never made the journey ... getting only as far as Syracuse and there he departed this life.'

'You know so much, uncle.'

'Ah, my boy ... you flatter me. I have to say ... it is not always *what* you know, but *whom* you know. I talk with informed friends ... amongst whom is Procopius ... We are blessed in that we have such a fine historian in our city ... Some say he will become Prefect. Friends ... your kindred spirits ... are important. What *you* know is so much a digest of what *your friends* know, my boy. Good communication ... that is so important in this life. Seek truth, but as we said earlier ... also be circumspect with that truth.'

'But despite all, uncle ... all the killings ... all the sadness ... all the plotting ... all the persecution of unorthodox Christians ... the Emperor *has* restored the Empire to its former boundaries, right across Europe and to the Black Sea. I would think also, he *has* continued the work of Constantine ... of making the Christian Church enclose the Empire with its embrace ... to bind it firmly. Has he not achieved what he set out to do?'

'Yes, my boy. It is indeed, much as he wanted, and certain things are to his credit ... but alas, the Empire is stretched and weak and many of its people impoverished. It cannot last as it is. Mark my words. It *will not* last.

It is not founded upon a rock, but upon strife and insensibility. I have to say also, neither is its state-religion ... founded upon a rock.'

'But Uncle Paulus ... will the religion not strengthen the Empire? And don't the scriptures describe the Church itself as being founded upon a rock?'

'My boy ... You are right to raise the question ... and it is a very good question. The teaching that you recall, I know well. According to Matthew, when Jesus said *'Who do you say that I am?'* Peter replied *'You are the Messiah, the Son of the living God!'* And Jesus continued *'... and upon that Rock I will build My church'* ... That rock ... It is the teaching-through-the-Messiah which is that rock, Martin. The teaching-through-the-Messiah is also to be through Peter. 'Peter' is derived from the Greek *petra* which actually means 'rock'. The Messiah's teaching is a teaching of love. It has simplicity and purity. As to the Empire's constructs, its dogma is different and something quite apart. Its Councils have been presided over and guided by Emperors who have much blood on their hands. There has been too much warring ... too much conversion by conquest, and too much killing of so-called heretics. The Empire's constructs are not born of love. The state-religion of the Empire is not founded of that 'rock' ... It is, I would venture to say, instead ... a 'rocky road' that the Empire takes! A 'stumbling-stone' within the teaching that the Empire has unfortunately placed there.

And yet Martin, the central flower of that Christian faith is still there ... midst the rocks of that rocky road ... within the adaptation of the faith that the Empire has made. There will be many ... so many good people who will see that flower clearly and who will nurture it regardless of diversions, regardless of dogma and death-threat. That flower of the true faith remains of good essence. That part is truly of the rock of Peter! But those parts of the Empire's *state*-religion that are *not* of the true faith, will confuse the unwary.'

'This is deep philosophy uncle. I'm not sure that I understand.'

'Look to the central flower of the faith, Martin. The teaching of Jesus comes *from* love and *is* love. Now look to the constructs added by the Empire's Councils. They simply do not come from love. They come from an Empire that is hostile towards many and which has within it, much political and economic strife. There has been so much killing. One cannot equate any of these things with love. The additions made to the religion by the state are to be seriously questioned for their worthiness.

Look also to the Commandments of the Christian religion ... in particular: *Thou shalt not kill.* If the faith is enmeshed with an Empire that has a variety of *killing* policies, and that same faith relies upon the Empire for its grand buildings and legislative matters; then its bishops cannot sensibly object to that Empire's military policies. But those military policies conflict with the very fundaments of the Christian faith. The position defies logic. It was Constantine's idea to bind religion to state. But unless the state itself, strives to observe all the laws and teachings of the religion, and upholds its purity ... then the concept is an impossible one. I will put it another way. For a state such as ours, which deals so much in death and contrived adversity, to be able to attach itself to a doctrine of love, makes about as much sense ... as ... as the notion that tarting is perfectly in order, but only as far as Alexandria!'

'Ah! Now I understand clearly, uncle. You have such a way of putting things! This has been quite a day ... a day when I have learned many truths ... and I do thank you for your patience. But what do you perceive of the future? Will it be long before the Empire fails?'

Paulus looked up somewhat wistfully into the branches of the fig tree as he spoke: 'I think, when Justinian departs, then there will quickly be changes.' Then he looked into the hazy distance and it was as if he himself were also far away. His words came as if half spoken, half thought: 'This Empire used to persecute Christians. The persecutions and martyrdom, in a way, strengthened their faith. Then the Empire embraced their religion and made alterations to it. Those who did *not* accept the religion were this time persecuted. This must surely confuse and weaken the faith. I fear that mankind is destined to remain confused for a long, long time ... for hundreds of years ... perhaps even thousands. And yet, there will always be those who seek out that central flower that still remains ... imperishable ... that will always flourish; and they will understand the message of love therein ... and profit by it.'

[It happened in much the way the learned Paulus had anticipated. Justinian died at 73, having reigned 38 years. His passing was the end of an era. Shortly before his departure, he completed legislative works that fixed the dates in the Christian calendar for Christmas day and Epiphany ... the manifestation of Jesus to the three Magi of the East. Following the passing of Justinian, the Empire moved steeply into decline. Procopius wrote of Justinian and Theodora, in a particularly candid manner, and for the last three years of his life, Procopius indeed aspired to Prefect of the Metropolis. Civil law systems of the present Western world have been based upon the work of that legal expert: Tribonian.

It is the militant Empire's adapted and adulterated version of the Christian faith, which has been adopted by the equally militant nations of the West. This 'developed' and 'dogmatic' version of the faith continues to this day, to confuse the understanding of so many. But the teaching of Jesus, with love at its centre (not militancy, conquest or greed), remains as a lucid living flower for all to imbibe and savour; and it is this that has been the object of true Prophecy.]

At that point
Where time has ended
And space ceased;

At that point
Where no personality is
And all ideas are gone;

At that point
There is a flower.
Pick it.

Raymond Christopher Davis 1993

PART 3

Birth of Materialism

The power that did create can change the scene
Of things, make mean of great, and great of mean:
The brightest glory can eclipse with might,
And place the most obscure in dazzling light.
Translated from the Roman poet Horace by John Milton, (1608 - 74)

In Europe and the West, the monasteries were for a substantial period, centres of light and learning. Then came the spectacular mushroom growth of the 17th century in many places of learning and elsewhere; growth in philosophy, the sciences, arts, invention and technology, with establishment of virtually all scientific disciplines and systems to suit what remained of that millennium. Voyages of discovery and colonisation led to the American colonies and their shared participation. Many would be revered for their genius. This burst of growth would continue at least into the next three centuries to reshape the world, also our lives.

Chapter XV

Interim

Prior to the materialism that was to come later, Europe struggled on into what became known as its Dark Ages; then perhaps things became just perceptibly brighter in the Middle Ages that followed. What had emerged after the glorious Greek civilisation and the dominant Roman authority, became a political and social melting pot, in which peoples migrated, fought and conquered. In the latter half of the 6th century, the old order declined as new powers emerged, and religious teachings spread.

St. Benedict had already founded an order of monks in the West, and monasteries had been established as seats of light and learning; and of this, the practical work of book copying was an important part. St. Benedict had vacated Rome at an early age to dwell in a cave for three years. He listened to the inner voice and meditated, away from worldly distraction. It was he who founded among other centres, the Monte Cassino monastery, where he once had audience with and admonished Totila, King of Goths. St. Augustine, at the bidding of Pope Gregory, crossed the Channel with forty others and landed in Kent. He was to establish Canterbury as the see of the archbishop of the English churches.

St. Columba sought a special place. He felt a guidance that came from within. It was a small party that travelled from Ireland with him, and they would eventually land upon the Isle of Iona, where a monastery would be founded. The place was indeed special. The place already had a residual energy from much more ancient times. It waited there. He with his teaching would reawaken that energy of the past; and from this base, he would be able to carry out his life's work, and reach the mainland peoples. Many monasteries were established across Europe. It was a time for this.

There was another of no insubstantial influence, who took the name Mohammed. Born at Mecca, Mohammed was at first a camel driver. That is how he began his Earth life. The Dark Ages, although much troubled, were in no way entirely dark, and the plague years that had ravaged Europe for more than half a century, eventually came to an end; but this not before its population had been halved.

Mohammed the camel driver became Mohammed the prophet. He dreamed dreams and heard the voice of the angel Gabriel. He listened carefully and wrote down what he heard, and his writings became the

Koran. The one universal God, is known to different populations by different names. To the Moslems who accepted 'submission to God' ... *Islam* ... he was Allah. The Emperor Constantine had conceived the *one* God religion as the device that would unite an empire. Now, it was another version of the *one* God religion that was separately uniting the Semitic and Arab peoples. Until this time, they had been peaceable tribes without a collective will. This would change. In its early form the Islamic faith was, unlike its *developed* Christian counterpart (and unlike the later *developed* Islamic religion), attractively simple. There were no grand buildings or priests, no mosques or minarets. It was a religion the people carried in their hearts. There was its code embracing love, honesty and humility. Followers would be mindful of their belief turning five times a day, to face towards the Holy City of Mecca, and offer simple prayer. That is how it began, refreshingly pure and simple; *as the source teachings always are.*

There was one other factor, a factor common to all religions and so very widely misunderstood: *the recognition of the indestructible spirit aspect of our being*. When the crucified Jesus, said to the respectful criminal: *'I tell you truly, today you shall be with me in Paradise',* he was clearly referring to that immortality of spirit. Likewise Mohammed, when he said that those who fall in battle as soldiers of the faith *will go straight to heaven*; his statement was also in keeping with that same immortality of spirit. The emphasis of Islamic interpretation, however, was that ... to die fighting for the faith, was a gloriously quick route to heaven; and that heaven was to be so much more desired than the hardships of life here on Earth. As a result, not only were the Arab peoples united, they were united in battle ... and in battle, they became the most fearless of fighters! It was the will of Allah ... the Jihad ... a holy war of deliverance!

Islam became a religion of conquest. Emirs with their green turbans and flowing robes, skilful with horse and scimitar, led their legions deep into North Africa, across Europe and into much of the Eastern Mediterranean. Jerusalem fell, the huge library at Alexandria was fired and its incalculable treasures lost to the world forever. Half of Christendom was taken. It was the way of the Jihad!

Eventually the Franks, the people of France, led by 'Charles the Hammer', halted their advance. It was the Franks led by his grandson, Charles the Great ... 'Charlemagne' ... who later recaptured much of Western Europe. At this time, there were again difficulties with the Papacy in Rome. There was violence on the streets of Rome. Pope Leo III was attacked and left for dead. He was bandaged and saved by friends, and fled to Spoleto, a city some sixty miles to the northeast. He then travelled to Paderborn, in what is now Westphalia, to hold counsel with Charlemagne. On his return to Rome, Pope Leo was well received, and those who had conspired against him were banished. These details led to an important consequence.

Charlemagne attended Rome and on Christmas Day of the year 800, he was crowned 'Holy Roman Emperor', in St. Peter's Cathedral, by Pope Leo. He was now seen as the *Protector of Christendom*, and the bonding of Western Church and State was reasserted. Now there would be two Emperors in Europe; one for what became known as the 'Holy Roman Empire' in the West and one for the old Byzantine or 'Eastern Roman Empire'. There were other significant moves. It was some time later in the year 1066, that Duke William of Normandy crossed the Channel and defeated King Harold. He was to unify England as a stronger monarchy that would become an influence in later world affairs. But it was the Seljuk Turks from Central Asia who were to take the next significant step.

Christians and Moslems at last settled more peaceably and those from the West were making pilgrimages to the Holy Land. But now, the Turks who had won Persia ... currently Iran ... and who had themselves become Moslem, were taking over from the older Moslem regime; and now it was they who threatened Constantinople. This prompted the Emperor of the Eastern Roman Empire to request aid from his Western counterpart. In response, the Papacy sanctioned a status of 'Holy War'. And thus began the Crusades.

The First Crusade (1096) consisted of four armies of knights led by French princes. They took Nicaea, Dorylaeum and Antioch; then stormed Jerusalem from a siege tower. Once within Jerusalem, they slaughtered without mercy and established what was called the Christian kingdom of Jerusalem. Within the space of two hundred years, there would be nine separate Crusades. The Papacy was involved in the first five. The Third Crusade was a most royal adventure, which included King Philip Augustus of France, King Richard Lionheart of England and Emperor Frederick Barbarossa of the Holy Roman Empire. The Fourth Crusade divested itself of all idealistic purpose and chivalrous ethic. It became a scandalous *mis*adventure that involved underhanded dealings, leading to conflict between Western Christians and Eastern Christians and to the actual sacking of the nominally Christian Constantinople by the Crusaders!

The general picture of the Crusades is in retrospect, a miserable confused mess. The overall result was failure. The only profit was expanded trade for the merchants of Venice. The Crusades created enormous and widespread hardship, havoc, suffering, death and injustice. They would have continued; there certainly remained much talk and the further planning. But the popes and the emperors so frequently quarrelled, and the kings of the West were busy warring amongst themselves. East and West remained divided. The religions centred on 'love and humility' were unhappily obscured by a confusion of violence entwined inextricably with the death wish of unconfined nationalism.

Following the Crusades, the Knights of St. John of Jerusalem continued loyal to their cause. When forced to retreat from the mainland, they fortified the island of Rhodes. Increasing Turkish naval power forced their further retreat. They became the Knights of Malta, fortifying that island from which they raided Turkish shipping. As the Knights of Malta, they remained a brotherhood of Knights of many nations, and a rearguard to the Western Christendom, in its retreat from the eastern lands from which had sprung its Christian origin.

The treaty of Mersen-on-Meuse (870), divided Charlemagne's kingdom into two parts. The western half, contained Gaul, a part of the old Roman Empire, and kept the language of that province. France thus has its language of Latin origin. The land to the northeast, was known to the Romans, as 'Germania'. That part of the Frankish Kingdom, was different in that it did not at any time form part of the old Empire. The language spoken was therefore not of the Latin, but the *lingua teutisca* or 'popular dialect'. *Teutisca* became *Deutch* and the land: *Deutchland.*

History repeated itself when a later Pope: Leo VIII sought assistance from a kingdom. He approached Otto, the Deutchland king, who had become a powerful leader of the Germanic peoples. In return for his services, Otto was made 'Emperor of the Holy Roman Empire of the German Nation'. [This strange politico-religious title seems to symbolise more than anything, the attempted welding together of State and Religion. The title would continue until General Napoléon Bonaparte placed the Imperial crown upon his own head, and declared himself heir to the Charlemagne tradition. This he did while Pope Pius VII, who had been summoned, stood by and observed (1801).]

Other extravagant titles were bestowed. Martin Luther's works on reform went against Papal doctrines. When King Henry VIII of England wrote a book that went against Luther's work, Pope Leo X, favoured him with the title of 'Defender of the Faith'. Ten years later, whilst attending to his matrimonial problems, this 'Defender of the Faith' saw fit to replace that faith with a different version of his own. He now established an independent 'English' state religion: The Church of England, with himself, Henry at its head; quite isolated from the Pope and from Rome. As of old, those who disagreed with this latest modification were dealt death in various harsh ways. The executions of 1535 included Charterhouse monks, John Fisher, Bishop of Rochester, and the ageing and retired Sir Thomas More. His resolute words as he mounted the scaffold: *'I pray you master lieutenant, see me safely up, and for my coming down, let me shift for myself.'*

Another title of note: Visitor-General of English Monasteries, this given to Thomas Cromwell. There would first be his visits; then followed the destruction and the sackings. It was a heavy-handed affair. Some 550 monasteries were destroyed and the lands taken by the Crown. As to the monks, 7,000 of them were turned loose into the countryside. Those who objected were executed. Leaders of the subsequent uprisings ... the Pilgrimage of Grace ... were executed. The acquired funds from the monasteries would build castles, dockyards, warships and the like. Lead from their roofs was melted down to make musket shot, a practice that would send the fine old buildings into rapid decline.

Just three years after the execution of his second wife, Henry had Parliament pass the Act of Six Articles. The articles were six doctrines for the Church, with severe penalties for their transgression. Marriage for the clergy was denied. Private masses and confessions were useful to the clergy. Monastic vows were binding. Clergy had the right to deny to laity, wine at communion. In communion, the bread and wine *were* the body and blood of the Christ, and denial of this was punishable by death. Protestants had their own name for the Act: 'The Whip with Six Strings'.

In England then, the monastic system was crushed, and the link with the Holy Roman Empire ended; and in its place, was now a new state-bound religion, with an insensitive monarch in command, who clearly would have none of the finer teachings for himself. Europe fared no better. Europe was being afflicted by an ever-deepening shadow: the shadow of the Inquisition. Many thousands were now being put to death on account of belief and religious practice. The simple message of love and humility still lay there somewhere within, and was understood by some. But to many, it remained heavily obscured. What had happened to that *simple* 'word' delivered to humankind in the Holy Land? And what of that 'third prophecy' of Fatima, which to date has never been divulged? Perhaps that prophecy connects in some way to this political smothering of the love and light of the message as received.

Chapter XVI

Century of Genius

At the turn of the 17th century, a new energy seemed to be pervading the Western world. It brought relief. Some kind of a change was long due and sorely needed. There had been too much erroneous thinking, too much misuse of power, excessive bloodshed. The mood was better, but death still stalked in the shadows; the Inquisition continued to hunt for those it foolishly chose to call heretics. But a more outward seeking energy now pervaded many places, as a quest for truth and knowledge gathered momentum. Those who were critical of religious unorthodoxy, often clung to the errors of tradition; and the punishment for being unorthodox, was too often beheading or burning. Sadly, it was the very seeking and the progression of knowledge that so often *meant* not conforming to tradition. How can one possibly progress to new ideas without being different? Earlier, Nostradamus had managed to elude the unwanted attentions of the Inquisition. Not all were so fortunate.

It was cold. It was February 17th of the year 1600. A new century had begun. Giordano Bruno had been used to better times than this. He had attended the courts of Henry III of France *and* of Elizabeth I of England! Bruno was an erudite philosopher, had delivered many lectures and had written many works of considerable merit, *and* he had even written a play of contemporary society.

'Good heavens! That was 18 years ago! It was Mocenigo's jealousy that had placed him in the position where he now found himself! He, Mocenigo it was who had talked to the Inquisition. That was just seven years ago. That was the time he had entered the jail of the Roman Palace Holy Office. He had stated and re-stated his case, but to no avail. Now he was under sentence of death as an heretic, by Pope Clement VIII. It had been a mistake to return to Venice. But the chair of mathematics at Padua University had become vacant, and would have been perfect for him ... and if only ... but that had been offered to Galileo ... a sound man, a good scientist ... He was pleased for him. It was he, Bruno, who had made the false step. He should have kept clear of Italy.

They were fools! They were fools in their thinking! It was really *they* who were in error ... and they handed out false justice in the name of their God whom they failed to understand. They were children wielding a power that was too big for them. He, Bruno, was able to take comfort from the fact that *he* understood ... understood the *one* God; their God; his God; and his God's creation, whereas *they* did not. *They* were too young, while he had grown to be ... to be the *philosopher.*

They hold to the view of Aristotle that Earth is at the centre of creation, while the finite heaven with sun and stars move around that centre. It suits *their* blinkered picture of heaven above and hell below and God seated in heaven immediately above Jerusalem, while angels push the great sphere of heaven around on its journey. If only they would read Aristotle properly! Read him properly! Aristotle reasons his case, but also concedes: *'the Italian philosophers known as Pythagoreans take the contrary view. At the centre, they say, is fire, and the Earth is one of the stars, creating night and day by its circular motion.'* Aristotle's very words! And *they* are Italians! The work of Copernicus, of Krakow, Poland, has for 60 years now, made it clear that the older Italian view was and still remains correct. The sun *is* at the centre of this part of the universe, and Earth *does* move around the sun. I, Bruno, have written and taught that the universe, in which this system lives, is truly an *infinite* universe. The God *also* is infinite, and I have taught that mankind should seek truth and virtue and make good the union of human soul with the Infinite One. I will not retract that belief. I Bruno, in the face of death, stand by my teaching!

I also stand by my other teaching ... on the more general concept of religion ... that there should and must be a peaceful coexistence of all world religions based on a mutual understanding and upon a freedom of reciprocal discussion. I go to my death as a true believer and I know in my heart, that I fear less than those passing sentence upon me. I can recall my own words at that time of sentence: *'Perhaps your fear in passing judgement on me is greater than mine on receiving it.'* So be it.

There is more that I could have done ... and I surely would have cherished the doing. Some further elaboration on the atomic basis of matter would have been worthwhile. As to space and time of the infinite universe, all motion within that vast system can only be seen as relative. That is clear to me. Such terms as *up, down, above, below,* become quite meaningless in the vast universal context. But it is of little account. Others there will be who will follow my work. It is begun and the thought has sparked. That is the important thing. Now my time is come. A prepared stake awaits ... a stake void of any Christian love or charity and, as to hope; that impassive stake certainly curtails all hope in *this* realm.

Now the flames. It begins. But why the gag? That, I had not expected. I shall not cry out; that is for sure. *Now* I have the greatest need of my power to think! Just for a short time ... until I meet our Maker. Think the thoughts! Think! Transcend this dismal place! So *this* was the death of that poor youth ... of the maid of Lorraine ... Joan of Arc ... Too young she was ... Too young! ... Too young for this! Listened to the voices, she had ... And followed their bidding ... Had listened and had gone to fight for the Dauphin; had put the English to flight! And later, it was *they* who burned her ... as a witch! For heresy! ... A mere slip of a young girl ... To listen to the voice within is no heresy! Unjust disgrace! ... Unjust! By what authority ... By what ...?'

A blackness came at that point when the burning could no longer be endured. And then ... And then ... he was in his space and time. Somewhere, not up, down, above, below, but elsewhere and nonetheless he *could* look down, and there the flames receded. No pain now ... and yet he still had the knowledge of it, a *memory* of pain. But that memory was now just overwhelmed by the caress of love and light that he at this moment was receiving ... a light, much brighter than the flames; and he could sense someone there, someone close, giving immense love ... It was all around him, and the source so very close. One seemed to be there … was there, whom he could not quite see. The love seemed to pervade his very being. And he *knew* ... he *knew* ... there *was* no death! 'I still have thoughts. That is my proof of continued being!'

His life and his death had opened the doors onto a brand new century. His clear logic had cut through the dross of those faltering times with the keenness of an Emir's scimitar. More philosophers were to come in this Century of Genius, each in his own good time, and each would make handsome contribution. Gotfried Leibniz invented the differential calculus for describing, in a quantitative way, rates of change: his gift to all subsequent students of mathematics. It was also he who attempted to rationalise a unitary system for the universe based on 'monads'; the same name as was used by Bruno for *his* 'atoms'.

Baruch Spinoza argued that all knowledge could be deduced from one key substance, which he called God or Nature. God, he describes as: *'this supreme substance who is unique, universal and necessary.'* But this new century was essentially a time for the *material* development; not a time of spiritual expansion. Yet Spinoza knew well enough that, in reality, all came from the spirit. This was to be primarily a *material* century, and the material development would be 'of the mind' ... of the thinking ... of the *constructs* of the physical mind. As Spinoza understood, the ideas that inspire mental effort may well originate in spirit, but this for the most part, would not be recognised in *this* period of our awakening. Each invention would be attributed to the excellence of its inventor, and the quality of that one's physical *mind.*

René Descartes invented analytical geometry, with 'Cartesian' co-ordinates. He discarded tradition. He emphasised the supremacy of science and suggested that the universe be subject to mechanical laws. In his philosophy, he would believe nothing unless it was a logical necessary truth. Through a process of at first doubting all ideas, he arrived at the ultimate first perception: *cogito, ergo sum* – 'I think, therefore I am'. He set a style for rational reason, and it should be noted that Descartes satisfied himself that we are all two-component beings, each comprising *body* and *soul*, the soul being the *true* person.

It was Francis Bacon who particularly advocated the scientific method. His comment on the status of science was: *'The sciences that we possess have been principally derived from the Greeks; for the additions of the Roman, Arabic, or more modern writers, are but a few and of small importance...'* Certainly Greece had contributed much; less so the Roman and more modern writers. But all that was now about to change. Western Europe would now steer its own version of the grand development in the wake of the achievements of ancient Greece.

It was the philosophers, with their power of thought and their ability to organise the thinking that swept the stage and prepared it, for great acts that were to follow. There have always been those few that stand head and shoulders above their compatriots, in the stature of their minds, in their ability to reason, while others marvel at that ability to seek and understand. These are the ones who feel strongly that spark of creation, as they address their gaze to the horizons of knowledge, to pierce the uncertainty beyond. On this planet, progress has never been a steady process. What *is* progress? Clearly, the gathering of knowledge and the good application of it, is a significant part. It is a growth, as is a tree. The tree of knowledge has its time of germination in the dawn of consciousness, and its time of maturity as the accumulation of knowledge nears completion. In between, the growth rings of the centuries are sometimes tightly knit and sometimes far apart. There have been many stagnant pools of time, during which little happened worthy of the mention. To compensate, there have been enormous leaps, towards that more complete understanding begun by those we call philosophers.

Thus it was at this time. Facts emerged. These were written into books; stored, treasured and researched. Some facts were seen to fit together, like the pieces of a great puzzle, and patterns revealing the system of things began to emerge. Only the most gifted, could see and appreciate the patterns. It was the piecing together and recognition of the patterns that so often led to one of those major strides towards our fuller understanding of the universe in which we find ourselves.

Baruch Spinoza was in his work, part theoretical and part practical. His philosophy was really a leisure activity, while he earned his living in a much more practical way ... making glass lenses. There was a growing demand for these. The optical sciences were developing and progress was diverse in the extreme. While Johann Kepler was discovering the laws that would revolutionise astronomy, others were building the first microscopes. The attention of these was being focused upon the minute details of our world and upon the cellular units of life itself. A variety of small forms of nature were being seen for the very first time; and these forms were often both intricate and beautiful; so that the enthusiasm for observation was being kindled and re-kindled.

None was more enthusiastic or widely seeking than Antoni van Leeuwenhoek. Born in the Dutch town of Delft, he had a humble start in life. Lacking the benefit of a good education, he was nevertheless an intelligent man and with such a powerful curiosity. During the day, he ran a small haberdashery business. At night, he became a self-taught, self-disciplined scientist, grinding lenses and assembling microscopes that were surprisingly efficient. He then used these with the utmost skill to unfold a great many of the secrets of nature. And he was *such* an observer!

Berkelse Mere lay to the southeast. The journey would take two hours. The waters of the lake were always clear in winter, becoming clouded in the summer months. The locals had their theories about the change and most, for no particular reason other than the inability to concoct a better story, put it down to the seasonal dews. The microscopist would magnify a small quantity of water, and see for himself and besides, it would be a good test of the new instrument he had just made. People had accepted casual belief on all kinds of matters, for hundreds of years without serious question. Why ... it would be in keeping with the very mood of these changing times if he were to carry out a test to see what he could identify in that cloud in the lake. It was a suitable job for a microscope. This would satisfy his natural curiosity. The sample, once secured, was taken back to his office-laboratory, where he could make a detailed study.

The light of the candle entered the tiny lens and he held the device to his eye, and there ... brightly illuminated, was a whole new living world ... there ... within the tiny water drop! He was seeing the green chain-like threads of the alga *Spirogyra*, some spiral thread-like growths, some earthy particles, swimming 'animalcules', that bustled around like they were crowds in town doing the shopping, rotifers that seemed to throb and comb the water with their cilia, and the single cell protozoa. *These* were causing the cloud in the water. But what a higgledy-piggledy confusion of thriving creatures! None had yet been named! He, the amateur scientist, was the very first to see. Were these life forms peculiar to Berkelse Mere, or did all waters contain them?

Leeuwenhoek was curious, and so he searched elsewhere, finding many single cell life forms: bacteria, yeasts, protozoa, and a good many organisms that were more complicated. He carefully recorded, with drawings, all, for he had become a scientist of the times, and was a part of the activity of discovery of this remarkable century.

Others also made microscopes. Robert Hooke, Eustachio Divini and Philip Bonnani all went on to make their own versions of more complicated compound microscopes. Hooke made his lenses by fusing small glass beads and he *also* discovered minute life forms. Marcello Malpighi of Bologna, made drawings of glands and tissue detail, and started numerous lines of investigation into animal and plant structures. The Malpighian tubules of the kidney still carry his name. Jan Swammerdam of Amsterdam excelled at manipulative work. He fashioned his own minute scalpels and instruments for insect dissection. He made detailed drawings of their body structures. He was consumed with such an enthusiasm that he worked both day and night with precious little sleep. By the age of 36, he was just burnt out ... quite spent ... and died a few years later. He devised a system of classification, laid the foundations of entomology, discovered blood cells and for many years, his drawings of insect structures remained the best the world had produced.

Meanwhile, across the sea in London, the Royal Society was formed, for the purpose of progressing natural knowledge. Papers were read, scientists corresponded, and a number of foreign correspondents emerged. One such correspondent was Regnier de Graaf, a physician of Delft. He it was who discovered the ovarian follicles, still known as the 'Graafian follicles'. But possibly his greater service was the encouragement he gave to Antoni Leeuwenhoek. He encouraged him to write to the Royal Society. In fact, both de Graaf and an eminent diplomat: Sir Constantijn Huygens wrote letters of introduction on behalf of the less educated man. As the result of this kindness, the Royal Society was eventually to receive no less than 400 letters from Leeuwenhoek during the course of his lifetime, describing many observations. As an observer of microbes, he was second to none. [Earth then had to wait 200 years for another to connect microbes with the mysteries of fermentation and disease. The one to discover this had been *named* well in advance in a prophecy by Nostradamus. He was the renowned French chemist: Louis Pasteur.]

Europe was becoming a great bubbling cauldron of discovery and experiment. Scientists experimented, measured, collected data and communicated amongst themselves. Great doors of comprehension were at last beginning to open and the gifted ones struggled to find new words to describe what could be part seen in the half-light beyond.

The Danish astronomer Tycho Brahé was a disappointment to his family, a family of noble lineage. Not only did he neglect a comfortable career in law to take up astronomy, a pursuit that was frowned upon as inferior and not becoming for a nobleman; he also married a peasant girl! If there was one thing worse for a Danish gentleman than getting hooked on and besotted with astronomy, it was marrying a peasant girl! Then he lost a large piece of nose in a duel. But he carefully fashioned out of gold, an artificial nosepiece, which he managed to colour to make it entirely passable. He kept for twenty years, an observatory on the small island of Hoëne, funded by King Frederick II. He became a dedicated and methodical astronomer and kept detailed and accurate records. Unfortunately it became necessary for him to leave Denmark in 1597, on account of increasing persecutions and jealousies contrived by his more orthodox peers, leading to the loss of his observatory. Life, for him, had its difficulties. In fact, modern Danes will say, *'I've had a Tycho Brahé day'*, meaning, 'I've had one of those days'.

Rudolf II, Emperor of Germany, was interested in astrology and the occult. This led to his desire to employ Tycho at an observatory at Banatek near Prague. Now the ageing Tycho had corresponded for several years with a young man named Johann Kepler, and just before the turn of the century, the younger man had joined him as assistant. It was a fortuitous and timely union. They worked together for just two years before Tycho departed this life. Kepler was able to use the accurate data largely collected by his colleague, to work out the details of motion of bodies in the solar system. He found that the planets went about the sun following *elliptical* paths! The sun was at a focus of each ellipse, and he found a way of calculating exactly how it was. Johann Kepler went on to revolutionise astronomy.

Thus far, the astronomical data had been collected and discoveries made, without the aid of any telescope. But that invention was now in the process of happening. Hans Lippershey was a German spectacle maker. On the day that he held up a certain two lenses and looked through them at a weather vane, he was just astonished at the size of it! He had discovered a useful device! But, lacking in imagination, he could think only of possible military application. It was Jaques Bovedere of Paris, who suggested another application ... to Galileo. It was Galileo Galilie who developed the device as an astronomical telescope and then turned it towards the stars. Once equipped with such an instrument, his discoveries were both rapid and numerous. On looking at the 'belt and sword of Orion', he found he was able to see, not just nine stars but more than eighty. The moon clearly had features that cast shadows and was not self-luminous, but shone by a reflected light. He saw also that the lightness in the sky known as the Milky Way consisted of many thousands of distant stars! The planet Jupiter was seen to have four satellites. As to the sun, hitherto it had been regarded as a symbol of absolute perfection. Not so; now it could be seen defiled by spots, and these moved to show its slow rotation!

Galileo was of an old Florentine family and was Pisa born and bred. It was at the youthful age of 18 that he observed the regularity of swing of a lamp in Pisa cathedral. This gave him the idea of the pendulum for clock regulation and accurate time measurement. He became the originator of an experimental science, in this period of advancement into which Europe now plunged. Following talks with his father's friend Ostilio Riccio, he had changed the course of his studies from medicine in favour of mathematics. This and his natural inventive instinct had steered him into the chair of mathematics at Padua. He was at Padua for a period of 18 years where he enjoyed enormous popularity.

Some of Galileo's discoveries in astronomy were sadly and as expected, seen as heretical by the Inquisition; as had been Bruno's work only a decade earlier. The matter came to light on one of his visits to Rome, when he was denounced for his scientific beliefs. But he had friends in high places and was now turned 70, and he had developed some infirmity; this being so, had he been more circumspect, the authorities might well have turned a blind eye. But he was quite outspoken in both the voiced as well as in the written word. In these circumstances, the authorities chose not to overlook the matter.

One issue at his subsequent trial was a letter he had written to the Grand Duchess Christine of Lorraine. In it, he supported Cardinal Baronius in his statement: *'The Holy Spirit intended to teach us in the Bible how to go to Heaven, not how the heavens go.'* (It was the same Baronius who had devoted two decades of his life to the writing of a massive 12 volume work for the Church of Rome, trying to prove that the Church had not deviated in doctrine or constitution, from the Christian Church of the 1st century! Needless to say, it was a controversial work!)

Following trial, the great man was required by the Inquisition to abjure his scientific truths on his knees, and was then sentenced to punishment at the will of the court. In fact it transpired that, Pope Urban VIII under pressure from the Grand Duke Ferdinand II of Tuscany, allowed him to retire to live in a retreat at Arcetri near Florence. Here, he was able to continue his researches, so long as he complied with the conditions of his release/parole. (The Grand Duke himself had a scientific bent. It was he who devised a liquid sealed-in-glass thermometer that was later improved by Fahrenheit, resulting in a type of thermometer still with us today).

It had been the Grand Duke Ferdinand I, who had, earlier in Galileo's life, appointed him Professor of Mathematics at the University of Pisa. He was in fact, in receipt of several kindnesses from that ruling Medici family. During those earlier days, he had investigated motion and gravity. While at Pisa, he noted that all falling bodies, regardless of their mass, fall with the same velocity! He managed to demonstrate this by dropping cannon ball and musket shot from the top of the leaning tower. Soon he had discovered three basic laws of motion. But the subtlety of the nature of gravity continued to elude him. He died on 8th January 1642 and was laid to rest in the chapel of Santa Croce in Florence. It was the burial of a famous and a well-respected man.

Later that same year, it was almost as if that famous and respected man had made the decision to reincarnate post-haste on account of unfinished business. One was born in England on Christmas day, in the little hamlet of Woolsthorpe, just a few miles south of Grantham in Lincolnshire. It was a curious year, one that also saw the outbreak of civil war in England, between Charles I with his Royalists, and Oliver Cromwell's Parliamentary forces.

The child was impatient and the birth premature, small and weak at first. It was said he could have fitted into a quart pot. He was scarcely expected by some to live, but the spark of life burned brightly within and the child thrived; and Isaac Newton grew to become the foremost scientist of his time. He might well have grown up to be a sheep farmer. The Newtons had for several generations, farmed in the region. It would have been the family tradition. But at the grammar school at Grantham, he showed skill and ability in making all kinds of mechanical contrivances, water clocks, windmills, sundials and the like. Even so, following the death of his stepfather, his mother withdrew him from the school, to introduce him to the matter of farm management. But in this, he showed no interest at all.

It is often surprising how important in the process of history, those people are, who sometimes lend a hand, or encourage, or just give timely advice. At this point in Newton's life, it was his uncle: the Reverend William Ayscough, Rector of nearby Burton Coggles, who so changed the course of history. It was by his encouragement that Newton was sent to Trinity College, Cambridge, where he could further develop talents that his uncle knew to be there. This he could do in reasonable freedom because it was now the fashion in England, that science should not be burdened by the dictates of religious authority. The philosophies of Descartes and Bacon had very much helped to steer the thinking in this direction. Newton, unlike Galileo, was to be spared that kind of interference.

Oliver Cromwell had also been an influence, by his favouring the Puritan stance. Prior to the Civil War, he had been Member of Parliament for Cambridge. As Lord Protector, he had been demonstrably opposed to religious persecution. All that was now thankfully very much in the past. But, as foretold by the seer, Charles I had been executed, and since then, Cromwell had himself departed this life. Cromwell's material body, however, had *not* been forgotten: at least, on 30 January 1661, two years and five months after his death, that material body was disinterred and hanged; then the head removed, and spiked upon a pole and exhibited above Westminster Hall. This, by authority of King Charles II and the clergy! This version of the faith so lacked the love and compassion of the teaching of Jesus, that the head of Church and its clergy vented their wrath on the bodily remains in this way! Then, in the summer of 1665, the Great Plague had begun to ravage London and would lay to rest 68,596 of its people.

One good thing came of the Plague and its spread to Cambridge. It arrived in the wake of Newton's Bachelor's degree. The students, to reduce the chance of infection, were all sent down. He now had two years (the years of the Plague and of London's *predicted* Great Fire), in the quiet of Woolsthorpe, for free thinking. He was able to ponder the problems of the times, quite uninterrupted by the structured pathways of academia. It is clear that during these two years, he achieved major discoveries *and* evolved a programme of study for much of his remaining life.

His achievements were many and mixed. He had an understanding of the disadvantages conferred on optics, by the chromatic character of white light and was inspired to build good *reflecting* telescopes. Independently of Leibniz, he invented differential and integral calculus, which he called 'fluxions', and other useful mathematical processes. At the youthful age of 26, he was appointed Lucasion Professor of Mathematics at Cambridge. He later became President of the Royal Society, Master of the Mint, and received a knighthood. But his greatest achievement, was that work embodied in the 'Principia', a full mathematical treatise on the motion of bodies, the calculation of orbits, whether elliptical, parabolic or hyperbolic and gravitational forces. In fact, this amounted to a reference work pertaining to the constructs and motions of the universe. He had dallied somewhat prior to publication, and was urged to go on by Robert Hooke, Christopher Wren and Edmund Halley, receiving much technical and financial assistance from Halley who greatly shared his interests.

Newton had deduced the 'inverse square law' from Kepler's third law, stating the fundamental truth: *every particle of matter in the universe attracts every other particle with a force proportional to the distance between the two particles.* He tested the law by applying it to the motion and balance of the moon in its passage about the Earth. He needed Jean Picard's new value for the distance of one degree of latitude and he corresponded with John Flamsteed regarding the required astronomical data. Flamsteed had been appointed the *first* Astronomer Royal at the new Greenwich Observatory. The *inverse square* theory fitted exactly! It was then, the same familiar gravity as causes an apple to fall to the ground, which balances the moon and the planets in their orbits! Many times he had sat watching apples fall in the garden at Woolsthorpe, and from that beginning, had come to understand the balancing of the universe by mechanical-mathematical laws ... or was it a previous life in Pisa, that had been the first influence? It makes no difference. The Principia was published as a three-volume major work and was enthusiastically acclaimed throughout Europe.

Despite fame and achievement, he retained a modest or natural philosophical quality. This may be seen in his words of later years: *'I do not know what I may appear to the world, but to myself I seem to have been only like a boy playing on the seashore, and diverting myself in now and then finding a smoother pebble or a prettier shell than ordinary, while the great ocean of truth lay all undiscovered before me.'* The statement seems to connect quite well with a philosophical poem by Rabindranath Tagore. One might picture him ... Newton ... child of the universe ... sitting before the great ocean of life, sifting pebbles through his fingers on a seashore:

> *On the seashore of endless worlds children meet. The infinite sky is motionless overhead and the restless water is boisterous. On the seashore of endless worlds the children meet with shouts and dances.*
>
> *They build their houses with sand and they play with empty shells. With withered leaves they weave their boats and smilingly float them on the vast deep. Children have their play on the seashore of worlds.*
>
> *... children gather pebbles and scatter them again. They seek not for hidden treasures ... Tempest roams in the pathless sky, ships get wrecked in the trackless water, death is abroad and children play. On the seashore of endless worlds is the great meeting of children.*
>
> Rabindranath Tagore *Gitanjali*

Chapter XVII

The Path of the Comet

> *When beggars die, there are no comets seen;*
> *The heavens themselves blaze forth the death of princes.*
> William Shakespeare *Julius Cæsar. Act II, Scene II*

He had grown up the son of a London soap boiler, but had had the benefit of an education at the St. Paul's School, and then Queen's College, Oxford. Following his studies, he had been able to realise his dream and study the heavens. He was an astronomer, and had travelled to St. Helena. From there he had catalogued the stars of the Southern Hemisphere ... a two-year project. 'Catalogus Stellarum Australium' had been published in 1679, and his work had earned him the title of Southern Tycho, not because he had had a bad day! On the contrary; because he was now respected for his excellent work, as had been Tycho in earlier times; by those who *really* knew him and had the understanding.

It had been quite literally the realisation of a dream. Before he ever made the voyage, he had *dreamt* of sailing towards St. Helena; and the memory of his dream-island had remained with him, as the reality came into view. He said afterwards, that the sight of the island as he approached on his voyage, was just as he recalled it from the dream.

Jean Baptiste Colbert had quite different talents. He was French with Scottish ancestry. His grandfather had been a bagpiper with the Scottish Regiment while in France. Colbert had served an apprenticeship in a woollen-draper's shop, and then rose to become Minister of Finance under Louis XIV. Like the much earlier John of Cappadocia of Roman times, he had revised a poor taxation system and was very efficient ... most efficient ... too efficient! He produced massive funds from merciless and overpowering taxation. He was hated, and seemed to be void of compassion. It would appear that tax collectors and reformers sometimes get unaccountably carried away with their fund-raising! At his death, there were those who would have gladly danced on the body and torn it limb from limb. The establishment of the day knew very well that this was the feeling, and accordingly, arranged the funeral at night under heavy military escort, to avert such a spectacle. But, money is money, and the ample public funds were put to numerous uses, not least the setting up of an observatory in Paris. Colbert had invited Giovanni Domenico Cassini to take charge. Cassini it was, who had measured the periods of revolution of planets, discovered satellites of Saturn and who had measured the tilt of the moon to its ecliptic. He was a good man, of that there was no doubt.

Now, in the year 1680, Cassini was joined by the Southern Tycho ... Edmund Halley ... and together they observed a good-sized comet, as it wound its way across the sky. In England, Newton was observing the same comet. There is also a curious connection with a fourth gentleman, William Lilly, an astrologer. In the last almanac to be written by his own hand (he became blind in his latter years and thereafter they were written *for* him), he had *predicted* this comet. That had been in his almanac of 1677. Astrology and the material science of astronomy might conceivably be seen as in opposition, but in this instance, they came together agreeably. The observers were puzzled by the comet's course, and did not yet understand the motion of these space travellers in the heavens.

Next came the great comet of 1682. Halley was now back in London, in his private observatory in Islington. At 0630 on 22 November he was observing. This was a *great* comet! This was a comet of inspiration! It really fired his interest. Later, Halley and Robert Hooke talked about the comet's course in relation to gravity. A friend, Christopher Wren, offered a small prize if one of them could *prove* that the comet was subject to gravitational control. Halley talked with Newton, and it became clear that Newton had already worked out the general details of the nature of gravity! (It was this interchange between the two men that led to Newton's publication of his Principia. It seems that having worked it through, he then needed some degree of persuasion to get the sizeable work into print). As to the comet, Newton was sufficiently cognisant to realise, that the comet seen approaching the sun in the November, would be the same one as was seen moving away from the sun in the December; albeit in almost the opposite direction. And that would make its path lie close to an hyperbolic curve. This he communicated to Halley, with the result that Halley now knew a good deal more about these cosmic oddities than hitherto.

But it was to take a few more years yet. Halley played a game of comparing comets that had been seen over the centuries, to see if he could identify similarities that might suggest regular returns of the same one. The one he had observed with Cassini could conceivably be that observed in 44 BC ... it was the one that followed the murder of Julius

Cæsar. It would have returned in 531 and 1106, giving it a period of 575 years. Further calculations however, showed the connections to be in error. No! ... He must begin again. It was a difficult task. *Then* he realised the comet of 1682 that he had observed in London, had a particular distinction. It went the *wrong* way around the sun ... against the rotation of the planets, as did comets sighted in 1531 and 1607! He plotted elliptical trajectories for these and found agreement! They had to be the same comet! He was able to predict its next return in the year 1758, giving an average period of 73 years. This next-return date was destined to be just 16 years beyond his life span. He would miss that reunion.

The years embracing Halley's prediction steadily crept by, and as the appointed time approached, interest began to seriously grow. But there was also consternation ... fear and feelings of sheer superstitious dread. Comets were still seen by many as ill omens. There still remained the old comet tradition, that of seeing them as supernatural messengers of ill tidings. On that occasion when the Turks had entered Constantinople in 1456, not only had a great comet appeared in the sky, at the same time, the moon had blacked out in total eclipse! Surely this was *indeed* portentous! A time to be much feared! Western Christendom certainly thought so. It took account, and further dreaded the possibility of a Turkish advance into Europe, and to the Ave Maria they added a prayer: *'Lord save us from the devil, the Turk, and the comet.'* Such irrational fears of the unknown still remained with a good many.

But the new scientific seekers were fired with a different logic. It was realised that, if the theory was correct, then the planets of Saturn and Jupiter would exert their own gravitational pulls at each passing of the comet, causing small deviations of both trajectory and time of the next visit. Mathematicians were at work producing updates on the exact timing for the next visit, making allowance for the small deviations. The work of Alexis Clairaut, Madame Lapante and Joseph Lalande gave the revised timing of April 1759 plus or minus one month, to reach perihelion (nearest approach to the sun).

Following the visitation observed by Newton, Halley, and by many others who cared to be out at night and look up at the night sky; the great comet had gone off on its lengthy path. It passed well beyond sight of Earth; beyond the orbits of Mars, Jupiter, Saturn, Uranus; even Neptune and Pluto. It continued beyond the domain of the planets, and far into the unimaginable void of space. Judged by our own everyday standards, the great comet would be travelling at no small pace. Even so, it would take the necessary years to traverse the domain of the planets, and then beyond. But what of pace far out beyond those planets? By what reference should one measure passage? The only reference here is the myriad of bright specks, so far distant that they seem quite still, and no warmth reaches out from their brightness. This is a cold, lonely, trackless, almost timeless place. Not quite timeless.

There is a time for comets when the outward journey ends. A time for hesitation and turning to face the distant host sun once more that distant larger brightness that forever exerts its steady pull. This place, the mathematicians call 'aphelion', a turning point ... the very edge of the ellipse. A time for slowing down and turning back, slowly and so very steadily at first but with increasing pace, slowly but gathering way, under the steady pull of the larger brightness. It is still brittle ice-cold, but in just a few decades the warmth of the host sun should again be felt. The outermost icy layers will respond to the solar caress; will run ... run free ... free of the frozen crystal shackles, to release and to spread a translucent shawl across the heavens; a new blaze to illumine the night skies of Earth.

Such had been the prediction, and as the cycle neared completion, there were those on Earth who enjoyed hesitant expectation, as night after night, they scanned the heavens. Many eyes sought the minute speck. It might just appear. It would appear if the prediction was correct, but it still could just be a matter of fancy. How certain can these scientists and mathematicians be? The calculations may be quite wrong. Not every hypothesis matures to a theory. Not every theory acquires proof. But theories are for testing, and in so doing, one must always hold on to a certain openness of mind. Many kept the vigil through the closing months of the old year, except perhaps, for the Christmas holiday. That time was after all, a time that the Emperor Justinian had set aside for celebration.

Dresden was the capital township of that part of Germany known as Saxony, with its elegant Renaissance-style Royal palace and its splendid Japanese palace. It was at this time, an acclaimed centre of art treasures. Augustus III had purchased the unique Modena Gallery of 2,400 paintings by Italian and Flemish masters. Dresden flourished ... flourished despite Saxony being caught up in the Seven Years War that beset Europe. Thankfully, the splendour of the palaces survived and within, their fine art collections survived. Johann Palitzsch also survived. He lived a country life, and farmed just outside the town. As a farmer, he is not especially remembered, but he himself would remember that some harvests were good, while others were not so good; but *this* year's harvest would never be forgotten ... that extra golden sheaf, so late in the year! Farming was not his only pursuit. There was his hobby. As an astronomer, he ranked as an amateur. Nevertheless, as an amateur, he was keen. After all, not every astronomer, amateur *or* professional, would be viewing the night sky at Christmas, and so it transpired that he, Johann Palitzsch, on Christmas day, was the *first* to see the tiny speck of light that marked the return of the comet.

Halley's comet continued its approach and passed nearest the sun on 12 March 1759, just within the limits set by the mathematicians. The great comet had returned, this time, and for the first time, a recognised traveller of the heavens and friend of Earth. It was a part of the creation and obeyed natural laws of motion, as do the planets. No more mystery ... no more doom portents. Halley's prediction had been correct, and the comet now carries his name.

Kepler had determined from Brahé's observations that the paths of the planets are ellipses. Newton had shown how these ellipses are a consequence of the law of gravitation. Halley's predicted comet return, had now come as a clear demonstration of the truth, of these fundamental principles.

Halley's comet had in fact long before this, been a friend of Earth and had already borne witness to many events of great significance to the world. As long ago as 239 BC, it had visited and observed the beginnings of a massive construction that was to be the Great Wall of China. Appropriately, it was the astronomers of China, who at this time observed the comet and made a *first* official written record of its passage. In the American continent, the Mayan peoples had just developed a base-20 number system incorporating a zero, and this would remain the most sophisticated counting system for many years. In India, the Emperor Asoka had united most of that sub-continent, which he was now converting to the Buddhist teaching. He would be styled by the later historians as *the Buddhist Constantine.* These were the happenings observed by the comet at this passage.

Passing again in 162 BC, it witnessed paved streets in Rome! Following an early persecution of the Jews and desecration of the Temple in Jerusalem, Judas Maccabaeus had retaken Jerusalem, leading his Jewish patriots against greatly superior numbers. The temple was purified and Chanuka ... the Feast of Reconsecration followed. And *Chinese* astronomers had observed sunspots (long before Galileo was to re-discover them for the West!)

Passing again in 86 BC, a Greek astronomer Sosigenes, was living at this time. He would later be a huge influence on future generations. His advice to Julius Cæsar would result in the adoption of the Julian calendar with its 365¼-day year. [This calendar, in effect, continues today, apart from minor adjustments in the correction mechanism for the fractional day, introduced in by Pope Gregory XIII.] The Chinese had been making paper for several decades; used for packaging and clothing at first, but the idea of *writing* on it would come in due course.

In 11 BC, the comet heralded the Christian era, which would be a major influence. At each passage, it witnessed historic happenings and changes upon the Earth. A progress was in motion.

66 AD - Hero of Alexandria nearly invents a steam engine. He has made a toy that rotates by the power of steam jets, (like a spinning, boiling kettle). From the start of the century, thanks to Ko Yu, the Chinese have the wheelbarrow.

141 - Ptolemy writes a text on astronomy that will remain in use as a reference through the Middle Ages. Chinese agriculture is now using a grain winnower *and* a multiple-tube seed drill! Tsai Lun has made a paper that is now being used for writing.

218 - More Chinese advances. Their mathematicians now use powers of 10 to express high numbers, and Liu Hui has calculated 3.14159 as the value of 'pi'. [Pi was of course, also *known* by much more ancient cultures and its ratio used in, for example, the design of the Great Pyramid of Egypt.] Porcelain will certainly make a lasting impact, and the 'whippletree' will enable two oxen to pull together and share a single load.

295 - Pappus of Alexandria, a mathematician and author, describes a number of useful technological devices ... the lever, the pulley, the cogwheel, the screw and the wedge.

374 - Books are beginning to replace scrolls for keeping the precious knowledge. At last, born in Alexandria, daughter to Theon, one who will become recognised as a *woman-philosopher*! Hypatia! She will succeed her father in the chair of philosophy at Alexandria. How they will flock to the lectures! Her teaching inspiring such a love of beauty, goodness and truth, and her students coming from all over the East. She will enjoy such fame! [But her end was to come tragically. Cyril, Bishop of Alexandria, saw Hypatia as a 'Satanic enchantress' and generated a powerful hatred of her teaching. He influenced others and a party of monks abducted her. Hypatia

was taken to the Cæsarian Church, stripped, murdered, her body torn apart, taken to a place called Cinaron, and burned! But the philosopher's teaching would live on. Others would be inspired by that same love of beauty. And she herself had been inspired by Plato, and taught his philosophy. The wonderful library of Alexandria fared no better and had already been ransacked by a mob led by Bishop Theophilis].

451 - Alchemy, precursor of chemistry, began its course at this time, a curious hunt for the elixir and philosopher's stone, an irrational quest evoking a material greed. Then, as the comet moved away from Earth's orbit, refugees who fled from Attila's Huns were constructing Venice. *This* would be a charming place! And the Chinese have use of the umbrella!

530 - The building of the monastery at Monte Cassino, founded by St. Benedict, is now under way; while the two renowned centres of learning in Athens, the Academy and the Lyceum, started by Plato and Aristotle, have been closed by the Emperor Justinian. Thus bringing to an end nearly 1,000 years of Greek philosophical tradition, an act *designed* to be against paganism! But happily, philosophy lives on and our perceptions of truth and progress are ever changing. It was Plato himself who said: *'And they see only the shadows which the fire throws on the opposite wall ... to them the truth will be nothing but the shadows of the images.'*

607 - It is the first birthday of Fatima, daughter of Mohammed. The Chinese can print pages from wood blocks. Persians develop the first windmill. China now has fire-lighting matches, toilet paper, and a sailing wheelbarrow!

684 - Glass windows, have for the last ten years been appearing in English churches!

760 - It is the year of foundation of the Turkish Empire, by a Tartar people. Abu Musa Jabir ibn Hayyan, the Arabic alchemist has the knowledge to prepare aluminium chloride, nitric acid and acetic acid. All is not lost in the alchemist's pursuit, as some *chemical* knowledge emerges from it. A newspaper has been in circulation in the Chinese capital these last twelve years!

837 - Wessex wars with the Danes. Europe has the crank handle for turning wheels, 1,000 years after Chinese first use! The Chinese have paper bank drafts (Precursor of paper money).

912 - The largest Benedictine abbey of Europe has been established at Cluny. Arab alchemists have learned to prepare alcohol by distillation. Chen Yin has invented gunpowder for the Chinese, and has warned that great care should be taken in its preparation, or you will have no house!

989 - The Chinese have invented the canal lock. Vikings have established a colony on Greenland.

1066 - A battle is in progress near Hastings. The Norman Conquest of England will have considerable influence. William I will be crowned on the Christmas day of this year. The comet as seen during this visit, will be embroidered as a part of the Bayeux tapestry.

1145 - The Chinese inventions continue! Now they have the spinning wheel, movable type face, are burning coal as fuel, and Tseng Kung-Liang has just published recipes for three different gunpowders! Their astronomers observe the Crab supernova! (It will continue to be seen as the Crab nebula by future generations).

1222 - A decorative window in Chartres Cathedral, indicates that the West now also has the wheelbarrow! Padua University is founded, where Galileo will later teach. In warfare, the Chinese are using shrapnel bombs.

1301 - The goose feather quill has now been in use for writing for half a century. Eyeglasses are being used to aid vision. The glass mirror is in use in milady's boudoir. In London, coin clipping is an offence; for which Christians have been fined, while Jews have been hanged! In their warfare, the Chinese now use the cannon, and for these last ten years in China, the Ming dynasty has replaced the earlier Mongol.

1378 - Troubled times. The growing sea trade has exacted its price. The Italian ships that brought to Europe, rats with fleas carrying the Black Plague have transported disaster. Europe is severely struck down, and in just half a century, has lost half her population. This disaster has brought the first quarantine station, set up in Dubrovnik, Yugoslavia. The steel crossbow is a new weapon. Following the death of Pope Gregory XI, the Great Schism of the Church is created in this very year. The problem will last almost 40 years, during which period there will be two Popes.

1456 - It is now a quarter of a century since Joan of Arc was burned at the stake. She was a part of those troubled times. This is that year of cometary fear and panic, when the moon was seen fully eclipsed as viewed from Constantinople. The Turks in that city convert the church of St. Sophia to a mosque.

1531 - Signs of an awakening Europe. Maps are being published for the first time with the new continent named: 'America'. Ferdinand Magellan has sailed around the world. Leonardo da Vinci has designed various devices including roller bearings, flying machines, a wheel-lock musket (first gun in the West) and a pendulum clock. Copernicus has written his sun-at-the-centre theory of the solar system, but has not yet published.

Certain species are on the move: turkeys introduced to Europe from America, maize introduced to Spain from the Caribbean and oranges have arrived in Portugal from South China. But this year ... this very year of the comet, there is further division in the Church, as Henry VIII forces the English clergy to recognise himself as Supreme Head of the Church of England.

1607 - The pattern of life has changed. The West has *come alive* in respect of the arts, sciences, communication, commerce and expansion. As regards interesting developments, the honours, for the past millennia have gone very much to the East. Now, the West has become a shining jewel of creative activities. In this very year of the comet, Jamestown, Virginia is established. This is the first English settlement on the American mainland. The American Colonies will eventually be making their significant contribution to this new age ... this new age that will bring many discoveries and inventions.

1682 - And now so much is happening. There is developing some understanding of the material aspect of the world in which we humans find ourselves; also some understanding of the heavens. In this very year of the comet, Peter the Great is made Czar of Russia, at present, with his sister Sophia as Regent. Soon now, he will come of age and will be able to devote great energies to political change that will bring Russia into the cultural arena of the West. He himself will travel to Europe and learn the ways of the West. He will work in the Amsterdam shipyards and learn about ships. Russia is destined to have a navy and merchant fleet, and to trade with the West, and to share the ways of the West. Peter Alexievitch is about to guide his people in all this.

Appropriately, this was the time that the procedure for making 'Champagne' emerged. It was Dom Pierre Pérignon, who kept the cellars of the Abbey of Hautvillers. He had noticed, as had many others, that the wine sometimes blew the corks. Pérignon found, quite simply, that a net of twine and a wax cover held the cork and prevented this, albeit a bottle would occasionally burst. On balance, the idea saved wine, but what was much more important, the life and lightness of the resulting wine found the instant royal approval of King Louis XV; and so it was that *Champagne* was born. Much later, it was the Dom Pérignon champagne that was to be one favoured tipple of the fictitious 'James Bond'.

The tree of knowledge of the *material* world grows faster than ever before. The growth now spreads. New buds appear, to form new branches in the arts and in the sciences. Many more names now appear in the records that have made their contributions. Just five more passes of the great comet should be time enough for the tree of material knowledge, as propagated by mankind, to reach a fully fledged maturity. A full maturity of knowledge is a *logical* goal. After all, was it not Lucretius in the 1st century BC who said: '... *things must be brought to light one after the other and in due order in the different arts, until these have reached their highest point of development...?*'

Chapter XVIII

This was the Time

The discoveries of the 17th century were so dramatic and numerous, that one can say of materialism, that quite unequivocally, this was its beginning. This was indeed *the time* of the initial burst of growth of Western materialism.

Like Halley's comet, Newton's great work: the 'Principia', has stood the test of time, being quoted by scientists across the centuries. His third law: *'To every action there is always opposed an equal reaction'* ... is as appropriate to rocketry in the present world, as to the considerations of Newton's day. In optics, he had followed the earlier work of Descartes, then went on to discover the spectrum colours and how they re-combine to give the white light of nature. He then attempted to describe its transmission in the *aethereal medium,* but it was his contemporary, Christiaan Huygens, a Dutch physicist, who was to originate the wave theory of light. (Francesco Grimaldi had described the details of *light interference* and *diffraction*, but had not connected these with wave propagation).

Christiaan Huygens was the son of Constantijn Huygens who earlier, wrote that timely letter to the Royal Society. Descartes knew the young man and predicted future greatness for him. In fact, his greatness was only fully realised *well* into the future. It was to be 150 years before his wave theory of light was fully accepted and its value properly recognised! Although Dutch, he wrote his Treatise on Light in French. It was written during 15 years as the first foreign resident of the new Academie des Sciences in Paris. As did Cassini, he took up the post at the invitation of Colbert. Despite being ahead of his time in wave theory, Huygens was nevertheless still honoured as a scientist of international repute within his own time. He had a practical bent for inventing things that were needed. He and his brother found a better way to grind lenses that overcame spherical and chromatic aberrations. He built improved telescopes and made further discoveries in the heavens. This lead to a more detailed description of Saturn's rings, and to the discovery of Saturn's satellite: Titan. Huygens devised a micrometer for accurately measuring the small angles between observations, and there was his accurate pendulum clock. These things all helped to build a good reputation as a leading scientist of this remarkable period.

But as to 'light'; while its precise nature was still being argued by those few with that particular focus, a Danish astronomer was now able to measure its speed of travel. It is curious that a country that, at the time, frowned somewhat upon astronomy as a pursuit should have produced such good astronomers! Ole Römer studied the moons of the planet Jupiter. Like the Earth's moon, they rotate with uniform motion around the planet; and he attempted to draw up a timetable for their passage. But an odd factor emerged. When Jupiter was further away from Earth, *the moons got behind schedule*, and in the season when Jupiter came nearer to Earth, *its moons were ahead of schedule*! He reasoned that light must have a finite velocity, and the differences in moon-rotation times, must result from the extra distance that light has to travel in its passage from Jupiter to Earth. An astute deduction! ... And the value he obtained was quite close to that calculated from today's much more refined data.

The West still struggled for better data in medical science. The origin of disease was not understood. In London however, positive moves were being made. At Gresham College, a dissecting school was set up. It was supplied with corpses from Tyburn Gallows. It was William Harvey who worked out in detail, the circulatory nature of the blood, and the book he published was eventually after a dubious start, well acclaimed throughout Europe. But for a time at least, his practice diminished, he received published criticism from physicians, and uninformed people regarded him as simply 'crack-brained'. The truth sometimes requires a little time to elapse before it can be appreciated. His book, once accepted, led to a conception of the important parts played by diet and exercise in *preventing* disease. (And, of course, it remains a valid argument today, that prevention is so much more satisfactory than cure). Richard Lower demonstrated blood transfusion. He was an early advocate of animal testing, and used dogs for his experiments.

Harvey was the seventh son of a Kentish yeoman. He studied at Padua while Galileo was there, then settled in London, marrying the daughter of Dr. Lancelot Browne, physician to Queen Elizabeth. His patients also included the notaries: Francis Bacon, King James I and Charles I. He had a bold directness. In his teaching he much preferred to instruct anatomy: *'not from books, but from dissections, not from the positions of philosophers but from the fabric of nature.'* Yet in his other great work on the generation of animals, he makes quite frequent reference to Aristotle's work. But then, it was a massive bridge that was being constructed between the Greeks of old and this century of new Western thinking, and Aristotle was so deserving of some recognition. In this time, as in any other, the services of physicians cost money and not all were blessed with coinage. It was largely for the benefit of the poor, that Nicholas Culpepper wrote his great 'Herbal'. This work provided a useful guidance for the self-cure of those in need, by means of the wayside herbs.

One physician of particular note was William Gilbert. Shortly after receiving his degree at Cambridge, he travelled extensively in Europe and his interests clearly extended well beyond his chosen profession. Gilbert was very much an experimental philosopher, finally settling in London where he was a good physician, and appointed as such to Queen Elizabeth. That was in the same year as the publication of his remarkable book on magnetism: 'De Magnete', 1600, at the very start of the new century. The book was hailed as the first important English work in physical science, and it used the word 'electricity'! ... *'We sometimes employ words new and unheard of, not (as alchemists are wont to do) in order to veil things ... but in order that hidden things with no name and up to this time unnoticed may be plainly and fully published.'* Gilbert was the first to use the term 'electric force', and it was his conjecture that electricity and magnetism relate. (It would be another 200 years before that matter became finally proved!)

Gilbert rose to be President of the College of Physicians and served on the committee that produced the Pharmacopoeia Londinensis, and the monthly meetings that he held were a precursor to the Royal Society. He was thus at the start of a number of worthy things. Galileo described him as *'great to a degree that is enviable'*. His greatness lives on, sadly not his library or his instruments. These material things were lost in London's fire.

It was Christopher Wren who brought to architecture the experimental spirit, and it was he who was Surveyor of Works and concerned with so much of the rebuilding, *after* the fire. In the early decades, it had been Inigo Jones who had conferred architectural beauty upon London. The Banqueting House at Whitehall was his masterpiece. Now, it was Wren. His complete plan for the rebuilding was not accepted, but he was nevertheless able to contribute in a fine and fitting way. He designed 52 new churches, of which St. Paul's remains his masterpiece, fulfilled royal commissions in respect of three palaces, and built two famous hospitals at Chelsea and Greenwich, and the Naval College also at Greenwich. Wren was an artist in architecture and very much a part of the grand scheme of these inspirational times.

Robert Hooke is not best remembered for architecture, but in this Restoration period, he designed Ramsbury Manor, an elegant Wiltshire country house. In 1666, he was Surveyor for the city of London, a remunerative appointment at this time, and he built Bedlam, as a physician's college. Hooke is much better known as Curator of Experiments and Secretary of the Royal Society. He displayed an outstanding inventive genius and is described by some as the greatest man of philosophical mechanics. Today's student of mechanics will certainly know of Hooke's law of elasticity. The universal joint was his invention. The red spot of Jupiter was his discovery, and furthermore, he was a wonderful participator in so many of the acclaimed advancements of the period.

Richard Boyle studied at Cambridge and the Middle Temple; then went off to Ireland with just a few pounds in his pocket to make a fortune. He was energetic and fared well, raised a large family bought estates, and became the Earl of Cork. Robert Boyle was the seventh son and fourteenth child of that family. It was Robert who became a founder member of the Royal Society and who attended some of the early monthly meetings. He had a sparkling mind and a way with words, whether he was speaking on scientific or theological matters.

Robert Boyle also made advances in chemistry. He improved the air pump, a recent invention of Otto von Geurick, Burgomaster of Magdeburg; and found the relationship between gas-volume and pressure, known to today's students of chemistry as 'Boyle's law'. Boyle researched many topics, including combustion, acids, bases and the nature of elements. In fact, he established 'chemistry' as a science, shaking it free of the clouding and confusing influence of that earlier tradition of alchemy. His way with words perhaps inspired others. In any event, some peers aptly described him as: *'father of chemistry and son of the Earl of Cork.'* He no doubt enjoyed that title, but was not one to seek self-aggrandisement. In fact it is on record that he chose to decline both presidency of the Society and a knighthood.

In mathematics, it was a Scot, John Napier, Laird of Merchiston, who, after 20 years of application, produced the device of logarithms, complete with tables and rules for their use. Henry Briggs, a Yorkshire man, later introduced a variation: base-10 tables, which became more widely used. It was William Oughtred who invented the slide rule. This most valuable tool would furnish laboratory and workplace for the next 330 years. (In fact, the world's technical data would be calculated using logarithms and slide rule, until the invention of the electronic calculator in the mid-20th century).

The additions to algebra, geometry and trigonometry during the 17th century have been many, and no doubt interesting if only one can understand them. But as to new departures and practical ideas of undying merit that emerged; these must include:

(1) The development of a *calculating machine* by Leibniz, with capability to multiply and divide, with construction of working models.

(2) The expression of the idea of *binary arithmetic* in a letter by Leibniz to Joachim Bouvet.

(3) The first book of *statistics* by John Graunt and William Petty. It includes life expectancy for London population.

(4) Jerome Cardan wrote a book on games of chance; and the firm of *Lloyds of London* was established; offering insurance calculated on expectation, and itself a living illustration of *probability* theory working in practice.

(5) As to *decimalisation*, it was Franciscus Vieta of Pitou, France who argued for decimal representation of numbers a little before the start of the century. Then the Flemish mathematician Simon Stevin gave an account of the use of decimal fractions.

These ideas would certainly remain an influence on our lives for a great many generations, the latter idea, rearing its head from time to time and always resulting in a partial alignment to that system, midst irritating muddle until good sense once again prevails. Hours and days are born of the universe and will *never* be sorted into batches of ten, albeit the years are sorted into centuries that have no meaning in relation to the heavens. And it would be unthinkable if those in Brussels today were to metricate the birth weights of British babies. To a young mother, every Avoirdupois ounce counts, whilst 0.02835 Kg is a meaningless fragment that the brain prefers not to encompass.

The metric system of measurement required a central standard of length. Gabriel Mouton, a vicar of Lyons, proposed the 'metre' unit, in the year 1670. A planetary standard for the metre was later agreed, as one ten-millionth of Earth's quarter-circumference. In order to calculate this, a measurement of the Earth's meridian was required. Giovanni Cassini, the same, who had watched a comet with Halley from the Paris observatory, made this.

In the field of medicine, there were those who developed important insights into diagnosis of illness and its treatment. Thomas Sydenham (the English Hippocrates) introduced proper descriptions for measles and scarlet fever. He very reasonably prescribed opium for pain relief, quinine for control of malaria and iron for anaemia. Thomas Willis related sugar-in-urine to diabetes. He also gave, at this time, an accurate account of the effect on the brain of the later stages of syphilis. The effect on the world of one suffering from such *megalomania* could be so catastrophic!

But, what of more down to earth things? What of manufacturing industry? This too was developing as learning and innovation progressed. There were now paper mills and weaving mills. Cotton goods were being made and the first calico printing was produced. Stockings were now an item of manufacture. A glass industry was making the first 'plate glass'. This was the time of the first pencil factory and the first fountain pen. The Cheddar cheese process began in the same year as London's fire. All these things, of course, developed together with the developing science, commerce and infrastructures.

This was the time when the banking houses of the West were established: the Bank of England, the Giro-bank of Hamburg. Bank notes and cheques came into use. Trading companies were formed: the Dutch East India Company, Hudson's Bay Company and the Merchant Adventurers for the export of cloth. The idea of finance by shares was created.

This was the time for the creation of a Colonial Office, the British Museum and London's Covent Garden Market. Following the new product and process developments, patent law was introduced, and the penny post (the idea of Robert Murray), parcel post, letter boxes, newspapers, newspaper advertisements, property insurance, street lights, fire engines and the first real trade fair at Leiden in Holland.

Major new book publications included the King James Bible (1611), Old Moore's Almanack and Samuel Pepy's Diary. The Chinese remained far in advance of the West in respect of books on plant knowledge and plant-derived medicines. Li Shi-Chen's great work: Ben-zao gang-mu published in the final decade of the previous century, describes in excess of 1,000 plants, and gives 8,000 medicinal uses for plant- and animal-derived materials. But now, there were also those in the West who saw the need for plant knowledge and classification. Nehemiah Grew published his 'The Anatomy of Plants' (1682) and John Ray's 'Historia Plantarum' followed. This was to lead to the wider systematic classification by Linnaeus that is essentially the system of classification used today.

Imported plants and plant-derived materials were having an enormous impact upon Europe; not least the potato (introduced into Germany 1621).

Cocoa and chocolate arrived from the Caribbean, and chrysanthemums from Japan. But it was the tea of China and coffee of Arabia that had such a trade and social impact. Chocolate also became a beverage. The first coffee-house in Europe was opened in Constantinople (1551). Then coffee-houses spread to Western Europe during the course of the following century.

'Edwards' was a successful London merchant. He arrived back in London with coffee procured from Smyrna on the West Coast of Asia Minor. It was a pleasant and interesting beverage, and his Greek servant Pasquet could prepare the most excellent cup. The difficulty was that he, Edwards, had so many friends; and when they got to hear of the new most superb beverage that he had obtained from the East, they all of them came round to see him; and they kept on coming; more and more of them! They multiplied! He became engulfed by his chatty friends with their ... his ... cups of coffee, and he lost his freedom and peace of mind; and besides he had a business to run. But he was an astute businessman, so like the businessman that he was, he had a good idea. In order to get out of the difficulty, he set up London's first coffee-house at Newman's Court, Cornhill; and had Pasquet run it. A brilliant stratagem! That was in the year 1652. The first coffee-houses in France followed in Marseille (1671) and Paris (1672), and of course, more coffee-houses appeared in London in the 1650s; not least Garraway's.

The earliest reference to tea in the English records is in a letter by Mr. Wickham of the East India Company (1615). It was the East India Company that initially had a monopoly on the tea trade. It was slow to become popular, partly on account of its initial extremely high price and of the high tax levied upon it. It therefore at first, only became known to the most wealthy. But although the price of the dry leaf was prohibitive, the price per cup of the prepared beverage would be more acceptable. Even so, a tax of 8p per gallon was to be levied upon the prepared ready-to-drink beverage!

It was the successful London merchant, Thomas Garway who, after receiving an extra large consignment of tea, set up the first tea-dispensing house (1657). He sold his beverage from 'Garraway's Coffee House'. Other 'tea-shops' then followed. It was it seems, trade monopoly, high price of the leaf, and high taxation that helped to motivate the spread of tea-shops in this period. Quite simply, people could afford a cup, but they could not afford to purchase the dry leaf. These trading conditions would not substantially alter until 1833 when the East India Company's Charter would expire. The trade monopoly would then end and the excessive tax on the product would be reduced in stages to a much more realistic level. The irksome bother of taxation as is familiar today, seems to very much have its roots at this point in time. There were other commodity taxes, as well as income tax and property tax, all introduced during the course of the 17th century.

This was the time of many adventures and explorations. It was Henry Hudson who first navigated into the inland-sea now named Hudson's Bay. William Baffin went more northerly; in fact, his journeys took him within 800 miles of the North Pole. No explorer would get closer until the advent of the 19th century! The New England colonies were being established in North America. The colonists were a strange mixture including militia, fortune hunters, convicts and those fleeing orthodox religion. William Penn founded the Quaker State of Pennsylvania. The Puritan group of 'Pilgrim Fathers' sailed from Plymouth in 1620, to Plymouth Bay, New England. But the first permanent British colony was founded at Jamestown (1607) and became the State of Virginia.

In the early days, it was Captain John Smith who was the able leader of the small fragile colony. He had much with which to contend. There were problems of idleness, ignorance and quarrels. He was a brave soldier of fortune, who realised the need for hard work and for making friends with the native Indians, and where they were concerned, he got into difficulties, was captured by the chief Powhatan, and would have been killed at his command. It was the chief's 12-year old daughter who rushed forward and entreated her father to be merciful. He spared the captain. The young girl's name was Pocahontas.

There followed a period of comings and goings; Pocahontas and her associates would visit the captain at Jamestown, and of course was shown great respect and welcomed. In the year 1609, she gave warning of a plot to kill him. Various intrigues followed, during which time, Smith returned to England. Pocahontas was led to believe that he was now dead, and in 1613 she married John Rolfe. One aspect of the marriage was the alliance: the alliance between the white man and the powerful Indian Chief. Powhatan was instrumental in cementing an advantageous period of peace for the colony. But one suspects Pocahontas' heart really remained with Captain Smith.

It was three years later when she travelled to England with her husband, and was presented at court, as was befitting for a respected princess. But now she again met Captain John Smith. It was clearly a shock to find that he still lived, and contrary to her expectation. It was a blow. Her life's path had been fouled by the prior false information. She hid her face away for several hours, unable to look upon the world that had now twisted and turned upon her fortune. Those hours passed, but the zest for life was somehow lost and did not return. Another four years and she had made the decision to return to her native Virginia. But she never embarked the vessel on which she was to return. Unhappily, she died at Gravesend, at the tender age of 22. But she and John Rolfe had one son.

Following uncertain beginnings, Virginia to the south, colonised under the auspices of a group of London merchants, and New England to the north, settled by the Mayflower pilgrims; became foundation states of what later became the *United States of America.* The settlers of those states, all had something in common. They all took with them the fabric of 17th century England: the customs and ideas, the language and songs, the farming methods and the laws. The new colonies were cloned from that stirring, awakening culture across the Atlantic.

Virginia would play a lead role in the new transatlantic developments. The founding London merchants secured a main cash crop from the colony ... *tobacco.* The tobacco traded well, became a popular commodity and a handsome tax was levied upon it. Although tobacco was a land-spoiling crop, there was no shortage of land; and plots could be moved and moved again as necessary. Once the colony had stabilised, there was money to be had for all, but as time progressed the system became corrupted and so problems arose. The despicable slave trade got under way, with men, women and children being brutally abducted from Africa and forced to work the plantations. This was of course, to become problematical. It was the nature of the taxes on the imports *to* the colony that became another major problem, especially the tax on tea. This would later lead to a breaking away of those carefully cloned American colonies, and result in their becoming self-governing.

[The war between Britain and her own American colonies over tax levies was a phoney war; perhaps the first phoney war. The majority of people in Britain did not want it and neither did many in the colonies. It was a war of attempted subjugation by a small number of powerful politicians at Westminster. If Edmund Burke had had his way, there would have been no war. His words still echo down the corridors of time regarding the results of treating colonists well: '*... no force under heaven would be of power to tear them from their allegiance.*' But they were *not* treated well or with respect, and war resulted. Virginia produced George Washington, who initially became Commander-in-Chief of the colonists' volunteer army, and then first President of the United States. Later still, Virginia was to produce another statesman: John Randolph, a peacemaker. He spoke out against the Anglo-American war of 1812, played a lead role in ending the slave trade, and himself saw to the freeing of 318 slaves and their maintenance in a 'free state'. He was descended of a line from the beginning of the colony; it is thought from Pocahontas].

This then was the time, when three separate new commodities, each with its heavy socialising aspect, were introduced into Britain and Western Europe. (Tobacco had already been introduced to Europe by the Spanish returning from the Americas, and Walter Raleigh had introduced tobacco to England just before the start of the century; but it had then taken a few years to become popular). Each commodity, with its stimulant and addictive effect, became a popular item as well as a habit. Tea, coffee and tobacco; even if acting in isolation, in the absence of all else, one of these would be sufficient to alter lifestyles almost beyond recognition, and to change the world! But there were three such items! This really was a time of such huge irrevocable and irresistible change.

It has to be said that there was the unsatisfactory side to the century's happenings. There were the wars, often over unimaginably trivial issues; and no reason for a war could possibly be more trivial or utterly stupid than 'the tax on tea'. There was the fearful slave trade, totally lacking in love for humanity. There were extinctions: several species of dodo, although the longer legged Solitaire bird of the genus continued to live through the 18th century; and the wild boar in Britain. Aztec and Mayan peoples were savagely diminished through Spanish conquest.

Religious controversy continued. William Penn wrote *'Sandy Foundation Shaken'*, a work that seriously questioned the doctrine of the Trinity. Penn was a non-conformist, and had been sent down from Oxford for that very reason. His father, Admiral Penn, came to agree with his son's simple Quaker view of religion, saying at his death: *'Keep to the plainness of your way, and you will make an end of the priests to the ends of the earth.'* Now, there existed a royal debt to Admiral Penn of around £20,000. It was this debt that was negotiated for a province in America to be called Pennsylvania. John Aubrey (Brief Lives) wrote at the time: *'... a province in America which his majesty was pleased to name Pennsylvania, the fourth day of March 1681, to which he is now going this next September 1681.'* William Penn travelled to America, and so, in settlement of a debt, the Quaker colony of Pennsylvania was established.

London's air pollution became sufficient to be critically attacked by John Evelyn. A clean air campaign began at this point in time. It was however, on the credit side, that there was so much. We must always be positive and look to the credit side: at the ideas, the inventions and worthwhile new things taking shape in all disciplines.

It was a Dutchman Cornelius Drebbel who successfully tested a manned submarine in the Thames, similar to an earlier design by William Bourne, an English mathematician. Giovanni Branca described the principle of the steam turbine. Denis Papin devised a pressure cooker and then went on to describe the steam piston and the steam engine. It was Thomas Savery who built a steam water pump for use in pumping water from mines, and who took out an early patent on that invention. Richard Towneley was interested in weather records, and invented the first rain gauge. Fine measurement in engineering was assisted by the Vernier measuring scale, conceived by Pierre Vernier, and by the micrometer that was due to William Gascoigne. (And how much more might he have done, but for his untimely death in the Civil War? William Gascoigne was struck down, while in his mid-twenties, at the battle of Marston Moor, near York).

Meanwhile, the French were making the preliminary moves as regards the bicycle. Jean Théson made a wooden quadricycle, which was really rather too heavy to propel by shoving with the feet. Then Sivrac reduced it to two wheels, but another century would pass before further development would make the machine take on more useful form.

Attendant to so much innovation, many new words were appearing in the language. Some have since become much used key words, basic to the fabric of mind; they include: *electricity, magnetism, conductor, insulator, gas, banks and shares.* As words, 'electricity' and 'magnetism' hold what one might even describe as an exaggerated place in the mind fabric, on account of the continued inability to understand the *cause* that underlies the *effects* which these terms represent. Until causal factors become recognised, such terms will be blanket expressions that simply embrace all aspects.

The word 'vacuum', had on the other hand, become quite well understood. It is a word simple to define, and it is easy to visualise empty space. But technically, the vacuum presented considerable difficulty in its generation and study. It had been Aristotle's belief that such a condition could never exist in the real world. The old attitude was that Nature simply abhors the vacuum and will have none of it. But now, a group of scientists all contributed to its study and its understanding. They were Blaise Pascal,

Evangelista Torricelli and Vivenzo Viviani. It was Pascal who concluded: *'the vacuum is not impossible in nature and she does not shun it with so great a horror as many imagine.'* During the course of his work, Pascal also invented a syringe for use with fluids. Torricelli devised the first barometer with its contained partial vacuum. It was Edme Mariotte who named it and so added a further new word to the 17th century vocabulary. Otto von Guericke was first to use the barometer to forecast weather. While the more serious scientific study was under way, he had been using his air pump to produce good vacuums in sealed devices, and then tried pulling them apart. He enthusiastically demonstrated to admiring crowds, that 50 strong men or *teams of horses* were unable to pull apart his vacuums. His pumped-out vacuums seem to have been *that* good, and *that* entertaining as well! He also demonstrated that a heavy piece of lead and a feather fall at the same speed in a vacuum, where they are free of any air friction.

It was John Mayo, a Cornish physician, who gave a good description of the chemical process of oxidation. [And it would be another 100 years before Antoine Lavoisier would be able to prove the matter by experiment]. One who contributed much to chemistry in a practical and preparative way, in this continuing Century of Genius, was the German chemist Johann Glauber. He studied European mineral waters and health spas, and he found that he could isolate sodium sulphate from their waters by evaporation. Like the earlier alchemist Geber of the 8th century, he believed in the existence of the 'philosopher's stone' and the 'elixir of life' ... that universal balm ... that cure-all that would bestow youth and ongoing vitality. When he succeeded in isolating sodium sulphate from the invigorating spa waters, he had reason to believe that he had at last found the elixir! But of course, it turned out instead to be just a good laxative and purgative. Nevertheless, his discovery when administered, brought relief to a number of people, and it was a sound positive step in preparative chemistry. Sodium sulphate is still sometimes called *Glauber's salt.*

Glauber went on to prepare potassium nitrate, which he declared to be 'a principle chemical of life', and stated that it should be used as a fertiliser. A document left at his death describes how Germany's agriculture could be improved, by using manufactured potassium nitrate, applied to the land. In that, he was correct. Crop yield was indeed increased by that procedure. He was thus the originator of the principle and policy of synthetic chemical fertiliser usage.

This then, was the time that would prompt changes in agriculture, so that even the land itself would change. In many locations, canals were being cut to extend waterways across that land. [The canal was not a new idea. Egypt had them in the days of Rameses II]. As London's fire burned, Pierre Paul Riquet was in the early stages of cutting the 'Canal du Midi' for a length of 290 Km, connecting rivers, to make a continuous waterway right across France, from the Mediterranean Sea to the Bay of Biscay. An imaginative project! Such canals would usefully extend the trade routes. But on certain highways, there were now delays as travellers were required to stop and pay tax at the road tolls. They were called 'turnpikes', after the spiked barriers being used to bar the way. [Today's motorway tolls are the update of that old 'turnpike' system of revenue collection, and the term turnpike in today's New World is sometimes used to denote a road that has a traffic problem!]

There were also land drainage schemes. The mathematician and surveyor, Jonas Moore, made his name by surveying and draining the Fens of Britain. He constructed banks to follow the same configuration as the old coastline, and was the first to effectively keep the sea out of Norfolk with a grand scheme.

This was the time of so much innovation, in science, technology, food and agriculture, towns and infrastructure. In the days of Lucretius, 'the arts' were seen as more extensive, embracing the true arts and sciences alike. Now, that the province of the arts has been redefined and is thought of as comprising pictorial art, literature, theatre, poetry and music; all expressions from within; perhaps this province is not strictly a part of materialism. Yet, the artist uses colours produced by technology and the musician, his manufactured instruments, while author and poet write of the ideas and happenings of the world about them. All is therefore connected and a part of the whole. The arts have developed just as remarkably during this generative period as has all the rest. The arts then, are a part of the grand pattern and must be seen as such.

The ensign held his standard high with pride. The colours of Amsterdam, the orange, the white and the blue, hung and broke sharply from the darkness of the great arch behind. That darkest dark weighed against the moving, fleeting shadow of the foreground, as the company scurried from the arch into the light, in response to the drummer's rappel. It was the 'call to arms', and in response, arquebusiers, sergeants with halberds and the pikemen came forward. Captain Banning Cocq and his lieutenant were striding to the fore. It was a perfectly natural sortie of the Civic Guard, as was evidenced by the barking dog at the drummer's feet. All was beautified by the balancing and enclosures of light and dark; for this was: *'The Sortie of the Company of Frans Banning Cocq'*, the finest masterpiece of Rembrandt van Rÿn, his captured impression of the living bustling moment, and a window on 17th century Europe.

To Rembrandt, the working of light and dark was something to explore and perfect, and his 'action group portrait' was a departure from the more postured standard portraiture. All great artists have their particular styles of brush and balance of the colour. At this time there were so many. They are names that have been treasured across the centuries of time: Peter Paul Rubens, Michelangelo Merisi da Caravaggio, El Greco, Jan van Goyen, Anthonis van Dyck, Diego Velázquez, Nicolas Poussin, Peter Lely and the first great Dutch artist Frans Hals. It was Jan Vermeer who to his great credit painted a number of single figures in fine detail, including *'a girl in a blue turban'*. There are others too, but those names mentioned here have made such impact that several of them will be known today, even to those of us who have only casual or no interest in the art of masters! Such is their fame!

This was also the time when music and its attendant pursuits enjoyed several new beginnings. At the start of the century, ballet was in its infancy (in Italy and France), opera became established (in Italy), and the Baroque period of quite exuberant music with expressive singing had just begun. Claudio Monteverdi became master of the madrigal, while Jean Baptiste Lully and Alessandro Scarlatti established operatic form complete with overture. Ballet reached a high point of development with dance arrangement by Pierre Beauchamp, music by Lully and words by Molière. In London, the Sadler's Wells company was formed. Baroque style in music advanced through the genius of such names as Claudio Monteverdi, Giacomo Carissimi, Arcangelo Corelli, Heinrich Schütz (who influenced both Bach and Handel), and Henry Purcell, who so excelled at writing music for special occasions.

Antonio Stradivarius is of course remembered for perfecting violin design. He in turn owed much to Nicolò Omati, to whom he was a young apprentice. The violins of Stradivarius remain the best that the world has produced for their tone. It is believed that he made at least 1,116 violins, violas and cellos. Others born into this century, given a little time, would have no small further effect upon the growth of music; those names born into the latter decades including: Dominico Scarlatti, George Frederick Handel, Johann Sebastian Bach and Antonio Vivaldi. What a wealth of the work of the Muse would *they* contrive!

But this was also the time of the *written* word, sometimes inseparable from the music. This was a time of plays that would be staged again and again across the centuries, a time of poetry and song, a time of great literature; also a time of worthy diaries to portray the daily life in elegant style. The immortal diarists of the day were Samuel Pepys, John Evelyn and John Aubrey. They tell us some tales! They tell us of the daily happenings, and of the theatres. The London theatres were having an intermittently difficult time. They were closed on account of fires, including the *great* fire, by the plague; and they were closed for the period of the Commonwealth rule by an imposed Puritan policy.

At a time when the theatres had once again re-opened, following these events, Pepys writes: '*... to the King's House to see the 'Mayden Queen', a new play of Dryden's, mightily commended for the regularity of it, and the strain and wit; and the truth is, there is a comical part done by Nell, which is Florimell, that I never can hope ever to see the like done again by man or woman.'* King Charles II also saw Nell Gwyn in the play and was delighted. Later, with Dryden perhaps at the height of his career, came 'The Conquest of Granada' in which Nell played Almahide. Speaking the prologue from beneath a huge broad-brimmed hat, it seems she had the king laughing, almost into convulsion!

Another style of Dryden combined with the writing of Sir Robert Howard in *The Indian Queen*, a semi-opera, in elegant combination with the music of Purcell, and his ode: *Alexander's Feast*, was likewise set to Purcell.

The century had many playwrights of much merit, and many of their plays continue on stage today. They have withstood the test of time. Some also wrote poetry, or acted, or wrote other works, so that it is sometimes difficult to say which was their best pursuit. The list of well-appreciated playwrights, must certainly include William Wycherley (*The Country Wife*, an early comedy of sexual manners), William Congreve (*Love for Love*) and Thomas Middleton, whose *Game of Chess* had the first long run in theatre, at the Globe. And Molière, a close observer of the details of public behaviour (*The School for Wives*, an acclaimed comedy); also Jean Baptiste Racine, France's leading tragic dramatist, who achieved a long run with *Iphigénie*, an adaptation of a play originally by Euripides, with a typically French addition of a love sequence. Le Grand Corneille was the *creator* of French tragedy. Some would say that, of his 33 dramas, *Cinna* was his best, while others would say *Polyeucte*.

Another who was writing at the start of the century was Ben Jonson. *The Alchemist* is a work of much carefully orchestrated humour. But of course, sharing the stage ... and at times, the Mermaid tavern ... with Ben Jonson in these days, was the greatest playwright ever, in terms of wit, humour, tragedy, and the sheer poetry of it all: William Shakespeare. His output over just a dozen years (1599-1611), include such memorable works as: *Twelfth Night, As You Like It, All's Well that Ends Well, Much Ado About Nothing, The Merry Wives of Windsor, Measure for Measure, Hamlet, Julius Caesar, Othello, Macbeth, King Lear, Timon of Athens, Coriolanus, Antony and Cleopatra, Pericles, Cymbeline, The Winter's Tale and The Tempest.* There are others too of course, equally well known, and mostly from a decade earlier. Many have discoursed upon the genius of the man. But it seems so fitting that, Dryden's words perceive beyond 'the man': *'He was the man who, of all the modern and perhaps ancient poets, had the largest and most comprehensive soul.'*

John Donne was an author of metaphysical poetry. Thomas Traherne wrote *'Centuries of Meditation'*. John Bunyan, Civil War soldier, Puritan minister and twice a prisoner for his religious belief wrote *'The Pilgrim's Progress'*. Jean de La Fontaine wrote *'Fables Choisies, mises en vers'*, a masterpiece of French literature, and John Locke's philosophical works helped to guide a young and developing Western democracy, reasoning: *'right to freedom of conscience, right to property and limitation of sovereignty'*, as the best way forward. John Milton wrote *'Paradise Lost'* and *'Paradise Regained'* and much more.

This was the time that Thomas Hobbes made his stern and pointed pronouncement upon the Papacy, seeing it as clearly as anyone, as the phoenix from those distant troubled Roman times: *'The Papacy is not other than the Ghost of the deceased Roman Empire, sitting crowned upon the grave thereof.'* But it was Thomas Jordan who observed in poetic terms, the brief spell of anti-dogmatic Puritanism that rose up with Cromwell's commonwealth:

They pluck'd communion tables down
And broke our painted glasses;
They threw our altars to the ground
And tumbled down the crosses.
They set up Cromwell and his heir ...
The Lord and Lady Claypole ...
Because they hated Common Prayer,
The organ and the maypole.
Thomas Jordan *How the War Began*

Other notaries born before the close of the century include Voltaire *(Writer and wittiest of all great wits)* and Jonathan Swift *(Gulliver's Travels)*. Daniel Defoe *(who after a period as political activist, as prisoner and as one in the pillory, thankfully turned to creative writing and wrote Robinson Crusoe)*; also Alexander Pope *(classical poet)*, Emanuel Swedenborg *(scientist, theologian and visionary)* and Henry Carey *(dramatist and songwriter)*.

The French writer Cyrano de Bergerac Savinien wrote: *'Journey to the Moon'*, and suggested rocketry as a means of getting there. (Johannes Hevelius had by this time produced the first moon map!) One final and fitting innovation at the close of the period was the first Eddystone lighthouse, constructed by Henry Winstanly (1698-1700), to illumine the new century. It would need two re-builds. Wood and stone are less durable than the written word, the brushwork and the music. *They* may ... the loveliest and the best ... live on. Just how much is there of that *century of genius* still alive in today's world, lurking midst the cobwebs, in the fabric of the mind? Just how many quotes, clichés, 'pearls' or 'joys forever' still form a part of our now?

Shall I compare thee to a Summer's day?
Thou art more lovely and more temperate:
Rough winds do shake the darling buds of May,
And Summer's lease hath all too short a date...
William Shakespeare *Sonnet*

To be, or not to be: that is the question:
Whether 'tis nobler in the mind to suffer
The slings and arrows of outrageous fortune
Or to take arms against a sea of troubles,
And by opposing end them?
William Shakespeare *Hamlet*

Drink to me only with thine eyes,
And I will pledge with mine;
Or leave a kiss but in the cup
And I'll not look for wine. ...
Ben Jonson *To Celia*

I have it here in black and white.
Ben Jonson *Every Man in His Humour*

Let us with a gladsome mind
Praise the Lord for He is kind:
For His mercies aye endure,
Ever faithful, ever sure. ...
John Milton *Psalm CXXXVI adaptation*

... Thousands at his bidding speed
And post o'er Land and Ocean without rest:
They also serve who only stand and waite.
John Milton *On His Blindness*

Faith, Sir, we are here to-day, and gone to-morrow.
Mrs. Aphra Behn *The Lucky Chance*

The end justifies the means.
Hermann Busenbaum *Medulla Theologiae Moralis*

Who would true valour see,
Let him come hither;
One here will constant be,
Come wind, come weather.
There's no discouragement,
Shall make him once relent
His first avow'd intent,
To be a pilgrim. ...
John Bunyan *The Pilgrim's Progress.*
Song of Master Valient-for-Truth

Gather ye rose-buds while ye may,
Old Time is still a-flying:
And this same flower that smiles to-day,
To-morrow will be dying. ...
Robert Herrick *Gather ye Rose-buds*

One should eat to live, and not live to eat.
Moliére *L'Avare*

We live and learn, but not the wiser grow.
John Pomfret *Reason*

Take care of the pence, and the pounds will take care of themselves.
William Lowndes *Letter*

Let all the world in ev'ry corner sing
My God and King.
The heav'ns are not too high,
His praise may thither fly; ...
George Herbert

A desperate disease requires a dangerous remedy.
Guy Fawkes *6 November 1605*

Wherever God erects a house of prayer,
The Devil always builds a chapel there;
And 'twill be found, upon examination,
The latter has the largest congregation.
Daniel Defoe *The True-born Englishman*

And with faint praises one another damn.
William Wycherley *The Plain Dealer*

'Tis better to have loved and lost, than never
to have lost at all.
Samuel Butler *The Way of All Flesh*

Give peace in our time, O Lord.
Prayer Book 1662

It is lawful for Christian men, at the commandment of the Magistrate,
to wear weapons, and serve in the wars.
Prayer Book 1662

I care not two-pence.
Francis Beaumont & John Fletcher *The Coxcom*

A horse! A horse! My kingdom for a horse. - *Richard III*

We have seen better days. - *Timon of Athens*

I must be cruel only to be kind. - *Hamlet*

The wheel is come full circle. - *King Lear*

Once more into the breach dear friends, once more;
Or close the wall up with our English dead! - *Henry V*

There are more things in heaven and earth, Horatio,
Than are dreamt of in your philosophy. - *Hamlet*

William Shakespeare Plays

God save our gracious king!
Long live our noble king!
God save the king!
Henry Carey *God Save the King*

This then, was the time ... of new beginning for the West, a time for verse and song and wise words. So many fragments ... parts of these would be adopted and adapted to form a part of the jargon ... of the fabric of future generations. This was the time for fresh starts in thought-organisation; fresh starts in the sciences, in technology, in the arts, and a time for the continued religious wrangles and revue; also a time of great endeavours ... and of the American Colonies. This was a time of new vigour, of rampant growth of the knowledge. The knowledge ... the fruit of the tree ... *must* have humanity's respect, or there would be disaster. If all went well, the process would run to completion, and humankind would rejoice in a newfound place in the great universe. This was the beginning; and this was the time that would set our culture on a collision course to meet with its self-contrived *destiny*.

And for that, just five more passes of the comet should be time enough ... but what then?

As from the power of sacred lays
The Spheres began to move,
And sung the great Creator's praise
To all the blest above;
So when the last and dreadful Hour
This crumbling pageant shall devour,
The Trumpet shall be heard on high,
The dead shall live, the living die,
And Music shall untune the sky.

John Dryden

Grand Chorus
Song for Saint Cecelia's Day

Chapter XIX

Milestones on a Road to Tomorrow

When Johann Palitzsh saw the speck that was the comet on that Christmas day, it continued its approach to Earth early in the following year. That was 1759, and the time of a rapidly changing world. What had transpired in the marvellous earlier century had laid such foundations! The few requirements that were needed to set into motion an *industrial revolution* were raw materials, a labour force and fuel; also a financial system to fund workshops and factories; and a transport system to connect with markets. These were all now available. It happened in England first; and the population there, had increased again following the plague years. Powered by coal, an inventive spirit and the steam engine, an industrial revolution now gathered momentum. Iron ore was to hand for iron and steel production, and the new colonies provided other raw materials including cotton, and the Lancashire cotton manufacturing industry was now being aided by the *flying shuttle*, and the first of the new cotton velvets was developed.

It was clear to see that, also in this year, scientific advancement continued on its course. Alexis Clairaut calculated quite accurately, the masses of the moon and of the planet Venus. Anders Celsius devised the 100°-temperature scale that was now here to stay. The first blast furnaces had been commissioned and were producing steel. 'Coke' made from the coal, could be used in place of charcoal to produce the high temperatures required of industry. Technological progress continued, aided by Philip Vaughan's invention of the ball bearing; while the idea of *casting*, extended to 'false teeth', that application being due to Philipp Pfaff.

Russia was now fast catching up with Western Europe. Moscow had a university. The United States had its first scientific society: the American Philosophical Society, established in Philadelphia by Benjamin Franklin. In this very year of the comet's return, the Bavarian Academy of Science was also founded. The western world's most respected scientist of the 20th century, who would long be revered, would have membership of this academy.

It was Kaspar Wolff who maintained that *vis essentialis* ... essential force ... is at the heart of all living matter, (and surely without question, it is within the hearts of the poets and the writers). Robert Burns was born in this year; also Voltaire. The admirable, amazing and philosophical Voltaire, after being imprisoned in the Bastille, after being cudgelled at the orders of an offended courtier, and after being exiled from Paris; now, at the age of sixty four, he would complete his splendid work: *Candide.*

> *There is a chain of events in this best of all possible worlds; for if you had not ... been involved in the Inquisition, and had not wandered over America on foot, and had not struck the Baron with your sword, ... you would not be here eating candied fruit and pistachio nuts.*
> Voltaire *Candide.*

When the comet returned in 1835, it was Dumouchel in Rome, who first saw it. Francis II, last to hold the title: 'Holy Roman Emperor', died at this time. In this same year was born Andrew Carnegie, a Scot, who became the industrialist who would do much to consolidate the American steel industry, and who without doubt, was with the *essential force.* He would become a pioneer and a powerful influence in shaping the New World. Carnegie would make a fortune from the industry and then would spread it well. He would endow 2,800 libraries and donate $350,000,000 to a variety of foundations. The wealthy Scot would also be principal benefactor of the Carnegie Hall, New York. (Curiously, this was also the birth year of Hetty Green, who became by repute the richest woman in the world, and a miser).

The United States now had a novelist whose writing was in the new American vernacular. He was Samuel Langhorne Clemens, although he chose not to use that name. Born in this year of the comet, he would return to spirit in the year of the comet's next return.

[In fact, it is on record that he spoke with a fellow writer, A. B. Paine in the year of its next approach, saying: *'I came in with Halley's Comet in 1835. It is coming again next year, and I expect to go out with it. It will be the greatest disappointment of my life if I don't go with Halley's Comet. The Almighty has said, no doubt, 'Now here go those two unaccountable frauds; they came in together, they must go out together."* It lit up the sky on April 20. He departed April 21.] Clemens had worked as pilot on the Mississippi river boats and was well familiar with depth soundings, and the call indicating two fathoms was: *'Mark Twain!'* It understandably followed that that would be his chosen nom-de-plume.

Davy Crocket made his move to Texas, to die at the Alemo just one year later; also the year in which Samuel Colt filed a patent on his new single barrelled revolver. This gun would be widely worn as a sidearm and would certainly leave its mark in the U.S.

In Europe, Hans Christian Andersen was publishing his first batch of tales. There would be more of these to follow. Victor Hugo had just completed *'The Hunchback of Notre Dame'*, which was to become a best seller. The French philosopher Victor Cousin coined the phrase: *'art for art's sake'*. Meanwhile, Charles Darwin was away in the Galapagos Islands observing the different 'Darwin' finches, and reasoning that they had all evolved from a common ancestor on the mainland, from whom they had become long since isolated.

It was now that William Henry Fox Talbot photographed Lacock Abbey in Wiltshire. It is a famous photograph. This was the *first photograph* to be taken in England using a familiar 'negative' process. It was an independent achievement for Talbot. (Others ... Daguerre, Wedgewood and Niepce had, it must be said, also achieved photographs slightly earlier, using their own independent techniques). Discovery is sometimes a *collective* happening, and may well sometimes involve some aspect of the *universal consciousness.* But clearly, in 1835, a well-processed photograph manifested for the first time in England.

Heinrich Caro, after discussing dye synthesis with William Perkin, began to establish dyestuffs as a major industry in Germany. The world would now have: synthetic dyestuffs, photography, the American libraries and a wealth of literature; and Joseph Henry had just devised a basis for the *telegraph*, which Samuel Morse would later perfect. All was now changing so very fast! What a world it would be!

1910 was a very special time, and the visit by our heavenly friend in this year, was also altogether exceptional. The head of the comet made its passage between Earth and Sun, and now Earth became gently enveloped within and caressed by the diffuse brightness of its far-flung tail. The exceptional visit seemed almost as if in salutation of the progress made by those on Earth. This was indeed a most special passage. On Earth, the best brains were still reeling and were quite unable to grasp at the full meaning of Einstein's relativity theory. Traditional logic said: *'In this system of things, why not bend (or manipulate) all else except time?'* But to fit the equations of his theory, *time* just had to be of variable speed! Time! Why, that would mean that those of us sitting around, here on Earth, would be a year older this time next year; *but* someone out there, speeding around the comet, might only gain ten months by then! How ridiculous! How contrary to our gut feelings as to how it should be! How very disconcerting! But that was not all. The familiar, comfortable, steadily-ongoing, *linear* time of the past, that had served Earth-dwellers so very wonderfully well, was now seen to be somehow intricately bound up with the material world; and this in such a way, that the issue of 'bent time' could no longer be brushed aside as no-concern-of-ours.

Distance divided by time, is speed (miles per hour, or feet per second, for example), so that 'time' is involved in 'speed'. And light travels at a speed we call 'c' (to save writing a huge number), and this, Einstein was saying, relates to material mass 'm', and 'E' the energy contained in the atoms of that mass, such that: $E = mc^2$. His neat equation firmly links the *variable* time to the *stuff* of the material world. There was to be no escape. Furthermore, *'c'* had been measured and re-measured, and was known to be huge, so that *'c^2'* would be absolutely enormous in this equation of mass-energy conversion. He was presenting to the world, a fundamental equation of 'creation'! Reading from left to right the equation indicates that *a vast amount of energy is required to make a small mass.* (But later, those interested in having superweapons with horrendous destructive potential, would seek to use the equation *backwards*, to make a devastating amount of energy from a small amount of mass). So be it.

He was driven by a powerful intuition. Einstein just knew that beyond mass and gravity field, beyond the electric and magnetic fields, beyond all; there was a unifying principle of the universe. Through his latter years on Earth, he sought to develop *a unified field theory* that would bring together, in equation form, all primary construct parameters of the great universe. But that final unifying principle was always to elude him, just as it eluded the more general philosophy of the West. That 'final frontier' that would reduce the entire universe to a set of linked mathematical equations was to remain out of reach. As the concepts stand, of mass-energy equivalence and of the unifying principle, it is interesting that the modern science of the West, and the ancient science of the East, stand together.

The Aghoris of the East have the same knowledge. And this is expressed: *'... and a scientist of this knowledge should use it for healing purposes, and should tell other scientists that matter can be changed into energy and energy into matter. Beneath all ... there lies one unifying principle which is still not known in its entirety by modern scientists. Vedanta and the ancient sciences described this underlying principle...'*

Swami Rama *Living with the Himalayan Masters*

Himalayan International Institute of Yoga Science and Philosophy.

[In fact, there are a few in today's world, who are able to exercise the gift of healing, and who are also aware of mass-energy conversion in its *dematerialization* mode. There is a sufficiency of *well-attested* literature now available in the West, concerning *spirit surgeons* working through *spirit mediums*, who are able to remove for example tumours and cancerous tissues; the removal of these items, involving their dematerialisation. This is a clear example of the use of mass-energy transfer for the purpose of healing. The essence underlying the relationship $E = mc^2$, may in fact be used for creation, destruction, controlled production of energy, or for healing. The choices are ours, and it seems the healing aspects have been known and practised for thousands of years].

Herman Minkowski now clearly saw *time* as a fourth dimension of the universe, a variable dimension, as are its linear dimensions that describe the spatial volume. Marie Curie, the first woman professor of the Sorbonne, in this year, published her *'Treatise on Radioactivity'*. Max Planck had already established quantum theory, and Rutherford and Soddy had made their statement that *'radioactivity is caused by one element changing into another'*. (So the philosopher's stone principle of transmutation does in fact exist after all!). Next year, John Archibold Wheeler would invent the term *black hole*, to denote a cosmic body, of such huge gravity that light cannot escape from it. Together with the accumulated particle and wave data, mankind now had the rudimentary framework of modern theoretical physics. Here lay a path, where knowledge and inspired thought have excellence, but misuse of them may well wreak havoc. Those in possession of this potent knowledge, and those with the political power to make decisions for the world, were now weighed down with awesome responsibility.

But we are fortunate in that not all matters are so serious as are the forces and constructs of our world and universe. The idea of the 'week-end' had become popular in the United States ... an early influence of the U.S. upon the world, and perhaps an inducement for the world to lighten up a little. The General Electric Company now marketed the first electric toaster. This was also the time of the first electric washing machines, neon lights, and manufactured rayon stockings. It was also the beginning of the plastics industry with Leo Baekeland's 'Bakelite'.

The United States would, from this time on, be a considerable influence upon the world. It was Major Frank Woodbury of the U.S. Army Medical Corps, who originated the use of *tincture of iodine* to sterilise cuts and abrasions. The idea of dissolving iodine crystals in alcohol and knowing that the combination would disinfect and achieve superficial skin penetration is really quite simple. Yet this must be one of the most widely used and dependable of material medicaments of the 20th century!

The Wright brothers had pioneered powered flight by means of the internal combustion engine, set in an airframe of wood, wire and canvas. This was sometime earlier than was credited by the media of the day, on account of the sheer disbelief by them that humans, especially relatively non-scientific bicycle mechanics, could achieve in this way. But local travellers on the railroad could see the Wright field, and their earliest flights, despite their going unreported. (A Frenchman, Clément Ader, had already managed to get a bat-like contraption powered by a steam engine, off the ground as early as 1890; likewise not reported at the time). Now, in this year, 1910, Eugene Ely became the first aviator to get airborne from the deck of a ship. Only the year before, Louis Blériot had flown the English Channel, and Henri Farman had made the first flight of 100 miles. Powered flight was here to stay, and the internal combustion engine would now power land and air transport for a full century.

Now came another pollution warning, this time from Charles Steinmetz. There would be water pollution from uncontrolled dumping of sewage into rivers. The increased burning of coal for electrical power production would foul the air. Appropriately enough, this was also the time that John Auer and Paul Lewis suggested that asthma could be caused through allergic reaction. These were prophetic statements for the western world, deserving of a more careful consideration. But in the face of such impetus of industrial development, who was there who would take heed of such warnings? The pendulum of change would have to first swing a good deal further in the direction of disillusion and despair, before any correction would be sought. Pollutions, asthma, respiratory problems and the more general toxicity problems would increase first. They would at least, serve to illustrate that to a very marked degree, we are indeed authors of our own diseases and difficulties in this life.

It was Mary Baker Eddy, who taught precisely this. She, like Mark Twain, was one of the new Americans; and again like Twain, having completed her life's work, she now returned to spirit in this very year of the comet. Her major work had been the founding of 'Christian Science'. She was another who in this different time, had listened to the inner voice, and had given a new teaching to the world. It was a teaching, still based on the old; but it was now more analytical to suit the thinking of this new era.

The style would not suit all, but enough would take heed and this new word would spread, and soon there would be a depth of understanding as the result. The message amounted to this: God is perfect. Mankind as created, is perfect. But coerced imperfection of the mind may manifest as disease of the body, as a kind of reflection from within. That in essence was it. That reflection may have a quality of illusion about it, or as Emile Coué across the Atlantic, might have said: *a quality of autosuggestion.* And certainly, the chemist Coué would agree whole-heartedly (and proved scientifically in his placebo experiments), that those suffering from disease can *imagine themselves well and be cured.* A good many in the West have since amply demonstrated that power of visualisation ... that power of thought. Such a thought-powered healing has, we know, been practised in the Himalayas and truly holy places for thousands of years.

It is without doubt, that so often disease is projected from within, and can also be corrected from within. But it is perhaps more acutely obvious when the waywardness of the more general consciousness of society, gives rise to a material poisoning of its environment. These poisons are then ingested, causing a variety of diseases. There have been the warnings to society from those who have been concerned; but society is slow to change its habits, and risks are taken far too often. It is blatantly obvious that industrial and traffic fumes can result in asthma and allergy. The smoke when processed tobacco is burned can result in lung cancer. Drinking water contaminated by sewage can lead to bacterial infections such as cholera. And in conditions of stress and unfulfilled living, the body can produce its own toxins and system of self-destruct. We are indeed in so many ways, authors of our own diseases. Further problems can arise from denying our bodies acceptable diet, through ignorance or through resisting the inner voice guidance. But it is well known by sages and by healers that *miraculous* cures may *also* be generated from within. Thought is all-powerful. The God-consciousness is all-powerful. And the religious teachings of Mary Baker Eddy through Christian Science encompass this. Improved communications should so much help to spread this vital knowledge.

Communications! But there would be wonderfully improved new communicating systems that would surpass anything we might imagine. The world now had *telecommunication.* In the last year, Guglielmo Marconi had received the Nobel Prize in physics for his work that had truly astonished the world. There was now telecommunication to ships at sea and across the Atlantic! Marconi had had the most amazing stroke of luck, in that long distance transmissions were found to bounce off the ionised *Heaviside* layer that encloses the Earth. He had pressed ahead *intuitively* (with due regard to inner voice no doubt), building two quite expensive installations at Cape Cod, Massachusetts and at Poldhu, Cornwall; without any firm knowledge of exactly how the transmissions would reach across the Atlantic. They were in fact reflected from the ionised layer. It worked! There have since been a good many that would reflect and think: *'he got lucky!'* But there were also certain guiding influences that helped his work.

Developments in *radio* ran parallel, and many contributed to its final form. History records, that the first radio-set, was built by Marconi and his instrument utilised a 'Tesla' coil. In this very year, 1910, a Frenchman Joseph Berthenod tested the first mobile transmitter; this was mounted on board an airship. The first kit-form radio receivers became available to the US public, and they heard the Metropolitan Opera with the voice of the great Caruso! But who *really* invented radio? Who had lectured and actually demonstrated its principle in Philadelphia as early as 1893, filed patents in 1897 (and delayed three years at that, due to a laboratory fire)? Who was it that had already worked the principles through and through, and had even filed patents on such finer aspects of radio transmission as independent-fixed-frequency of transmitting stations, to avoid their mutual interference? And why was he such an *unsung hero* of those times?

Nikola Tesla, truly a genius, standing at the forefront of experimental science and a thinker, well ahead of his time, was born in Croatia and became a naturalised American. Perhaps he nonetheless, continued to be seen by many in authority as a *partial* alien. Tesla did not receive all the credit, financial reward or the acknowledgement that was deserved. Brilliant and accomplished though he was, he was also a foreigner and a loner; not that he particularly minded being a loner. His own thoughts were complex and fulfilling and left little spare time for socialising. But then, one year he was actually cited as a Nobel Prize winner. Was this to be recognition at last? Well no, although there had clearly been the leak, the news was published in the press and he was interviewed; official notification was never to follow. Apart from being talked about, it all came to nothing. Nikola Tesla, one of the greatest and most accomplished of scientists, was in fact one to be 'talked about', by those who would take the trouble to study the facts and consider them for themselves, and talked about he still is:

'But how then did he see this world of ours?'

'Ah ... well! As *he* saw it, the world was alive! The world was a place, quite literally alive with a wild multiplicity of electrical vibrations. The 'vibration' was at the centre of all things and was at the centre of his life's work, and he just loved it.'

'And not just electrical either. He understood mechanical vibrations too. Took friends back to his laboratory to stand on mechanical vibrators for toning up the body ... had Mark Twain at it once. He really enjoyed the feeling ... but he stayed too long and the shaking got to him ... had to rush off to the toilet without delay. Too much rhythmic vibration can have that effect it seems. It can be like that! Tesla himself had already made that discovery ... and he *had* warned him. But then, there's nothing quite like finding out for your self ... is there? But to more serious aspects, he must have been the first to understand metal fatigue. He made vibrators that could be fixed to a steel bar, and after a set time, it would break ... fracture! He understood.'

'But you know, so far as radio is concerned, he worked out the tuning of electrical resonance and designed a system of *wireless transmission of intelligence* as early as 1893. Then, I think it would have been in Century Magazine, he wrote: *'Stationary waves ... by their use we may produce at will, from a sending station, an electrical effect in any particular region of the globe.'* ... or something to that effect. That was in June 1900! The statement of a true visionary...'

'Of course, he disagreed with a few people in his day ... Einstein no less ... on his relativity. Certain things *can* travel faster than light ... That was a part of his belief. And he believed that all matter is derived from the primary source ... the aether that pervades all space ... And you know, I think he could just be right about that.'

'Yes! And I believe he made a statement on that: *'Nor would any explanation of the universe be possible without recognising the existence of aether and its indispensable function.'* Yes, a statement against the thinking of this century, but I agree, he could well be right! Nowadays there's a great deal of wavering on the old idea that space is nothing. You can't be forced by your theories to bestow all kinds of properties on the space between the stars, and still call it nothing!'

'But he *excelled* at the practical ... worked out radar ... guidance systems ... basics of the cyclotron and energy-beam projection...'

'He lived a good life, but departing when he did ... 1943 ... of course some of *that* work went via the FBI straight into classified files ... and so again ... no credit given for *those* items.'

'He never married ... well ... married to his science he was ... must have been lonely at times in the big city ... in New York ... used to walk the streets and the parks late at night, but seemed to enjoy it mind you ... did his clear thinking then ... and fed the pigeons. That was a nice touch ... fed them ... took care of the injured ones ... the broken wings and legs. He *was* capable of love. He loved his Manhattan pigeons ... especially the white one ... with the grey wing tips. She would always come to him...'

'But going back again to before 1910 ... his big dream ... the *big* dream ... 'beamed-electric-power'. Those huge 'factory sized' tuned coils he made! They produced all sorts of weird light effects ... And *ball lightning* as a side effect ... which he saw to be a nuisance! Stuff that we still don't understand too well even today, he was actually making accidentally and finding it a nuisance!'

'Of course ... he designed the motors and the alternators ... the electrical power system of alternating current that we have today! We owe him for that. We all of us owe him so much! But of course, he wasn't satisfied with a system that had to rely on wires going everywhere. He wanted to *beam* power like it was radio! And he did! ... over short distances at least.'

'But he had this idea of a standing wave *through* the Earth. That was his dream when he built that big Wardenclyffe plant ... the finance ran out and it was never finished ... that one. He thought the wave would pass along the Earth's diameter. But someone later worked out it's more likely to travel an arc between diameter and surface. Of course, the structure was there at the time of that Tunguska fireball in Siberia ... that blue fireball that flattened the forests ... 1908 ... You don't suppose ...'

'No ... He couldn't have ... could he? The timing though ... that would be right...'

'It was never finished ... so he couldn't have could he? The project just wasn't finished.'

'No ... but just supposing ... anyway, what a man!'

'Brilliant!'

1910 was such an eventful year! Arthur Evans had just completed his excavations of the palace of Cnossos on Crete, which had produced such cultural delights. H.G. Wells had just written *'The History of Mr Polly'*, E.M. Forster had just written *'Howard's End'*, and now there was Mary Pickford! It was the birth of a *film* industry! Florence Lawrence ... the Biograph Girl ... had been the first *film star* to enjoy having her name actually made known to an appreciative public. Gertrude Lawrence got mobbed after the release of a report of her death ... the first movie-publicity-stunt! But it was Mary Pickford who then won such popularity as to be hailed as: first 'universal star of cinema' and 'America's Sweetheart'. The five-cent admission *nickelodeons* had rapidly increased in their number over five years, and by 1910 there were 10,000 of them in the US. Britain had its equivalent *penny gaffs*. The Gaumont palace opened in Paris, with 5,000 seats ... the largest cinema yet.

In the early days of the US cinema, the various strictures and the attempted levying of royalties, were quickly to result in Hollywood becoming a centre for the developing film industry. It had dependable sunlight, excellent locations, and the Mexican border was to hand just in case one needed to quickly escape across that border from royalty hunters. This new cinema (that now followed on from that first ever photograph) was to become a new and splendid leading art form that would continue with vigour, in a wild multiplicity of styles and configurations. It had all developed so very quickly, from the invention of the Lumière brothers and their first motion picture of 1895, to this year of widespread commercial cinema in which Thomas Edison now demonstrated for the first time, simultaneous moving picture with sound. The film industry had arrived!

This 20th century would now be overtly and wildly different from any other that had preceded it. There would be just no comparison! But there was also a sadness ... a specific date that has to be accounted ... 18 November 1910; better known simply as 'Black Friday'. Britain had continued unbalanced, as a male-dominated society that denied its women any political vote. An oversight perhaps? Well, no, not exactly an oversight. There were plenty of women who desired to have their say in the affairs of the country, and who spoke out and worked to that end. They became the 'Suffragette' movement. On Black Friday, as Suffragettes marched on the House of Commons, police intervened, and there was a riot. The media described the scene as 'disgraceful'. There was battering and bruising, and 200 arrests were made. This was the start of the road to equality, but it was to be a lengthy road. Three years later, Emily Wilding Davison stopped the King's horse in a race at Epsom, in the Suffragette cause; and died as the result. But it was not until the General Election of 1918, that women would be allowed to vote, and even then only if they had reached the age of 30. Men could vote at 21. It would be 1928 before voting *equality* would be allowed. It was to take 18 years of campaign and protest from that Black Friday, to establish voting equality! Fairness for the fair sex eventually came about, and it was such a long climb down for male intransigence. But a clear and balanced logic was finally to prevail. The eventual result, although tardy, had an obvious righteousness about it.

There was just one more happening of 1910 that, at the time seemed trivial and not worthy of the mention, even sordid perhaps. It passed without notice at the time, and was only later accounted by investigative historians; but it would alter the shape of events that were to follow, and should therefore be included. The happening was in the nature of a transaction that occurred in Vienna.

Chapter XX

The Vienna Factor: 1910

The month of April brought with it an improved feeling of optimism. Winter was past and spring and summer embraced months that were easier for the outdoor girl. Hannah was very much an outdoor girl ... a girl of the streets ... a tart: since leaving home, had known nothing else. She generally walked to catch the eye of the travellers and tradesmen around the vicinity of the station, the *Nordwestbahnhof*, which had good promise of prospecting for the greater part of the year. The trade was steady at 50 heller a time, in doorways and side streets or between sheets if she was lucky; but it was not a circumstance that would ever lead to riches or even modest comfort. It was a meagre existence that depended on a number of liaisons every night, and it was in no small measure, a risk profession. But for now, while she still managed to hang on to that certain alluring flush that makes a young woman a young woman, it remained a reliable business.

She was Jewish, not that that meant a great deal. Religion was not a subject that came into her thoughts in any meaningful way. But she was only too aware, that to be overtly Jewish, in this city at this time was to be in some kind of a political shadow. Vienna had become a centre for growing anti-Semitic feelings; perhaps Europe's foremost centre of the anti-Jewish leaflets, books and vulgar slander that were tossed around at this time. The stuff was everywhere: in the streets, in the shops, in the cafés, and anti-Jewish feeling cast with certainty a sad darkening shadow on these days. She ... Hannah, was not especially troubled by such things. She was *more* troubled by the faintly pink rash that had appeared over her lower abdomen. If only it was something as simple as measles, but she knew it was not. Nonetheless, she was a sensible girl, with a certain down to earth quality. She was only too well aware that venereal diseases were the major risk of this trade, and so, she had been to see a doctor and seek advice. The syphilis required treatment. Thank heavens there was now a mercurial remedy for the disease! This was said to be completely effective. The remedy would quickly benefit her, and the rash would disappear. Her treatment would not of course, be of any benefit at all to those she had been with over the past few weeks.

Hannah would have been with a good many during that period in which she carried the disease. Those who had already 'brushed' with the syphilis and had been treated at some time, would now be immune to a further exposure. Any fresh contacts would now have become infected by her and would be incubating the bacterium, and these would simply have to fend for themselves. She remembered the young men over at the hostel at 27 Meldemannstrasse near the Danube, in the 20th District, because they were regulars, and because it was fairly comfortable in there. The hostel was, of course, strictly for men ... no women allowed; but the janitor would always let her in for a few cigarettes, and she usually took a break there, and stayed an hour or two.

There were three of them; two were teenage and the other, a little older, around 21. She had got to know them a little. The older one, Adolf, was different. He was definitely the interesting one ... no money ... no regular job ... but interesting. He had paints. He liked architecture, painted postcards of buildings and street scenes; had a friend Reinhold who sold for him on commission. He seemed to be able to sell the cards in taverns and at the fairs. Adolf also painted sales posters for shopkeepers, and they both did odd jobs too; carrying bags at the station, shovelling snow, that sort of thing. But the three at the hostel always had difficulty scraping together their 50 heller.

They spent little or nothing on clothing. Adolf had an old black overcoat that had been given him by Neumann, a Hungarian Jew who dealt in second hand clothes. A small payment received for paintings and such sometimes meant ... cream cakes and reading newspapers in a café, which Adolf loved. Despite poor means, this one had a certain liking for *style.* No smoking and no alcohol, that was just a silly self-indulgence and waste. But disporting oneself in the cafés and confronting the various ideologies had life and style! He was a one for noisy debate, and likely to go into a rant on some political issue. Others would react. Some would laugh, some would complain and some would be impressed.

There were times when he was not averse to receiving a little influence himself, and he had been especially impressed by a film at the cinema ... the new film-showing cinema which had now reached Vienna! Kellermann's *Tunnel* it was. The film portrayed a political agitator who delivered rousing speeches to the worker masses and thereby won their following. It had clearly made a deep and lasting impression, because he had gone on for days afterwards, extolling the virtues of *the power of the spoken word.* Of all the roads to fame and glory, there was something fine about this particular road. The amount of political power that could be had, by cultivating such a delivery of the well chosen words! The spoken words ... the worker following ... the power! They linked together ... as a road ... as a glorious highway! One day ... One day! ... He might just take that highway. Then he would go into one of his quiet brooding moods, and spend long hours at the public library; and afterwards seek sustenance at a soup kitchen. Yes, this one was different ... He was certainly different ... no doubt about that.

But Adolf had then fallen out with the other two. It was over Hannah. He had procured her services for himself one afternoon, in the slightly squalid comfort of the hostel; but then was unable to pay. In fact, he got his two friends to produce the hellers for him. They paid; then threw him out. It had been outrageous behaviour! As he landed in the road, he turned and shouted obscenities. They hurled his few clothes, paints and brushes after him. It was a terrible scene. But it passed.

As is the nature of the aftermath of quarrels, the two young men cooled down. In fact they decided to go off to the station, collect Hannah and bring her back to the hostel for their own amusement that evening. On the previous occasion that they had been with her, they had both noticed the redness on her body. They had thought ... just the rigours of the business ... too much cheap soap, a residual heat rash perhaps and maybe a flea bite or two. Like a good many young people in this early part of the century, they were not street-wise and not at all well informed, despite a degree of promiscuity.

It was perhaps two weeks later when Adolf returned to the hostel. God knows where he had been in the meantime. Perhaps sleeping out. He would not have been averse to sleeping rough and it would not have been the first time. As to the altercation, the heat had long since gone from their anger and there was no longer any retained animosity. He undressed for the baking of his clothing in the oven. This was the ritual de-lousing procedure of the establishment. It was at this time they noticed the faint pink rash that Adolf had, which was rather similar to a pink flush that they themselves now had about their abdomens. They did not at this time connect any of this with Hannah. After all, this was sometime later than any transaction that any of them had had with her.

But as fortune would have it, the two young men did eventually seek out a doctor. This was after the disease had progressed a little further, with the swelling of lymph glands, skin eruptions and leading to a general feeling of languor. This was also after they had finally gone their separate ways from Adolf. The treatment that they received was in time to intercept and to arrest the disease from what would have been the further and far more serious damage to their bodies. They were really extremely fortunate to have its progress checked in time, and could only pause and wonder how Adolf had fared, but he was now out there somewhere, on his own. It would be his own decision whether to seek out a physician or take his chance.

The two young men from the hostel on Meldemannstrasse went about their lives and lived on into the 20th century, despite the difficulties of their youthful misadventure. They survived the rigours of World War I and of World War II, and so, were later in a position to recount the way things had been that time in old Vienna.

As to Adolf, he in fact remained in Vienna until the spring of 1913, increasing in his little eccentricities, in his hatred for the Jews, and dislike of priests, Social Democrats, the 'unintelligent masses' and the Imperial Hapsburgs. He joined the 16th Bavarian Infantry Regiment in 1914 and served as a meldegänger, running the trenches and battle zone with despatches between Company and HQ. This was throughout the course of World War I. Following that episode, he cultivated for himself 'the power of the spoken word', and took that road to fame that had been his dream, and he became Führer of the Third Reich. World War II became a part of that dream, but he had to share it with the syphilis spirochaete, that continued to ravage his body in its third stage of bodily violation. His personal physicians were able, with medication, to slow down the advancing stiffness of joints and the course of the megalomania. But it was impossible to fully arrest these symptoms, once in progress. It was the megalomania that fired the man towards the harshness, the brutality and the rashness that so misused the power that he had contrived. In the latter stages of the war, he passed to spirit by his own hand in the Berlin bunker, 30 April 1945.

'Yet Vienna was and remained for me the hardest, though most thorough, school of my life. I had set foot in this town while still half a boy and I left it a man, grown quiet and grave. In it I obtained the foundations for a philosophy in general and a political view ... not until today have I been able to estimate at their full value those years of study.'

Adolf Hitler *Mein Kampf* Translated by Ralph Manheim. Pimlico

'But the power which has always started the greatest religious and political avalanches in history rolling has from time immemorial been the magic power of the spoken word, and that alone.'

Adolf Hitler *Mein Kampf* Translated by Ralph Manheim. Pimlico

'His hatred of delegation was based on distrust. Like all megalomaniacs he was fearful of rivalry, of any other hand than his own on the reins of power.'
Alan Wykes *Hitler* Pan/Ballantine 1973

'There have been no profound transformations, and such changes as have occurred are less marked in the religious field, notwithstanding the tremendous efforts of the Christian missionaries ... The white races did, of course, give some things to the natives, and they were the worst gifts that they could possibly have made, those plagues of our own modern world - materialism, fanaticism, alcoholism and syphilis.'
7 February 1945 *The Testament of Adolf Hitler.*
The Hitler-Bormann Documents Cassell 1961 *(Written in the Berlin bunker, in the last days).*

'A fire was kindled from whose flame one day the sword must come that would regain freedom for the Germanic Siegfried and life for the German nation.
And side by side with the coming resurrection, I sensed that the goddess of inexorable vengeance for the perjured deed of November 9, 1919, was striding forth.'
Adolf Hitler *Mein Kampf* Translated by Ralph Manheim. Pimlico

(There is some ambiguity in the date. He was impassioned by and despised the abdication of Emperor Wilhelm II on November 9, 1918. That event preceded Germany's capitulation. The Treaty of Versailles that followed, he equally despised. The date of its signing was November 11, 1919. The precise date matters not in terms of vengeance. Either way, it would seem that the path leading us to World War II was already being trodden in 1925 when the first volume of *Mein Kampf* was published.)

PART 4

Aquarius: A New Age

From the Silence of Time, Time's Silence borrow.
In the heart of To-day is the word of To-morrow.
The Builders of Joy are the Children of Sorrow.
William Sharp *Triad*

Looking back on the 20th century, one can perhaps heave a huge sigh, and reflect upon its complexity; its vast array of machines and machinations. A period of confused rampant growth in all things: arts and sciences, commerce and advertising, politics and legislation, population and mixing of cultures, communications extending to satellite relay, systems and systems applications, wars and life-wasting weaponry ... computers and all things material. Will it never end? And what about quality of life? Was Lucretius right? Shall we reach a high point in accumulated knowledge? Will society become just too stressed out to be able to live with itself, and can we in any event handle the advancing knowledge with anything like adequate wisdom? All valid questions that we might well ask of ourselves. About such matters, three things are reasonably certain:

(1) Life *is of necessity* subject to change, without which there might well be little logical purpose to it. In addition, many would argue that change must in general, head in the direction of beauty and perfection to be of any value.

(2) If a full change of direction becomes *necessary* for our culture, then it will automatically happen in some way or other. This will be a certainty regardless of whether or not we actually like the idea at the time.

(3) Any such change of direction may well be steered either by our selves, or by influences from beyond our material being, or by both. (There is of course, much more to this universe than just our *material* selves and the stars, and as we head into the 21st century, this fact must become much more widely accepted).

It is true also that, in the latter 20th century, there were a good many who looked back in pitiful sadness upon two inglorious world wars, and they knew with utter conviction, that mankind could never indulge a third, and expect survival to be a part of that package.

Chapter XXI

1986: Year of the Signs

Another comet year, and this was a curious time of political intrigue, anti-nuclear protest, and mixed with a rising awareness of supposedly clandestine illegal activities, perpetrated by Secret Service agents at the behest of various governments. But media-growth was an increasing factor, and the press and the media-in-general were giving political happenings a plentiful coverage ... all a part of the rising awareness. A developing curious state of affairs may be traced, that really began two years earlier. An erudite paper on the subject of radioactive waste management, and sharply critical of the DOE White Paper 8607, was read at the Sizewell enquiry on 13 September 1984. It was Rob Green who read the paper, in the absence of its author, his aunt; she having been brutally and mysteriously murdered six months earlier.

Hilda Murrell was a 78 year-old authority on roses and a Cambridge MA. She had informed friends that for some reason she feared for her own safety. She also let it be known that her paper for the Sizewell enquiry was now complete. This paper referred to radioactive waste as the worst industrial pollution ever created by man and she argued that even if energy were needed as a desperate measure, the creation of such a pollutant would still not be justified. Then, it would appear from various subsequent reports, she returned to her home on 21 March, surprised intruders, or so it would seem, grappled with them and received injuries. Her body was later found dumped in a copse, six miles away, together with a bread knife (thought to have caused some of her injuries), having been driven there in her own car which was left abandoned at the roadside. Cause of death was attributed partly to injuries and partly to unattended hypothermia. Her death by no means resulted from a standard 'discovered break-in'. There was no normal set pattern to it. One could not help thinking that it had the look of a crime-gone-wrong, with a desperate attempt to make it look like something else. The car, as seen by witnesses, was being driven jerkily and badly. It was driven away from the house and past the police station! This part of the misadventure was clearly carried out in haste at considerable risk of discovery.

The official statements and evidence that ensued following the murder were of an unsatisfactory nature. They contained numerous unreasonable contradictions and discrepancies, and three police officers were to become suspended as enquiries continued and the mystery deepened. The investigations appeared to progress but the culprit was never found. Theories of political intrigue were voiced. The idea of political foul play was strengthened when it became known that her telephone had been 'fixed' to prevent outgoing calls. Later, on 26 January 1985, her Welsh weekend cottage was burned down, and *that* telephone would also appear to have been 'fixed'. The next day, the Observer newspaper printed a story about Sizewell objectors being under surveillance.

An aspect of society was to become known increasingly as *the establishment*, and those who openly probed and questioned the ways of that aspect of society were to be known increasingly as *subversives*, and there were certain subversives known to be under *surveillance*. These were the ways and the terms of the times. Hilda Murrell would have been classed as a subversive by the establishment. She was against nuclear missiles and a member of 'Tories Against Cruise and Trident', and like a number of sympathetic citizens at that time, was sending donations to the women's peace camp at Greenham Common. Then there was her Sizewell paper. Moreover, she had a good bond with her nephew Rob Green. During the Falklands war, he had been Commander Robert Green RN at GCHQ Cheltenham. Green was there at the time of the controversial sinking of the Argentine cruiser *General Belgrano*, with the loss of 368 lives, and of any last hope of a peaceful solution to the Falklands confrontation; and he would have been privy to highly confidential communications material. Needless to say, to certain establishment personnel, this family connection might have been a great worry.

There had in fact been an information leak concerning the movements of the *General Belgrano*, but when it came, it was to emerge from quite a different source. It was a senior civil servant Clive Ponting, who was subsequently charged under the Official Secrets Act in respect of the leak. He had deliberately made known the contents of a certain secret document. This was just as well, because the truth was that Parliament itself had actually been misled in statements made to the House, on the manner in which the sinking took place! At the trial, Ponting's duty was deemed to be first and foremost to the State - that is, to the Crown in Parliament; and his motive had been to see that the State was *not* misled! This was deemed to be a strictly honourable stance, and a jury had accordingly, on 11 February 1985, found him 'not guilty'. The verdict was unexpected. Some viewed the result as unbelievable, some viewed it with relief, and some with a certain joy that justice had come down on the side of openness and individual conscience. On the side of conscience! Subversion is often in the eye of the beholder, and in these times, it was depending so very much upon exactly where the beholder stands.

On the other side of the world, a converted trawler named *Rainbow Warrior* was going about her business in the SouthWest Pacific, ferrying passengers. She, the flagship of the little Greenpeace fleet, was in the process of transferring, in several sailings, the inhabitants of one of the Marshall Islands to another in that same group. The population numbered 304. They and their effects were being moved from Rongelap, in the same latitude as the better known Bikini Atoll. Following US atomic weapons testing several decades earlier, it was evident that Rongelap remained sufficiently radioactive to be causing health defects in its population and to be responsible for a number of coconut palm mutations. Due to the radioactive fall-out, this place was no longer the paradise island that it once had been.

The population's new home would be the little island of Mejato, previously uninhabited, and lying 120 miles to the south. The task of transporting was completed in good spirit and the islanders were left optimistic and grateful, on their new island home. That concluded the final mission of Rainbow Warrior, before making for New Zealand to a berth in Marsden Wharf, Auckland. The next campaign was to be a 'small boats' protest against the French underground nuclear testing beneath Moruroa Atoll, east of Tahiti. It was a controversial matter. Some were in favour of the nuclear programme and some, especially those living in that region, were understandably very much against. The local police in Auckland were just a little uneasy, and on the lookout for any strangers with odd behavioural leanings, who might just be potential troublemakers.

As midnight approached on 10 July 1985, two improvised explosive devices (IEDs) thudded into the tranquillity of the night and ripped through the hull of the Rainbow Warrior. Within minutes, she was at the bottom of the harbour; and alas ... crewmember and photographer, Fernando Pereira had been killed by the second IED. When the news broke next morning, the world was shocked. No one had expected *such* high handed measures as ... blowing up a Greenpeace boat, with disregard for life! The New Zealand police were aware, however, that certain foreign individuals, supposedly on holiday had been acting strangely. There were reports on file, and they knew immediately where to begin in the hunt for the saboteurs. Thanks to their efficiency and persistence, and the support of Prime Minister David Lange, the outrage was quickly and without any doubt, attributed to the French Secret Service, or more correctly the DGSE.

There was a team consisting of two using false names and false passports, posing as a honeymoon couple, but failing to act out the rôle with any degree of enthusiasm. They had flown in on an Air New Zealand Boeing 747. Another team of four had sailed from Nouméa, New Caledonia, travelling south, on the yacht Ouvéa, bringing with them the explosives. A further man was present who co-ordinated the operation. A woman infiltrated the Greenpeace entourage purely as a spy, and there were various telephone calls made to a secret number in Paris, which I understand the NZ police were advised did not exist, but which responded quickly enough when the number was tried. It seems that at least eight individuals were concerned with the sinking of the Rainbow Warrior. Prime Minister Lange took a positive stance and demanded retribution. Suddenly eyes and hearts all over the world were tuned into New Zealand, as detectives were drafted into Auckland from far across country. Many, many lines of enquiry were explored with some degree of success. One could not expect total success. It was a tricky multinational situation with contingency planning by the saboteurs and obvious backup.

The affair ended as a mixture of cop-out and fair cop. The odd 'honeymoon couple', Major Alain Mafart and Captain Dominique Prieur were arrested and charged. Prior to trial, they traded a plea of *guilty to manslaughter* in return for having the original charge of *murder* dropped from the charge sheet. The charges of *immigration irregularity* and *conspiracy to cause explosions* remained. They were each sentenced to ten years imprisonment. Had the yacht team returned their chartered craft to its owners, then they also would have been arrested. Their part in the plot had been worked out. They did not in fact return the craft. It seems likely that they scuttled her and boarded the French nuclear submarine *Rubis* that was known to be in the area. It transpired that Nouméa Yacht Charters sought to sue the French government for loss of the Ouvéa. They were diverted towards private settlement in the region of 990,000 francs, with the French Ministry of Defence; thus avoiding for themselves, the embarrassing prospect of legal proceedings with DGSE crewmembers being subpoenaed for court attendance.

Three crewmembers that were trained DGCE frogmen using false names and credentials, had their covers fully blown and are unlikely to leave France again. The fourth man, well travelled with a well-stamped valid passport (giving the group a measure of credibility) is likely to remain similarly domiciled. The Greenpeace infiltrator, had moved on to Israel, was tipped off that her cover was broken, and managed to escape arrest by fleeing for France.

Vice-Admiral Lacoste, in command of the DGSE, was sacked. Charles Hernu, French Minister of Defence, resigned.

The whole episode was quite clearly a Secret Service job that went very badly wrong. In the final reckoning, it was a mess that managed to retain very little in the way of its original pattern of secrecy, and the humiliation had to be borne. It was the result of fair-minded citizens opposing irrational incursions spawned by a sad misuse of power. Signs of a changing world, in which an event in Auckland harbour became relayed around the planet by next morning! The emotion of it somehow tapped into the consciousness of all. It was not an *internal* affair and the amount of *cover up* that was possible, was consequently limited. In this changing world, it was now much more difficult for a national power to use such high handed tactics and escape challenge. People-consciousness was now a factor in world affairs, and there were now world systems to make that factor quickly connect with news media almost anywhere.

[A decade later, when yet another series of French nuclear tests were being conducted beneath Moruroa atoll, a rising *peace-consciousness* was in many minds everywhere. Moreover, in Tahiti and the nearby islands, what had transpired just ten years earlier was still held firmly in memory, and so, street riots in Tahiti would be a natural consequence. Of course! ... There would be formal objections to the tests from some of the world's prime ministers. Of course! ... There would be condemnation of the tests by the world's media. Of course! ... There would be stern warnings about cracks in bedrock releasing radioactive chemicals. And of course! ... There would be some that chose to boycott French goods as their own personal objection to the matter. The world was and is a changing place. The need for peace, the now obvious uselessness of yet more superweapons, and the stark necessity for keeping radioactive pollution out of living space and away from food chain, were thoughts now in the minds of so many. The nuclear-bomb-testing in the South West Pacific could now easily be described as an idea showing a marked *obsolescence* ... a power-politics dinosaur, now a seriously endangered species, having one last, final kick.]

In 1986, there were distinct signs of the East-West Cold War at last coming to an end. The Cold War period had been predicted by the few, sadly observed by the many; and its cost accounted in horror by those who felt the pain of the world's underprivileged and starving communities. They could so easily have been helped by such funding. The people of both East and West had their peace campaign organisations. These had now reached a peak of activity. In the USSR, it was the Soviet Peace Committee that (from 1958) published its magazine 'XX Century and Peace' in five languages, (the English version available in London). In this very year (1986), it gave photographic coverage of the massive peace march through Moscow. Only the language of the banners made it any different from the CND marches through London. (Like the SPC, CND had also been formed in 1958). Clearly there was now a sufficient peace-consciousness for around ¼ million people to meet and march through the streets of their respective capital cities; then congregate in the parks for speeches. Civic authorities and police had to make whatever arrangements they could, for traffic and crowd control.

Not all in the West openly identified with the pacifist and anti-nuclear groups. When compared to other moieties such as major political parties or football followers, they remained minority factions. But it was abundantly clear from street crowd reactions, that the peaceful demonstrations of peace-activists were approved and applauded by many others. Clearly then, the SPC in the East and CND in the West, represented the tips of larger icebergs of fast rising peace-consciousness. This, in just three years, would lead to a material manifestation ... the dismantling of the Berlin Wall, which had practically and symbolically divided East and West for half a century. This event was seen by all to mark the official end of the Cold War period. The way was now clear for a partial decommissioning of nuclear arms, radical re-thinking and re-structuring ... this being not without its own problems. A direction-change ... by whatever agencies ... had been initiated, and 1986 could be seen as a 'watershed' year at the interface of difficult and corrigible times.

The main objectives of CND at this time, might be briefly stated as follows:

(1) The ongoing aim of reducing nuclear arms world-wide.

(2) To alert public awareness of the nuclear status quo, and to clarify what was being done in the public's name and by means of its own funding.

(3) To simply stand up and say 'No!'

The CND calendar for 1986 was a busy one, including as major organised events:

6 February: A one-day blockade of RAF Molesworth by 6,000 in freezing adverse weather conditions. (This was the first anniversary of the removal

of a peace camp from the site and surrounding it with razor wire; a first move in making it the second American cruise missile base in Britain, after Greenham Common).

15 April: Following the bombing of Libyan targets by American aircraft from British bases, there followed protests to the US embassy, a candlelight vigil in Downing Street and a huge demonstration in Oxford Street. Particular objection was centred on the inevitable civilian casualties resulting from the attack.

17 April: The launch date of the 'basic case' information campaign. The information publicised included a listing of the 50,000 nuclear weapons held as world stocks and data on the British missile systems. What had not been generally clear to the public prior to the campaign, was the size of the escalation of nuclear stratagem in replacing the Polaris system with new Type 640 submarines armed with Trident D5 missiles. Since each missile warhead could be loaded with up to 14 independently targeted nuclear bombs, the total complement of four submarines would likely be in the range 512 to 896. This would represent at least an eightfold escalation on the old Polaris system.

8 July: Parliament was lobbied concerning British participation in the American 'Star Wars' initiative. This was seen as a ridiculously expensive attempt to raise the stakes in East-West nuclear confrontation, and a lamentable waste of endeavour and resources. Publicity was important. The people should know the implications. Isaac Asimov is reported as describing Star Wars as a device to make the Russians go broke; but we would also go broke, it being very much a John Wayne style stand-off.

Summer period: This was an active time. The four-day Glastonbury rock and folk festival organised by farmer Michael Eavis and helped by CND volunteers, was an excellent annual fund raiser; attended enthusiastically by 20,000 people. On the nuclear front, sites were required by the industry for dumping waste materials. Four villages had been named as possible locations, but of course there were those who raised strong objection. Hundreds turned out to blockade each site and prevent NIREX from making test drillings. After all, who wants nuclear traffic and dumped waste in their own back yard? The present design of nuclear process seemed to be beset by three major problems: bomb-making material as a by-product, quite large amounts of *hot* active waste to dispose of, and the thankless and expensive task of decommissioning old worn-out plant, once its safe active life was at an end. What an awful task to bequeath to the next generation! It was by no means a clean route to efficient energy production in the present state of the art.

Bruce Kent, chairman of CND, led a walking party from Faslane (nuclear submarine base in Scotland) to Burghfield (nuclear warhead factory in Berkshire). It was a long and well-observed walk that carried with it a potent anti-nuclear gesture. George Galloway, Director of War on Want joined the party, and the exercise meant more publicity and more than £100,000 raised; this to be divided between CND and War on Want projects in Nicaragua and Eritrea. It was good to see the connection being made between on the one hand, waste on weaponry, and on the other, those desperately in need of help who were starving. It somehow seemed to put a spotlight on the wild eccentricity of a world in which proliferation of weaponry was taking precedence over compassion for starving populations.

5 October: In the 'Hands across Scotland' event, 'Parents for Survival' organised a human chain linking hands from coast to coast. This was to symbolise friendship between East and West and the desire to stop the arms race process.

30 November: Following considerable groundwork to expose and advertise the frequency with which nuclear convoys were now using the motorways and A-roads of Britain, the television companies and newspapers suddenly combined in the cause in quite a big way. One news report read: *'As thousands of CND protesters set out yesterday on a national day of action to expose secret nuclear convoys, a senior Tory MP said that in wartime they would be shot.'* The statement at least served to illustrate just how attitudes can change. The various convoys and vehicles included loaded cruise missile launchers, Polaris warheads, flasks of spent reactor fuel and trucks transporting uranium. A regular missile convoy route was from the Greenham Common base to Salisbury plain, for practice deployments.

American Cruise missile convoys in general travelled at night around 1 to 3 am, to and from their exercise sites; an approximate monthly happening. The 'Cruisewatch' division of CND monitored movements of the massive 8-wheel-drive launchers, always in convoy with one control vehicle, a bevy of heavy trucks and support vehicles, and police escort fore and aft. Despite the hour, Cruisewatch always managed to muster protest teams with placards, flares and lanterns. In general, around one thousand would stand in small groups at the roadside, along the convoy route. Their cars would be parked off the road, in lay-bys and on verges, and their registration numbers would have been noted by a police patrol.

This was the quiet time; the scene prepared. Away from the roadside, in trees and hedgerows, nature's wild ones still slept, until it came by. The passage of a convoy would always be a mechanically noisy, gear-grinding with smells of hot oil, light-flashing, military and a heavily atmospheric ... affair.

Vanloads of police would always drive ahead of the column and police teams would line the roadside, between its passage and protesters. They were there for their own aspect of peacekeeping that linked with law and order and with Anglo-American protocol. Regular protesters would often genially pass the time-of-night with these officers, with whom they had no dispute; this in the quiet spell just before the distant roar and the lights came into view, snaking their winding way around a distant hillside. The night air held a heavy strangeness, as people of such differing beliefs, met in the commitment of one shared belief in protest. They met beneath the stars, by the light of flares and headlamps; some simply to maintain a silent vigil, while some saw fit to shout their views; as drivers raced their gears to keep the convoy spaced on an upward grade.

The messages on boards leapt out from shadow, faded again, then lived the more brightly as more lights came onward. Tilting a little or thrust in gesture, mostly brief, a jostling living verge of: *'Cruise out!'* ... *'No not this!'* ... *'Yanks go home!'* ... *'Thou shalt not kill!'* ... *'Love - not war!'* ... *'No nukes!'*, and Albert Schweitzer's axiom *'Reverence for life!'* was there. A camera flash or two leapt from the roadside ... and from a missile launcher's cab. There would be photographs in scrapbooks both sides of the Atlantic ... Better that than holocaust. It was all over in minutes ... just minutes, then police teams scrambled, seeking their vans again, to get on past the convoy to another demo point. That the protest was registered somehow satisfied conscience and fired the hope that things would someday change. A mixed group ... teachers, scientists, mothers, agricultural workers and others, had all stood there to say 'No!'

It was now done and time for bed. But some would turn their thoughts around and later set them down on paper ... the local press would sometimes publish:

Friend, maybe you abhor it, or maybe you approve,
But you haven't tasted terror 'til you see the convoy move.
For those who speak of 'Peace through strength' have often never seen
The shadow-shapes behind their words; reality, obscene
Steel coffins brought from underground when concrete tombs gape wide...

Wrapped in their shrouds of camouflage, with living death inside.
The Dogs of Death: four Hounds of Hell on every launcher's back...
Tonight they prowl the dead of night, a phantom hunting pack
Unleashed into the world of men, to burn and kill and maim:
It's on our quiet roads this night ... once every month the same.
And you may sleep and never know how close has Death passed by...
But some still keep accusing watch beneath the moonless sky,
With crackling radios, crumpled maps, to plot the racing course
Down silent roads; and nerve themselves to meet its fearsome force.
To watch the snake of headlamp eyes come winding through the night:
Red lights pick out control trucks for each dark, demonic flight,
And the blue strobes flash like lightning from police cars in the lead
(To cry "You traitors!" is unjust: not all approve the deed).
The motorbike outriders pass, and Hell comes close behind,
Twelve juggernauts of sombre steel: twelve monstrous hulks that grind
Towards and past us, roaring by, and though their engines growl
We hear the slip-streams racing surge, a bitter banshee howl
As each one passes ... tail lights glimpsed, then fading in the gloom
That swallow up all traces of this cavalcade of doom
So that, just minutes afterwards, no one would ever say,
To walk upon the silent road, that Death had passed this way.
So whether you abhor it, friend, or whether you approve,
Come watch with us the next dark night the convoy's on the move.
John Pritchard *'Cruise-Watch'*

The objectives of peace campaigning were achieved in reasonable measure, in so far as such things are ever possible. Change is a swinging pendulum ... and the period of swing is in accord with the full set of influences, and the full process just takes time. But on 26 April 1986, there was an event that impressed upon the world the dire reality of nuclear hazard in a way that all the peace campaigning of that year could never do. The Chernobyl nuclear power station in the Ukraine exploded. It was such a major disaster; and despite incredibly brave and sacrificial, selfless effort by Russian work teams, the radioactive cloud escaped, contaminating pastures and food chains across Europe, and went on to reach high locations in the UK. Many in the Ukraine continue to suffer the terrible effects of the radiation exposure.

The media went wild with concern and condemnation. But this was an out-of-control accident concerning just one of the world's several hundred nuclear reactors ... in relative terms, quite a small event. The two bombs dropped on Hiroshima and Nagasaki at the conclusion of World War II had been much more devastating. The modern nuclear ICBM weapon would be much more powerful than both of these together. But the small Chernobyl event came as a short, sharp reminder of the *reality* of nuclear threat. If so much fuss was to ensue from so little, then how can one ever begin to accept the idea of even the smallest limited exchange of ICBMs? If Chernobyl had a purpose, then it was to vividly demonstrate to post war generations just how utterly unthinkable is the risk or the use or misuse of nuclear weaponry in any shape or form.

[At the turn of the millennium, the situation was that an area of about 1,500 square miles around Chernobyl remained an exclusion zone, this so far as habitation and food production were concerned. The soil remained radioactive, largely on account of caesium-137 with a half-life of 30 years. To a degree, it became a test area for soil recovery. Useful findings were that: (1) cannabis can be grown as a crop to produce good 'clean' hemp fibre. The plant waste may then be burned to a radioactive ash, thus removing from the soil and collecting, 1% of its radioactivity, and (2) mulching and use of potassium fertiliser may reduce radioactive contamination of plants by 30-40%.]

Tragedies were not confined to the East in 1986, the American 'Challenger' rocket exploded in flight on 28 January. It steadied things. The hype of international space attention faltered, and the 'space race' aspect of serious solar system exploration, dropped from media headlines ... a further step away from East-West confrontation. In Britain, over-zealous cost trimming had spawned unsatisfactory animal husbandry; and this in turn led to BSE or 'mad cow disease'. This would take its toll of Britain and the West by stages. Now, it quietly progressed, but the full awareness of the consequences would not be realised for another decade.

There were the usual honours published during the year. Knighthoods may be expected or they may be tuned to an orthodox punctiliousness of purpose and might even go unnoticed at the time. But occasionally there is an award that catches the imagination and one might well exclaim: 'Ah ... yes!' There was one particular 'Ah ... yes!' knighthood in 1986, awarded to a Boomtown Rat, and the recipient especially well known to those who followed the New Wave pop music of the day. The previous year, Bob Geldof had received a calling concerning the starving millions in Africa. Somehow, he had managed to combine strength of purpose and his connections, to do something about it, and this had led to the Live Aid launch of 13 July.

> *'I stood stock still, my hand raised above my head, my fist clenched in unconscious salute. In front of me stood 80,000 people. Somewhere, invisible, behind them, another billion people all over the world had joined us. Together we held our breath.'*
>
> Bob Geldof *Is That It?* Macmillan Publishers Ltd

That was it. It was a fine example of people-media interaction, with the satellite link between Wembley and Philadelphia and world-wide connections. It was the biggest party ever, and massive funds were raised and continue to be raised. Later, he had travelled across Africa to see what could best be done about distribution of supplies, that sometimes got stuck in storage depots, while people continued to die daily, still without food. He helped to keep things on the move.

More and more the world was being seen as a place of resources: resources that could be used either to produce weaponry and war-zones, or that could be used to feed and rescue starving millions. While one half, through weaponry, had the funding to actively blaze their own trail to oblivion; the other half were starving and already just about there. Bob Geldof himself put it in a nutshell when he said quite simply: *'They can't eat arms.'* The people-media interaction was now getting to this problem and acting to a large degree beyond the influence of government. [Governments would manage to claw back some control over charities through introduction of state lottery systems that included an apportioned charity allocation. The system would produce a good taxation sum and the state would generally benefit in some way from the placement of the funds allocated to charitable causes ... within the state]. But media, Greenpeace, CND, SPC, Live Aid, Band Aid, School Aid and other charitable events/funds that followed, were all acting people-to-people in a simple direct way. It was all a part of the new consciousness that was having an effect, and it was itself a part of the grand change. The collective response was in part, a freshly felt 'oneness of spirit' ... a collective consciousness. All humankind belonged to the same club ... one huge global club! A new era was emerging.

The newly emerging era was certainly well marked in the Philippine Islands. The Philippines are prominent in SouthEast Asia as the region's only strongly Christian community (following 333 years of Spanish influence and missionary induction). Now, after a politically difficult period, a change of government followed the 'People Power Revolution', February

22-25, 1986. This was a peaceful, prayerful and successful revolution. On Sunday 23 February at Camp Aguinaldo, government tanks, trucks and armed soldiers confronted armed rebels. But the people (unarmed) took up their position between the factions ... tens of thousands of them. They stood, knelt, sat and prayed. They showed love and kindness to the soldiers, who were plied with handshakes, hugs, soft drinks, food and flowers. Through direct communication and eye contact, their hearts were won and the revolution was bloodless. President Marcos left the country. Mrs Corazon Aquino took office as the new president and restored democratic rule. What followed was a revised set of governing principles known as 'The 1986 Constitution'. Some of its principles deserve mention because they illustrate so well the world-wide uplifting of consciousness.

Principles included as part of the Constitution are:

- The Philippines renounces war as an instrument of national policy.
- The Philippines is declared a nuclear-free zone.
- Abolition of death penalty.
- The state shall protect ecology.
- Civilian authority is supreme over military.
- The state undertakes to promote agrarian reform.
- The state shall maintain honesty and integrity in public service.
- There shall be separation of church and state.
- Foreign bases to be banned from 1991.

It is an exemplary set of policies that deserves some prominence. It is a credit to those in office and to the consciousness of the people, that the importance of separation of church and state matters is now recognised.

As if to underline the last item listed above, Mount Pinatoba (or Pinatubo as it is more often spelled today), after having rested dormant for 400 years, erupted in the June of 1991; this totally destroying the remaining huge American military base at Clark, Zambales that had occupied 130,000 acres. (Clark and the smaller naval base at Subic had delivered unimaginable quantities of bombs during the Vietnam War. The bases have been described as the hub of an air war that delivered a greater tonnage of bombs than was used throughout World War II. It is reported that two million US military passed through the bases yearly and numerous service industries had developed, including hundreds of cocktail lounges, hotels, motels, discos and an estimated 40,000 prostitutes. The area north of Manila had changed beyond recognition.)

The eruption was massive, destroying the remaining base and sadly also causing widespread distress in the Negrito homelands, leaving large numbers injured, dead or homeless. The dust cloud affected sunsets and climate around the world.

Alongside these various happenings in the world, material developments continued to proceed vigorously and the microchip, liquid crystal, printed circuitry and computer, all contributed handsomely to the material progression. Wonderful intricate devices were being created by individuals and teams of individuals, working together to make the world a better place. The following statement, made between the world wars, both appreciates the value of creativity in the individual, and observes the senseless abomination of war; and none would put it in a more forthright manner than does its author:

> *The really valuable thing in the pageant of human life seems to me not the state but the creative, sentient individual, the personality; it alone creates the noble and the sublime, while the herd ... brings me to that worst outcrop of the herd nature, the military system, which I abhor. That a man can take pleasure in marching in formation to the strains of a band is enough to make me despise him. He has only been given his big brain by mistake; a back-bone was all he needed. This plague-spot of civilisation ought to be abolished with all possible speed. Heroism by order, senseless violence and all the pestilent violence that goes by the name of patriotism ... how I hate them! War seems to me a mean, contemptible thing: I would rather be hacked in pieces than take part in such an abominable business. And yet so high, in spite of everything, is my opinion of the human race that I believe this bogey would have disappeared long ago, had the sound sense of the nations not been systematically corrupted by commercial and political interests acting through the schools and the press.*
>
> Albert Einstein *The World As I See It*
> Trans. Alan Harris, 1935 John Lane The Bodley Head Limited

Chapter XXII

Harbingers in Cornfields

Throughout the 20th century, there had been curious sightings in the skies, curious because they did not seem to relate to anything that was known or to anything that was as yet understood. Prior to the advent of the nuclear age, the sightings were few and infrequent and not of any great concern. Some occurred during the course of World War II. At the conclusion of the war, the *lights* that had sometimes flown alongside Allied squadrons and had been named by pilots: 'Foo Fighters', were discovered with some considerable surprise *not* to have been a part of German reconnaissance. German intelligence on the other hand, was equally surprised to learn that similar *lights* that had on occasions flown with their own squadrons, were not of *British* manufacture. They became one of the war's mysteries. For want of a better term, they were officially called 'unidentified flying objects' or UFOs. From then on, UFO sightings were to become much more numerous.

In the decades that followed, we of course launched many objects skywards ... aircraft, spacecraft, satellites, weather balloons and rockets. It was no surprise at all that strictly rational critics said of UFOs, that they must be one of these items or maybe some trick of the light, with the implication being, that to think otherwise would make you a crank or crackpot. There are of course, people who make up stories and just love to be in the limelight of the *crackpot zone* anyway. They enjoy being at the centre of attention. Then again, there are those who would guide sections of *establishment* press into highlighting obvious and declared crackpots in order to deliberately discredit the whole bandwagon of more serious possibilities; and so protect the public from what might otherwise be seen as *alien panic.* In this way, the whole idea of UFOs, saucers, mother ships and observation globes became entirely confused. But there continued to be observations of mystery objects by people whose word should really be seen as unquestionable; for example, there were reports from airline pilots, police officers and a number who became clearly affected physically or emotionally by their experience. And we must not forget the Foo Fighters. There were no crackpots in those days. The world was a serious place devoid of such diversion, when the Foo Fighters were flying.

There is a little-understood phenomenon that needs to be screened out from general UFO sightings; a phenomenon that produces light effects in the sky. I refer to EQLs or earthquake lights. Luminous effects of various shapes sometimes appear in the sky just prior to, or at the time of earthquakes. It is an energy release from rock of a form that is not at all well understood or defined analytically by today's science. Such luminous energy is also released at times in the vicinity of geological fault lines (where there may be mere stress in the absence of any measurable earth tremor). The phenomenon is in itself of great interest and studies have been made.

There could just be connections with the ancient concept of a *hidden sea of energy* that underpins a variety of observed effects ... the *ch'i* of ancient China and the *kurunba* of the Australian Aborigine ... and the material world. But of course, EQLs do not display overt intelligence, do not respond to police officer's torches and do not fly around one TV mast after another! In any event, regardless of the precise nature of EQLs, there would appear to be strong connections between EQLs, geological fault lines, ley lines, ancient sites (stone circles, standing stones, earth works, old churches etc), UFOs and crop circles. A, geographical at least, association of these factors should be born in mind. It is as well that we throw all factors that might be related, into the mixing pot, prior to our analysis.

But before proceeding further, it would be as well to state three fundamental truths, which I am sure any honest-to-goodness scientist would agree:

1. The inter-stellar distances of the universe are so vast that, before any significant space travel is possible for ourselves, we must first learn to exceed the speed of light (186,000 miles/second). Otherwise it will take in excess of four years to reach the nearest star and we simply never manage to reach any other galaxy.

2. As indicated by particle acceleration data, we cannot exceed the speed of light using ordinary matter (atoms and molecules), as we know it. Ordinary matter, by its very nature, just *has* to keep within the confines of light velocity.

3. A culture that aspires to serious space travel will have probed beyond the confines of ordinary matter, will know *other* states of matter and will have greatly advanced in many ways compared to ourselves. They will have advanced in respect of such matters as love, knowledge and communication. Primitive factors such as personal greed, arrogant

patriotism, wars and ignorance will have long since been left behind. (The 'star wars' type of science fiction is merely Earth morality transposed to space, and is as much make-believe as Toad dressed in a tweed suit in Wind in the Willows. It simply has no reality content).

Any culture with the capability of space travel is therefore *not* to be feared. If there is such a culture that can travel inter-stellar distances, then the timing of their interest in ourselves would appear timely indeed. The latter half of the 20th century has been a period when we have developed nuclear strategies that have taken us close to nuclear conflict; that have headed us towards destruction, not only of ourselves, but of all life on this planet! It would be entirely understandable if others were concerned for our future and the future of planet Earth. Perhaps then, we should view UFOs, if they are real, as a blessing and *not* as a reason for being scared. So why fear *caring* beings that have advanced that much?

There is now a wealth of evidence to validate UFOs, and evidence that connects UFOs with corn circles. Perhaps then, we should also give the subject of *corn circles* our proper attention, and not be fobbed off by the inevitable set of crackpots and crackpot stories that attempt to invade their credibility. We owe it to ourselves not to allow our intelligence to be belittled in such a manner. Equally, it would be prudent for us to allow for the possibility, that any inter-galactic travellers are in turn, influenced by and subservient to, other guiding consciousness within the cosmos. The universe is a vast and wonderful infinity that extends enormously beyond our very limited vision of it.

The facts concerning crop circles cannot be explained away, as the capers of nocturnal vandals with rope and ladder, a big bundle of airline tickets and well-stamped passports, as a certain element of the media would have us believe. Let the facts speak for themselves. During the 15-year period to 1992, circle sites numbered more than 2,000, each site often containing a group or pattern of circles. The known sites span five continents. The majority of circles have been formed during the night and discovered next morning. As to their formation, they have been formed in a three dimensional mode as a *twisted spiral*, prior to the final flattening process.

There is an *energy* factor involved and a residual energy remains in the circles after their formation, the sense and detail of which is dowsable. (It may be dowsed using pendulum, rods, hands or hazel twigs. These merely extend the human energy-body that is doing the dowsing and the energy being dowsed is akin to that human energy with which it interacts.) There would appear to be some similarity of *energy pattern* with that which lies within ancient stone circles. UFOs or lights have sometimes been observed in the night sky at the time of circle formation.

There have been large numbers occurring in England with a particular concentration in the Wessex Triangle where there is also a concentration of stone circles and ancient sites. UFOs have their favoured 'entry ports' through the atmosphere and to the planet that depend upon astronomic and certain energy considerations.

A further point that should be mentioned is the intermittent simple clue, indicating that the circles were *not* made by mechanical means. Quite often, where the design has crossed wheel tracks left by a tractor, the pattern is seen to have run off course a little, giving a small but significant kink in the otherwise perfect shape. If the design were the result of the mixing of energies, the plant energy plus other applied energies, then this would be understandable. It would be the result of the absence of plant energy at the precise location of the wheel track. There would be an energy imbalance. If the design were made by mechanical means, then such an aberration would be unlikely.

The early circles were of simple shape, just large circles, smaller ones and rings. It was possible to expound theories based upon weather vortices to explain their manufacture; but that they formed on perfectly still windless nights was always a problem that could never be satisfactorily explained by the weather vortex theories. The early circles had nothing in them to fire the imagination of a would-be counterfeiter. (To call oneself a cornfield-artist and make simple circles would be just silly ... silly both in terms of motivation as well as artistic talent). By comparison with what came later, they were boringly simple. But then some 1989 circles contained new features not seen in those earlier years, and in 1990 came the most amazing, delightful pictograms and extended designs. Some were truly objects of surprising beauty and from then onwards, there was just no question of these formations being seen as natural phenomena. They were *unnatural* and they were the construct of an 'intelligence'. There was now no longer any doubt of that. They were becoming more complex and subtle with each season. And so far as the media were concerned, they also became more controversial.

There would be attempts to explain away the 'intelligence' designs as the work of 'cornfield artists' who spend their time travelling about the country at night. At a glance, this answer may seem plausible to some, but of course leaves all simple circles with no artistic merit, unexplained! And if it takes eight years to graduate from making simple circles to something having more form, such an occupation would surely be boring beyond measure! Furthermore, to assign the circles of one decade to weather vortices and the designs of the next, to cornfield artists, would be quite absurd. This is a matter that the media have so far appeared to ignore. The formations have clearly evolved from simple circle to complex design over a period of more than two decades, and all have their same source. The attempted bipartisan explanation is in the final analysis, consistent with cover-up.

Proper investigation is time consuming and not without its difficulties, apart from the irksome problems of hindrance from occasional hoaxers and wild reporting. Nevertheless, it was to become clear that the grain from circles had undergone subtle changes. The electrical conductivity of the bract tissue around the seed was altered. The growth rate of the seeds was different and in general, plants grown from circle seeds were more robust. Both American and British laboratories agreed that the DNA structure within crop circle plants was detectably altered. In addition, there has been evidence of altered soil chemistry and decreased nematode populations. Surveys concerning visitors to circles reflect a variety of physical, emotional, mental and spiritual effects and sometimes a momentary loss of consciousness has been reported.

There also appeared to be a mystical connection in all this. A number of ancient prophecies refer to this precise period 1987-2011 as a period of transition during which consciousness has to be raised, prior to entry into a new era. The Hopi elder Dan Katchongva says that we must be alert for the signs. Mayan prophecies refer to a time when the *sacred symbols* will become freshly understood. The writings of Hunbatz Men, founder of the Mayan Indigenous Community refers to this period of huge change in consciousness, and indicates that we shall have fully entered the new Earth era by 2013. Oh Shinnah describes the period as one of great purification, to be completed by 2011 and marked by the appearance of a new star. These are old shamanic prophecies that show a beauty of cohesion. It was in 1986 that there was a council of indigenous peoples from all over the South American continent, held at Machu Picchu, Peru. The decision was then made to re-open the ancient Mayan centres of energy and influence. The following year, shamans and elders joined together to open and re-activate sacred sites world-wide, this to assist progression of humankind through the transition and into the new era!

In 1989, there was again a gathering to re-activate the ancient Mayan centre of Chichén Itzá, Yucatán. This was to assist in the reprogramming of our DNA, considered necessary in the transitional change! It is the indigenous peoples who have preserved links with their ancient past; have maintained their bond with the planet. They have the sensitivity and awareness ... the connected oneness with source ... that the rampant materialism of the West, has smothered for many people (but not destroyed). Through their continued strong link with the collective unconscious or what lies beyond, the indigenous peoples have been able to assist in the process of change, whether or not those in the West have awareness of it. There are some indeed that have that awareness. The re-activation of the ancient energy sites was quickly followed by a burst of detailed eloquence in the crop circles that appeared in the vicinities of ancient sites in England. There would seem to be a world-wide resonance with respect to Earth energy and connections with those ancient sites.

Developments in the 1991 circles included a new *curly* or *spiral* element. A formation near Stonehenge was a human-like pictogram with curly hands, curly feet and curly ears. It was referred to as *'Mr Curlyman'*. A different design near Winchester had similar curled appendages. One near Popham airfield had the suggestion of a double helix (the essential structural principal of DNA!), and there were snail-like designs. (The snail being symbolic of spiral form). A number of designs incorporated an unmistakable *ladder* reaching across an arc ... symbolic of going up, or of raising consciousness perhaps. As is a common enough practice in *spirit communication*, a positive symbolism was being presented in the designs. The subtlety of the entire picture was now taking a huge bound, this time well beyond the domain of any childish prankster.

A design at Chilton Foliat, Hungerford quite clearly resembled *chromosome splitting* as in cell division, and in this instance the residual energy within the pattern was strongly dowsable. One at Barbury Castle unmistakably used sacred geometry symbolism. The doctrines of the Cabbala would have been born of early Jewish mysticism. The *Sepher Yetzirah*, or Book of Formation, is likely to have been written in the early AD centuries. The sacred geometry of the Cabbala has undergone a number of variations and applications over the centuries. It has been seen as a powerful symbolism for creation and transmutation, transmutation of spirit in its Gnostic sense. Later, in the days of alchemy, it was seen to symbolise the transmutation of base metals into gold. In the nuclear age, concern was more for the transmutation of Uranium and post-uranium elements into baser metals, lead being the stable end-product of the full natural radioactive decay process. Whatever the exact meaning, this pictogram concerned 'transmutation', and the large central sphere, in the coding of the Cabbala, would be the presiding Godhead.

The alchemical wisdom and its origin are obscure today. A verse from the Tabula Smaragdina runs: *'It ascends from the Earth to Heaven, and descending again, is new born to the Earth. In this way it takes unto itself the power of the Above and the Below.'* The sense of the verse seems to go along with the idea of 'Earthly consciousness' being re-presented from 'above' in symbolic form.

At Ickleton near Cambridge, on 12 August nearly at the end of the season, a huge Mandelbrot fractal appeared; a precise shape, born of computer-calculated mathematical equations and fairly modern, being known to our culture since the sixties. It signifies the meeting point of order and chaos. Within the Mandelbrot is order; without is chaos. It signifies 'creation' out of the universal chaos, a deeply meaningful symbol concerning life and all that is.

The crop was harvested, leaving the Mandelbrot intact. Then 13 days after its formation, there was a mysterious fire that destroyed it. The local pub talk was of military interference or in any event, the work of outsiders. But it had been there and it was photographed and recorded ... these are the important facts of the matter.

The 1992 season continued with spirals, snail symbols as well as repeated earlier patterns. Crescent moon shapes appeared both in isolation and worked into pictograms. But the quantum leap for the year was at Silbury Hill, where a perfect Dharmic Wheel appeared. The Dharma is the sacred law of the Hindu tradition. The wheel with its eight symbols, is a statement on the shape of the Ultimate Reality, and this wheel has at its eight points, the more ancient of the symbols that are recognised by today's world. They include the antlered head of Kernunnos, Lord of the Forest, depicting the animal spirit. They include the crescent moon of Sulis as the birth womb of spirituality and the key of Mapon that unlocks the door to spirituality. Each symbol has deep meaning and comes from our distant past. At the centre of the wheel ... the Godhead. The individual symbols also appear as part of the season's pictograms across Wessex, giving a grand co-ordination of imprint to the entire display.

The 1993 circles told a similar story. The spectacular pictogram of the season appeared at Bythorn, near Huntingdon. It was a pentacle, set in a pentagon, set in a ten-petal flower. Traditionally the human frame relates well to pentagonal geometry (as was illustrated in drawings by Leonardo). The mathematical devices of *pi* and of the *Golden Mean proportion* and their embodiment in ancient architecture has long been viewed as connecting humankind and cosmos. The pentacle is an ancient symbol of the five-fold nature of man. The points of the pentacle are also known to witchcraft, where the area so marked would be cleansed or protected. According to prophecy, we are about to enter a fifth era with a different consciousness. The design has been arranged such that there are just two possible positions for the pentacle within the flower. (If it rotates 36°, there is a perfect new position for it). It can therefore be seen as another symbol of change for man, in relation to his position in the cosmos. Whatever the precise interpretation, it is without question, again a potent symbolism using the ancient imagery that is firmly established as a part of our culture and of planetary collective consciousness.

In 1994, a number of designs seemed to indicate a progression, taking the form of a necklace of spheres of increasing size. One such design at East Dean, West Sussex, consisted of five spheres, the fifth and largest (or nearest) of which, contains a crescent moon ... the 'birth of spirituality' sign of the Dharmic Wheel. Another reference to our entry into a fifth era and a more spiritual age perhaps. A spider's web design at Avebury had the same ten-pointed character as the Bythorn flower of the previous year. The four strands of the web enclose and progress to a glorious encircled centre, consistent again with progression from fourth to fifth. Its being enclosed by an outer circle rather likens it to the Native American Indian *dream catcher*, in which the web was seen to catch the good dreams, which then found their way to the hole at the centre. The device often had a feather that would hold that dream. The necklace of spheres near Devizes, Wiltshire, terminates in a large head-like structure, which has led to its nickname: 'the scorpion'. But the head is enclosed by a crescent moon, and it has a further small crescent attached; again consistent with a symbol of progression and of new spiritual birth.

There were further elaborations in 1995 as well as continued themes. There were more crescent moons, and a four-crescent pattern appeared at Exton. An interlocking three crescent design appeared at East Meon. A design with one crescent appeared at Overton. A formation of the 'progressing spheres' type arrived near Danebury Hill Fort near Andover. A 'bent pentacle' was seen at Kingsclere (in form, like a flexible pentacle being rotated with its points trailing) ... The five-fold nature of man *on the move* perhaps. A set of concentric but eccentric rings appeared near Lancing. The eccentricity gave the three-dimensional illusion of a striped wide-based cone. There was a new type of pattern at Cheesefoot Head that seemed to be based on a sine wave-modulated circle, introducing the idea of oscillation or frequency.

But at three locations, astronomical maps appeared which seem to draw attention to the inner planets of the solar system. At Stockbridge, quite simply the sun surrounded by the asteroid belt was depicted. At Longwood Warren, we had a more complete map showing the sun, the asteroid belt and the orbits of the four innermost planets. The planets: Mercury, Venus and Mars were marked on their respective orbits; Earth, the *third* planet being clearly and curiously omitted from its orbit. A similar map appeared at Tichborne, except that all four planets were marked in an alignment configuration with the *orbit* of Earth, this time omitted. Whatever the detailed meaning of these astronomical maps may be, one can be certain of one thing. They draw attention in no uncertain terms to planet Earth. Quite clearly there is a concern for Earth.

In subsequent years, the designs have become more diverse, more intricate and bigger. At Windmill Hill in 1996, a three-armed spiral made up of 194 circles graded in size, measured a thousand feet across. At Alton Barnes a DNA double helix design based on 89 linked circles, was nearly 650 feet long. On 8 July 1996, and I understand between 5.30pm and 6.00pm,a Julia set fractal (swirl) design appeared beside Stonehenge. It was made up of 149 circles and measured 915 feet. Its formation went unnoticed either by those attending Stonehenge or by those driving along the nearby A303, yet there is evidence that this formation appeared within a 30-minute period.

The designs of the following year included some that, although two-dimensional, could easily be seen in their effect as three-dimensional. One such design of 1998 near Tawsmead Copse, Wiltshire, was a 21-sided compact figure 400 feet in diameter.

Although the crop circle phenomenon is by no means restricted to just cereal crops, it is the cereal crops that are favoured. This is perhaps understandable. The formation *is* an *energy* phenomenon. There is no doubt of this, and each individual cereal plant has its own energy field (which may be demonstrated by Kirlian photography). A wheat field, with each plant reaching to the same height, may be seen as a smooth sheet of energy, and a perfect large-scale *energy* writing pad. Each plant can be manipulated by applied energies acting on its own energy, altering plant microstructure in the process, and leaving a residual, detectable energy within the circle. A plausible explanation maybe; but what makes the crop formations so beautiful ... so eye-catchingly captivating?

A number of interesting studies have been made of the various designs and it seems that several mathematical principles contribute to their beauty. Gerald Hawkins has shown that the area ratios of some circles conform to the diatonic music scale. John Martineau has studied the 1987 quintuplet at Upton Scudamore. This formation has a particular beauty of geometric symmetry. (If a circle is drawn to enclose and touch the four satellite circles, and an eight-pointed star is constructed within, then the central circle becomes exactly inscribed within the octagon so formed by the star structure. Other constructions also result in *perfect fit* arrangements). He goes on to compare similar harmony in the orbits of planets in the solar system.

A factor in the beauty of such works as the Great Pyramid and the Athenian Parthenon, is the dimensional use of the phi-ratio or Golden Section. It seems that one dimension in the ratio 1.61803 to another gives *pleasing* proportion to the eye; a fact realised and used from ancient times and a part of sacred geometry. In much later times, a number series known as the Fibonacci series was discovered ... a series such that each number in the series equals the sum of the two preceding numbers: 0, 1, 1, 2, 3, 5, 8, 13, 21, 34, 55, 89 ... The series identifies quite closely with nature. Its form is found in patterns of plant growth, in flower petal arrangement, in fir cone design and in planetary orbit ratios. When a graph is plotted of Fibonacci numbers against their successive-number-ratios, the reducing-wave-form graph quickly approaches and aligns to the value 1.61803 ... the phi-ratio! The phi-ratio would therefore appear to lie at the heart of the Fibonacci series. And it must itself also be intricately bound as an integral part of nature!

A number of the crop circle designs contain elements that are in the phi-ratio, or approximately so. A particular example is the 1993 Bythorn flower, in which four of the circle-diameters are in a phi-ratio series. The petal arc diameters and the pentacle side length also fit the series. Parts of the 1994 'scorpion' are in the phi-ratio, while the East Dean formation has diameters that approximate to a Fibonacci series relationship. There is clearly subtle mathematics in the various formations that in some measure helps to describe the format of their beauty. It is not however, the general 'synthesised' brand of mathematics, but that which lies deeply embedded, and wrapped in Nature's cloak. And the mathematics underlying various formations reveals a bond with Nature herself ... often seen as the Earth Goddess ... as Gaia ... as Artemis ... as Demeter.

Could it be the Earth herself who cries out? She has good reason to. If the rain forests were re-established, if the spoiled regions were restored, that would still not be enough. All would be to no avail without a reawakening of that *inner dreaming* ... that underlying creative resonance. Have the subtle patterns of the circles reawakened spirit or inner dreaming? And does whatever process is involved include a feedback from our own planetary collective consciousness?

Remember too the ancient festival of Eleusis ... how *death and rebirth of humankind was inextricably entwined with death and rebirth of the corn. And the corn was of Demeter, she with the golden tresses that waved so like the corn itself. In communion they would share the unleavened cakes bearing the motif that was the head of Demeter*. What better place could possibly have been chosen for any such message to humankind? And those of us who have read Homer, Plato, Aristotle or any ancient Greek philosopher, will be aware of the *Greek connection* with our present culture. Those names of that earlier civilisation continue to be viewed by ourselves with much reverence and admiration.

Crop Circles diagram 1986 - 1995

At some risk of confusion, the diagram that follows attempts to show 27 crop circles and how their complexity has changed over a ten-year period. It is of course, a very small selection picked from the many. As illustrated, black simply depicts the standing corn and white, that which is laid. The small circles that often appear adjacent to the main configuration are shown as white specks. They are variously angled 'bird's eye view' impressions.

Beginning with the top row and going from left to right, they are:

Row A: *1. 1986. Cheesefoot Head. A single circle with ring.*
Its simplicity is typical of the previous ten years.
2. 1990. Longwood Estate, near Winchester.
3. 1990. Etchilhampton, near Devizes.
4. 1990. Allington Down.

Row B: *5. 1991. Hungerford. 'Splitting chromosome'.*
6. 1991. Barbary Castle. 'Transmutation' symbolism.
7. 1991. East Kennet. 'Fractal'.

Row C: *8. 1991. Cheesefoot Head. 'curly' design.*
9. 1991. Amesbury. 'Mr Curlyman'.
10. 1992. West Draycot. Design with crescent.
11. 1992. Silbury Hill. Dharmic wheel. (One sign of the wheel omitted on account of spoilage by ground-water).
12. 1992. Tawsmead. A single large crescent.

Row D: *13. 1992. Alton Barnes. A snail-like design.*
14. 1993. Devizes. Some simpler designs still continue.
15. 1993. The Bythorn 'pentacle-flower'.
16. 1993. Windmill Hill.

Row E: *17. 1994. West Stowell. Two-armed spiral.*
18. 1994. Near Devizes. 'Scorpion' with crescents.
19. 1994. A crescent in the fifth circle.
20. 1994. West Overton. 'T'ai chi' pattern.

Row F: *21. 1994. Avebury. Spider's web.*
22. 1995. Cheesefoot Head. Frequency-modulated circle.
23. 1995. Kingsclere. 'Bent pentacle'.

Row G: *24. 1995. Longwood Warren. Solar system. Earth missing!*
25. 1995. Tichborne. Solar system. Earth orbit missing!
26. 1995. East Meon. Crescent moon design.
27. 1995. Exton. Crescent moon design.

Crop Circles 1986 - 1995

Crop Circles (post 1995)

These are examples of later and particularly large designs. Starting at the top of the page:

1. *1996. Windmill Hill. 3-armed spiral of graded circles.*
2. *1999. Hackpen Hill, Wiltshire. Double crescent, 3-armed spiral.*
3. *1996. Stonehenge. Julia set fractal.*
4. *1996. Alton Barnes. DNA double helix.*

This formation measured 1,000 feet across, almost 1/5th of a mile!

Chapter XXIII

Earth Energy

As early as 1910, I. Galli had published a report listing 148 observations of atmospheric light phenomena that had been previously recorded in Italy. Further research in the sixties by John Keel, positively linked various atmospheric lights to earthquakes. Ragnar Forshufund made connection between the incidence of this type of 'UFO' light and sunspot maxima. There is no question whatsoever about earthquake lights (EQLs). They exist. They are seen from time to time along the Earth's fault lines. Along those stretches where the rocks are under stress, a kind of *energy* is released and it becomes manifest as balls of light or some such effect. The EQLs therefore, offer some measure of proof to the would-be sceptic, that the subtle lines of earth energy at these locations also share a place in reality. There is also a serious possibility of an interaction with sun energy, resulting in peak incidence during the times of sunspot maxima.

Those who are sufficiently sensitive are able to feel the subtle earth energies. The Aborigines of Australia would 'know' and travel the songlines of their country. Such a way was natural to those *tuned* and in close touch with the earth. A good many in the old days, were close to earth and nature and knew her ways so well; not a scientific understanding, but a 'knowing' that came from the shared oneness of creation. Many in the West have now lost that sensitivity, but not all. There have always been some that still have the ability to *divine* water or *dowse* the subtle changes below the surface, within the planetary crust. Some may seek extension of their natural gift by means of hazel twig, pendulum, rods or some other contrivance. The energies are there, for those who feel their gift and care to use it, to seek out whatever lies below.

But it was the extreme conditions of the ice ages that had a particular and lasting effect upon the landscape of the British Islands. The passage of engulfing glaciers as they advanced from the north, reached half way and more, covering virtually the whole of Wales and the Midlands; but never encroaching the Severn estuary and lands to the south. Those lands, which were to become known as Wessex, were central to that unspoiled region. To the north, life and its structures were of necessity intermittent; signs of prior occupancy being scoured and scraped, and the landscape held in frozen condition. In earlier times, there was no Channel dividing

Britain and Europe. Migrations came freely. Wessex was a land of forests, plains, downlands, rivers and lakes, inhabited by elephant, lion, elk, mammoth, bear, pig, hyena, deer, bison and humans. Life was here from *distant* times and the humans, for at least half a million years. That is what makes this part of Britain of a different nature, the continuity of life.

The land shape, the tracks, the energies, all remained steady in the absence of any catastrophic influence. Just how far back do the tracks and landscape lines go? Were they made by our early ancestors, or were they first the tracks of animals? Who can tell? Their origins may well be remote. As to the standing stones, the circles, the dolmens, the holy wells and other associated structures along the path, in relative terms, they would certainly be more modern. But their makers, the ones who placed them, would still nonetheless be 'knowing' of the energies, and would have felt the special path, bonding earth-energy and nature.

There were the straight tracks and there were the leys and very often they were the same. That is, they were travelled *and* had the energy. In the old days, these were the routes that were felt and walked.

The major ley that runs across the region has a double aspect. It was dowsed, tracked and studied in depth in modern times by Hamish Miller and Paul Broadhurst. Their journey took them from Carn Lês Boel and St. Michael's Mount in the extreme southwest across to Hopton on the Norfolk coast, in what became, in its overall and general shape, a straight line running 27 degrees north of east. The line passes through such landmarks as St. Michael's church, Trull; Burrowbridge Mump (with its ruined St. Michael church); St. Michael's church, Othery; Glastonbury Tor (with its St. Michael tower), and the great Avebury ring forming a part of the ancient Serpent Temple. The 'St. Michael Line' is an earth-energy line. It is of a winding, meandering *serpent-like* energy. (Straight in its overall alignment, but meandering in the *detail* of its course.) It seems to have been important to the early Christian Church that such energy should be subdued ... conquered. Therefore its early churches built along that line were dedicated to Saint Michael, the *dragon- or serpent-slaying saint*, and some to Saint George (of similar disposition), with suitably fashioned tributes in stone to depict the slaying of the earth-energy ... of the *serpent*. At that time, the early Christian Church and its masons must have been fully aware of the serpent energy, and so, arranged their churches along the line and dedications as they then thought fit.

[Equally, on the other side of the world, Australian Aborigines had their awareness of the *Rainbow Serpent* energy; their serpent being an energy symbol, representing the sacred body of the Earth ... and being the creative energy of Dreamtime. In the Mayan culture it was the *Vision Serpent* that stood as the symbol of path between material world and the other-world. The symbolism was extended to the Vision Serpent's body penetrating the mountain, just as the king's spiritual path should penetrate the pyramid floor to reach the heart of the Earth.]

The ancient cultures all held a ritualistic respect for the serpent energy, each recognising the Earth connection in its own particular way. But not so, the early Western Church, which was contemptuous of arcane belief. There is of course, ample evidence for the enmity that existed between the early Christian Church and older belief systems. Moreover, it is a sad loss to us, that much of the Avebury Serpent Temple has been destroyed over the years as the result of this enmity. (We in present times are indebted to John Aubrey, who drew attention to the temple in his 17th century writings, and to William Stukeley who then recorded its details at a time when it was still a good deal more complete than it is today. We are also blessed with 20th century revival of proper interest and the marking of positions where original standing stones once stood).

The serpent-slaying symbolism in the churches, probably relates to *Revelation 20, 2-3*, where the angel overpowers ... *'the old Serpent, who is the Devil ... and hurled him into the pit ... so that he should no longer deceive the nations.'* But the term 'serpent' of course, has been widely applied in our language (for example, to that which is of winding character whether it be a body of water, an earth energy line or a musical instrument). Clearly, the serpent of Revelation has a very different meaning. Unlike a ley line, the serpent of the Bible would *'deceive the nations...'* which has to make it something quite apart. One can only surmise that the serpent-slaying symbolism was used quite simply, and without justification, to put down the religion for which the Serpent Temple stood. But in the latter 20th century, the scheme backfired and became supporting evidence in the rediscovery of the ley line, also revealing with clarity that there must have been knowledge of its presence at the time when the churches along its length were built.

The St. Michael line passes through a series of features that include dedicated churches, standing stones, stone circles, mumps and places of power. During the period of study by Miller and Broadhurst, the line was discovered to have a dual aspect. A feminine counterpart, aptly enough named the 'St. Mary Line', running alongside; crossing the St. Michael Line at special points, the two lines joining and then running together through the two stone circles within the Avebury ring. The church dedications along this second line are to St. Mary. Along *her* line lie the holy wells and places of healing, barrows, mounds and the greatest of all constructed mounds ... Silbury Hill. The two lines are of quite different character. St. Mary, of course, is the feminine aspect of the Christian faith, and as such, shares the maternal loving and protective qualities of the Earth Mother. But perhaps the female line is in part at least, the office of Sulis, the Sun Mother Goddess. It would be *she* who rises on May Day above the Norfolk coast to beam her rays along the line from east to west, and it would be she who pours her warmth into the waters that emerge at sacred places as the holy wells and healing waters. Where the energies of the two lines run together within the Avebury ring; that is the midpoint of the system ... a fulcrum of the forces ... the meeting of the energies of Earth and Sun. Such is the origin and the nature of Avebury.

In ancient times, the central hub of the yearly cycle was Beltane ... the fire festival celebrated on the first day of May; a time for renewal; a time of fusion of the deities of Sun and Earth; a union that would ensure both germination and harvest. Pilgrimage and the lighting of fires formed a part of the custom and ritual across the land. But at Avebury, the centre of the lines of power extending to coasts in east and west, *there* at Avebury, was a main centre of pilgrimage ... where the power lines converge within the great serpent temple that those with the knowledge had placed there, within the landscape.

It is clear from William Stukeley's record, that a megalithic avenue wound between low hills, from the vicinity of Knoll Down, crossing the River Kennet to meet the great Avebury ring. Emerging from the ring again, it then followed a curving course the full distance to two concentric rings that form 'The Sanctuary' on Overton Hill. Here, in The Sanctuary, has been found a crossing point of the two lines. The St. Michael Line continues its course along the megalithic avenue and into the great ring. It then exits to follow a course that crosses Windmill Hill. The St. Mary Line leaves The Sanctuary on quite a different course, passing through West Kennet Long Barrow, the sacred and cyclic Swallowhead spring, through the beautiful chalk-structured mound ... Silbury Hill, and into the great ring. Emerging, it then passes through the church at Winterbourne Monkton, crosses the St. Michael Line on Windmill Hill and leaves the area via the Long Stones ... the two remaining stones of the megalith avenue on the Beckhampton side. (Of the original 600+ megaliths comprising the temple, a total of 76 remain today).

The Beckhampton Avenue would appear to have marked the course of a further (dual) energy line from the great ring to Knoll Down, where it divides into two spirals and terminates. Such is the Serpent Temple ... several miles of it, marking the course of the energies and set into the landscape. The temple adheres to the landscape and the land feels the sanctity of the temple and has *connected* benefit.

According to legend, Sulis is the 'Sun Mother Goddess'. Likewise, legend portrays Sun Goddess, Mother Goddess, Earth Mother and Corn or Grain Goddess as being much intertwined, and all aspects of a single female deity. All entirely understandable, since without sun, there is no nature, there is no corn and nothing to 'mother' save the barren earth. Hence, all are naturally aspects of the one. In the Gaelic, even the word for sun is *Greine or grain*, and the Sun Goddess is *Dia Greine*, and so the connections are found in language too. In general, the Grain Goddess is in any event held to be a direct expression of the Mother Goddess, known by different names to different peoples of different times. In ancient Greece, she was Demeter. Earlier, she was called Ker, a three-in-one Goddess. She being the *maiden*, also the spark (the *life germ*), also the *mother*. It is she: Ker, who has the sister Rhiannon ... Rhiannon who rides her white mare between worlds when the doorways to the other-world are open. And it is Rhiannon's white mare that rests upon the downlands of the landscape surrounding the Serpent Temple.

Did the energies of the temple then in some way facilitate a doorway to the other-world? If so, then that would explain why four white mares lie waiting upon the downs within just four miles of the Avebury circle. One awaits on Hackpen Hill following the Ridgeway to the north, one on Milk Hill near Wansdyke Path to the south, one on Cherhill Down following the Beckhampton Avenue and earthworks to the west, and a fourth close by the River Kennet and Marlborough to the east. Further white mares may be seen on the hills that lie more distant. Perhaps the Beltane festival that celebrates the union of energies of Sun and Earth also concerns the union of the two worlds. (The ley energy would be akin to the energy of the human energy-body, since it can be dowsed by it. And any raising of the aura frequency would favour psychic potential).

They would begin their pilgrimage in good time, many walking the high 'Ridgeway' to take a place in the temple landscape, and to go in procession along the marked megalith avenues. The flat-topped Silbury mound with its terrace was built central to the ceremony; a well sited place of control within temple and within landscape. A straight line from the Knoll Down spirals (the serpent tail) to The Sanctuary bisects the mound, and a straight line sighted from the West Kennet Long Barrow to Windmill Hill, again bisects the mound. It was indeed well placed, with all extremities of the temple itself being visible.

We can imagine the scene ... April was out, and the early hours of the new month were just extending beyond silence. As the eastern sky began to lighten, the sequence of dawn chorus sounds heralded the moment. A light brushwood fire was well prepared with the dry wind-blown grass and lightest of kindle at its base, awaiting ignition. It would take from the *tein-eigin* ... the forced-fire. The greenwood square frame for giving power to the axle-tree stood ready; its central spindle thrust into old oak. It was the *sure-fire* way. The dried agaric, resulting from nature's own recycling of her spent birch trunks, was placed at the centre and would respond instantly to the first spark. Nine men stood ready, bent to their machine. An expectant hush, which the bird-calls now penetrated with their true liquid clarity. A golden edge feathered the horizon ... seen from the mound ... and the sign was given! The axle-tree creaked as the nine pressed it into motion, racing around, like the maypole that it was. The axle screamed and sparks showered ... a bright glow ... and a waft of blue smoke trailed as it was quickly but with due ceremony, transferred to the waiting kindle. Then the roar of fire as flame found crack-dry twigs and old pine needles to tempt the quickening heat; just as the first true rays cut across the heavens from the distant Sun Mother. A perfect union of the lights!

This was the moment of fusion. Earth and Sun; Sun Mother and Earth Mother, would fuse again their energies of life and growth. It was the fusion too, of Nature's material aspect, of which humanity must be a part, with 'spirit legions'. This was the time for awakening Nature's devic entities. They would watch over the buds and flowers in the months ahead. Humankind would also find spiritual refreshment, sharing the joy of an enriched landscape, finding new energies of a shared consciousness; human consciousness, the energies of Nature's spirits, and enjoining a full connectedness. Rhiannon's white mares scattered through the hills well symbolised the journeys into spirit. The *power* of the *energy-flow* was felt and was real! All would be refreshed, blessed, healed; and all would enjoy the oneness of spirit of it all and the oneness of their own collective spirit selves. All would have the *full connectedness*, and right across the country, hilltop fires would focus the fusing of the energies ... and the Earth's current would stay strong. It would of course stay. This was a part of the *energy system* of the *living planet*. This would always be.

In 1987, *The Ley Guide*, Paul Devereux & Ian Thomson, was published. (First published 1979 as *The Ley Hunter's Companion*). The book includes seven example leys, which are classed as *holy hill* leys. These in general include hills with ancient chalk figures or earth workings aligned with Christian or Christianised shrines, and sometimes there is a known pilgrimage tradition. In each alignment, there are five to ten features, which frequently include such items as tumuli and barrows. They are short *visual* alignments in the existing landscape. But of course, their energy lines may well be much longer than the line of 'markers' that remain visible in today's landscape.

The three map-diagrams that follow, illustrate:

(1) The St. Michael - St. Mary line and how four of the holy hill leys seem to cluster around Avebury, one being the energetic Old Sarum ley that passes through Stonehenge.

(2) The area with chalk hill figures and the Avebury temple.

(3) The area of high crop circle incidence.

Some Ley Lines of Southern England

The St. Michael Line (ref. Colquhoun, Miller and Broadhurst) and short 'holy hill' lines (ref. Devereux and Thomson), drawn with slightly exaggerated length.

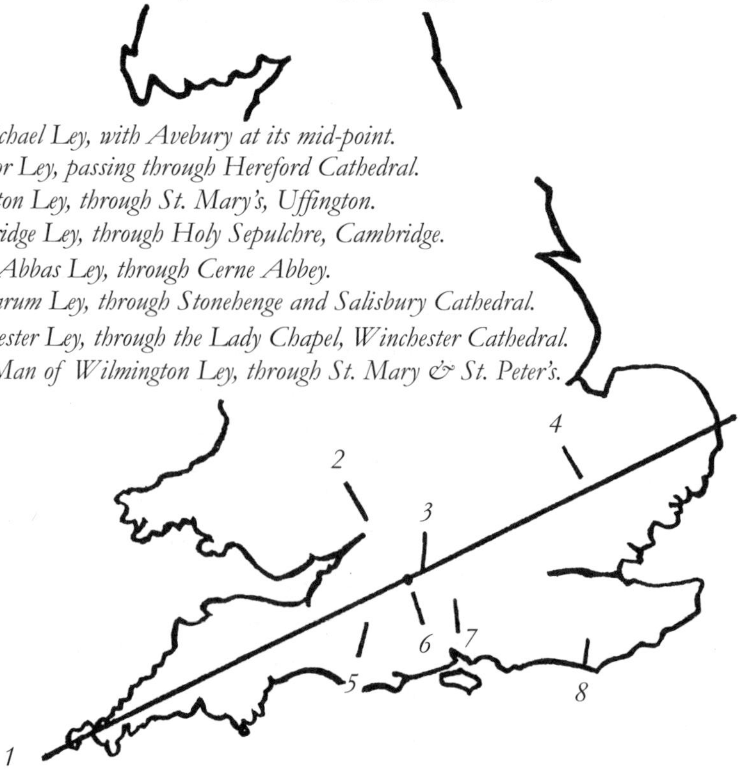

1. St. Michael Ley, with Avebury at its mid-point.
2. Dinedor Ley, passing through Hereford Cathedral.
3. Uffington Ley, through St. Mary's, Uffington.
4. Cambridge Ley, through Holy Sepulchre, Cambridge.
5. Cerne Abbas Ley, through Cerne Abbey.
6. Old Sarum Ley, through Stonehenge and Salisbury Cathedral.
7. Winchester Ley, through the Lady Chapel, Winchester Cathedral.
8. Long Man of Wilmington Ley, through St. Mary & St. Peter's.

Avebury: the Ancient Landscape

The Temple (Knoll Down - Avebury Ring - The Sanctuary. Ref. Wm Stukeley)
St. Michael - St. Mary Lines (Ref. Hamish Miller & Paul Broadhurst)
Alignments, White Horses, Tumuli (shown as dots), Barrows (shown as dashes)

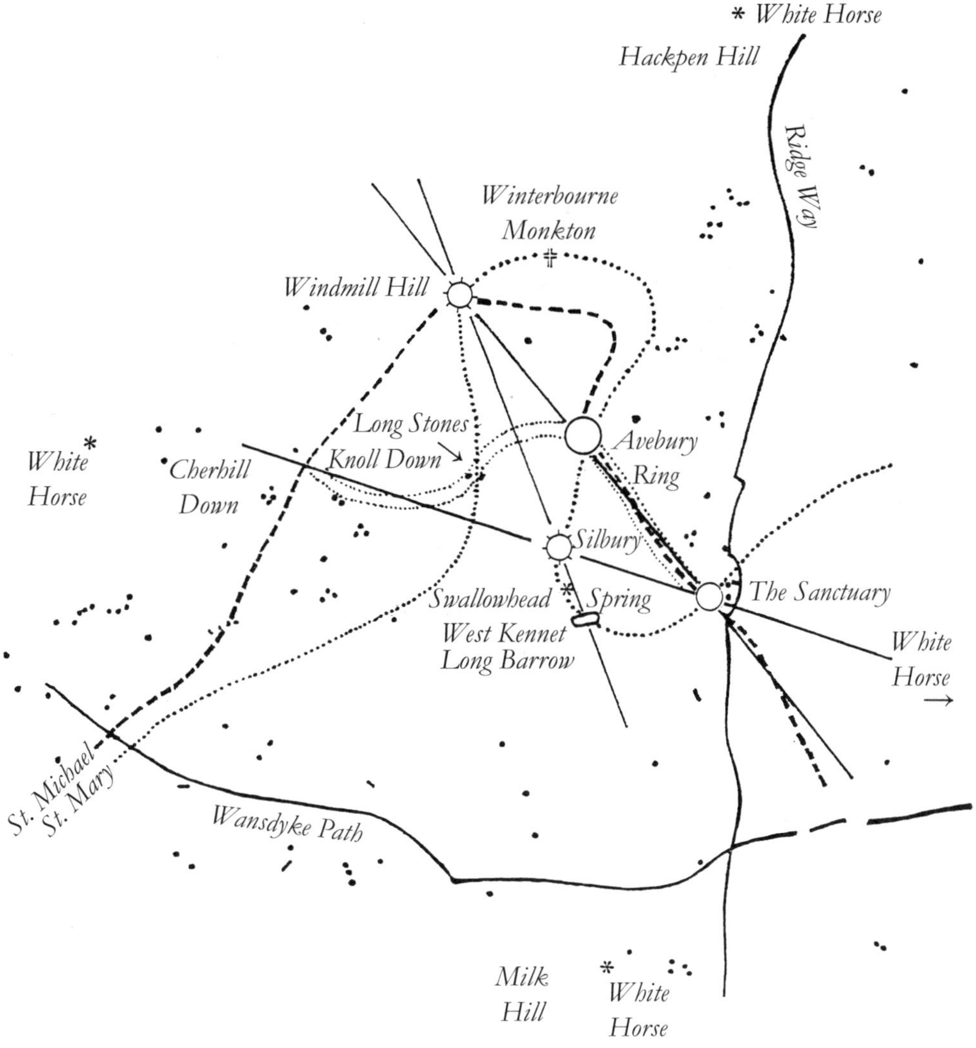

Incidence of Crop Circles in England

Crop circles regularly occur in the squared areas of the map, with a particularly high concentration around the middle part of the St. Michael Ley Line and Avebury.

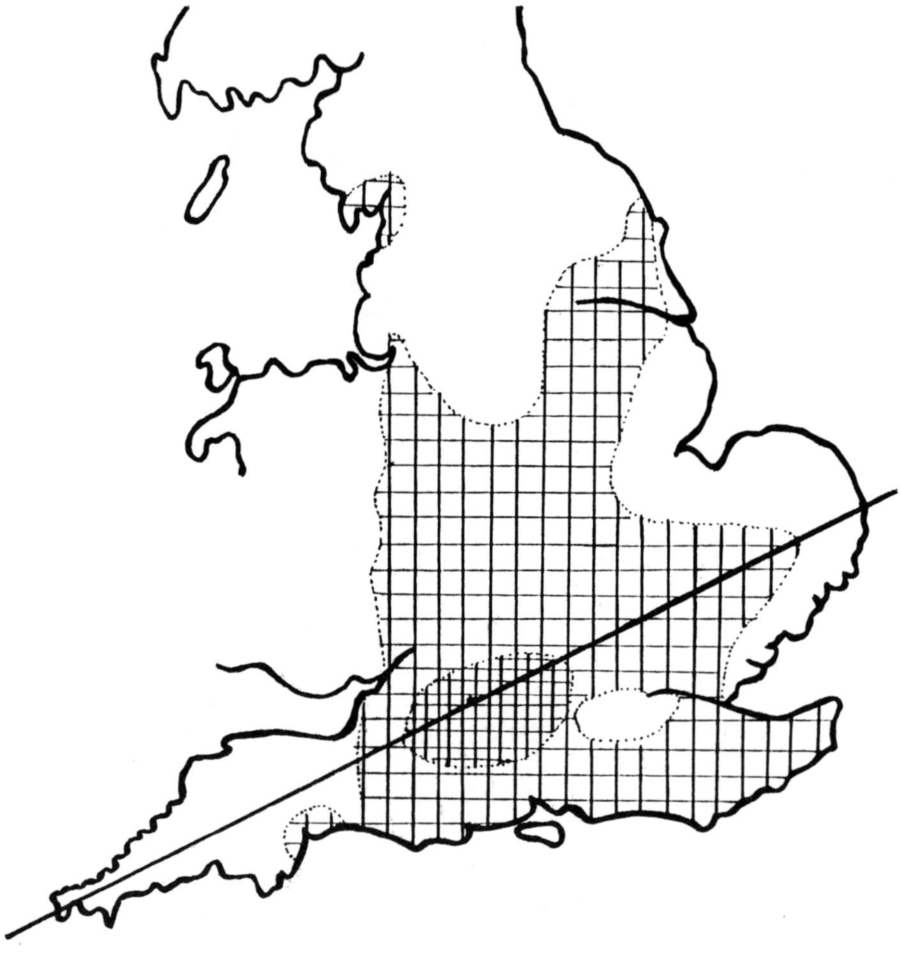

There would appear to be a quite remarkable correlation between crop circle placing and the ancient landscape. Furthermore, it is on record that, during the summer of 1988, 51 crop circles appeared within just seven miles of Silbury. On the night of 14 July, five of them appeared *on* the St. Mary Line, between the Swallowhead Spring and Silbury.

The authors of *The Ley Guide* also draw attention to the Nazca plateau of Peru and the Western Cordillera of Bolivia where ancient long straight (artefact) lines also occur in the landscape. But the similarity with British leys does not just stay with the lines themselves. The Long Man of Wilmington is thought to be one of our more ancient chalk hill figures. He holds two poles and is 237 feet in length. He has been around sufficiently long for there to be several legends concerning his origin.

There is a figure from similar ancient times in Peru. There, he is known as the *Staff God*. The representation from the Raimondi Stele, Chavín de Huántar, shows the South American version of the Staff God in splendid detail. Here, he has ornate head-dress, the mandatory two staffs, and a huge endowment of the serpent energy; which includes a coiled twin-serpent representation at the very top. (This device generally denotes the dual nature of the serpent energy). The Staff God frequently occurs on beautiful burial wraps with a less ornate head-dress. A similar Staff God figure also appears as the central figure on the Gateway of the Sun, at Tiahuanico, Bolivia, and he was painted onto the Tiahuanaco pottery. Like the stone circle builders, these people were also experts with stone, both at Tiahuanaco and the more ancient site at Puma Puncu. Fitted blocks weighing up to 130 tons were used to form temple bases. Later, the Mayan staff rituals held at period ends may have a derived symbolism from the Staff God.

The several links between Britain and the indigenous and ancient peoples of the Americas are intriguing. Their prophecies concerning world transition seem to relate to the progression in pattern of British crop circles. The straight tracks of South America have been compared to Britain's leys. There is evidence that the Staff God from ancient times was known on both sides of the Atlantic. The Hopi, who have preserved their culture on the high mesas in the north-east of Arizona, have a prophecy that concerns the red brother and the white brother taking their different paths. The red brother developed in spirit, while the white brother attained a quite different technical development. The two would meet again to unite their qualities, and the synthesis of those qualities would exceed in value that which had gone before.

As the days of change and transition unfold, a flower of synthesis may well open to bloom with a resplendent beauty.

South American Staff God

Outline drawings that compare stance and general bearing with that of the Long Man of Wilmington. The detail of the South American representations contains many serpent pairs.

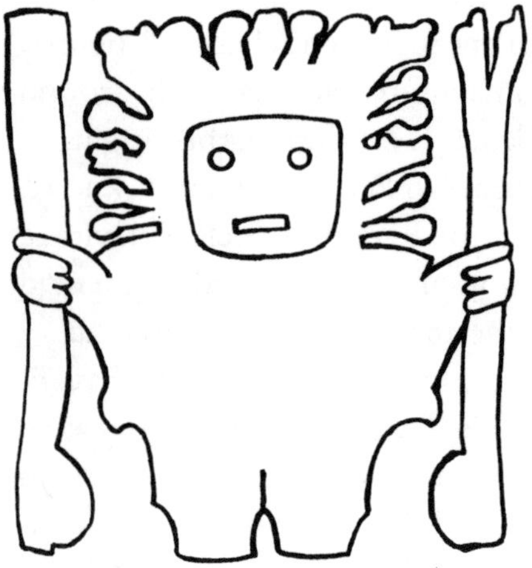

As he appears on the Gateway of the Sun at Tiahuanaco near the southern shore of Lake Titicaca, Peru.

On painted cotton textile dated c. 1200 - 700 BC from Carhua, Paracas Peninsula, Peru.

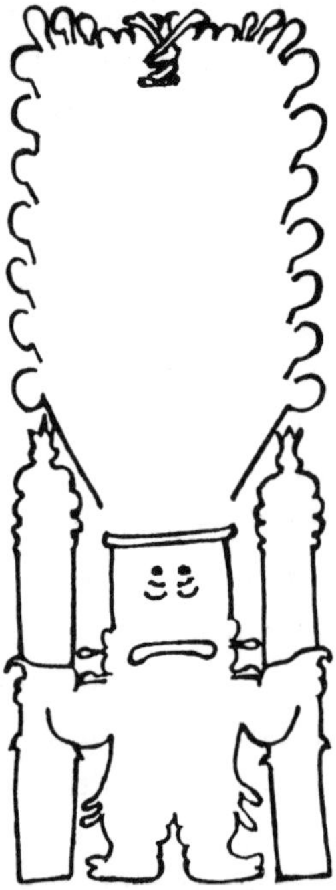

A low relief design on the Raimondi Stele at Chavín de Huántar, Peru. It is a highly detailed masterpiece and the elaborate head-dress has many serpents including a coiled pair at the top.

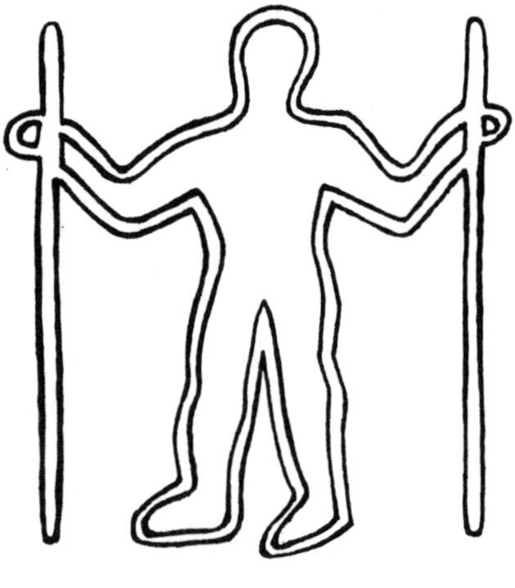

Long Man of Wilmington, cut into the chalk of the South Downs, East Sussex.

Chapter XXIV

Beyond the Technical Reality

The physical world is a wonderful place, and this I feel certain, we would all agree. The technical and artistic achievements of past millennia, are doubtless a natural outcome of our interaction with the physical world; but there must clearly be something more than just its visual material aspect.

Peering beyond what is technical, beyond the material world, beyond light and its more general concept of electromagnetic wave form; we understand little. That is, beyond the bounds of our very limited science, there is much with which we in the West remain unfamiliar ... and some would say: 'Why should it be otherwise?' ... or ... 'When the details of the material world can be proved so readily, why waste time on anything else?' We are each entitled to the view that we choose to take. Yet, there is ample evidence of many worlds of possibilities that lie just beyond the doorways that enclose our material perception. We do not understand Earth energies, but for a host of reasons, know them to exist. And there is the knowledge that other souls, in the not so distant past on this planet, have been much more familiar with those energies than we ourselves, they that sited the early churches for example. That is one doorway which we have ventured to peep through ... albeit just a small peep. There are many other similar doorways worthy of our exploration.

Some of us are more sensitive to the non-material than others. But we all have the natural inherent ability to develop ... enhance ... tune ... that ability that waits within. We are all able to observe the traffic that passes through the doorways of our primal perception. It is possible for us to learn much from the accounts of others; we can learn from books written by those who 'know'; the sages, the holy men, healers, philosophers (perhaps more from East than West), and those who have found themselves imbued with special gifts. We can learn from our dreams and in quiet moments, from the voice within.

How many of us have been visited by close ones who have departed this life? How many have been reassured by an etheric envoy that a child lost early in life, continues to live happily in another world beyond? Some have been fortunate enough to have an extended period of grief assuaged in this way. There are many such accounts on record. Some visitations have been to ordinary loving folk; some to holy men who have rejoiced in once again having sight of departed masters. Sometimes a dialogue ensues. It is a common enough occurrence, and was clearly accounted at that time when Jesus the Christ left this Earth. But such accounts are by no means confined only to the scriptures. In fact, such visual visitations are most certainly a continuing phenomenon in today's world. There is clearly more to human form than just the material body. Some descriptions of visitations are brief but sincere, while others carry a wealth of detail. No account of such a happening is more vivid than that given by Paramahansa Yogananda, when he was visited by his dead and departed master Sri Yukteswar:

> *'Angelic guru' I said, 'your body looks exactly as it did when last I wept over it in the Puri ashram.'*
>
> *'O yes, my new body is a perfect copy of the old one. I materialize or dematerialize this form any time at will, much more frequently than I did while on earth. By quick dematerialization, I now travel instantly by light express from planet to planet, or, indeed, from astral to causal or to physical cosmos.'*
>
> Paramahansa Yogananda *Autobiography of a Yogi*
> Self-Realization Fellowship, Los Angeles, 1998

As appears to be the case with a number of masters from the Himalayas and the East, Sri Yukteswar could dematerialise or slip out of his material body, even while he was still in his Earth life. Even in the West of course, there are quite numerous accounts of 'near death' with 'out-of-body' experiences. In the modern hospital operating theatre, there are from time to time *temporary death* situations. Those coming back or regaining physical life, report that they have seen their own (material) body from above with the concerned medical staff in attendance. Knowing that gurus, through their regular meditation and training, can achieve the out-of-body phenomenon in a controlled way, it is not surprising ... *fitting*, one could say ... that it also sometimes happens by accident. And it is a fact that many of the shamans of earlier cultures first went out-of-body as the result of accident or illness. In fact, we have to observe that the separation of material and etheric bodies has been well documented throughout history. (It is also interesting that the words of Sri Yukteswar endorse the view that space travel may be achieved with efficiency if we first dematerialise ... that is, dispense with 'matter' ... dispense with the atoms and molecules. In his afterlife situation, he will in any event have a body of subtler, much less dense matter and of raised frequency.)

One must therefore in this life, accept the multiple nature of the body. There is no question of it being comprised of just material aspect alone. But one might equally well reach the same conclusion from reflecting upon thoughts, dreams and that voice within from which we may receive guidance while in quiet, meditative mood.

Where dreams are concerned, there are some that just process the entangled thoughts of the day, while others may be of a more *special* nature. I am aware of my own *special* dreams. They are quite rare, always in colour, and on waking I have the feeling of having had one. They may be meaningful or revealing, or they may be out-of-body. One can travel far in the dreamstate. (But however far one travels, there is still an attachment. Throughout an Earthly life, although one speaks of *material* and *spirit* parts, they are as one, and remain connected, but the connection knows no bounds. Full partition only happens at death, when the material body is discarded.) There are certain dreams on record, that can only be described as both spectacular and historic.

On the night of 10 May 1812, it is understood that the British Prime Minister, Spencer Perceval experienced a powerful dream in colour. It impressed him, yet it was unbelievable. In the dream he was confronted by a man, who wore a dark green coat with brass buttons. The man waved a pistol, and it was happening in the lobby of the House of Commons! The man was menacing. A shot was fired, and all became blackness. Next morning, he recounted the details of the dream to family and friends; but who was there who would bear him such animosity? He left for work as usual. That day at around 5pm in the lobby of the House of Commons, he was shot in the heart and killed by a man wearing a dark green coat with brass buttons. He died instantly. There was little reason to the assassination. The man bore him no personal ill feeling. John Bellingham was a broker and had suffered trading losses for which he had applied to government for redress and this had been the source of his discontent.

It was one evening in the year 1865. The President's wife spoke with her husband, knowing that something troubled him. It is reported that after some persuasion, he ... Abraham Lincoln ... talked in a general philosophical way about dreams; then specifically about a powerful one ... the one that now pervasively occupied his thoughts. He said to her: *'Somehow the thing has got possession of me ... and like Banquo's ghost, it will not lie down.'* He went on: *'... I suddenly heard subdued sobs as if a number of people were weeping.'* He described how he tried to figure what was happening and had wandered in his dream from room to room in search of a reason. In the

East room, he came to a corpse, wrapped in funeral vestments and attended by mourners. He asked: *'Who is dead in the White House?'* And was told: *'The President. He was killed by an assassin.'* A few days after giving account of the dream to his wife, Abraham Lincoln attended a play at Ford's Theatre where he was shot and killed by John Wilkes Booth.

Our dreams may well have an aspect of timelessness about them, and those dreams sometimes describe events that transpire in our future. That is the way of things. The dreamstate is free, and simply does not have the shackles of time dependency, that our more familiar day-to-day Earth lives must yield to.

Much knowledge is available to us from the sages and holy men of India and the Himalayas. Their tradition, teachings and disciplines have resulted in a clear sightedness and closeness to source. Out of many wonderful teachings, Swami Rama's words are an inspiration:

> *A prophetic vision is the rarest of all visions. It flashes from the source of intuition and is therefore beyond the concept of time, space and causation. Such a vision sometimes is received by the laymen accidentally. But those who do meditation and truly have attained the fourth state of mind receive such guiding visions consciously.*
>
> Swami Rama *Living With The Himalayan Masters*
> Himalayan International Institute of Yoga Science and Philosophy

The fourth state of mind follows on from the states of waking, dreaming and quietly sleeping. Its traditional name is *Turiya* ... the state beyond. There is no doubt that meditation is one of the doorways that can be opened onto other worlds beyond the material. The guidance, progression and influence that may be achieved through meditation is well documented. Meditation in its primal, most fundamental form is a prayer of knowing. Its nature and extreme value will be immediately appreciated in considering the following words of a teaching master:

> *In meditation you are allowing the human aspect of you as you know yourself now, to be forgotten and the soul to come forward. You go deep within that spiritual light, that spiritual knowledge which has the answer to all questions. Therefore I say to you, to meditate is the answer to all things … all things spiritual.*
>
> Salumet

At the risk of being overdramatic, I would like to illustrate the reality and the power that meditation can have by reference to an ancient scripture. Let us consider for one moment, the fact that many adepts and masters of the Himalayas, are so *in touch* that they *know in advance* their hour of departure from this Earth life. They are that much *at one with source.* And, needless to say, they are well able to handle such knowledge without emotional complication. Accordingly, when their time comes, they invite close ones to sit with them, bid farewells and possibly make last requests or arrangements. It has been known for those having specific knowledge to even go a stage further.

The phenomenon known as 'spontaneous combustion' (sudden and virtually complete destruction of a living human body), in general remains very much a puzzle to materialists of the West. This was not so in the ancient East:

> *There is another very rare way of casting off the body. By meditating on the solar plexus the actual internal flame of fire burns the body in a fraction of a second, and everything is reduced to ashes. This knowledge was imparted by Yama, the king of death to his beloved disciple, Nachiketa in the Kathopanishad. All over the world, instances of spontaneous combustion are often heard about, and people wonder about such occurrences. But the ancient scriptures such as Mahakala Nidhi explain this method systematically.*
>
> Swami Rama *Living With The Himalayan Masters*
> Himalayan International Institute of Yoga Science and Philosophy

The *internal flame* referred to, is clearly not ordinary *material* fire. It is of the 'energy body', or at least, the non-material body ... and the ancient scriptures are fully conversant with this. In any event, with a little thought, it is a reasonably straightforward matter to deduce this fact. Where ordinary *material* fire (fast oxidation) is concerned, the most difficult part of the body to burn, is the central bulky part with its wet stomach contents. But in instances of spontaneous combustion, this part is always consumed to ash. Parts that get left are extremities such as a hand or foot. In spontaneous combustion, the energy of the process is clearly *within* the central body ... and the main chakra energy centres, lie within and along the main body and not at its extremities.

The reference merely serves to illustrate in no uncertain way, the potent reality of meditation and the tangible effect that it may have. It is no mere imaginative flight of fancy. Thought is powerful. It is difficult in today's world, to see any sense in the seeking of spontaneous combustion. In the context of the previous ancient culture, there was some point and no harm, as will be referred to later. As to the general virtue and validity of meditation in principle, if it is practised with due respect, in a proper loving attitude, then only good can result. (Let me also point out that no one is going to self-destruct from *this* cause without firstly becoming a rather special kind of adept, and then acquiring the specific ancient knowledge!)

In some parts of the U.S. where *Transcendental Meditation* (TM) has been practised by some for several decades, a number of statistical studies have been completed. It is clear from these that in townships where more than one per cent of population regularly practises TM, crime rate falls, medical requirements and hospitalisation fall, and community life generally improves. Some would equate this to *power of thought,* some would describe it as a *collective consciousness* effect, and others would see it as a resonance that affects the *implicate order* that underlies the *explicate* (material) world. But the eloquently postulated mechanisms are unimportant when the facts simply speak for themselves!

Transcendental Meditation directed to the common good can benefit the world! Of this there is no doubt. 'Yogic flyer' is a term used to indicate a modern TM adept. A mass session of TM held by yogic flyers in Washington in 1993 is claimed to have reduced local violent crime by 25%. In 1999, it was suggested to President Clinton by John Hagelin, a Natural Law Party presidential candidate, that 7,000 yogic flyers could powerfully assuage the Balkan conflict ... a measure that would be many, many times less costly in every sense than military confrontation. The proposition was not taken seriously. The political world was not yet ready to recognise or value such methods. But unlike those who favour air strikes and ground troops, as a scholar of the Yoga Sutras and a quantum physicist, Hagelin would have been well placed to understand their potential. (Prayer that comes from deep within is powerful and may be seen as projected thought. Yogic flyers meditating together could produce a concentration of such powerful projected thought. That is the principle.)

In probing the regions that lie beyond our material plane, there are a number of possible doorways that one may use for access. But having gained access by one or more doorways, it is then reassuring to find just how many aspects and ideas begin to fit together. The following quotation makes a few such connections:

> *What psychics see clairvoyantly also confirms the research that Jung and others have made into the collective unconscious, whose many layers now seem almost incontrovertibly to include traces of past life memories.*
> Roger J Woolger *Other Lives, Other Selves ... A Jungian Psychotherapist Discovers Past Lives* HarperCollins Publishers Ltd

Through the doorway of regression hypnotherapy, emerge accounts from patients, of *past lives* ... often accompanied by descriptions of how things were at that particular time. It is often the case that an irrational fear or hang-up in *this* life, relates to what has happened in a previous life ... and sometimes it may relate specifically to the nature of the *past life death*. An irrational fear of water may be found, in regression, to relate to a death by drowning. An inexplicable limp may be found to relate to a smashed leg on some battlefield leading to a traumatic death.

Sometimes it is possible to remove such hang-ups and fears by regressing the patient to the moment in question, in such a way that the emotion of the situation can be released. If the patient can come to terms with the situation just prior to the moment of death, then a permanent cure of this life's problem may well result. The *emotional blockage* will have been removed. In such instances, *proof* of the *past life* may be seen in the *cure* that results. In the literature, there are many case histories of cures being affected by regression to a past life situation which had left an unresolved crisis, or in which life terminated in shock without release of emotion. It is a quite well known form of therapy today. Healing through past life regression has a success rate. Regression therapy does not *always* produce the healing that is sought, simply because there are sometimes reasons why an emotional blockage should remain in place, but in a number of cases it works.

If by removal of the emotional blockage, the soul's progression via the present life is enhanced, then regression therapy can be successful. This is the criterion. The soul's progress is the all-important factor. In some instances of attempted regression therapy, information from a source other than the soul may possibly be given. (The patient becomes a spirit medium instead of regressing per se.) The test of true regression is the cure ... removal of the emotional blockage.

Past life memory is not always absent. It is usual to be born into this life with no conscious memory at all of what has gone before, but it is not *always* so. There are rare accounts of some retained memory. In my travels, I one day met a thoroughly rational scientist who would read and talk with his two-year-old daughter at bedtime. One evening, she began talking about a time when she had propped heavy wooden ladders in trees and had spent all day picking apples. A cloth would be tied over her hair (in kerchief style) while harvesting the apples and it was hard work. Needless to say, the memory could not possibly have come from the two-year-old's present life. But she had done it, and it was held in memory!

Logic dictates: if past life memory exists, then past life also exists, and the principles of reincarnation and the ongoing status of the indestructible spirit naturally follow. The Tibetan Book of the Dead embraces this, and presents a very clear picture of the cycle of death and rebirth. At the moment of death, the spirit (or soul-fraction) passes into the *timeless* other realm. The circuitous path that it experiences is now timeless, while as like as not many, many years pass on Earth. Eventually, at a suitable stage and when the soul is ready, it is reconceived for a new physical life. The reconceived spirit then takes on whatever karma and samskaras (a Sanskrit word for dispositions and emotional blockages derived from past lives) and these will be in place at the time of rebirth. At birth then, the new-born child is already imbued with samskaras from unfinished business, not only from the last death, but possibly from previous lives as well. It is understandable that the Tibetan lamas place a heavy emphasis upon the value of quiet death with undisturbed final moments of Earthly consciousness.

The path that is taken between death and rebirth is sometimes called the Great Wheel of Existence, and is drawn as a circle. The circle would also be drawn with a diameter, pointing upwards from the *death* point at the lower edge of that circle. This diameter is known as the Great Vertical Path. Those few great ones who attain supreme illumination, are able to release *all* karma. They are now beyond the need for any further Earthly reincarnation. The Great Vertical Path is for them and them alone, who now have a total transcendence and an 'undying' immortality. (There is self, and yet there is firstly the shared *oneness* with source ... like the single facet of a huge diamond. The consciousness in all its aspects is of the whole diamond.) Regarding the soul's further development, there is no point in more returns to Earth. The one possible reason for a further Earth incarnation from such a soul, would be a special mission to teach ... as a Master ... as a Messiah ... as a Christ.

We should note, to avoid any confusion, that so far as we on Earth are concerned, there are two types of immortality ... with and without repetitive Earthly incarnation. Within the Christian religion, many who have read the Holy Bible, believe that Jesus came from spirit, incarnated in the flesh, returned to spirit and continues in spirit. This leads them to a belief in the second type of immortality. Despite Bible text that quite strongly hints at *re*incarnation, they do not quite take on belief in the first type. If, however, their reading extends to the 1st century texts of the Dead Sea Scrolls and Nag Hamâdi library or to the Jewish Cabbala, then their belief is very likely to embrace the principle of Earthly reincarnation, in line with other world religions.

In the discourse between Jesus and his disciples, *Matthew **17**, 10-13,* it is clear that Elijah and John the Baptist were regarded by them as incarnations of the same spirit. And through history, many revered or well-respected ones have, in their different ways, expressed belief in Earthly reincarnation. They include the philosophers Giordano Bruno, Plato and Socrates, Henry Ford, Leo Tolstoy, Walt Whitman, World War II General George Patton, several American presidents, Mahatma Gandhi, the England football manager Glenn Hoddle and of course Jesus the Christ.

The Masters returning to Earth, to teach humankind, know the doorway that surpasses all other doorways. They are well conscious of the *oneness* of source whence they come. Their teachings are virtually infallible, and will be seen clearly as such by those who are ready to receive. Only subsequent misunderstanding and bad presentation by confused, mortal humans are able to mar such heavenly wisdom. Unfortunately this can and does happen.

The pattern of existence that fits the available data may be described in an oversimplified way as follows:

(1) Spiritual life is ongoing and immortal.

(2) The continuously evolving essence of that life is the soul.

(3) To assist with its progression, small fractions of the soul may incarnate and live physical Earth lives (as many times as is necessary).

(4) The soul has evolved to its present state as the result of past Earth lives and progression in spirit.

(5) A part of the soul that continues in spirit is sometimes referred to as 'the higher self'.

(6) A sufficiently advanced soul will have no further *need* of physical incarnation.

(7) Not all beings of the cosmos have 'Earthly' life as part of their development.

(8) The paramount factor in life is the soul's progress.

If this is truly the basis of existence then what about spirit circles? Are they able to communicate with those who have moved on through the process that we call death? There is ample evidence that this is so. Much of today's evidence is not only as witnessed by those present; it is also recorded on tape, for the benefit of others.

Let us now consider what one might loosely describe as a *spirit circle* ... but this is a vague term and such things require definition. The type of circle I have in mind would include a knowledgeable and experienced one who presides and at least one experienced spirit medium. The objective of the group would be to promote the common good in some way, by communication between the worlds of spirit and the physical. This is still a loose definition, but at least it does exclude anything of a frivolous or exhibitionist nature. Such a group could be seen as a true and worthy doorway to other realms. It may transpire that a group, with years of dedication and experience, establishes substantial connections so that its portal becomes a busy and treasured thoroughfare ... treasured equally by those above, as by those below.

The circle may well include some who are gifted in clairvoyance, or clairaudience, or who give power. The key members of the group will be the spirit mediums (instruments) and the president (who takes charge and initially at least, interviews the visiting spirits). Transactions usually occur with instruments in semi- or partial-trance and with the visiting spirit using the instrument's vocal chords. The instrument may or may not have any awareness of what is said, depending on depth of trance and conditions. It is most important that all meetings are conducted in an atmosphere of love, humility and respect. This type of arrangement (requiring organisation by those above as well as by those below) becomes a most versatile and interesting doorway between the worlds.

A group of this general format, meeting regularly, may:

(1) Exchange messages between relatives and friends across the divide.

(2) Receive guidance in regard to ailments, (as did the shamans of earlier times).

(3) Enter into philosophical and informative discussion with highly developed spirits of greater knowledge. (Such exchanges can be wonderful in embroidering or confirming items of which one already has some degree of knowledge or inner belief ... or indeed for clarifying erroneous ideas from the past. This is *not* a vehicle for obtaining knowledge for which mankind is not yet ready! This of course would contravene the group's integrity; also the ethic of cosmic progression).

(4) Learn of the nature of spirit realms and locations, and the ways of the ongoing life.

(5) Learn of possible potentials of circle members as regards such individual pursuits as mediumship, clairaudience, automatic sketching etc.

(6) Give counselling and assistance to *spirits* who, for a variety of reasons, may have problems that temporarily stay their further progression. Such assistance may be preferred or may be more directly to the point, than

alternative spirit realm procedures. The counselling is seen by those who have a familiarity with such matters to be a valuable option. (The following chapter is devoted to examples of this type of work ... known as 'rescues').

(7) Enjoy the love and the knowledge that life continues across the divide and it is all so near. Knowing also that departed loved ones are still in touch, and that when it is time to make the journey, the traveller will be met.

(8) Receive inspired teaching that will lead to a more perfect understanding of the divine message, (the same divine message as has been taught by incarnate masters such as Jesus and Buddha).

(9) Learn of the work and dedication of other wonderful beings of the cosmos who are pure energy beings and who have not themselves experienced Earthly or physical life.

There are many pathways in life and such meetings may not suit all, or some may simply just not yet be 'ready'. Motivations and timing become evident in various ways. What are the dangers? It is important to have rules. A properly orientated and well set-up group as outlined, should encounter no great difficulty. The personalities and love within the group should be self-protective. Such a group will be recognised on the other side, where the doorway will be watched over by a *gatekeeper* to enhance safety and smooth operation. Any mischievous spirits ... and there *are* some in realms close to Earth ... would or should be dissuaded from slipping through. On those rare occasions when a notorious spirit from lower realms is being counselled to aid his progression, the group may well be informed of additional protection being installed from the other side. It is important to have a good working relationship (without which certain things simply will not transpire).

This is the point at which to mention the Ouija board (The 'yes-yes' in both French and German board). It *is* a possible doorway to spirit realm ... but *uncontrolled*! The board is of course inanimate and there are no gatekeepers! You may find rationality if your approach is *honest*, *unselfish* and with due humility. It is entirely down to you. Much depends upon the personality of the operator. But if for example, all you want to know, is the winner of the two-thirty at Newmarket tomorrow, then you may well encounter an extremely angry spirit. He might well decide to teach you a lesson, and rightly so, for being so unfair to bookmakers, acquisitive and self-centred ... and you will then never wish to see the Ouija board again! So be warned.

There are times when those in spirit may have the desire to deliver messages, literature or music to the world. They may feel their work on the Earth plane was left unfinished in some way. Perhaps, while on Earth they taught incorrectly, and have the wish to make amends. Perhaps it is simply a part of their work or mission in 'afterlife', to help us. There are various possible motives for delivery of *automatic writing*. All that is needed is for the motivated spirit to establish a channel with a willing mortal. Establishing a channel may take a long time, perhaps several years. One such collaborating mortal was the Reverend G Vale Owen, who in 1913 began writing down the spirit communications of Zabdiel:

> *It is not on myself that I would fix your mind, friend, but on the messages proceeding from me to you, and through you to our fellow-Christians fighting their way through the mists of controversy and doubt and misdirected zeal ... For it is of primary import to everyone that he realize that the (spirit) existence before him is no dream ... but it is indeed the fuller life developed, and the life for which the earth life is both a preparation and beginning.*
>
> Rev. G Vale Owen/Zabdiel *The Highlands of Heaven*
> The Greater World Christian Spiritualist Association

The communications of Zabdiel make interesting reading and he includes several statements that are surprising. His reference to space and matter is interesting. The most illumined scientists of the post-1986 period have now thrown out the fallacy that the space between the stars is just an extensive zone of nothingness. One cannot call space 'nothing' and at the same time confer properties upon it! A rare few might even agree with me that 'space' is *the* most fundamental part of the universe. Stephen Hawking's theorising on black holes and Grand Unification, more than hints at space *not* being empty:

> *The answer, quantum theory tells us, is that the particles do not come from within the black hole, but from the "empty" space just outside the black hole's event horizon! We can understand this in the following way: What we think of as "empty" space cannot be completely empty because that would mean that all the fields, such as gravitational and electromagnetic fields, would have to be exactly zero ... the uncertainty principle means that even "empty" space is filled with pairs of virtual particles and antiparticles. These pairs would have an infinite amount of energy...*
>
> Stephen W Hawking *A Brief History of Time*

In 1913, the language of Zabdiel was understandably different. Space was then called 'aether', sometimes spelled 'ether', but the gist of his message had a similarity about it:

> *If you were to endeavour to build up a machine for the manufacture of ether, and the conversion of it into matter, you would find no substance to your hand on earth of sufficient sublimity to hold the ether, which is of a force greater and more terrific than any force which is imprisoned within what you understand as matter.*
>
> Rev. G Vale Owen/Zabdiel *The Highlands of Heaven*
>
> The Greater World Christian Spiritualist Association

Zabdiel speaks of the interconversion of space and particles and the problem of the huge unmanageable quantities of energy; the energy of space exceeding that within the atom! Hawking theorises on space being filled with virtual particle-antiparticle pairs and the problem of their infinite energy. It is my impression that both authors are discussing space-matter interconversion and the huge energy content of space, and in 1913, the spirit communicator was well ahead of his time by our standards! [Although Einstein had acquainted the world with mass-energy conversion, that is $E = mc^2$, the equation as presented concerned just the *energy* of the atom, as opposed to its *space plus energy equivalence.* As space was counted as *nothing* at that time, Einstein's equation seemed then of course, to be sufficiently complete!]

It is a well-known fact that some people have the gift of healing, and they will say that the gift is not of themselves ... they merely channel the healing energy that helps others ... Quite so. The healing energy may improve health in a number of ways, joints become less painful, strains and torn muscles heal faster and so on. This is all fairly well established and accepted. *Spirit doctors* and *spirit surgery* are much less generally known or accepted, but nevertheless they also have a firm place in our reality. Just as there are accomplished medical practitioners on Earth, so it is in spirit. A spirit doctor is in fact, one more type of spirit communicator, who may seek to communicate his skill through a willing and suitable spirit medium. When this happens, the spirit medium *appears* to have medical skills that bring about wonderful cures, though he may have no medical training whatsoever.

Some spirit surgeons working through their mediums have been professionally observed ... put to the test ... and their work documented. Being what they are gives them the opportunity to work in different ways to conventional Earth plane doctors. They may, for example, either make or not make incisions; the use of antiseptics and stitching seem to be unnecessary when incisions are made; and removed items may or may not be simply dematerialised. Either the energy-body or the physical-body may be worked upon, and subsequent healing of any incisions, is very fast. There is photographic evidence of the latter. Internal manipulations may be carried out without the need for incision, if the spirit surgeon 'goes inside' using instruments of *his* own non-material plane. Any commentary during an operation may well be the voice of the spirit doctor, not the medium (who may be in semi- or partial or full trance, according to the preferred status).

In 1913, the same year that Zabdiel came through the Rev. Owen, Fr. Francisco Alves Correa was ordained as a Roman Catholic priest. Some years later, he was visiting 'Arigo' who had been imprisoned by the Brazilian authorities for witchcraft. It was unusual for a Roman Catholic priest to be visiting a prisoner convicted of all things, 'witchcraft'. Fr. Correa looked at the man, and now, was able to see him quite distinctly because, Arigo ... *had* it been Arigo, or the spirit within? ... Arigo had operated on his eyes with that old penknife of his, when he had been nearly blind from cataracts. He saw him so clearly now, and gazed upon him with a great tenderness. This man before him could heal ... he worked miracles! He had restored his own sight! It was a curious world that could imprison such a man ... for *witchcraft*! It was a strange world that saw his particular way of healing as within the art of witchcraft. Fr. Correa was confused. He did not understand; but instinctively knew that it was right for him to come and offer solace and hope, and to thank Arigo for the restored sight that he now enjoyed. It is reported that his words were:

> *This is why I came here to thank you. I hope God will give you the strength to bear this trial. You will leave here to perform still greater things. Be strong, for suffering is part of the law of evolution.*
>
> John G Fuller *Arigo: Surgeon of The Rusty Knife*

Arigo was extremely popular midst those who knew him, and following the Appeal, he was released from prison. And one of those little coincidences ... I find that his Appeal number is firmly entrenched in my own mind ... because, by a curious chance, it has also been my telephone number for a good many years! On release, Arigo was able to perform still greater things, just as Fr. Correa had said.

Dr. Adolpho Fritz who died in 1918, was the one who worked through Arigo. As a spirit doctor, he had good organisation and was supported in his work by a team of spirit medics. While Dr. Fritz was able to make incisions with Arigo's penknife, I suspect that for anything more delicate he would have used the instruments of his own world (invisible to ours). It may be that the penknife, was only ever a steadying devise or a means of making his work appear more down-to-earth and less magical to the people who watched. He was able to cure cataracts, glaucoma and to remove growths by surgery. Arigo cured further tens of thousands by diagnosis and prescription. He was able to work at great speed, and many cases were dealt with in little more than the time taken to scribble the list of required medicaments. There were operations on public notaries including the President's daughter; also on record, is the removal of a bulging growth from the arm of an American doctor, in ... minutes! There is photographic evidence from this operation, to show the growth, the incision, and the subsequent rapid healing. Dr. Adolpho Fritz and his team continued to do outstanding and valuable work on this plane until Arigo died in a tragic road accident.

Dr. Adolpho Fritz is just one example of this type of between-worlds healer. There are many others, throughout the world, including some in the West. Modern UK examples in the 1990s being, Dr. Lang working through George Chapman, one known as Paul who works through Ray Brown and Dr. Joseph Kahn working through Stephen Turoff. Such doctors often work very fast, and may see as many as 50 patients per day. But then, it is often the case that one practising spirit doctor is supported by a team of spirit doctors, who are able to enhance his performance. The spirit doctor working through his instrument, is very much a partnership. The spirit has to get to know his instrument and adjust procedures accordingly; after all, he is only human ... or ex-human, however you wish to view it. I understand that it took Dr Kahn a period of time to mellow into a *friendly* professional manner to suit modern times. (He had begun with a more austere approach, perhaps more reminiscent of the World War I Austrian Jewish doctor, that he had been in former Earth life.) A spirit doctor's performance can be as good as his own expertise, enhanced by his team, and aligned to his adaptation.

The Earthbound instrument may well have a wife or assistant who supports, and it may well be necessary for them to maintain part time at least, ordinary employment to pay the bills. (Arigo was a government office receptionist for a few hours each day). It is possible that, with due recognition, we on Earth *could* make such instruments better supported in the work that they do. This in turn may then lead to such 'healing doorways' being better appreciated and more widely used. Perhaps this world is not yet quite ready to admit medical teams from the other-world to assist the various national health services in an officially recognised capacity. As we move further into Aquarius however, these doorways may open wider, and they could have a fuller and better recognition. The physical Earth might then benefit from the extra love and care and awareness that this brings.

Working against this, as general awareness expands and consciousness is raised in the decades ahead, medical aid is likely to be required less. The need will simply go, as error is replaced by gracious living and *dis*ease gives way to ease. In the twentieth century down-to-earth parlance, we shall stop stressing ourselves, poisoning ourselves, abusing our stomachs and fouling our otherwise tranquil planet. We shall also stop fighting each other for every last unit of wealth and living space. These must be cited as the reasons, together with attendant unawareness, for the sadly over-heavy medical needs of the twentieth century. Meanwhile, in the interim years, any help from the other-world can only be seen as a blessing and a means of restoring good health to many.

Monsignor Robert Hugh Benson ... son of Edward White Benson, Archbishop of Canterbury ... died in 1914. While on Earth, he wrote a book entitled: *'Necromancers'*. He was later unhappy concerning its subject matter and this led to a further book being delivered to Earth by his spirit self, as a channelled work through Anthony Borgia. The resulting book is a valuable *first* hand account of how things are in the spirit realms and how life continues therein:

> *The percentage is low, deplorably low, of people who come into the spirit world with any knowledge at all of their new life and of the spirit world in general. All the countless souls without this knowledge have to be taken care of, and helped in their difficulties and perplexities. That is the principle work upon which Edwin, Ruth and I are engaged. It is a type of work that appeals to many of the ministers of the church of whatever denomination. Their experience upon earth stands them in good stead, and all of them - perhaps I should say all of us! - know that we are now members of one ministry, with one purpose, serving one cause and all of us possessed of the same knowledge of the truth of spirit life, without creed, without doctrine or dogma, a united body of workers, men and women.*
>
> Anthony Borgia *Life in the World Unseen*
>
> Reprinted with permission of 'Two Worlds', London

Before proceeding with the next chapter, this is a good point at which to remind the reader that this is essentially a book of factual truth. It has to be said however, that in certain of its earlier chapters, there are some passages that are contrived dialogue ... albeit firmly based upon the history, so far as it is known. There are also contrived scenarios ... equally based upon the known history. In certain other accounts, (living) people have been given fictional names, as is sometimes standard practice and necessary. The book otherwise is comprised essentially of fact. The main content of the five chapters that follow, are transcripts of tape recordings of spirit conversations. The conversations with 'Salumet' are reported verbatim, the only manipulation being selection of material from a huge quantity of transcripts and tapes, accumulated over a five-year period. Certain other transcripts have been slightly reduced where the original recording was indistinct, or where there was a tendency towards repetition.

Occasionally, a sentence may seem 'quaint' or not quite perfect English. Sessions are conducted in very heavily subdued lighting, so that all questions are put 'off the top of the head'. There are no notes or cue boards! And there must be the occasional instance of 'language unfamiliarity' across the veil. In order to preserve accuracy and authenticity, I have not attempted any correction of the dialogue. It is simply as delivered at the time.

In reporting the dialogue of spirit communication, I have used *italic* script within quotation marks to indicate spoken passages. I have not for the most part, indicated who is speaking. The dialogue is mostly between our President and the visiting spirit, so that the speaker is really self-evident. I hope that you will agree with me that this presentation helps the material to flow. (And in the general narrative, the use of italic script for single-word emphasis, is continued as in previous pages.) Some passages are *mixed dialogue*, and I have therefore used a further aid to define which is channelled spirit and which is normal speech. Sections introduced by '~' are always the channelled speech.

Chapter XXV

The Kingsclere 'Rescues'

Just as the doctors who are progressing their lives in the realms of spirit, may choose to use their skills for the benefit of those of us on Earth; we on Earth, may also set up teams to assist those in spirit. Although little publicised, this in fact happens. The two directions of assistance between worlds form a part of *our* reality. I refer to the 'rescue' groups, which are quite rare, but which provide a counselling and healing service, that is valued by those 'above'; and is found to be both interesting and rewarding by those of us 'below' who provide the service. But of course, to talk of *them* and *us* is really quite absurd. They *are* us! We are all in the same club! We are all spirit beings; the only difference, is that we on Earth wear the material overcoats. These, of course, are normally cremated or buried at the time when we go to join ... *'them'*.

Whilst upon Earth, we are time-bound ... locked into the biological processes and travel modes that are all subject to a *timed* system, in which ageing is a one way passage. As soon as we shed the material overcoats, time in some way no longer has the same control; and that seems to be one major difference between *our* being here and *our* being there. It should also be mentioned that recognition of time in the physical world, the systems for its measurement and our adherence to them, are entirely of physical mankind's making.

During *our* transition period here on Earth, into the new age, there are some of us who understand this well enough; but none understand with a greater clarity than does Leslie. He presides over several different groups during the course of a week ... groups for healing ... for spirit communication ... and for the 'rescues'. He has the experience and the expertise; for he has been engaged in such between-worlds work for more than half a century; a field of activity that remains, even in the period of change ... strange or even unknown to a good many. But it all comes as second nature to Leslie, who in his mid 80s, still possesses a fine mental agility and good vigour. At the time of writing, Wednesday evenings would be set aside for 'rescues'. It would always be a 7.30 p.m. start. *Time* may not have the same meaning on the other side, but *they* know *our* schedules, and are able to keep to them, even on those occasions when we adjust to British Summer Time!

The room kept for 'the work' is quiet with heavy curtains at the window. Up to twelve ... sometimes thirteen chairs ... line the walls, and there are two standing microphones. The tape recorder would be out in the hallway so as not to disturb. Leslie would say *'Hello friends'*, addressing those 'above' as well as those seated. A few brief words of chat ... perhaps some news of a happening during the Monday meeting. The light would be dimmed to extinction. It would now be darkness and quiet for ten minutes or so. There would be silent mental greetings and silent prayers. Any stray thoughts would just ebb away as the energy built ... an energy that could be felt. Some would slip into partial trance. Then the dim red light would gently soothe the darkness and it would be time for Leslie to move about the room to see if an 'instrument' was *with visitor*. He peered here and there, and always knew, and would formally address the spirit: *'Good evening to you…'*

The Monday evenings *began* in similar style. At these meetings, Eileen, a 'developed medium', would frequently channel one we know as 'Salumet' ... a highly evolved and loving spirit who had become a much respected teacher and a very dear friend. He would bring enlightened teachings to aid spiritual growth, from which we ourselves would benefit, and as many that would subsequently listen to the recorded tapes or read their transcripts. In addition, during the course of an evening, other spirits would likely drop by for a chat, or might deliver messages, or may help to guide the evening's events; and sometimes a 'rescue' would come through. There were several mediums in the group, and on some occasions, as appropriate, Leslie himself would be *used*. There would always be something happening ... sometimes several communications simultaneously. One had the impression that there were always some that would like to come through to say *'hello'*, if scheduled business should be concluded leaving a little spare time. Frequently, the unexpected happened. The time of the session was *never* wasted.

The evening of Monday 10 June 1996, was one of those different sessions, not that anyone was ever able to foretell exactly what was going to happen next. That aspect of the meetings was always a fascination. Leslie began by explaining that Eileen, although feeling well in herself, had a throat condition that left her without voice this evening; and it was not expected therefore, that she would be used for speech by Salumet. The period of darkness had just begun. He continued to address those in the room: *'... I may as well tell you now ... We had a very, very bad rescue session Wednesday. One of the Chernobyl people ... blown to bits...'*

'Oh dear!' someone quietly exclaimed.

'Heather said she felt as if she had got a big gap between the top of her legs and the bottom of her chest ... and her hands were blown off. He came through really very, very distraught ... Really one of the worst she's ever had, and they sent somebody through afterwards to thank her especially ... for taking it.'

'Oh dear! ...'

'You were able to relax the spirit?'

'Oh yes ... yes...'

'An incredible experience ... that must have been.'

'Oh yes ... It was ... of course, it was virtually instantaneous. I knew ... I don't have to tell you how I know ... because I don't know myself how I know ... but he had gone into the danger area with some mates ... workmen ... comrades ... knowing that they would never come out. It was a desperate attempt to stop the explosion ... just those few seconds too late.'

'Very brave ... modern day heroics.'

'Yes. I had a vivid impression of what they had done ... gone in, knowing it was a forlorn hope ... but at least try.'

'He was one of the team that went in?'

'Yes ... '

Next, came a slight pause, and up to this point, it had been just our own somewhat muted conversation and Leslie's account. But now, there was the heavy respiratory sound that, on those occasions when he himself was 'used', preceded a spirit communication through Leslie. There followed on from the altered breathing, the new voice: ~ *'I say to you my friends ... you did not witness what this one has just spoken of. You can be assured that it all stems from the work you and your friends do in this Temple of Love. It was a* **tremendous** *experience for the lady concerned. We cannot express sufficiently our gratitude, or even our admiration, for taking on such a task. We know that it left her somewhat depleted, but that was taken care of. But I wish to tell you, as I shall tell the others at their next meeting, that the* **group** *whose representative came here and was dealt with as usual, are now well on their way to accepting the new conditions in which they find themselves.'*

Someone in the room ventured: *'Wonderful!'*

~ *'I felt it was only fair that I should come to tell you this ... to confirm once again that you cannot possibly know while you are in the physical plane, the tremendous work that you all do to help those just across the border. We can only ask that you continue to give your time, your energy and your love in these matters. For this we thank you in advance, for all that still remains to be done...'*

Someone said: *'We thank you. God bless you.'*

~ We ask God's blessing upon you all. Never fear that you will be left with any definite reaction after such a 'rescue', as you call it. All will be resolved. God be with you all my friends.'

In unison: *'God be with you.'*

~ 'And thank you! Thank you! Thank you!'

There followed a brief silence during which the spirit left and Leslie resumed his 'self' posture. Then, moving across the room, he greeted a 'control' spirit who was with Sue: *'Good evening to you.'*

~ 'Good evening ... You were not expecting that, were you? Oh ... that was a little shock, but it was felt necessary to bring information to this group concerning events of the previous time.'

'Yes ... that's the first time that's ever happened.'

~ 'Yes. It was felt that the time was right, while you were discussing the matters concerned ... We apologise to you if you were taken somewhat by surprise.'

'No ... no apology necessary at all...'

~ 'We know you are used to our ways, and we did not think that it would bring discomfort to you at all.'

'No, not in the least. I am only too pleased that you told my friends here, about it...'

The comings and goings of the evening then continued in a more general manner, while Salumet on this occasion worked 'silently' with Eileen.

The above is a good illustrative transcript for us to begin with. It says much about the work. It illustrates the depth of feeling, mutual love of humanity that has no between-worlds barrier, and the importance to the soul of continuing life's path after crossing over. The principle is revealed, of 'unlocking' the predicament of the one, who can then go back to release the similar difficulties of the rest of the team. The 'counselling/healing session' (if I may call it that) for the one, can so often be referred back, to help the many.

The difficulties of transition from Earth plane to spirit, frequently arise out of 'erroneous belief', 'body-dysfunction', 'crime and guilt', 'violent death' or combinations of these. In 'violent death', there may well be no chance for release of emotion, and vivid memory of lost body-parts may be held onto so strongly that life becomes impaired in the next world, until the matter can be resolved. (And that impression of missing body parts is also communicated to the instrument.) It also follows that, if one has no belief in any form of afterlife, then this lack of belief can make the spirit blind to the fact that physical death has occurred.

The vast majority of rescues, as one might expect, concern ordinary people, quite unknown to the world's media, known only to their circles of friends and colleagues. There have been some however, who were public notaries, the infamous, those featuring in news headline events, or those concerned in well publicised disasters such as Chernobyl. Many visiting souls were coming to this special meeting place, and this was not the first time that the room of these transactions had been referred to as a 'Temple of Love'.

But why should those leaving Earth plane, have to return in this way to confront their problems? Cannot such problems be adequately met in the realm of spirit? I believe the answers to these questions are, firstly that they do not *have to* return, and secondly, all adjustments *can* be made in spirit. But in certain instances, the 'referral' system can be more expedient ... simpler ... more direct. It may also be the situation, that in this century, catastrophic deaths, as occur for example in the worst motorway crashes, in technological disasters and in nuclear explosions, have an increasingly problematical bias, when viewed from spirit. It is always so much more satisfactory when death is the natural, gentle process without violent complication.

So perhaps the more pertinent question may be: *Why should we* ***not*** *lend a helping hand to those souls in need; thus helping them to progress along their paths more efficiently?* It is often said that we are here to help each other. This is very true. The same is equally true up there; and on such occasions when those up there, are able to meet with those of us down here, then the same is true again. As has been stated, we are all of us in the same club. Since we are all one, it is appropriate that we increase our awareness of just that, by reaching across the Divide in this way. Helping, healing, loving gestures ... can only contribute to the greater good and the wider awareness.

Many spirits who are 'brought through' are children who have had terrible disabilities during their Earth lives. If one were born without arms, or without control of arms, then he/she will have no (Earth life) memory of arm movement ... of gripping ... of writing or holding a pencil. Although the spirit body is perfect, it needs that memory in order to be able to trigger full use of that perfect spirit body. It is a very direct solution to slip the spirit child into a medium, and get it to use the arms of the 'borrowed' body and feel arm movement. The child can hold a pencil and draw lines! The resulting expressions of joy at being able to do this are a delight to behold. The child then returns, and has that memory to work with, and can achieve normal arm movement in spirit. It is a simple direct solution ... at least it always has been when Leslie does it. He always seems to know exactly what to do and say. The one 'healed' child is then able to return and help others with similar disability. It works!

Similarly, those with speech difficulty can be helped to acquire belief in their own ability to talk freely. Those who have had the spastic condition while on Earth can be helped to discover, through instruction while in the 'borrowed' body, a perfect body control and movement. The extreme joy displayed when they discover they can *do it*, is something well worth seeing. And of course, they carry that limb function, or that speech fluency with them when they return to spirit.

I remember a time when four boys had been tragically drowned while canoeing off the coast in worsening weather. One of them came through in a puzzled state, ~ *'How did I get out of the water? Where am I?'* It was gently explained to him that he had been brought here for a chat ... *'and have you ever wondered what happens when we die?'* The conversation slowly moved on until he had sufficient awareness of what had happened, and knowledge of the ongoing nature of life. He was an intelligent boy and full of questions: ~ *'Will I be able to see my mother and father?'* Leslie explained how he would receive instruction so that it would be possible for him to be close to them ... and how they would feel and *know* his presence. The exchange was well done. He now had a fair understanding of it all, and I shall always remember the boy's final comment: ~ *'Why don't they teach us all this at school?'* Why not indeed!

Death can be a curious and distant thing. So many in the West have such a poor understanding of the process, apart from the physical curtailment of body function. There is often little or no conception, of what lies beyond. This may lead to the spirit refusing to believe that death has occurred. ~ *'I experience thoughts and observations ... therefore I remain alive and am my usual self ... How could it be otherwise?'* That is a frequent attitude. ~ *'And yet, something has changed. What can it be?'* Others in spirit will be aware of the problem. Friends may slip the 'living' spirit into the borrowed instrument body, and a dialogue is then possible ... with Leslie.

The spirit may look down (with borrowed eyes) in the dim conditions prevailing and be able to make out 'rings on the fingers'. ~ *'Whose rings are these? What are they doing on my hands?'* The situation may sometimes become almost droll. The spirit would be carefully told about the death, and about being brought here to have what happens explained to him ... Some, however, would still much prefer to believe that there had been no death, and someone must have been playing games and ~ *'putting rings on my fingers!'* All eventually come to accept that they are in the position of being able to borrow the physical body of another, for the purpose of the counsel session. It is sufficient for some to feel the hair, and find it to be quite different from their old familiar head. The light may be turned up just a little for some, and they may be shown a mirror. It must be strange when an 'elderly man' in spirit, sees himself as a rather more youthful young lady! But, as is often said ... 'seeing is believing'.

I recall one memorable evening when a young boy came through one of the female members of the group, she being in the flush of mature womanhood. He was attempting to understand, but at first, got mixed up. He thought for one moment, that having died, he was now being given a new body and this was it. He thought that there must be some mistake, because on looking down, he became quite visibly flustered and embarrassed, saying: ~ *'Well ... what are all these* ***extra*** *bits?'* He was much relieved to learn that this was just a temporary arrangement, and the maleness to which he had become accustomed, was not under any threat. Many young boys *would* I think feel quite attached to their familiar male prowess!

Not all rescues require words. It was one evening in October 1993. There had been, it would appear, an horrendous motorway accident. One that had died instantly in the crash, seemed to be emotionally 'locked up', and was quite unable to speak. A friend had brought him along to see if he could be helped. Leslie talked to both, who were with separate instruments. The problem was that, in the suddenness of the crash, the one now silent had no chance for the release of emotion. Eventually it came out as a succession of huge heaving sobs. In the conditions of the healing, there seemed to be some tuning into or sharing of that release. Several of the group had tears streaming from their eyes. And that was it! That release was all that was necessary. He just 'unlocked'.

(It would appear that, just as one in Earth life, through hypnotherapy, may be regressed to a past-life-memory situation for the purpose of *emotion release*; so too can those in spirit return to Earth life, via the Medium Rescue Service, for the very same purpose. The Tibetan teachings correctly embrace the importance of quiet death. Nevertheless, the samskaras resulting from catastrophic death may still be corrected or averted, through these practical procedures. There is both the clinical and the spiritual evidence that emotional blockage can be relieved.)

Since time is not the same in spirit, those who are ready for, or who will benefit from rescue, may not relate to *our* modern times. They may have passed over ... years, or even centuries earlier. We should remember another factor too; that the group who meet, share a mixture of abilities, including clairvoyance and clairaudience which often feature in the rescues in a strongly significant way.

There was one evening that I remember, when R said: *'I see three ladies ... They look like witches ... in a circle ... They want release ... They are coming through over there!'* ... pointing across the room to D's corner.

Leslie was now aware that D had a visitor, and approached: *'If you are white witches, we can help you ... or if you ask for help, we can help you...'*

The first gave her name as Susan. It was clear she wanted to leave the darkness that had enclosed her for so long, yet she was fearful of coming into the light. It was a big step. Her fear was visible. The voice trembled and the chair was seen to shake! The time was right for her step, but she needed coaxing ... reassuring. The chair continued to shake ... eased a little ... then shook again ... violently. Then: *'Open your eyes ...There it is ... light. You are safe. You are with friends. All is well.'*

Her two colleagues were Jane and Sally. It became clear that they were equally fearful, but wanted to leave behind the blackness of their circle, to be in the light. The fear and shaking began again. The group extended loving thoughts ... love ... welcome ... strength ... above all ... love. Sally came through, then Jane. All three were now out of that dark place ... and quite clearly with such relief!

'You are safe now ... with friends. Look above you. You will see blue lights approaching. Do you see? They will come to your heads. That is the light of your salvation. You are free now.'

It seemed as if they had retracted into a darkness of their own making, for as long as it takes in non-linear time terms, whatever that may mean. At last, with some difficulty, they were capable of facing their predicament and moving on. And to me, on reflection, the situation of it all seemed rather symbolic, but that is exactly the way in which that particular rescue transpired. Understanding may sometimes be difficult and in any event unnecessary. But there is a passage in St. John's gospel that might just connect: ...*men loved the darkness rather than the light, because their practices were wicked. For every one who acts vilely, not only hates the light, but shrinks from it, so that his doings may not be detected. But he who does right comes to the light, so that his actions may be displayed; because the origin of his conduct is in God.*

John 3, 19-21

There are souls in much deeper difficulties that are in the process of recovering their lost ways. One must never lose sight of the fact that a soul is a soul. However dark its deeds may have been, however many the atrocities, however much repentance is needed; a spark of goodness is always there within. It may have become heavily clouded, but *always* it has the chance to grow and shine through. This recognition is a fundamental law of the cosmos, which manifests in various forms within the teachings of every Earth religion. It is consistent with ... forgiveness ... immortality ... love. At whatever level of growth, a soul can be helped if it is 'ready', and if it has attuned to a desire to move on. Until it has taken those first steps in repentance, it will not be ready to move. But once it is 'ready', then from whatever level, wherever it may be, even the lowest realms ... it ... can ... be ... helped.

It was on Wednesday 15 May 1996 that one came through who gave the French name of *Raolf.* He had been 'caught up' in the terrible and misguided system of the Inquisition. He had tortured to secure 'conversion of faith'. It was a business in the sense that he was paid to do it. He had a kind of belief in what he did at first ... no doubt induced by some of the erroneous ways of that period, but of course, as time progressed, he came to doubt and to see it's falseness. His work was not really the salvation of souls that it was supposed to be. His gown was blooded, but not by his own blood. A part of his subsequent suffering related to what mercy he might expect, when he had shown so little himself. It was a sorry dilemma. But he could now see that it was *his* turn to make confession, instead of receiving it from others. He was repentant and ready for a positive step. The bad memories would eventually go, when he had made proper amends.

The crux of the matter came with the question that was put: *'Are you willing to work to compensate for the evils that you did when you were on this Earth?'*

~ *'Yes ... If I am given a chance to make amends ... If I can be put in a position to make amends ... If I can be put in a position to learn and help others, I will do my utmost to try and make amends.'*

'That's what our (spirit) friends wanted to hear. It will be a long road for you. Do you understand that?'

~ *'Yes.'*

'And you will meet many whom you sent over in pain. ***That*** *you will have to suffer and face too ... and ask their forgiveness. Are you willing to do that? It won't be easy ... You now realise you are very much alive don't you?'*

~ *'Yes.'*

'You know that what you used to teach about death being near, was nonsense ... The soul is indestructible ... When the physical body dies, the soul goes on living in the next plane of life ... there to face the results of living in the physical world. That is what is facing you now my friend. You will now leave the Earth for the second time. On this

occasion, you will go with the knowledge of what lies ahead of you, and that you can come out of the darkness ... Others ... will guide you and show you the best way that you can begin that work.'

~ *'... How did you find me?'*

'I didn't. My colleagues found you ... my colleagues who work in your plane of life ... I am going to let you go now ... Good bye to you ... and our love goes with you...'

(The above is part of a tape transcript. A few phrases towards the end have been omitted because they were indistinct on the tape. This was a busy evening, with several overlapping dialogues in places, making it difficult to decipher, especially towards the end).

An obvious question that arises out of this work is ... *what about language and translation?* It is my experience that there does not seem to be any one simple rule concerning language. A number of our visiting spirits who had Earth lives in China, North America (native peoples) and elsewhere have clearly made it their business to learn English and no doubt other languages. These have achieved varying degrees of fluency. I am aware of other visiting spirits coming through in foreign language that no one in the group could understand. I know a Danish lady who has channelled both in English and in Danish. (She understood the Danish when she listened to the tape afterwards, but none of us understood at the time.) On other occasions, there seems to have been an 'automaticity' of appropriate language that leads me to the tentative conclusion that direct speech in appropriate language can on occasions be 'arranged' on the other side. I imagine this would depend upon the nature of the communication or mission and its control format.

Many of the rescues are a pleasure to observe ... especially when they arise out of suffering or some difficulty of transition, which becomes alleviated. The rescued spirit then generally expresses such relief and happiness, and one can so easily share in that happiness. But on those rarer occasions, when there is serious business ahead, there may well be advance warning and suitable preparations for a difficult rescue. In fact it is true to say that, in this work, successive evenings may be wildly and almost unimaginably diverse.

I do not pretend to understand the process by which Leslie is sometimes guided in his questioning and counselling. I believe it all derives from what is termed 'clairsensience'. He becomes aware of facts to be used. As to the clairvoyant images, it is like seeing fragments of another world ... of another vibration. Images may be visible to several of those present, who are able to draw each other's attention to details. And when it comes to the soul that at last begins a journey that will lift it out of a difficult domain; one can just be thankful that there is *always* that option to go forward, whatever the conditions that prevail; however dark the shadows that surround. *Always* the option to go forward is there to grasp.

There is always a scattering of those less obvious rescues that one would hesitate to categorise at all. A military man, an ex-rifleman, once came through. I can identify with him easily enough, because in National Service days, I found that I was for a time, a rifleman myself ... not as the result of any ambition ... but on leaving school following the war years, I was conscripted. It was simply expected! ... And that is often how military placement happens.

At first it seemed as if this rifleman might have just dropped in for a casual talk about nothing in particular. It eventually transpired that there was a problem to be talked about and worthy of the visit. Our visitor had been a career man and had become a 'crack shot'. He had spent time at the range, had worked at it, and enjoyed his status as an expert marksman. In times of war, there were on occasions, special tasks for this man. When under fire from a distant hill, for example, the Commanding Officer might require him to 'pick out' that distant troublesome target, and it was all down to him ... his expertise. He had attained a certain admired status. In a way, upholding his status as a crack shot, had become the central feature of his life. The problem was that now, in the spirit realm, there were no guns, no killing and there was no point whatsoever in being a marksman. The wind had gone clean out of his sails, and he was now at a loss to know what to do. It had not at first been revealed, but he did in fact have a problem, and this was it.

The matter was discussed, and it soon became obvious that he had the ability to enthuse ... not only about his shooting ... there were other things to which he might equally apply such enthusiasm. There were country walks and flower identification and wayside features; in which, in fact, he did have more than a passing interest. In time, he might lead such walks, and pass on that enthusiasm of his, to others. This seemed a good adaptation of his talent, and a constructive way in which to proceed. He became happy at the thought, declaring that he had found the chat most useful.

Upon departing, he left a message for others. It was: ~ *'Don't do something in life that comes to a dead end. Do something useful and ongoing that will serve you later. And don't move so far away from natural life, that the life loses purpose.'*

Chapter XXVI

Voices From Our Past

There have been evening meetings when a spirit who has had Earth life in another time and perhaps another country, has joined us and talked freely about that life. To receive such knowledge in this way is always an immense privilege and there might even be a significant historical content in what is said. The same spirit may even return to us again on subsequent occasions, and would, in that event, become recognised by speech and mannerisms; and one may get to know him/her by name. To illustrate what I mean, let me first refer to a conversation that occurred in 1979, between Leslie and 'Long ... Shadow', a North American Indian. (His name, it seems, should include a substantial pause between the two words, and to address him merely as 'Long-shadow' invites correction.) We pick up the dialogue that has centred upon the hunting lore of his people:

~ *'... We go hunt. We ask chief: 'which way go animal?"*

'And he knew that, did he?'

~ *'Yes. 'Those kind animal go* **that** *way ... Those kind animal go* **that** *way.' Yes. He know ... close ... close.'*

'And you think he was helped by his spirit friends?'

~ *'Yes.'*

'I thought so. He would be given instructions as to where they were?'

~ *'Yes.'*

'This doesn't surprise me.'

~ *'Brother of chief go look ... come tell.'*

'His brother in spirit?'

~ *'Yes. Go look ... Come tell. That way that one, that way that one.'*

'And that was because the chief was interested in the welfare of his people ... and also knew that help could be given by his brother?'

~ *'Yes.'*

'He didn't say: 'That is silly.' He said: 'I believe' ... And he got help?'

~ *'We not wish to go straight there, kill. No. We enjoy ... you call sport; but all old fathers ... old ones ... old ones ... have to feed. So when old ones need meat, chief ask brother ... brother say: 'that way ... that way'. When not old ones need, we don't ask ... No ... We go sport ... For old ones we must get meat ... must get meat.'*

'It wasn't sport. It was serious work...'

~ *'Yes, yes. Not take chance lose meat ... not take chance.'*

'I understand. And always you were told which way they went?'

~ 'Yes ... brother go look.'

'This is most interesting ... and you always looked after your old ones?'

~ 'Always do chief tell. Chief know need. Chief know need because brother tell chief ... and we do.'

'This doesn't surprise me. I'm very interested to know that this could be done. And this could still be done in this world here, if people accepted that guidance could be given. If they believed that they could be told by those in the spirit world, then they would have less problems here. They would know how to act, as you knew how to act.'

~ 'You would understand ... if **all** *hunting, go chief ... say: 'that way, go kill'... Not good for hunter ... Not good enjoy sport of hunting to kill ... Not good all time.'*

'No ... It must only be done when necessary.'

~ '... Not good all time ... both ways.'

'Our people now hunt with the gun ... You know what the gun is?'

~ 'Yes.'

'... Hunt with the gun, not because they need the meat, or because old people need the meat. They hunt for the pleasure of killing, and we don't like this.'

~ 'That what I say. Not good all time. Not good all time. Sometime kill ... sometime sport.'

'Did you ever hunt the animals or chase the animals and not kill them? ... Just for the pleasure of the sport and tracking them?'

~ 'Me? No ... No.'

'Nor your people?'

~ 'Some ... yes.'

'They would track them and not kill them?'

~ 'Yes. I not think good to do.'

'You don't?'

~ 'No. I think animal right to live ... right to enjoy life. When time come ... need old people feed, then they go; but not ... I don't know the word ... They say tell him 'not **worry** *animal' ... Yes?' [It appears he was advised at this point by a control, on use of the word 'worry'].*

'Yes, I understand.'

~ 'No ... not good meat. Not good meat if all time chase ... No.'

'This is very interesting, Long ... Shadow.'

~ 'We don't want him too clever when we **do** *need him, for the old ones ... no. No ... that not reason. Animal have right to enjoy life.'*

'Until the time comes when he is needed for others?'

~ 'Yes ... Then only kill that one how much need. Not more.'

'And did you give thanks when you killed?'

~ *'Yes.'*

'I thought you would.'

~ *'Thank brother feed old ones. Thank chief ... get message. Thank brother for good place. Thank animal have allow us have him feed.'*

At this stage, Long ... Shadow, became quite emotional and another came through who went on: *'That one very honest man. That one was, you understand, very upright man. He did whatever was necessary to be done. He knew that he could not allow emotion to come into his work. He did have thought about animal ... yes. He did not like to kill animal ... no. But neither did he wish to see old people wasting away, getting too thin ... no ... could not be allowed. If the spirit tell him to chief: 'these people must have meat ... you must kill', he did, but he did not enjoy ... no.'*

It is a heart-warming narrative from those earlier times in North America; which amply describes a sensitivity of approach to the need of killing for food. That sensitivity embodies a belief in guidance and a respect for the animal. Both attributes need much re-establishment in today's world. Some of us have that sensitivity, and it is of course, embodied in Albert Schweitzer's axiom: *Reverence for life.* The knowledge is certainly known and accepted by those of us who look within and listen.

The two dialogues that follow are interesting in that each has a precise historical content. This in itself makes them worthy of their inclusion here. But in addition, and as will become evident, they have been *arranged* for us, to teach us a little about the nature of our ongoing life in spirit, and how that life relates to this physical realm.

The evening of 20 November 1995 was a truly memorable evening, and a much-treasured meeting. The tape recording itself carries deeply emotional passages, the feeling of which cannot possibly be, adequately transferred in transcript. But one can at least write down the words, and let imagined emotion rise to whatever level beckons.

The visiting spirit has a firm place in the history of the West. It should be pointed out that this particular visit had been attempted on an occasion several months earlier, but 'conditions' had not been quite right then. It had been agreed on that occasion, that a further attempt would be made at a later date when conditions would hopefully be more favourable. No name was given in words, but one of those present had 'sensed' an identity. She did not speak the name, but wrote it down, sealed it in an envelope, and handed it to Leslie for his safe keeping.

It was an 'arranged' visit. Following formal greetings, Leslie ventured with: *'Our mutual friend Salumet said you would be speaking with us tonight.'*

~ *'I would wish to speak in your language of today.'*

'Thank you.'

~ *'I come to you ... to show you all that the spirit of one long gone, can return.'*

'Yes. We believe this implicitly.'

~ *'I speak to you on the last memory of my time (on Earth). And perhaps I will become a little more accustomed to speaking with you.'*

'Thank you. We look forward to hearing what you have to say.'

~ *'I would like to tell you that some points raised about my death are not so accurate as they may seem.'*

'That doesn't surprise me.'

~ *'Now ... as I return to these vibrations, the memory returns.'*

'Hmm.'

~ *'I must tell you that I have attempted to return before to you, some while ago…'*

'Thank you.'

~ *'... when I mentioned to you about your seating, and I would need more room. Do you recall?'*

'Yes. And you did ask for a hard seat didn't you?'

~ *'Since that time, I have discovered that it is unnecessary.'*

'... And your instrument was very aware of the clothing you used to wear too.'

~ *'She will be this time too...'*

'Good.'

~ *'...But I have tried to modify it for her, to make it a little more comfortable.'*

'And you yourself are quite comfortable now are you ... with us?'

~ *'I am indeed.'*

'Thank you very much. I shan't interrupt again. We now await for you to talk as you wish.'

~ *'I want to say to you, that my last day upon this Earth is still very vivid in my memory, as I return to you. It was a beautiful bright February day. The sun shone, and to all intent and purpose, you could feel that spring was around the corner. Are you understanding my words?'*

'We are ... It is very, very clear.'

~ *'...Because it is difficult to gauge for me.'*

'We hear them very clearly indeed.'

~ *'That is good ... I awoke that morning after a very sleepless night; because you see, there was much noise throughout the previous night. I was ready to meet ... how you would have termed then ... my Maker. I truly believed myself, that I was completely composed. I promised not to shed a tear ... that I had to be strong for those who had cared for me in those long dark days ... Dear Jane and Elizabeth ... to them I owed so much in those last dark days. I will have to ask you to be patient, because memory torments me, even now...'*

Leslie, quietly: *'Of course, we do understand.'*

Then, with much emotion and a deep, deep sensitivity, yet with a wonderful clarity, she continued: ~ *'I truly believed that I left this plane of existence with goodness in my heart ... even for Pollay (?)! ... How wrong I was! ... How wrong I was! ... That when I met my Maker ... as I would have said in those days ... did I discover how much I had loathed that gentleman! He was a jailer ... Oh hatred! ... I am sorry to display these emotions. I did not feel I would ... but you have to realise that on returning ... how painful these memories become.'*

'I can quite understand. They must be a burden to you.'

~ *'What I want to say is this: Much has been written about the words I uttered on my last breath. It is said that dear Jane and Elizabeth thought I uttered the words: 'Sweet Jesus'. I tell you now, that I had been praying, as my head lowered to the cushion ... I prayed earnestly to be taken quickly.'*

'Of course.'

~ *'As it struck my neck ... I was saying the words: 'Je suis! Je suis!' ... 'I am! I am!' ... And so, I left behind the Earth plane torment, which had me jailed for so long. No one knows ... No one knows ... that my sweet dear little dog was gathered amongst my underskirts. How could they know? ... How could they know?'*

'Of course not.'

~ *'And this is something else I want you to know ... that only those close to me would have known ... that my dear animal was known to me as 'Piers' ... Dear, sweet animal. I know it has been written, that when I was disrobed ... that those who watched ... and can you ... can you ... imagine the humiliation to be disrobed in front of so many?'*

'Of course.'

~ *'I was dressed intentionally ... intentionally I must say ... in red undergarment ... not ... not to hide the blood as it has been written ... but, being a devout Catholic, I wore the colour of the blood of Christ.'*

'Yes. I understand.'

~ *'So I was preparing myself to meet our Saviour ... But on going there, I was shocked at my own stifled deep dislike and hatred for some of those who treated me so badly.'*

'Yes.'

~ *'I have to tell you also, that whatever has been written about (Queen) Elizabeth ... she really did not move to sign my life away.'*

'No. So I understand.'

~ *'This has to be made clear to you.'*

'Thank you.'

~ *'She also was unaware of the treachery of Pollay (?), who was indeed an evil man.'*

'Yes. Have you met him since you have been gone?'

~ *'I have not. I would not wish to. But I have come to terms and have forgiven him all. But I did not meet him ... face to face ... I think you would say. Is that the words? I did not wish ... I have much in memory of those last hours ... and now they have been spoken.'*

'Now you can go in peace.'

~ *'But now I have to tell you why I have come...'*

'Thank you.'

Then followed an instruction for us, an instruction that will be of interest to any that have wondered about such things as the apparent multiplicity of spirit. How can a spirit be comprised of a set of 'past lives', yet be one? And how is it possible that such past identities can meet with those of us who are currently fixed in the material present?

~ *'Because ... Thank you for your help ... I am so appreciative of it ... And I know you will be rewarded for it ... I want to tell you now, why it has been important ... not the words I have spoken to you ... but to tell you that the person that I was then, has subsequently returned in another form to your Earthly plane.'*

'Is that so?'

~ *'Salumet has told me that he wanted you to realise what he has told you ... that you are more than one.'*

'Yes indeed.'

~ *'And whilst I retain the memories of those painful times within that lifetime; that* **part** *of me returned for the betterment of others. And so he hopes we all can share this time, to know that we are not just one.'*

There followed some discourse about preparations for the visit, and the lady's presence having been 'felt' earlier in the day, while those preparations were in hand. Our visitor then continued:

~ *'I feel much stronger now.'*

'Good. We are delighted to hear that. I hope that our combined love and presence has been of assistance to you.'

~ *'It has indeed. And I want to let you know of the time difference of which I come. We are speaking ... can I give the year? ... To let the others know how long ago I existed here?'*

'Yes. Please do.'

~ *'I am speaking of the year ... 1587.'*

'1587 ... And would you care to tell my colleagues your name?'

~ *'It's unimportant ... but...'*

'Yes. If you would ... for them...'

~ *'I was known as ... Mary Stuart.'*

And Leslie, quietly: *'Yes ... Queen of Scots.'*

~ *'But I have to be honest and say that truly, my heart belonged in France.'*

'In France?'

~ *'Yes. But it matters not now. These facts are well dispatched. I hope that all of you in this time find your world religions much more humble ... that people no longer suffer for their religious beliefs. Because, truly, that is why I was put to death.'*

There followed some talk of the Queen's son James, and then the exchange of pleasantries at parting. Finally, Leslie was saying: *'It has been a wonderful experience for us ... Thank you ... God bless you.'*

It had indeed been an evening to be treasured. And within the sealed envelope, what of the name therein? What had been sensed during that previous visit had in fact been perfectly correct. The legend was *'Mary Queen of Scots'*. It was nearly a year later when I was putting together this chapter, which involved transcribing from the tape of that evening, and reading for comparison, the detailed and informative biography by Antonia Fraser. At that time, Ann and I were taking a break for a few days with our camper van. We stayed in Chester and travelled into North Wales. Ann had business at one of the Chester hotels, extending over three days, while I was ensconced (through the day) in the camper, in the hotel car park; paying visits to the hotel's coffee lounge and offices from time to time. There were several royal portraits in the hallway leading to the lounge. The one that caught my eye, was a picture of Mary Queen of Scots. It was she! And we exchanged some long thoughtful looks. Each time I ventured past, it appeared to me, that she was looking down and conveying a reassuring feeling that she was really not so far away.

'My heart belonged in France ... it matters not now ... These facts are well dispatched' ... are words well spoken. Mary was born of a French mother, Mary of Guise, on Scottish soil, and crowned Queen of Scots at Stirling when a babe of 9-months. The alliance between Scotland and France concerned the French monarch King Henry II (The same who received the accurately predictive letter from Nostradamus.) The Scottish Parliament gave its assent to the marriage of Mary to King Henry's son Francis ... the Dauphin. Mary was then to spend her happiest years (6 to 19) in France, with the French court exceedingly well disposed towards her.

'The little Queen of Scots is the most perfect child that I have ever seen.'
King Henry II of France

Her heart *of course*, remained in France; and it comes as no surprise that her last words should be spoken in the language of that country.

Mary's troubles began when she left French soil and sailed for Scotland. In the long and difficult years of captivity that were ultimately to follow ... *'dear Jane and Elizabeth'* ... were Jane Kennedy and Elizabeth Curle. It was they who were closest to her during those difficult years, and who shared her bedchamber. The day-to-day lives of Mary and her entourage were much influenced by the jailers, in whose charge they were placed. Towards the end of 1584, they had been in the charge of Sir Ralph Saddler, who held a reputation for being in general, fair and considerate; but not their subsequent jailer. Mary's pronunciation ... *'Pollay'* ... can only mean 'Paulet' ... Sir Amyas Paulet. It was from early January 1585, Mary and those who cared for her were transferred to the dreary, hateful and less well appointed Tutbury Fortress, where they were in the custody of that particular jailer.

> *... the care of her person was handed over to a new and infinitely more severe jailer, Sir Amyas Paulet, who became in time as odious to her as the masonry of Tutbury itself. Under these doleful circumstances, with very little to cheer her as she surveyed her prospects for the future, Mary Stuart entered on the last and most burdensome phase of her captivity.*
> Antonia Fraser *Mary Queen of Scots.* Weidenfeld & Nicolson

Such is that part of the recorded history. The noise through the night preceding the execution was from the tramping of the guard's boots outside the Queen's room, and the hammering. The hammering was to make the raised wooden platform in the great hall, where the partly concealed, almost clandestine, yet watched by some 300 spectators ... deed, was to take place. The Queen's bearing must have been truly regal as she approached the great hall. The entry of her servants was at first barred, and she had to plead with Paulet. Mary pleaded a detailed case for their presence in the hall; declaring her disbelief that it could be the instruction of Queen Elizabeth ... her own cousin ... that she should die alone with none in attendance.

Mary was finally allowed to have six with her, including of course Jane and Elizabeth ... her closest. It was necessary to vouch for them ... that they would not cry out or behave unseemly. It had been suggested to her that any servants present might not only cry out, but might dip napkins in her blood as keepsakes! ... And this would be inconvenient! But the six were finally allowed into the great hall. When the time approached and

Mary's servants crossed themselves while the tears flowed, Mary had the strength to turn and gently admonish them ... in French: *'Ne crie point pour moi. J'ai promis pour vous'* ... Her statement being in effect that they should keep the promise she had made for them.

At the moment of departure, the Queen's lips moved, with her final words of that life ... again in French. That was with the first blow of the big axe. The delivery was not straight. It was the second blow that severed. It was the executioner who held the head aloft while lips continued their movement in death, and he declared: *'God save the Queen!'* But the head fell away from the auburn tresses, now seen by all to be a wig; and at this, spectators were quickly and appropriately hushed to more respectful silence ... But then, certain nobles at the front, saw fit to break the energy of that silence. They breached it with raucous shouting; their shouted politics, including such flouts as: *'So perish all the Queen's enemies!'* and *'Such be the end of all the Queen's, and all the Gospel's enemies!'* But those who heeded the inner voice and understood the sham, just let the tears flow in a silent sorrow. Theirs was a humble and a much more understandable feeling that carried with it, due respect.

When it was time to remove the remaining adornments from the red-clothed body, the little Skye terrier ... Piers ... that Mary had loved so, in those dark and desolate days, saw fit to take up a position of vigil, between the blooded shoulders and the head of his late mistress. Nothing would entice Piers to move elsewhere. It was a deserved embarrassment to those responsible. As if it were a cleansing of guilt following murder, all traces pertaining to the Queen was burned, all blood scrubbed clean, the wretched blooded block was burned, and the weeping women removed and locked in their rooms. The executioners were not allowed to keep their perquisites. Those in charge would not run the risk of any possible Holy relic remaining from what might be seen as Catholic martyrdom. Even Piers was washed ... more than once. But the loyal little terrier only ever wanted the one mistress; and so, refused to eat and quickly pined away. Perhaps the little dog showed more love and feeling than a good many that were privileged to be present through rank and legitimate process.

Lord Talbot was dispatched from the fortress in the early afternoon, for London. He delivered the news to Queen Elizabeth next morning. She received it with indignation and distress. Such is the gist that may be derived from the historical accounts.

It is well that such encounters through the doorways between worlds are reported. It is not only educational in respect of the ways of the spirit;

it also sheds a fresh light on elements of history, and of course, the history books do not always get the facts quite right. How could they? They can only be based upon what we think the ears hear, word of mouth, and memory. How could they get it all completely right?

On the evening of 29 April 1996, we experienced the privilege of the arranged visit of another great lady. On some occasions, the process of communication between worlds has a somewhat 'cloudy' or unclear start, as if the procedure is not quite 'automatic'; but the situation steadily becomes clearer and more comfortable for the visitor, as things get under way. This was one such occasion, and I include that initial part of the dialogue, simply to illustrate that these things are not always of a perfectly simple straightforward *Dr Who-like* nature. Apart from the two who would be involved in the channel, the rest of us were asked to talk quietly amongst ourselves, to help facilitate the passage of the one. A control then spoke, saying: ~ *'Now we are ready to bring forward the one who awaits.'*

'Thank you very much indeed.' Then there followed a silence, which lasted two or three minutes.

~ *'Your silence and expectation is commendable. I am so pleased to be here with you.'*

'We are certainly very pleased to welcome you. And we appreciate you coming to talk to us.'

~ *'I have to admit to you, that all at this particular moment in time, does seem confusing, but hopefully it should clear ... and I will be able to give you the information that I intended to give.'*

'Thank you very much.'

~ *'I was not prepared for this confusion of thought on entering this life.'*

'I understand that it is very confusing for the first few moments when one returns to the physical. I am also told that it does clear itself as the voice continues to be used.'

~ *'Yes. I am happy with the instrument, but it is like swimming through a sea of fog at this moment.'*

'It must be very difficult for you.'

~ *'I will try to recall, if you will bear with me.'*

'Certainly. I was going to ask if there is anything you would like each of us to concentrate on, to assist you, to clear the confusion?'

~ *'I ask only for your love please.'*

'Right. Well we can certainly give you that.'

~ *'It is strange to be touching such rough material...'*

'Yes. I suppose it must feel rough to you now.'

~ 'Yes. It is not unpleasant, but is strange. I was not prepared for it.'

'Is that so?'

~ 'So please bear with me...'

'Yes, of course.'

~ '... And we will begin conversation.'

'Yes. We will be happy to go along with whatever you wish.'

~ 'I am also trying to adjust the voice, because I know it is not how I would wish it to be.'

'It is quite clear incidentally.'

~ 'If you are happy with it, then we could continue.'

'Yes, we are quite happy. You are speaking very clearly.'

~ 'Then, do you know why I have been sent to you?'

'No, we don't. Salumet said that we would have somebody coming, whom we would find very interesting. That's all he did say.'

~ 'I am deeply touched that those words should have been used about me. But of course, the reason behind my returning, is the teaching that you have received ... that I am in fact a cut ... **cut of the personality** *of the whole, which is returning in different time and different body.'*

'Yes. Salumet has explained something of that to us.'

~ 'It is not that we wish to impress ... that we wish to give details. We do not need to give you evidence of life after what you call 'death'. That is not why we return, because you have gone further than that.'

'Yes.'

~ 'So, the reason behind this return visit, is to show you that the personality can cut itself from the whole and make a return.'

'Thank you.'

~ 'I will try to bring forward some facts as you may bring to memory, and help you to recognise who I am.'

Before proceeding further, Leslie explained that all was being recorded, and how this meant that many would subsequently be able to listen.

~ 'Let me say to you all, it is good to be amongst an audience once again.'

'Good.'

~ 'This happened many times in the lifetime which I have come to speak to you about. It was quite normal for me, and I accepted it too easily as being the normal ... So once again, to be amongst all the people, does indeed seem strange ... because, as of course ... as I have gone on in this side of life, I know how unnecessary this was. But of course, it was my life's plan at that particular time, and I do accept it now.'

'I understand.'

~ *'Firstly, I would like to give you my name, although, I do realise that you probably will not recognise it.'*

'Yes...'

~ *'I was known as Sophia Augusta Frederika.'*

'Sophia Augusta Frederika ... Really?'

~ *'Yes.'*

'Really! Thank you! I **do** *recognise it.'*

~ *'But, of course, to others throughout the world, I would have been better known as Catherine.'*

'Mm ... Hmm.'

~ *'... But I have to say here and now ... I always objected to changing my name ... and always I was known as Sophia when I came to this side of life. I rather resented the intrusion on my birth name, but being a woman, I had no say in these matters of state.'*

'No. Unfortunately, in your time, that was so, wasn't it?'

~ *'Indeed it was ... And of course, I was a young slip of a girl, and did not dare to speak out.'*

'No. I imagine you do very differently now, where you are...'

~ **'This** *is what I come to tell you ... All of your life's troubles does not mean too much, when you come to the larger side of life. Everything comes into perspective. You see your life's plan. You see the pit falls, and you see the good points of it all. And of course, you learn from your many lives. You understand this of course?'*

'Yes we do.'

~ *'I had much to regret when I left this life ... or at least, the life I am speaking of ... because, in your yearly terms, many years have gone by. But I speak only of this time in order that you can make recognition for yourselves and to understand that time is not the least important, when it comes to the continuity of lives.'*

'Yes. This we are beginning to understand. Incidentally, if I might say, your voice is now very much clearer. I hope the confusion has lessened.'

~ *'It is clearing.'*

'Good.'

~ *'We were hoping that the control would have been greater this time, but we must always work with what we have.'*

'Yes. I understand. Thank you.'

~ *'It is strange how these things become misty. You would assume that all would be natural in memory ... but it is not so. I am recalling just the few times of this lifetime which I can tell you about. They obviously made a great impact on my life when I lived here. So may I tell you a little?'*

'Please do! You are doubtless aware of the intense silence. Everybody is anxious to hear you.'

~ *'My childhood was mainly uneventful. I believe I was a loved child. But my mother had great promises made for me. Her ideal was to see me married well. So this is how my name came to be changed, much to my annoyance at the time. The decision in my life was made partly in 1774. This is the time we go back to. This is my first strongest memory ... when I was taken from my homeland, a small Duchy in Germany ... influenced I might say by Frederick, who was a strong powerful man at the time. I was transported, by my mother, to Russia. I have to tell you, I was terrified at the prospect. I was a petite young woman aged only fifteen ... Can you imagine what it must have felt like? ... To be transported from one's homeland and the bosom of your family ... to be confronted by a woman so strong ... so powerful ... as not one word was uttered in her presence?'*

'The Czarina...'

~ *'The Empress.'*

'Yes.'

~ *'I have to tell you, she was not unkind to me. But also, she did not show affection either. To one so young, it was indeed disturbing and distressing.'*

'I can imagine. Why did they take you there?'

~ *'Because I was to become betrothed to the Empress's nephew.'*

The nephew of the Empress Elizabeth was Peter Feodorovitch, grandson to Peter the Great. On the death of the Empress, on Christmas day 1761, he was briefly to become Peter III Czar of Russia. The historical record is that, at her death, it was Prince Trubetskoy who announced, *'Her Imperial Majesty Elizaveta Petrovna has fallen asleep in the Lord. God preserve our gracious sovereign, the Emperor Peter the Third.'* But after a promising start as Emperor, he embarked on policies that were unpopular with the Church, the army, and the people. In particular he irrationally eulogised King Frederick II of Prussia. After shedding much blood in six years against Frederick's armies, the Russian people were happy enough when Peter made peace. But to name a Russian ship of the line 'Fredericus Rex', to refer to Frederick as 'Our Master' and to toast him at banquets to the roar of 50 cannon fired twice, was seen as alarmingly eccentric. Increasing distaste for his policies and irrational ways led to his removal from power within just six months.

The young Princess Sophia had travelled from Anhalt-Zerbst with her mother, to become his bride. That she should be required to enter into the Greek Orthodox Church, was, in Russia, then held to be a condition in such a marriage, to a foreigner. There would certainly be many difficulties for her; not least, the maladjustment of the youth she was to marry. On this, it is known that she wrote at the time: *'My disposition is such that my heart would have belonged entirely and unreservedly to a husband who gave me his love.'* But that was not to be ... that love was not given.

We now listened attentively, as Sophia ... Catherine continued:

~ *'I was instructed in the Russian language, which I have to say, at that time, distressed me. I was instructed in the orthodox religion ... I was instructed in so many things in such a short space of time. Also, my name was changed to Catherine and I was betrothed to Peter. He was a thin, gangly, pock-marked young boy, only one year older than I. But I would happily have joined him with love, if only he could have shown an affection; but that was never to be. The memory now distresses me, when I think back to the love I left behind within my own family at home.'*

'Were you never able to visit your family?'

~ *'My mother stayed with me and frequently wrote back to my father. But I was so unhappy.'*

'I'm sure you were.'

~ *'... But I could never show it, because of course, I was constantly told how great a ruler was being bestowed upon me, and one day I would become a great lady. I never wanted that, but fate and circumstances were due to bring me just that. I am speaking to you now, about the human element of this woman. I am speaking to you about the feelings within her heart; that one never spoke aloud at the time ... because, as a young woman, so young in age, she was terrified to say one word out of place.'*

'Yes.'

The history books of today of course, cannot possible convey with any measure of accuracy, those feelings within. A pause then followed, before our eminent visitor again continued:

~ *'The next memory that comes to me ... is of the marriage ceremony. I was taken to the Empress's room, while she took charge to dress me ... to be duly instructed ... and so, then Peter and I were transported to the great cathedral ... The Virgin of Kassam. I remember thinking how appropriate that name was, and how terrified I was ... to become the wife of this 17-year old boy.'*

'I can quite understand. It must have been a terrible experience for you.'

~ *'The cathedral was beautiful ... and will always be imprinted on my memory. It took several hours ... Such a wedding was indeed spectacular. We returned to a banquet feast. Can you imagine* **so** *much food? ... But the worst part for me was the obligation to dance with so many old noblemen.'*

'Really?'

~ *'I was horrified. Even now, I can feel myself quake from the thought.'*

'Are you not able to ... clear these memories and give yourself peace of mind?'

~ *'Of course, they have been gone for many years. It is only the return to this physical world, which brings vivid, not only the memories, but the pain as well.'*

'I see.'

~ *'Of course they have gone. When I leave here, they will be gone forever.'*

'They will be gone forever ... good!'

~ *'I am not in pain now you understand.'*

'No ... We are pleased to hear that.'

~ *'But the memory is* **so** *strong.'*

'I ask the question because we did have a communicator from an earlier age than yours even, and who told us afterwards that her visit enabled her to clear her mind completely of the traumas that she had suffered. And we were hoping that this might be the case with you as well.'

~ *'No. I have none of these problems. I fully accepted when I came to this side of life ... I knew what I had done ... what I had done wrong. And I knew what had to be done. There are many memories, within a lifetime, that have to be faced up to.'*

'I see.'

~ *'... And I will tell you now, because it took me many, many of your years time to fully accept what I had done. Although I did not actually raise my own hand, I was responsible for Peter's death ... So, of course, those who caused the hurts sorely distressed me when the news came. But I knew in my heart, that that was what the state would need. You see, by then, I had become a worshipped lady throughout the land. The people wanted me to rule, because Peter was a weak infantile man. And I have to say ... his mind was not fully there. He was subject to many stormy outbursts ... and he did not please the people, because he was in favour of Frederick ... who was a powerful, in Peter's mind ...* **ally**. *And the Russian people ... they could see that he couldn't be a good and strong leader. So you see, the power came to me, without even my soul wishing or desiring it to be given.'*

'Yes.'

~ *'But once ... once you have the adrenaline flowing through your veins ... once you have the feel of power, and the adoration of your people, then your life can take a turn for the worse.'*

'I quite follow you. Yes.'

~ *'This I had to face up to...'* Then in a more reflective and more gentle voice ... ~ *'I had much to face up to...'*

Perhaps, in Russian politics, it was not so much a crossroads as an impasse. However one views it, the point in time is well acknowledged by historians. Vincent Cronin puts it thus:

> *'Catherine in short was determined to dissociate herself from Peter's Prussian-style State, the unpopularity of which she had experienced*

first hand as a girl, and she made this clear to her increasingly wide acquaintanceship at court.'
Vincent Cronin: *Catherine, Empress of All the Russias*
First published in Great Britain in 1978 by Harvill. Copyright © Vincent Cronin, 1978. Reproduced by permission of the Harvill Press.

The historians, of course, present the hard facts of the matter, and make whatever connections, as may seem relevant. The feelings of the heart do not in general, find their way into the books that are written. But whatever the presentation, the power settled away from Peter, who it appears was not receptive of it. And of course, such a position of power can be a lonely place. There was something to be said on this also:

~ *'... I was a warm-hearted pretty young woman who desired the love of a man. I do not deny ... I do not deny this. Neither do I feel grief about it, because you see, circumstances dictated all this. And I found love ... I have to say ... and I must say to you ... that it is not well known or understood; that Peter fully accepted a child as his own. In fact my own (three) children belonged to different men. This I am not sorry for, because I loved each and every one of them ... but I have to say ... if life could have been different, I would have chosen another pathway.'*

'Yes ... you didn't wish for the power that was thrust on you...'

~ *'No ... When I looked back over that lifetime, I could see I had done much good. But people ... some thought I had wronged them and not least my own son. And that was my parting memory and one that caused me continuous grief. But at times, because, although my peoples call me 'Catherine the Great'; to my own son, I was neither a good mother, nor heroine. He despised me because, you see, he always believed Peter to be his true father. On my death, he instructed that Peter's remains be dug up and be brought ... to be together ... and he...'*

At this point, Sophia ... Catherine, while speaking of her son Paul who succeeded her ... became very emotional and the recording is indistinct. But then her voice again became stronger:

~ *'... Can you imagine what it was like to watch this from this side of life, and to be unable to comfort him?'*

'It must have been a terrible time for you.'

~ *'It was, but it opened my eyes to what I had to accept...'*

'... And I believe I am right in saying, that though you didn't wish to have the power which you **did** *have ... in the main you used it for the benefit of your people?'*

~ *'The people were so glad...'* The tape is difficult again at this point, as she speaks with sensitivity of how it was with Peter. Then continuing once more with: ~ *'He was a simple man, given to strength but little knowledge ... And so, I had to take control ... not only of all the peoples, but of the future of Russia ... ... He was like a little boy. All he wanted was to play with his soldiers and his castles and to hunt with his dogs ... He was not ready for man's work ... to rule over his country ... to take a wife ... work. You have to understand, that in this time, you had no say in what your fate was to be.'*

'No, but it would seem that it was necessary for you to take the part you did in that life, because of Peter's shortcomings...'

~ *'I understand that now. It is the one thing that I have accepted. I reigned for 34 years of your Earth time, and most of them were good.'*

'Yes.'

~ *'... And you see ... I truly loved the first man I had my first child born with. There was no one to match him ... But he was sent away on diplomatic purposes, because of the rumours within court.'*

'I see. So that happiness was taken from you also...'

~ *'I* ***know*** *now, it was this that made me strong ... ... And I have to say, that since that lifetime, my heart has been heavy, not only with what has happened in Russia, but in my homeland of Germany. But I think I would be right in telling you that the nations of your world are becoming much more sensible ... that they are beginning to recognise that love of all mankind is truly what your lives are about.'*

'It is beginning, and for that we must be grateful.'

~ *'I do believe I must depart now ... I thank you for allowing this time. I thank you for the opportunity of memory. I thank you ... and I say to you all ... love one another, as you would those closest to you. Know that all in your lives can be good if you so desire.'*

'We all hope that you can retain happiness now. Is that possible for you?'

~ *'I am happy. I am happy. I do this only because it is instructive to you. All my memory has disappeared in the life that I now lead. I am only a small fragment of the life that exists now...'*

Some warm farewells continued with a fading power, as is often noticed at the end of a long session. Finally, Leslie was bidding our farewell which appropriately included: *'We can't find enough words to thank you for having come here tonight, and for what you have told us ... ... Our full love goes with you.'*

It was now abundantly clear to all, that this was a wonderfully open, sensitive and progressed spirit, that Salumet had 'arranged' to be with us. Sophia now forms but a small part of this progressed spirit ... and the term 'part' remains without full definition. Although accessible in terms of personality and memory, 'part' is an expression that is doubtless far too separatist a perception. That personality surely has to make a more subtle contribution to the soul than to be just an isolated fraction. If some of us have youthfully imagined at one time, an afterlife where one fortuitously bumps into Earth's notaries on some kind of metaphysical merry-go-round; then it is now time to realise that it is just not like that. There are, without any shadow of doubt, cosmic subtleties, that lie out of reach of our Earth-bound comprehension. To attempt to understand such things in terms of our *material science* and our *dictionary* is difficult. Yet, in his teachings, Jesus appears to have referred to our past lives as previous images that neither die nor are at the present time manifest:

> *'Jesus said: When you see your likeness, you rejoice. But when you see your images which came into existence before you, (which) neither die nor are manifested, how much will you bear!'*
> *The Gospel According to Thomas.* Nag Hamâdi papyrus.
> Trans. A. Guillaumont, H.-Ch. Puech, G. Quispel, W. Till and Yassah 'Abd Al Masúh. E. J. Brill.

It was, as stated, the one we know as Salumet, who arranged the above visits. In the chapter that follows, we meet and have conversation with that one who travels to us from a much higher vibration and who is able to make such arrangements.

Chapter XXVII

Evenings with 'Salumet'

The *future* already exists; at least, as seen from spirit, and as seen in trance by Nostradamus, St John, Cassandra and others; coincident with past and present. If there were to be in our physical world, an atomic holocaust, then it would already be imprinted in that future ... our future ... but it is not. Misdirected *free will* steered us for one fleeting moment in that dreadful direction. Thank heavens there are other realms of existence that may come closer at such times, and help to divert!

Souls in other realms are an influence, as much an influence as we part-physical beings ourselves, or more so if necessary. There are indeed times when others may come close and be a stronger, more powerful influence ... which is and has been a blessing. This being so, then our collective future, in both Earth-bound physical progression as well as beyond in spirit, can and will continue to remain for us ... a foreseeable future.

In Earth time, it was 2,000 years ago when Jesus the Christ incarnated in the physical, for the purpose of a teaching that centres upon 'love and peace'. The time was then right for that particular mission. Similarly, all other missions by incarnate *masters* have also centred upon a teaching of that same love and peace. Too often, sadly, our lives have fallen short of this teaching; and regrettably, resulting religions have dogmatised, jumbled and deleted passages from the *Divine Message* as received, rendering it confused and spoiled. The error has been made worse by enmeshing that distorted message with the political State, a process begun in respect of the Christian mission to Earth, in the days of the Emperor Constantine.

The present era is a time for further missions. Spirit realms move closer, and masters again walk the Earth, Sai Baba and Mother Meera to name but two. It is all a part of the present campaign of *influence* that unfortunately has become necessary due to our waywardness. Not all masters, who bring the spiritual message, choose to incarnate. The ways of spirit are numerous, and not limited to the process of childbirth into physical life. I believe I would be correct in describing he whom we have come to know as 'Salumet' as a master from a much higher plane of existence. The *channel*, through Eileen, an able and experienced spiritual medium steadily developed over a lengthy period. Then, on 27 June 1994, Salumet came through to us for the first time. He was on that occasion, able to give us a name to know him by and to deliver the cheering message:

~ *'We are reaching the point where your world will ...* ***will*** *be a better place. Do not doubt these words.'*

We never doubted the voice that was 'vibrant' with so much love and compassion. Visits became weekly, the channel became stronger, and sessions became longer. We quickly came to love and cherish this one, from whom so much love and sensitivity emanated, much knowledge and wisdom also. This one was truly a teaching master who understands the ways of Earth and the ways of spirit, and all the subtleties of time and how it links with prophecy; conversant with the ways of healing, power of thought, and the value of prayer. His teachings were to be all embracing. We would keep returning to the topic of 'power of thought', that generative principle that underpins and furthers the entirety of creation. At the time of writing, his visits are now into their fourth year, and there is a great wealth of recorded tape and transcript. Sometimes Salumet has delivered teachings; sometimes he has provided answers to invited questions, which have been both varied and profuse. We are greatly indebted to Leslie for ably presiding and putting questions and at appropriate times inviting questions from the floor.

The accumulated data, includes a great deal about life in spirit, progression of the soul, between-worlds transactions, life's chosen path, transition at physical death, the standing of world religions, the value of meditation, healing; as well as a great many details concerning our Earth and its history and the present state of our civilisation. (Much of this may hopefully one day be presented as several volumes that all will have the opportunity to read. Already, there have been many, many hours devoted to the process of transcribing.) The percentage of material that can be selected for just one book chapter is of course minute. I should also make it clear that, the material that follows in this chapter has a distinct bias. It has been selected for its relationship to topics raised in preceding pages, and to help clarify what is happening to Earth at and around the time of the millennium change ... very much a selection of the more down-to-earth subject matter, one might say ... and relating more to our earlier communications. Accordingly, a good proportion of the questions, but not all, I have been able to put to Salumet myself, a privilege that I humbly and gratefully acknowledge. And at what better point to begin, than with a question that relates to our beginning ... chapter I, concerning Homo erectus?

Q: *'About 2 million years ago, there were people we now refer to as 'Homo erectus' ... perhaps longer ago ... our timing isn't always accurate. The fossils indicate that their voice boxes were not as developed as ours; but would there have been a similar type of spirit communication, between them and spirit realm in those days?'*

A: **~** *'Let me answer that for you. Spirit has always been. And of course, even with man in his 'younger days', if you prefer to say it that way; spirit communication had always existed, because man is spirit. I wish you could all understand that. You are spirit first; you are a human being second, if you like. So of course, spirit communication has always been. How could it not exist?'*

'That is put beautifully ... clearly. Thank you.'

And Leslie was often quick to add a point: *'If I might follow that George ... Apparently you've not read or if you have, it may have escaped your memory; that the backs of the craniums of those people were much more developed than ours are ... because that was the seat of psychic expression and communication. That is why it was so developed. I'll let Salumet correct that if it's not so.'*

A: **~** *'I was going to say, it is the one area of your evolution which has gone backwards in man, rather than forwards as you think you have. The psyche has always been there, and in earlier man it was much more advanced. Yes, you are correct.'*

Q: *'It's a great privilege to be able to put questions to you like this. Some of us have a fascination for the great stone circles in our country ... like Stonehenge and Avebury...'*

~ *'Yes...'*

'... which were built perhaps 6,000 years ago in our time. They may have energy connections. They may have communication connections. We don't really know. Is there anything you can tell us about the stone circles?'

A: **~** *'Yes, I understand. Yes ... First let me say, there have in past times been groups of people with extended knowledge, far beyond your own comprehension. We can devote more time on another occasion to that. But first, picture these people with their extended knowledge, of energy patterns, of all kinds of vibrational energies, on your Earth plane. You are quite correct to say it has to do with energy. It also was a form of worship. You have to remember that, all over your Earth, there have been many gods to worship. Each and every group of people have worshipped in their own individual way. The stone circles were erected for this very reason, many, many thousands of years ago. I hope I can bring one of those people sometime, to speak to you ... May I?'*

In amazement: ~ *'That would be wonderful!'*

A: **~** *'They were a people, really not of this world; but of an extended knowledge, which helped them to create what you term: 'these wonderful stones and masterpieces'. But let me say, I will try to bring you someone who can give you so much detail.'*

'We would greatly appreciate that, because I've many times been amused at the theories put forward as to how the stones were erected ... when to me (Leslie) it has been a simple matter of understanding forces which **we** *do not understand.'*

A: ~ *'Yes ... that is the problem. The energy forces that exist on this Earth are not comprehended by the normal human being.'*

This seemed to stimulate a multiple exchange that then led to a question on UFOs and space travel:

A: ~ *'Yes ... there are other life forces beyond this galaxy. There are beings of extremely high knowledge and wisdom. They are not as you would know a human being, but they possess the qualities of love and great spiritual awareness. They come ... yes, you are correct ... there is much spoken about UFOs as you call them. But yes, within the whole universe there are people who exist, who to you, would seem to be ... masters in travel and knowledge.'*

And 'the floor' quickly responded: *'Yes indeed ... And that would apply to 'corn circles'. They are formed by entities invisible to us ... Yes ... the crop circles may connect with UFOs. They form in the crops that are grown at this time of year (July 11 1994), forming very beautiful circular patterns.'*

A: ~ *'I can categorically tell you now, there* **is** *the connection. I am not prepared to tell you what the message is. That is for mankind to become aware of, in his own time. But yes, there is a connection ... Again, we get into the Earthly vibrations ... the coming together of both. But I will not tell you what the message is meant to be. If mankind does not have sufficient awareness, then who am I to interfere?'*

'It is nice to know that there is a message. Thank you.'

The subjects of UFOs and our increasing awareness soon returned again, in the November:

Q: *'... Recently, in the last few days as a matter of fact, in our television media, there has been a very marked interest in UFOs in the north of our country; in Scotland, to be precise. So much so, that a community there has organised a gathering to discuss it further, and ask the government for further information, which they believe is being withheld. Can you give us any further information on that?'*

A: ~ *'I will try ... I think what you speak of, is nothing new in that area of your country ... But of course what is different, is that awareness has become more profound.'*

'Indeed...'

A: ~ *'It is not that suddenly there are more craft. It is just that people's awareness, as I have said ... has become more profound. They have become aware. It is not unknown to your government here, or in other countries.* **It is not something new, but something they have been aware of for quite some time.** *I would say to you, even from the beginning of your century.'*

'Is that so? So long as that?'

***A:** ~ 'I think if you were to face your governments ... And I say that is now happening, because of the interest shown by the ordinary person, your governments can no longer deny what is happening.'*

'I'm very pleased to hear that, because I and many others like me have been of the opinion for a long time, that there has been what we call a 'cover-up' in these matters.'

***A:** ~ 'It is understandable only in the way that your governments have been afraid of the fear it would cause amongst your communities. But of course, they deny the intelligence of the common person. But no longer can they deny what is known, because, as you have said, the 'people power' will insist upon truth. As I say, not only in this country but in all your world, these sightings have taken place. It is not uncommon, and it is not new.'*

'So there has been a general consensus of opinion throughout the world, by the government leaders, that nothing should be published?'

***A:** ~ 'I say they have been afraid.'*

'Yes ... they are afraid of 'panic stations', to use our expression...'

***A:** ~ 'I believe I have said to you ... If you were to speak to the people who have travelled into space (our own astronauts), they could tell you much, much more than has already been spoken of.'*

'You've certainly said that. And the inference was that they have seen a great deal more than they have been allowed to tell.'

***A:** ~ 'They have been instructed not to speak, but I can tell you, amongst some, it has caused some major problems.'*

'Has it?'

***A:** ~ 'It is awareness that cannot be denied.'*

'Quite. And can't be covered up for very much longer, I imagine?'

***A:** ~ 'Because of the increased awareness then, it will all become much more open, and people must at last make their own judgements, and they must stop and think.'*

'Good. We're very pleased to hear that.'

***A:** ~ 'But, it is nothing new.'*

Later in the same month, we returned to the related matter of 'corn circles', suggesting in the question as put, that a field of corn is like a sheet of energy, suitable for writing in, *with* energy. Although the subject had been broached before, it seemed sufficiently important to justify seeking a few more details. [We had by now become sensitive to two principles ... (1) that our teacher would be careful not to bestow knowledge for which mankind is not yet ready, and (2) certain knowledge already with mankind, might well be usefully extended. Our existing knowledge could be simply demonstrated, by the way we phrased questions. Sometimes, we would feel our way delicately.] Some prior discussion of the energy consideration led to Salumet's response:

~ 'Is there something specific you want me to talk about? You wish me to name the energy that is being used?'

Q: *'Well, you may say there is a more subtle message in the corn circles than simply indicating another energy, and indicating a 'beyond Earth' intelligence ... or would those factors be the main message in the crop circles?'*

A: ~ *'The messages you seek within these circles, as I have said ... are left by those space travellers who come to your Earth plane. I believe I have told you why they come. We have been concerned of how mankind has been abusing this Earth. I have told you that this is why we have gathered at this particular time. Of course these space travellers have knowledge that far exceeds your own. The energy used within your corn circles, is one that is not known at this present time, but of course there also is the energies of your Earth. The energies of your Earth, plus the corn, plus the energy used to flatten it. It is a combination of each energy. It is not one single energy being used. If all that exists is energy, does it not make sense that each energy is an individual energy in its own right, as each of you are individual? Can you see that?'*

'Yes.'

A: ~ *'So, I say it is a combination. But the energy used by the space travellers, is an energy as yet unknown to your Earth peoples. I have said to you, I will not say what it is at this present time, because I intend to bring someone to you who will give you much, much more detail. But I wish you all to see that all of life is indeed energy. Do you understand that?'*

'Yes. That does make it clearer. Thank you.'

Some kind of unknown or at least 'non-textbook' energy, would also have featured in the building of the huge stone buildings and circles of prehistory, and Leslie asked a question about that:

Q: *'We did speak about 'unknown forces' building the pyramids and other extraordinary buildings. It has often been discussed ... the methods of construction and building, and the erection of those stupendous blocks of stone. And I've said before, stupid ideas have been put forward. So far as I am concerned, there can only be two answers: either dematerialise the fabric, and re-materialisation in a new position, or actual levitation. Are you able to let us know which ... or whether both of those methods were employed? I think of the Inca and Aztec nations particularly, and their stupendous monuments.'*

A: ~ *'Yes ... Let me speak on that. Let me say firstly ... materialisation, dematerialise ... they are possibilities. It continues today. But, as I have spoken previously, there were races upon your Earth much more knowledgeable. And yes, the simple answer is ... levitation.'*

'I thought it might be.'

A: ~ *'I needn't go further on this subject. Materialisation, dematerialisation ... this basically is what happens with healing today ... when you speak of your 'psychic surgery' ... but that is a different matter. These ancient peoples as you call them ... I call them 'very young' ... but let me say, their knowledge far, far outweighs anything that you have today. And yes, levitation was a way of constructing these huge, huge monuments.'*

This led to the subject of 'power of thought' and how a small group such as that in our room, might in the past, have summoned up the power for levitation. A dialogue continued:

~ *'Again we come back, as I say, to power of thought. Of course ... what* ***is*** *levitation?'*

'Yes, just the power of thought.'

~ *'I must stress to you all again ... the power of thought. It really is an incredible thing!'*

'Yes...'

~ *'I wish I could express to you in words just how powerful it is. In fact, one time I think we might try something within the room...'*

'That would be wonderful!'

~ *'I don't say it will be successful, but I am happy to try it with you.'*

'Well, we appreciate that very much indeed.'

~ *'I can't tell you how* ***powerful*** *thought can be.'*

'Well, we certainly look forward to that in the future.'

~ *'Do you know of the men who can lift themselves just by a thought?'*

'Yes, I've heard of them.'

'So why, when you think of the mass ... the weight of the human body; why would anything like a block of stone be any different?'

In our exchanges, the nature of *energy* and the result of *power of thought* would return again and again. But, over the centuries, one of the persistent problems to beleaguer and beggar mankind, has been that of war. It seemed only reasonable therefore to pose a question that embraced this old malady:

Q: *'I wonder if you could tell us something about 'war and peace'? Out of love must come peace, not war. And yet, war is a condition ... a condition which may bring the best out of people* ***some****times. So it's slightly confusing, but some of us feel that 'peace' is the only way in the world. Can you say something on war and peace?'*

A: ~ *'I will try. Of course the perfect world should have perfect peace. That is why, when I speak of religion ... it has caused more problems than it should have done. Wars are caused by man's inhumanity to his fellow man. They are caused by greed and many other things. There can sometimes be good from these wars; but ultimately I would say to you, they are bad, and not much good comes from them. Perhaps the* *fellowship of man together on one side is an area of good that results from wars, but of course that is something that should be taking place in any case. Man, as I have said, has much to answer for. So often we hear the cries of the people: 'Why does God allow such things to happen?' I put it back to you. Why does* **man** *allow these things to happen? They have moved away from all that is good and noble. Their lives have become one of want, of greed, of hatred, and anger. Too often through your ages, have we seen the results of your wars all over your Earth; not only in your times, but in times gone by. Men killing men. What do these actions show? ... It shows how poor in spirit you have all become. It causes great sadness in our side of life, when we see how much hatred abounds. You were not placed upon this Earth to hurt another human being. But you will say to me I know: 'What of these people who wish to steal another's lands? What of those tyrants? They cannot be allowed to roam free!'* ***I say to you once again: People power ... thought power.*** *You have within yourselves the power to change your whole existence upon this Earth. Wars are damaging not only to the people, to the countries, to your world as a whole; but the repercussions rebound within the space that surrounds your world. You cannot see these 'waves of hatred' as they travel through your space. This is perhaps another subject we can go into ... but wars are damaging. They can never be good, and even the peace that follows, is one of false hope. If you could only see those people who come to our side of life, those who have suffered because of wars, each and every one of you would strive, would do your utmost, to be peaceful. Peace, really should be your heritage, whilst upon this Earth. And that is what we too, are striving towards ... peace for all of mankind.'*

It was truly a magnificent sermon that seemed to embody all our confused innermost thoughts, and to present them in some degree of order. The prospect of the *space* that surrounds Earth, being polluted by our 'hate-waves', has to be seen as one huge sobering thought.

A question that we came back to more than once, was that of the nature of time; and it may well be that this is the most difficult subject to explain or discuss, through the doorway between our worlds. Leslie began this topic:

Q: *'Well, I am going to ask a question relating to something we were discussing earlier. Often we are told ... When I say 'we are told' ... Let me clarify that ... Often one can be told what is going to happen in the future. Am I right in presuming that, if that is possible, then the event has already happened, otherwise it cannot be known?'*

A: **~** *'Your presumption is partly correct.'*

'Partly?'

A: **~** *'Yes. All things are known. All things have been. But do not forget ... you are on a cycle of time. Therefore, without being too complicated in my explanations, I will say only this: What is to come, is past. What is past, is the future. We are on a never-*

ending cycle of events. Can you follow? It is difficult for you Earthlings to understand this. Time ... time is a complicated matter. But I will say: there are those of you who can see what is ahead ... not because it is the future, but because it is there. It is the past. It is the present. It is the future. It is one whole ... a never-ending cycle of events.'

But despite the complexity to us, at the very least it confirms that there is something very subtle about the nature of time. It is acknowledged that there are indeed seers who know what lies ahead. It was just two weeks later when I was able to put a question concerning the seer Nostradamus, and in one sense, it might be regarded as a question having some measure of connection:

Q: *'...It is about the nature of prediction. A long time ago, in the year 1503, a man known as Nostradamus, a Frenchman was born. And he is regarded as one of the best seers or prophets of his day. He wrote many things, and he appears to have written a number of good predictions for the present time, and for our future. He talks in particular of three periods of Anti-Christ ... uprisings against the teachings of Christ. The first Anti-Christ was named as Attila, a long time ago. The second Anti-Christ, he regarded as the period of World War II, which began in 1939. He also talks of a third Anti-Christ, which has not yet happened. Perhaps ... there are indications he was predicting a third world war, with nuclear forces. With our free will and positive thought, perhaps that can be averted. Perhaps it already has. Would you care to comment at all on that?'*

A: ~ *'I will. Let me place the question back to you. What is Anti-Christ?'*

'I would think 'Christ' stands for 'love and creation', and Anti-Christ would be the opposite ... 'hate and destruction'...'

A: ~ *'Nostradamus as you call him, was indeed a man of vision ... a great scholar of his time. But a man reared with religion. That is where the term 'Anti-Christ' comes from. Do we know what 'Christ' means?'*

'I take 'Christ' as 'Jesus Christ' and...'

A: ~ *'Let me put you right my friend, before we go further. It was not exclusive to Jesus ... the word 'Christ'. He should have been known as 'Jesus* **the** *Christ'. Let me explain a little further. What do you think it meant? ... 'Teacher'. That is the true meaning of the word 'Christ'. Therefore, let us go back to Nostradamus. He was influenced by the religion of his time. He was a great visionary, and of course, with his extended views and knowledge, he could predict events to come. You speak of 'nuclear disaster'. Your world has been heading for that for some considerable time. Let me say to you all ... There has come the time when many of us, and I speak as, let me say ... a master. Does that make sense to you please? ...* ***Many masters have come to tread this Earth plane at this particular time. There will not be a nuclear holocaust! That is our mission at this time in your evolution!***

That will not occur! *But let me tell you, the Earth is changing. And now we get to deep matters again. We spoke earlier of the Earth having an 'etheric' ... an etheric body. That is the one that will be filled with love and change, and that is why we have descended at this time, to bring forth the knowledge to help that transition. Does that answer your question?'*

'Yes, and that is wonderful to know. Thank you very much for that.'

The statement printed in bold italic, I am pleased to be able to say, was delivered with some considerable emphasis of voice; and was to be reiterated on several other occasions. And as to Nostradamus, it was good to receive confirmation that he is regarded as a true visionary, able to predict events.

The questions that were put to our very special teacher, were wide ranging and wildly differing. The one that follows, concerns an historic explosion that has, over the years, evoked much scientific curiosity:

Q: *'In the year 1908, there was a large explosion in the atmosphere over Tunguska in Siberia. There have been many theories about this. But I think the most plausible theory is that a comet approached the Earth and exploded in the atmosphere. Can you tell us anything about that?'*

A: *~ 'Let me say to you this ... It was an atmospheric explosion. It was not a comet. It was merely nature taking her natural course.'*

'Hmm ... Thank you. It's surprising...'

~ 'Is that enough for you?'

'I'm always interested; because this particular explosion which flattened (many) hundreds of acres of trees, has been a puzzle to those who like to think about problems of this kind.'

A: *~ 'They need to look to the Earth to find the answer, not the skies. It was a combination of atmosphere and Earth together, which created that particular disaster.'*

'I would imagine a build-up of energy of some kind?'

A: *~ 'Yes ... a 'clash' ... I think you would call it, in that particular area. You have to look down underneath the Earth, and you have to look to the atmospherics in the sky ... in the air. Together they can create ... how would you say ... a bang ... a bang?'*

'Yes. That's quite right ... or an explosion.'

A: *~ 'Am I faltering in my words? ... Yes. But they would need to investigate more, deep under the Earth, to find the answer. It was not from the skies.'*

The pattern of damage to the forest trees had always indicated a huge explosion high in the atmosphere, (entirely in accord with what had been said); but there remained the problem that there was no crater and no debris to be found. The presence of such items might have positively related to comet or meteor, but the evidence was always lacking. None of the old causal theories put forward by scientists had fitted the known facts neatly. Then there was a further much-thought-about curiosity, across the world in South America:

Q: *'May I ask about the Nazca plateau in South America? ... Which is a large flat region where there are huge lines running across it, and huge pictures, which can really only be seen from high in the atmosphere. We feel that may relate to a previous, older civilisation, or to extra-terrestrial beings. Can you tell us anything about that region?'*

A: ~ *'Let me speak on that. I have said before, there have been civilisations upon this Earth, who have had superior knowledge, far superior to that which you have now. The lines on the plateau that you speak of, were in fact directional lines for those people who travelled in space. I think I have spoken before that there were travellers from this Earth, because of their extended knowledge. This also applies ... It did not happen in just one area of your Earth, but in many. Particularly, we have spoken of the Egyptians ... the South Americans ... all over. And I too can say ... around your North Pole area, there was a civilisation with much, much knowledge. And still there is yet to be discovered the remains of that civilisation. It was a directional point, if you like, for space travellers to home on to. Is that helpful?'*

The answer said what some of us had thought (thought within, at least) concerning the Nazca plateau ... and more. But I wanted there to be no confusion as to the origin of the space travellers, and so:

'Thank you. Can you say if the space travellers were from Earth, or from elsewhere, or both?'

A: ~ *'I have said ... they were of this Earth.'*

'Thank you.'

It appears then, that the theories which some have been bold enough to voice, of past civilisations, of their advanced knowledge, and of their aspirations to space travel *from Earth*; form a part of the grand prehistoric pattern of our reality. The topic was pursued, partly in the interest of seeking a little about what happened to those earlier peoples ... only to find that *their* history somehow 'boomeranged' back to our own present predicament...

A: ~ *'I have said before there has been no intermingling of people on the Earth, and of space travellers. That has not happened. People who travelled ... you have to remember we speak of a long time ago ... when knowledge was so great. I have to say, you people on the Earth now, have really gone back to ... how will I say? ... times of 'babyhood' in your growth. You have gone backwards, instead of forwards. It has been such that these peoples have been 'wiped out' ... I think you say ... because of many* *things; because of Earth tragedies, because of nature herself, because of what you call 'progress' ... which many thought was the way forward and was in fact, the way down.'*

'So in part they were destroyed by ... persecution?'

A: ~ *'They destroyed themselves, partly ... partly by nature ... partly because they became too egotistical in their outlooks. I would say, mainly they destroyed themselves.'*

'Thank you. So you are now gathering to try and prevent a similar happening then?'

A: ~ *'You are heading towards a similar disaster. That is why we have gathered, so that this cannot and will not happen. It will not happen. It cannot be allowed to happen this time.'*

'Thank you for that. We can never thank you enough for what you are doing, of course.'

A: ~ *'Many times throughout your history we have gathered ... we have tried to impart our knowledge to you, which mainly has been rejected. This time, it has been decided, that the force of the gathering must be so that you cannot turn backwards.'*

'And you have the advantage that many people on Earth nowadays, are much more willing to listen to outside influences, and be controlled to some extent by their knowledge of outside influences, though they will not often admit it?'

A: ~ *'That is true. We see that people now are prepared to listen ... listen to that influence which is imparted to them ... although they are loath rather to speak about it. But slowly ... slowly, we are gaining momentum.'*

'That's certainly very encouraging for us to know. Any other questions for Salumet?'

Q: *'Yes. You seem to be repeating to us, that we are in a long steady state of decline. Most of us feel that, in many senses, society is improving. I find it very difficult to understand how, for example, there is this original knowledge which was lost, and where that knowledge must have come from. And why it is that we lack the original knowledge. I would be willing to say, I think all of us find it very difficult to understand where the source of this original knowledge arose ... why we ought to be in such a state of depravity from the point of view of knowledge?'*

A: ~ *'When man originated, he started off with very little knowledge. But always on your Earth plane, there have been, I would like to say, 'Masters of knowledge'. They are people who have come to this Earth plane, not as simple people, but as people with ... already extended knowledge ... if you like. Originally, some of the people settled here, came from another time. We are beginning to go into difficult subjects, but I will try to say as plainly as possible, how this occurred. In earlier times, there have been people on this Earth plane, who have travelled through space. Let me say, your Earth is very young as far as the planets go. I think you would agree on that, would you not?'*

'Yes, I'm sure.'

A: ~ *'I have said there are other places who hold ... I don't want to say* **superior** *beings, but beings with knowledge, who far outshine your own. They were placed upon your Earth to guide ... to impart the knowledge they had already obtained. So you see, although you had man, who knew very little, you had masters of knowledge too. These are the people who inhabited those places that you find difficult now to recognise. It was nothing for them to travel in space. The object of their lives here was to teach, was to encourage; was to help mankind gain the knowledge that 'they' already had. So you see, that was the beginning. But what happened, was that these settlements became greedy, became egotistical, and wanted to outshine each other. So in the end, what had to happen was, that they actually destroyed themselves with their own superior knowledge ... In the same way that man has now gained sufficient knowledge, that he too can destroy himself. I speak of your nuclear energy. They have the knowledge ... they have been guided to use ... and they have misused. So although you think you have gained in knowledge, you have in fact done the very same thing that those previous settlements of people have done also. The knowledge they had became too great for them. They misused it, and it was taken, and they lost all that they had gained. That is why we have gathered ... to prevent the same thing happening. You have been reaching a peak of knowledge. You had already started to travel to space. You were beginning to reach the point of extended knowledge ... and I am sure if you spoke with your astronauts who have travelled in space, they could tell you much, much more than they have already divulged to the ordinary people on your Earth. So you see, it is almost like something that is repeating itself, and we cannot allow it to happen.'*

'So, it's a question of having the spiritual maturity to be able to control what we have invented and learned.'

A: ~ *'Yes. The knowledge that is given to you must be used for the wellbeing of all the peoples of the Earth ... not for segregated communities ... not for the people with the knowledge. Knowledge that is given to you, is meant to be used, for the good of the Earth. Man has increased his intellectual power, but that does not mean he has grown in his soul growth. In fact, very often it can mean the very opposite. Life should have progressed, when these people of knowledge lived on your Earth. It should have been the beginning. It should have been a paradise on Earth, as you like to call it sometimes. But unfortunately, that did not happen. And I have to say once again, their own egos, power and greed, lost all of their knowledge, until they extinguished themselves. Is that helpful to you?'*

'Yes. Thank you!'

I would say at this stage, that the above section is sufficiently complex for me to have benefited by reading it through a second time. I have now the very strong feeling that this is an accurate logical account, and that it explains so very many factors in our planet's past ... and this is the sense in which it was delivered. It is plain fact, provided for our interest and in answer to our questions ... not an excuse or crutch for us to lean on in any following woeful state. That would not be the point at all. In any event, the reader should by now know that Salumet's teachings are very much delivered as presentations in love and knowledge. The final phrase may possibly seem quaint, but of course, when *'they extinguished themselves'*, they would return to spirit, where they would again become familiar with the knowledge that had become obscured in their failing physical existence. (The knowledge would exist in spirit, but would not now be known on Earth. My feeling is that that would follow.) The questions relating to our ancient past, were to continue with:

Q: *'The Noah's Ark story may have a truthful source. And there does seem to be some evidence for a boat-shaped structure on Mount Judi in the Ararat range, which has had some investigation. Are you able to comment as to whether that actually* ***is*** *Noah's Ark, in that position?'*

A: *~ 'At the time you are speaking of, there was indeed a ... how shall I say? ... 'vessel' made. But if you are speaking of the story as a whole, then no ... it is rather a figment of someone's imagination. The story comes from an older ... how shall I say? ... story, if you like, although there is an element of truth. There was indeed a vessel at that time, which was for all intent and purposes, called 'Noah's Ark'. There has been found this vessel, I believe the one you are speaking of, which has been dated back to those times. When Jesus the Christ was alive, many stories circulated. When these things were re-written, many centuries afterward ... how will I say? ... they were elaborated. Much was added, and much was left out. So if you want to believe the story as a whole, then I say to you, that vessel is the one that is intended to be. But the whole story of Noah's Ark, gathering the animals two-by-two, is rather a fairy tale.'*

'Yes. Thank you. That's a lovely explanation.'

A: *~ 'But yes, there was a vessel around at the time, but it comes from an older version of another story.'*

'Yes, I think there was another account of that story, written in the Epic of Gilgamesh...'

A: *~ 'Yes. It goes back much ... Let me say to you: Your Christian Bible holds many things which have been put together; sections from here, there, and everywhere. It made very good reading, I think. But as far as truth goes, you cannot accept it all. But indeed, the vessel you speak of, is a genuine one.'*

The available topics that might conceivably be included in this chapter seem almost limitless, but let me for now, conclude with a question from one of our number whom we see as, I think it is fair to say, more intellectual than most. The question was in fact put at an earlier stage in the sequence of meetings:

Q: *'I would really like to ask who you are; and I realise that is not an easy thing to answer ... but I often hear communicators say 'we' ... and I think to myself, well ... who* ***are*** *you? ... in relation to us, and who are you in yourself?'*

A: ~ *'My friend, that is just the type of question I would expect from you...'*

Leslie added midst a little laughter: *'It's been bothering him for some time!'*

A: ~ *'I will try to explain to you. 'I' ... 'I' come to you as a single entity, because it is easier that way to communicate. We are using one body ... but 'I' as you put it, I am not 'I' as you would know it. I am a combination of many things ... Are you following me?'*

'I'm trying ... yes.'

A: ~ ***"I"*** *come to you, because that is the way of communication that you on Earth understand. I am a 'conglomerate' of beings.'*

Leslie: *'Might I extend that question by asking ... and I think that is in the enquirer's mind too ... by asking, did you at one time live upon this Earth as a physical being?'*

A: ~ *'You have to understand my friend, things are not all they seem. Part of me ... yes ... has lived on your Earth at one time. We are getting into deep subjects again, but I will endeavour to answer. We spoke earlier of a 'diamond' ... I am one facet of a diamond, who has chosen to break from the rest to come to you at this time, to teach and to instruct you ... Therefore I am not the 'I' alone. I belong to the 'we'. That is the simplest way I can find to explain to you. I am more than 'I'.'*

It was an answer best thought about (also, there is an axtention to the above answer embodied in Appendix VI, this being a further conversation with Salumet that took place at a later date). In those more distant, more progressed realms of spirit, I think I would be right in saying: there is a much more perfect love, a tranquil peace, a natural humility, wisdom embracing extensive knowledge and a compassion that knows no bounds. In this realm, there would be a merging or diffusion of spirit (mere words become difficult) so that singular identity becomes in some way shared. He comes as a single facet, but has the knowledge and wisdom of the entire diamond. That is how I visualise the domain of Salumet. And to reach Earth plane from his natural habitat, I have learned that he has to adjust from a higher, to a much lower vibration. Here on Earth, we are accustomed to the lower vibrations and to dense matter. Such is our own more immediate ... local ... reality.

The above chapter holds so much the character of an evening with Salumet that it seems fitting to close with a prayer in our usual way. There have been times when Salumet himself has offered the words:

~ Eternal Spirit, we thank you once more
For this gathering; for this meeting of like souls.
I thank you for using me as your vessel
To speak amongst them.
I ask that a blessing be placed on each and every one,
That they safely be returned to their homes this evening,
That your light and your love look over them
Until we meet again.
God bless you all. Amen.
Salumet *1 August 1994*

Chapter XXVIII

A Being of Light

The communication that follows, is something that will assuredly be of some concern to us when our present Earth lives come to an end; when we are in transition between worlds; when the 'material body' gets left behind, and the spirit-self is free to move on. When that time comes, we leave much behind us, but there is also so much more that lies ahead, as we are certain to discover. Then again, there is also much that is of a non-material nature that we take with us. The time of that transition, may yet lie far ahead, and in the meantime in this life, it is important that we each fulfil our present life plan; and indeed fulfil that life plan to the very best ability of each and every one.

Eventually that time of our departure, will come; and when it does, death will no longer be feared or viewed with such uncertainty, since we now have some knowledge of what lies beyond. That saying: 'knowledge dispels fear', is one which carries much truth. But what of the actual process of transition? What of that very passage between worlds?

It was on 5 June 1995 that a spirit came through Eileen with, at first, some degree of uncertainty. The lady was unfamiliar with using physical voice and naturally required some reassurance that we were able to hear and understand her words sufficiently well. Then, following the reassurance given, she continued:

~ *'Firstly ... I am glad to join you all. I have been aware of this moment for some time, for which much preparation has taken place.'*

'Yes ... I am sure it is not easy for you to do these things. And we do appreciate the trouble you go to.'

~ *'Salumet thought you would be interested in hearing what I do within our world.'*

'I am sure we will be most interested.'

~ *'In fact I do more than one job ... I think you would say?'*

Our visitor went on to explain that she was an 'Escort of Light' ... and we did not at first understand the meaning of this expression, and this led to the first unveiling of our visitor's most delightful sense of humour:

'An escort of light ... ?'

~ *'So you understand what that is?'*

'Er ... Mm...'

~ *'No?'* Then, midst her own very amused chuckles: ~ *'I'm being told: 'They do not ... that is why you were sent!'* Then in what might be termed in theatre as 'an aside', she said: ~ *'Yes alright! I'm finding myself now...'* Then to her charmed audience she resumed: ~ *'What I do and what I mean by an 'escort of light' ... Perhaps you will recognise it when I say: I am the unseen 'being of light', when people travel the tunnel of light?'*

'Oh! Now we are with you!'

~ *'I am the vision of light that awaits the passing.'*

'Oh! That's lovely, and we do thank you for the effort you put into this. We've heard about it so many times.'

And again with humorous tone: ~ *'I think we are the unknown entities of the spirit world.'*

'Yes, yes, you are!'

~ *'So many times when these things are recalled, we are referred to as: 'I think I felt, or could feel someone there, but we were not sure."*

'That's quite right. You are absolutely correct in all that. We have heard it so many times.' (Both from spirit communication, as well as from some that have had near death experience.)

~ *'Well ... I have to tell you ... I am* **not** *unknown ... I am real!'*

'No. We quite believe that ... and so that is your main task?'

~ *'That is my main mission ... yes.'*

'Yes. 'Mission' is a better word.'

~ *'It is no task. It is work. It is growth. It is peace ... unending love.'*

'And now I am going to ask on behalf of all my colleagues here ... Why is it necessary to have a tunnel? Is that to conduct and direct energies between the two planes of life?'

~ *'Yes. It is to buffer the soul. It would be too much of a shock ... too much of a ... energy shock.'*

'Yes.'

~ *'It needs to be buffered. And that is the reason why most ... I could not say all ... but most people, feel that love energy surround them.'*

'Yes. I see. And it is concentrated by what we call a tunnel?'

~ *'You see ... within this so-called tunnel, it is energy of love ... I prefer to call it ... It is seen as a tunnel because of the state of the soul ... at a particular transition state.'*

'Mm hmm.'

~ *'That is all. But we remain unseen, because the soul at that time needs to be protected.'*

'I follow ... and I quite understand that it would be a shock. So you appear then, just as a light ... to the newly passing soul?'

~ *'To those of a little more awareness, I and others sometimes appear as a very, very dull image of what they assume is a person ... but they are never sure. It very much depends on the awareness of the passing spirit.'*

'... I think I would be right in saying that it is not necessary for every soul to pass through the tunnel?'

~ *'Of course not ... Of course not. Some find themselves immediately in our side of life. It is not something that is experienced by all by any means. But of course, we know of those who will experience this, and you see, in the in-between state of what you term 'life' and 'death', sometimes it is necessary for us to show ourselves as a bright light.'*

'Yes. That would overcome I would imagine, any attempt there is **not** *to leave this plane? The fact that there is a bright light could attract the reluctant soul?'*

~ *'Yes, of course, that is one of the objects of it ... That there are those within their bodies who will fight to the very last to remain within their physical overcoat.'*

The conversation moved on, and Leslie referred to his own dear wife's passing; she feeling at that time, what she was able to describe as ... just a 'puff of wind' and then she was in the plane of spirit. Then our most genial visitor was saying quietly: ~ *'What or who do you suppose was the puff of wind? ... I have many guises. You see, whichever way, whatever happens, in the transition stage ... we are always there ... whether we are known of, seen or unseen.'*

'Yes. I imagine that she was feeling an 'enfoldment of love' to welcome her...'

~ *'Yes ... and you say those words beautifully. We are an enfoldment of love. That is what I am. I feel so emotional when I say those words whilst using a physical voice. It is something of beauty. I have experienced much ... much joy ... much sadness ... from those on your side of life. But believe me, the joy it brings to those who work together ... it is something to behold.'*

'Yes. I think we are quite unable to imagine the extent of joy that is possible in your world.'

~ *'You cannot. One day perhaps you will. But we speak of such a long time of development, before you could achieve such.'*

Our lady of light then moved on from the subject of our transition, to tell us something of herself, and with our eager encouragement, something of what led her into her current profession:

~ *'We come from a state of what I can only term 'Supreme Love'. I believe you term it 'Bliss'. Yes ... that's the closest word.'*

'Yes, I think that is the closest we can get to it.'

~ *'Once that stage is reached, then there are many options open to us. I will speak a little of what I felt at the time of deciding ... of how I wanted to continue with my growth. I was introduced to a gathering of many, when one speaker stepped forward, who would give me inspiration for what I had to do. I had a choice:*

- I could continue as I was.

- I could teach others. Many would come and gather around me to seek. By this I was most humbled.

- But henceforth came the 'speaker of light', and approach me he did. And without going into too much detail, he showed me that the way that I should go would be, to come back; not as someone visible and known who would be grateful for such things; but to return through many spheres to help those who are lost ... who are lonely ... who need help. Can you understand how shattering this realisation was to me? ... Because you see ... even in the state of bliss, there existed an element of 'vanity'. Not vanity as **you** *would imagine the word to mean ... but you see ... to have people come to you for (one) to teach, is a very great privilege ... and I ... I don't know the word to express to you ... In my ignorance I suppose (I) thought that this was my soul's way of growth.'*

'Yes, I understand.'

~ *'So I was left for a time to reconsider, because ... I had said to you ... it was my choice. I had the choice and I realised, this was the way I must go. Do you see? ... To become an 'escort of light' ... not to be seen ... not to be recognised ... but to have someone know that you are something ... was indeed a very big experience for me.'*

'Yes, I'm sure it must have been. You mentioned coming back through the spheres. But, coming back to a lower sphere, if I can use that expression, does not have to be a permanent condition for you, does it?'

~ *'Not at all.'*

'You go back to your own sphere that you have earned?'

~ *'I return often, to replenish ... to be amongst those I should be with. I need to do this.'*

'Yes. I can understand.'

And then followed the 'best' between-worlds joke:

~ *'We all need to do ... I think you would term it: 'to recharge your batteries'? ... Someone just told me: 'Say that and it'll be fine.' ...* ***Recharge our batteries!'*** And whilst laughing: ~ *'Yes ... It's quite a comparison, don't you see? Yes ... I am telling you: I am a 'being of light' and I need to charge my batteries! It is quite amusing!'*

Then followed a period of general and quite unrestrained mirth while Leslie managed to say: *'Yes. It is an expression we can completely understand.'*

And our guest replied: ~ *'Yes. I'd rather forgotten how amusing you beings could be ... I had long forgotten. That is not to say we do not have* ***our*** *fun...'*

The dialogue continued; but it is perhaps good that this chapter should end on this very happy note. It is true to say that recourse to humour can often help us in our daily lives. Some might even rely heavily upon it ... and, as is often said: *'you, at times, just have to see the funny side of life'*. It is also good to know, reassuring perhaps, that appreciation of humour continues on the other side. Laughter and shared happiness have their places there, just as they do at the interface between worlds.

Through time, so many souls would have been enfolded in love at their passing, by our lady of light and by her fellow beings of light. One may now look back to that time of the 'death march' on Bataan with some element of detachment, because more than half a century has since passed. When the 17,000+ died in heat and pain and in miserable exhaustion, the beings of light would have comforted, would have escorted, would have enfolded and would have been there for them at their passing. They would have been there to buffer from the harshness of it all ... to *love* their passage. Their pervading love would quickly quench and soothe the awfulness of what had transpired. And that is one beautiful thought to hold.

Chapter XXIX

The Encoded Torah

Time, even as we perceive it upon Earth, may seem sometimes to have an illusive, almost will-o'-the-wisp quality about it. Within the collection of writings that we call the Holy Bible, are histories from different points in time; assembled from texts that have emerged over more than one millennium, and some stories have their mythic origin in a very much more distant past. A diversity of histories and teachings, have all been fitted into the one book. There are divisions within its pages ... New Testament ... Old Testament books of the prophets ... History of the people of Israel ... Torah. The Torah or Pentateuch consists of the first five books of the Old Testament. Tradition ascribes them to Moses and their original language is Hebrew. They lie at the heart of Judaism, and tradition has it that the books were given to Moses *letter-by-letter.* The Torah has always been accorded a special reverence; in the synagogue, being kept in the ark and only removed for reading at Sunday services. Within the Torah itself is the instruction given by the *'Ever-living'* to Moses on Sinai:

> *'Then you shall place the covers upon the top of the ark, and you shall put into the ark the evidences that I will give to you.'*
>
> *Exodus 25, 2*

And a little further on:

> *'And hang the veil below the books, and bring there, within the veil to the Holy of Holies, the Ark of the Witnesses. Then put the covers upon the ark in the Holy of Holies.'* *Exodus 26, 33-34*

Clearly, in scriptural lore there are indications of unusual origin and of value beyond measure. And great care has been exercised over the intervening years to preserve original form. Now, as we enter a new age, the Torah is about to exert its intended influence from within its mystical text.

One may think of the five books as containing a hidden book within itself, and there are references to this inner work and to the time of its uncovering, in other pages of the Bible. The revelation of future events to Daniel ends with the words:

> *'... and seal the record, until the fixed period, when many will travel and knowledge will be increased.'* *Daniel 12, 4*

And then:

'I heard but did not understand, - so I asked, 'My Lord, what will come after this?'
But he replied,
'Go away Daniel, because that is hidden and sealed until the fixed time." *Daniel 12, 8 - 9*

And John wrote concerning his visions of the future:

'I also saw upon the right hand of the Occupant of the throne a book written inside and outside, sealed down with seven seals. And I observed a strong angel proclaiming with a loud voice, 'Who is worthy to open the book, and to break its seals?'
And no one in heaven, or upon the earth, or under the earth, was able to open the book, nor yet to gaze upon it.'

Revelation 1, 1 - 4

In his vision, John was allowed to glimpse a little of the future, as the book's seven seals were removed one by one. What he was able to see is accounted in Revelation/Apocalypse. As the result of removing its first four seals he saw the rampages of the four horsemen of the Apocalypse. They, symbolic of conquest, wars, famine and death from various causes, have been discussed earlier, in chapter ten. That has been our history. According to Revelation, it was the Lamb, symbol of all sacrifice, who was empowered to open its seals, and the Lamb's opening of the seals formed a part of his vision. Planet Earth's spirit entities ... those who watch over and guide planetary evolution, whom according to John, include four Beings and twenty-four Elders ... sang their new song to the Lamb:

'You are worthy to take the book,
And to open its seals;
Because you were sacrificed,
And have purchased by your blood for God
From every tribe, and language,
And people, and nation…'

Revelation 5, 9

It seems from the vision, that the Lamb's sacrifice embraces the rampages of the four horsemen; also various catastrophes. The seals, during the course of our passage through history, would be removed by stages, as the various experiences transpire. Only then will we (by then, a further evolved humanity) be *worthy to take the book and to open its seals* for ourselves. He describes, in his vision, the opening of the seventh and final seal, as a process orchestrated by seven angels with trumpets. As the third angel sounded a trumpet, a further catastrophe was signalled, and the star named 'Wormwood', fell and contaminated a part of the Earth, (as accounted in chapter X). The time period for the opening of the seventh seal is clearly *now*. Such was the vision on the Island of Patmos more than 1,900 years ago.

A number of learned ones across the centuries have since sought the Book within the Book. They searched the Bible for some kind of code within its pages. The 13th century sage Rabbenu Bachya wrote of his own early useful findings. Isaac Newton devoted much time to the quest. Later, it was the Great One of Vilna, Lithuanian Rabbi Elijah Solomon, who made the prophetic statement: *'All that was, is, and will be unto the end of time is included in the Torah, the first five books of the Bible.'* There is evidence that the Great one of Vilna had a measure of understanding of its hidden format, and was able to access information that seemed to be from beyond the normal workings of the physical mind.

In the mid-20th century Rabbi HMD Weissmandel of Prague, Czechoslovakia, discovered the first positive indication of a 'skip code'. He found that, if he looked at the original Hebrew letters of the Book of Genesis, and skipped fifty letters from the start, then another fifty, the word 'Torah' was formed. He examined the Book of Exodus, the Book of Numbers and the Book of Deuteronomy, all with the same result. In order to further his study, he wrote out the 304,805 letters of the Torah in 10 x 10 squares. The process of opening the sealed book had begun. But ordinary mathematical process was insufficient to be able to dig at all deeply into its cipher.

Then, in the final decade of the old millennium, a mathematician Dr Eliyahu Rips, following the indicative work of those earlier pioneers, was able to reveal the fuller nature of the hidden code. His work has concerned the making of a computer programme that:

- Maintains all the Hebrew letters in their correct order,
- Arranges the letters into pages or blocks of all possible line lengths.

It is possible, with the computerised arrangement, to read the letters horizontally and vertically (as with a crossword puzzle), also diagonally. The computer programme has a keyword search facility, such that all positions of a keyword may be found (for all possible orientations and line lengths). Furthermore, the computer-arranged blocks of letters can then be examined for incidence of 'proper' words and phrases in horizontal, vertical and diagonal orientations, which relate to the keyword. The programme is used very much in the mode of: inject a keyword and observe the read-out. If for example, the keyword *'Einstein'* is entered, then I understand that the read-outs are *'they prophesied a brainy person', 'science', 'he overturned present reality'* and *'a new and excellent understanding'.*

This work, together with some of the Torah's encoded truths, is accounted in a book by Michael Drosnin entitled 'The Bible Code', published 1997. A further book of the same year entitled 'The Truth Behind The Bible Code' by Dr Jeffrey Satinover, provides a wealth of related information and statistical analysis of the mathematics involved in reading the encoded data.

It would appear that the sealed book was so designed that its seals should be removed in present times ... in the computer age; a feat that would have been impossible before the advent of suitable programming technology. The *'fixed period'* is the present time, some 3,200 years following its writing, a time when *'many will travel and knowledge will be increased'.* In its original Hebrew, the Torah represents an enormous source of 'historical' data covering those three millennia and beyond into our future. The encoded truths can be significantly accessed, only through today's and tomorrow's computer logic.

When such eminent names as Shakespeare, Newton, Edison or Wright Brothers are entered into the computer programme; then the achievements of those notables are briefly and accurately stated. If *'computer'* is entered, I understand the read-out is *'to shut up the words and seal the book until the end'.* The word *'Holocaust'* is encoded more than once. At one location, the year date of 1945 is given and *'Japan'* appears as a double read-out. (There were two bombs.) In another place, the read-out against *'holocaust'* is *'in the end of days'* and *'code will save'.* There is very much more contained in the two above named books on the Bible Code. They are both lengthy and detailed works.

Unlike humankind's mental logic, the computer logic, once programmed, is infallible. We can entirely rely upon the computer to seek out the truths of the sealed book without human distortion or bias.

Some likely implications of this inspired discovery are:

(1) Those who encoded the sealed book must either have used a sophisticated computer or worked in a different dimension that somehow obviates such a requirement.

(2) Its designers saw all time as one, as it is seen in spirit (but unlike Earth's earlier seers, they had a full knowledge of our contemporary terms such as airplane and computer).

(3) A free-will factor prevails, such that certain events at least, are not entirely fixed. Certain events may be seen as probability rather than prediction. This leads to the point that follows:

(4) Our days on Earth could or should have ended in holocaust, but *'code will save'*. It would appear that the Bible Code is one of possibly several devices/influences that will help to steer us away from oblivion. This timely knowledge, and the code itself, must significantly enhance our awareness and belief in other spirit realms, in the Divine Source whom many call God, as well as in our own spirit selves.

(5) It of course goes without saying that the proof of prophecy is well endorsed by the discovery.

(6) The Bible Code is not a device for divining the future. By its nature, it is for use in a retrospective sense. Its use when applied to more recent events may nevertheless help determine our rightful path. It is likely that much is yet to evolve from its discovery.

The Kingsclere Monday Group held an unusual meeting on the evening of 25 August 1997 ... unusual in that both our markedly developed mediums, Eileen and Sue were on holiday, and so it was decided that we should have a discussion evening. All had read the reports on Michael Drosnin's book, published in the Daily Mail newspaper of 28, 29 and 30th May, and I had read his book during the course of the previous week. It was an obvious subject for the discussion of that evening.

We sat in total darkness initially, as is our normal practice at the start of a session. Within a few minutes, a control spirit quite unexpectedly came through Leslie. He seemed pleased with our evening plan, and indicated that although the power was low on this occasion, they on the other side would nevertheless, with our agreement, like to participate in the discussion. He further indicated that as like as not, it would be another who would come through, who would be well versed in the particular focus of debate. We of course welcomed such participation. The scene was set. Our friend withdrew. Leslie himself was again with us. The light was turned up, and our own exchanges began.

We were short on facts in regard to a particular matter ... how the encoded Torah came about. So far as we knew, the five books that comprise the Torah, and likewise the Commandments, were simply given to Moses by God. There were questions asked amongst ourselves, but that these things were entrusted to Moses, was really the extent of our knowledge of how the books came to be. At this point there were the signs that another was coming through. We accordingly dimmed the light and waited a few moments...

What follows is a slightly abridged but otherwise verbatim discourse delivered to our gathering by our visitor through Leslie:

~ '*... We do not wish to classify the words under any particular heading. They originate from the Great Creator. And the Great Creator as you well know, has many, many, many helpers; and they take command from his wishes.*

You have been told on numerous occasions that the Great Creator is energy, in many, many, many forms. And many of these forms are beyond your awareness or understanding or even comprehension. They will not be clear to you until such time as you have developed much, much further upon the spiritual pathways before you. But through the Great Creator's energy, energy is dissipated through others who have attained much nearer perfection in their spiritual lives. It is they, regardless of their name, their country, their race, their habits, their clothing, their wealth, their poverty. It is they who are responsible for the original writings that you now classify under different names.

There is only one source and that is from the Great Creator of, not only this planet, not only your lives, but of the universe. Keep ... this ... in ... mind. You tend to put even more significance upon the Creator if you imagine the power of the thought that is there. So do not give credit to any one person, to any one dozen of our people. It is due to the thought that has been relayed, from the Great Creator, to the thought patterns and energies of those worthy to write the words required to be written.

We do not make the mistake of giving the credit to any one person in one time. It is the combination of many events that is culminating now in your awareness, which is encompassing your world.

It is unfortunate that in the human race, that the application of a word often indicates infallibility. And if such-and-such is in the Bible, then it must be so; if such-and-such is in the Torah, it must be so; if such-and-such is elsewhere, it must be so. All that must be so is that it need not be so! Because though those worthy people were entrusted with the tasks of writing the word from the Great Creator, they were not infallible. Unfortunately, they were at times using their own thought patterns to colour what they wrote.

... It was known that many mistakes would be made in the interpretation of the (Bible) writings. It was also known that, at this period in your physical world, your scientists would produce the means of discovering the 'Book within the Book'. You would not, as human beings, up to this time, have had an inkling of how to deal with the information that is now available, and which will fall upon you in the future. Your machines, that I think you call computers, will verify much that has been imagined. And because of the power, which they will have, you as human beings becoming enlightened ... not yet, but **will become** *enlightened. (And) because of the energy*

inherent in those machines, will be able to accept what is said, because you know they cannot lie.

Any misinformation, which will be placed in there, will in due course, itself be segregated and be shown to be false. This is something you have to look forward to. You do not realise the power that is, and can be generated in these new instruments. They ... will ... seek ... out ... falsehoods ... in ... their ... own ... capacities. Keep this in mind. They will not in future be subject to interference ... to human dictatorship. The ultimate truth is at stake.'

'Yes, we can be grateful to the computer logic ... and can rely on it.'

~ *'It is logic my friends, such as you have no comprehension of at this stage. 'Computer logic', known as a result of direction from the Great Creator, overcomes what is called 'human logic' ... not in your lifetime, but it will come. And falsehoods will no longer be tolerated. Are you understanding this?'*

We affirmed ... but of course, there was much to digest, and I think we all had the feeling that our minds were a little slow in comparison with our most welcome guest.

~ *'You talk much about the Millennium, but you cannot have any conception of what the Millennium will bring to this planet. Some of you will begin to see some of the beginning. But most (of the changes), I am sorry to have to tell you, will not be apparent upon this Earth, until you have joined us in our world; when you can then look down and remember what is being told to you now; because you quite possibly, in your enlightened spiritual awareness, will be part of the creative necessity which is planned for this Earth ... Now, do you have any questions?'*

There was a brief pause, during which I felt concern for Leslie. It had been a lengthy session, and the throat was becoming noticeably hoarse. And so I ventured: *'I would just like to say ... that is all very good news ... and very good to hear. We have our confused thoughts on things. It's very good to have things made clearer.'*

~ *'I am glad to hear that it is clearer for you ... because I must confess myself ... I did not fully understand what is going to be given to this planet. There is a limit to what I am permitted to know ... because I too can be fallible, and to tell you too much, may be incorrect. Therefore I tell you what I am permitted to tell, and hope that it will give you courage to continue in your work; and to enlighten you still further for your journeys upon your respective spiritual pathways.*

Now, if you have no more questions, I will withdraw and give this throat a rest. It is becoming uncomfortable for the instrument.'

'Thank you for your participation, which is appreciated.'

~ *'I will tell you one last thing I am permitted to say...'* Then, in a whisper and with enormous emotion, which Leslie afterwards said that he also had felt within himself: *'I ... was ... one ... of ... the ... original ... writers ... given ... power ... by ... the ... Great ... Creator.'*

'That is wonderful news.'

~ *'God bless you.'*

'God bless you.'

Leslie, on returning, partook of a glass of water, and our physical world discussion continued in a diminished and much more ordinary style.

The incomparable value to the world of the Book within the Book, is plainly evident, and will doubtless become more so as time moves on. The time of its emergence, according to both statement and biblical prophecy, is now. It is also clearly evident that the computer and its new breed of logic are here to stay and will exert enormous influence in the new millennium. And in further sophistication of the instrument, we may look forward to a computer logic that has been honed to unquestionable truth! How wonderfully fortunate it is that our human fallibility and waywardness should have been allowed for in the Grand Design!

Curiously, the admired Persian astronomer-poet of the 11th century appears to intuit a 'Book of Fate' and knows that the world would have to be recreated in order to alter our inscription in it!

Oh if the World were but to recreate
That we might catch ere closed the Book of Fate,
And make The Writer on a fairer leaf.
Inscribe our names, or quite obliterate!
Omah Khayyám of Náishapúr *The Rubáiyát*

Chapter XXX

The New Millennium

The millennium change had come and gone. As an event, it had been somewhat artificially constructed; in the sense that is, of its having been contrived out of the system chosen for calendar dating. The precise date of the year 2000, was special only in terms of the numbers assigned to the years, the year length and the imposed zero point of the sequence of those years, that marks the time of the birth of Jesus. The chosen year length of 365¼ days had arisen out of a discussion between the Greek astronomer Sosigenes and the Emperor Julius Cæsar in the year 46 BC. In the year 1582, the calendar was clearly out of sync due to the ¼-day being approximate, and Pope Gregory XIII made adjustments (deducting ten days from that year and introducing a structure to the leap-year system). He ordained that, every hundredth year from 1600 should not be counted as a leap-year except every fourth hundredth year ... so that the year 2000 would in fact remain a leap-year. Such is the construction of our present calendar.

But there is another factor that should also be considered: the precession of equinoxes, a process that is continuous in our heavens. This process, unlike calendar dating, *does* in fact, have a tangible and subtle meaning. It exerts an influence, and it has effected a *real* change for Earth quite close to the year 2,000.

The planet Earth always continues its slow shift in relation to the heavens. This shift is in relation to what appear to us, to be distant, fixed star clusters. It is this movement against the 'fixed' star clusters that brings about the changes of Zodiac sign. The sun will now begin rising in that part of the sky, known from its star configuration as 'Aquarius'. The symbol for Aquarius is the Water Bearer, who portrays the distillation of wisdom from knowledge. Wisdom can only of course, be used wisely, and must be poured out for the universal benefit.

For the previous 2,160 years, the sun had risen in the adjacent star cluster 'Pisces', depicted by the two fishes. Christianity, one of the formal religions spanning the period, also used the symbol of a fish. In a similar way, the much earlier Sphinx of the Egyptian desert which looks towards the eastern sunrise, with its lion body and human head; was appropriate to that much earlier age when the sun rose in Leo. The Sphinx, a trustee of the legacy of a past great civilisation, older than the Egyptian dynasties, continues its vigil; and is symbolic of that civilisation when the sun rose in Leo. The age of Leo had begun 2,160 x 6 = 12,960 years ago; almost exactly one half of Earth's *full* precessional cycle, distant from today. That time was equally just half the 'star clusters', or signs of the zodiac, away from the new Age of Aquarius now imminent.

So now the new Age of Aquarius would dawn, with both astronomical as well as astrological significances. In fulfilment of a prophecy of the changing times, a new star had appeared in the heavens. (There was also, of course, that prophetic vision of St. John, early in Pisces, in which he foresaw the history of the next 2,000 years and potent signs. These signs would proclaim the revelation of the *book within the book* and changing times.)

We had been on the cusp, whether one sees it as a change of millennium, a change of astrological sign or indeed as a fulfilment of prophecy. Such times are useful for review and for making plans; similar to new year resolutions only much more so. The period of transition had been a useful necessity, and it was not without its enjoyable aspect. There had been some radical rethinking that appeared somehow to have been inspired ... whether by raised consciousness or by a 'power of thought', confronting the end of an age ... Who can tell? Perhaps a new openness propelled by an overt and unquenchable *computer logic* had something to do with it. The pervading, new logic of the computers, unlike the old corridors of power and systems within society's structure; had no closed doors. The new system was refreshingly different, open and free from any traditional encumbrance. Whatever the root cause or causes, a light had seemingly begun to probe some of our floundering society's enigmatic shadows. The light in question probed both within and without.

Viewing our conception of the universe, the *big bang* theory was now seen as something of a departure from useful science, but not without an acknowledged usefulness in terms of thought-adventure; likewise the *steady state* theory. (These have by no means of course, been the only theories, to be jettisoned from the 'ivory towers' of expertise, after a sufficient dalliance. This, over the years, has been a part of the nature of our science.) A point now perhaps more fully realised, is that the part of the universe that we are able to observe, although vast in comparison to mere planetary distance, is minute when compared to the *whole* universe. Imagine the observable universe as a grain of sand on a sand dune, the dune representing its entire expanse ... and a wind blows. How can one say that the condition of the single grain gives a picture of the whole dune? The whole is simply beyond our scale of comprehension; unless of course, we somehow manage to leap the hurdle imposed by 'time', and view things from an altogether different perspective that sees beyond the *red shift* of our science.

We stand at the threshold of space travel and scratch at the understanding that goes along with that. Yet there is still much to do in looking after and repairing our own planet. There is much still to accept as we unravel the complexities of past great civilisations. They once existed, with a knowledge peculiar to their own development, and sometimes going far beyond our own understanding, or off on some quite unfamiliar tangent. The acceptance of past events on our planet was to form a part of our increasing awareness. The writings of such authors as Immanuel Velikovski, Andrew Tomas and Erich von Daniken, although in a number of ways speculative, were now to be looked at much more seriously. Awareness has wide horizons. *Seeking* was now less restrained and *convention* less of a shackle. The ivory towers of learned establishments now had far less rigid ramparts.

Political systems remained with some variation the world over. But one became aware of a gulf, not so much between the parties of politics, but between government and people. There had on occasions, in times of extreme need, been coalition governments that were subsequently regarded as successful, sometimes wonderfully so. Sunday, 12 May 1940 had been one such occasion.

> *'At this point in history one of the greatest administrations which has ever governed the United Kingdom was in the process of formation.'*
> John Colville *The Fringes of Power*
>

That particular coalition led by Winston Churchill had continued until 26 July 1945. And now, once again, that same style of regime had become popular; after all, a coalition provided the opportunity to use the best people regardless of party ... and in such a challenging, changing world, there was without doubt a need for the best. A separate small affiliated unit, in part *think-tank*, in part *watch-dog*, in part *liaison*, ensured that government continued to act in accord with the wishes of the people, and that the people properly understood the necessities of government. It improved confidence. It was an improvement on the old *compete with parties in opposition* system, that had in some measure lost its way through excessive argument. (In the distant past of old Roman times, the Blues and Greens had joined *for* the people against Justinian. Now it was that the parties of politics joined simply *for* the people, and all would benefit from that unity.)

As time moved on, the 'confidence unit' became less of a watchdog and more of a think-tank ... And out of that function had come, a really exciting change in transportation. The electric car together with its attendant package of legislation (and the attendant legislation had been so necessary to ensure acceptance). The 'Superlite' range of electric cars had made such a difference ... such a joy to drive, such a contribution to road safety, so economic; it had come upon the scene as a breath of fresh air from across much troubled waters.

The petrol engine had dominated the scene for a full century. The early versions of road vehicles had been born of steel and glass and petrol; and their late 20th century progeny were still essentially of these materials. Tradition, being afraid to make drastic change, had kept it so. But there were problems ... of pollution, of needlessly high energy-consumption, rising steel price, maintaining continued oil production and its transportation, road congestion, of ever-increasing accidents and insurance attitudes, road upkeep and motorway extension. The list continued to grow. There was much to stimulate the developmental change that eventually, simply had to come.

A focus had rested upon the ever-increasing accident rate. The insurance companies, quite rightly, could only reduce charges if accident rate could be brought down. The more pedantic critics even questioned use of the term *accident* for an event, the frequency of which had become highly predictable. Scientific papers were published under the general category of Motoring Psychology, which explored such areas as *traffic systems, human response* and *Highway Code influence.* Then accusing fingers were eventually pointed at *high momentum change on impact* as the major cause of serious injury. Having vehicles weighing a ton or more, built of steel and glass and holding potentially explosive fuel; travelling at speed in such close proximity, was directly inviting trouble. Any reduction in the momentum of a travelling vehicle should improve safety and at the same time conserve energy. Momentum equals *weight times speed*; so in order to reduce momentum, it was not necessary to sacrifice speed. If the *weight* could just be reduced, then speed could remain. A much lighter vehicle was the answer.

Resilience was the other factor. Engineers talked of *elastic* strength and *yielding* structures. (When a tennis ball is hit about at similar speeds to a travelling car, it, having tough flexibility, comes to no harm as the result.) A small, resilient, lightweight car that could travel in narrower motorway lanes, was the solution to all problems. Extreme lightness was also required of an *electric* car, in order to suit the increased need for energy conservation. The lighter the car, the easier it would be on its power source and the energy consumed, and minimal energy consumption was a major influence on design. Legislation kept them to an unladen 120 Kg, which was not a difficult matter for a fibre and expanded plastic construction with a coloured shrink-wrap skin. The heaviest part of the vehicle was its battery. And the cars could be plugged into a mains-supply for recharge.

Designs that emerged were a huge step away from what had been the tradition; overall form being slender and rather fish-like. They were of sharp-shape fore and aft to convert any old fashioned head-on collision into a sliding deflection. Shape and fins helped to stabilise, ensuring that they hugged the road at speed. Many were two-seaters, and not wide enough for two to sit side by side exactly. The driver would face ahead as was necessary, while the passenger reclined, a little in front and to one side of that position facing rearwards, with a large front-facing mirror for his benefit. The passenger position fitted the overall design concept, was excellent for conversation, and the *backwards-facing* arrangement with snug back support, had additional safety merit.

The old 'petrol, steel and glass' machines were now looked back on as a technological symbol of the old century. These new 'Superlites' were seen as a symbol for these more progressed times. Not only were they a joy to drive; they were safe, user-friendly, conserving of energy as well as motorways, and non-polluting. Furthermore, being light and so designed, they could be parked on end in a very small space, which was in some situations, an added advantage. More usually, they would be parked on their wheels with the simple ground-anchor locked in place. This had its security aspect as well as holding fast in windy weather. Attendant legislation had greatly reduced car-theft crime; in fact, it was now almost non-existent. The absence of steel in the structure had meant that Superlites might be easy to break into. But the computer-linked system of traffic observation, that instantly identifies any vehicle in motion without its matching coded key-card, was now a near perfect protective system; the instant location leading to rapid beamed power-cut and apprehension. It has all been built into the protective regulatory system; likewise a maximum speed was fixed within the design.

Theft in its various aspects had been an increasing problem of the latter 20th century. A series of marketed, approved, automatic *hit back* anti-thief (as opposed to anti-theft) devices had helped to reduce crime rate. They consisted of a mixture of ideas: dye dispensers, bad smells, fluorescent stains, instant adhesives, subtle within-car noise blasters and the like. They all of course, had to be foolproof. That was a matter for well-thought-out design. Their overall effect and real value was to make the criminal appear more in the image of a wayward fool. Prior to that, certain films, unwise publicity and law court procedures had come close to bestowing more of a cavalier 'mask' upon the criminal. The *hit back* devices were instrumental both in crime prevention, as well as in removing that false mask. It all helped to divert society into better living ... more positive ways of thinking ... less thought wasted on aspects of fear and defence of chattels, home and vehicle. In the past, too often it had been the innocent who suffered, while the wayward prospered materially. This was changing.

But beyond all this, the Superlites were such a joy! The heavy commercial vehicles had their own motorway lanes. Their more significant differences, compared to earlier times, were the large lightweight compression pads carried at the front, and their sustainable alcohol-based fuel. Fermentation industries now produced the fuel, the burning of which was far less polluting than petrol or diesel. The compression pads were a collision safety factor, and were much less costly to replace than damaged metal parts. It all contributed to a better world. Times had changed. The big motorway pile-ups, with horrendous injuries, death, twisted metal, broken glass and fire, were now thankfully only remembered as a horror of the past.

These were a few of the changes as Earth entered and consolidated in Aquarius. There were changes in major industries and in work deployment. The conventional power industry required energy from sun, wind, water, and from the atom by cold and hot fusion processes. Decommissioning took place, of old nuclear plant, nuclear submarines and missiles, and there was the reclaiming so far as was possible, of old nuclear test sites. Some radioactive materials could be recycled. All had to be made safe, and this was an exacting and painstaking process. Those who worked in this sector were revered, as had been the bomb disposal experts of previous more violent times. Some materials just had to go into very long term holding vessels, at locations where they could steadily continue their decay, whilst causing no harm. New developments in dematerialisation might one day help. Radiation dangers were now fully realised and well considered. New energies, not previously accounted by the scientific textbooks were finding recognition and application.

The planet itself had been crying out for attention, and at last, some appropriate measures were now being taken. Much was happening in the rain forest conservation areas of the Amazon basin and the Far East. In the West, many forests were being restored. All motorway margins now had trees, improving the air, reducing unwanted noise and improving beyond measure, the look of the landscape; even lowering stress levels. The timber that resulted, was a sustainable crop. To harvest a tree was not a crime, just so long as more were planted and cared for, than were cut down ... and a good mixture of species grown.

The Animal Bill of Rights had had a marked effect upon conditions for farm animals. It had been quite wrong to box them in small cells, to deny them adequate movement, to exclude sunlight, to fail to provide pastures, nature's food supply and natural surroundings. It had been so disgraceful and lacking in compassion. Equally it had been wrong to feed processed carnivore parts to herbivores. Children's illustrated books always show farm animals in a natural setting, 1930s-style, with smiles on their faces and swishing tails. That is how it should be, even if economists throw up their hands and say: *'But we can make more money the other way! And* **you** *will have to pay a higher price! And the nation must be fed, therefore standards must go!'* The controversial issues had been argued in long debate, and it was said: *'If money rules, then we all end up eating dirt and drinking foul water ... it's cheaper!'* But sufficient disease in the shape of BSE, E. coli infection, Salmonella, organophosphorus poisoning and other induced maladies, had demonstrated tragically, that changes were indeed much needed.

[The economists had been wrong ... too restricted in their view of the world. Profit should never be evaluated in terms of monetary return alone. There are other factors that should enter the equation ... health, beauty, pleasure, and of course love which concerns all things. These ingredients should each be seen as a part of the profit of the well-designed commercial venture. It was a credit to this new age that these items had indeed entered the equation; an aspect of the developing awareness.]

The animals must have man's respect. This is essential. An eminent North American Indian chief once stated the wisdom:

> *'If you talk to the animals*
> *they will talk with you*
> *and you will know each other.*
> *If you do not talk to them,*
> *you will not know them,*
> *And what you do not know*
> *you will fear.*
> *What one fears*
> *one destroys.'*
> Chief Dan George

While the system was under extreme stress, compassion and thoughtful reflection had resulted in more of the population adopting a vegetarian regimen. Vegetable markets and vegetarian restaurants prospered, and many found this to be *the* way. Nor was this the pursuit of just the more compassionate ones. Some were attracted by the reduced risk of disease, while at the same time, the lower cost of a vegetable diet was appreciated. And there were those who were put off by reported use in meat production of steroids, antibiotics, tranquillisers and beta-blockers; or perhaps they just felt so much at risk from a system that had deviated too far from nature's time-honoured and familiar ways.

There was at this time, a degree of control over the *false flavours* in foodstuffs. Very young children usually have good natural instincts regarding what to eat. Even the newborn baby will cling to the mother's breast, knowing instinctively that this is *exactly* what is required. If this natural food supply is denied, then similar alternatives will be accepted, providing they mimic body temperature, nipple shape and approximate taste. The substitute might just work out. But at a later stage, the child might then have been confronted by junk foods; possibly dubious commodities, having flavours that were something quite apart. This would confuse 'instinctive' choice! Natural instinct would have been duped, and the child, in the absence of parental guidance to the contrary, would then have been in danger of selecting food on taste, and not according to body-need. The link between instinctive choice and body-requirement, is an important one, and is now recognised. In previous times, there was the danger of the very young getting hooked on inappropriate foods before the age of reason.

The effect of bad diet could become a problem either quickly or slowly, sometimes taking half a lifetime to become apparent. The young had been observed to suffer more and more from hyper-activity, allergies, sugar-excesses and infections of Candida albicans. A measure of control over false flavours, has helped to improve the situation, and in general, schools now exert more and more guidance in respect of good diet ... so very basic to health ... so important for children, and indeed for all of us.

False imagery in advertising had also come under scrutiny. Drinks, rich in sugar are not at all to be recommended for thirst quenching on a hot day. Yet their sales imagery had contained the freshness of snow and ice and implied wonderful refreshment. Such things were misguiding for the young ... and so advertising had to become more realistic in terms of logic and ethic.

Those who have studied clinical nutrition know the devastating effect that excess sugar and sweet food can have:

'The more sugar consumed, the more upset the body chemistry can become.'

Nancy Appleton Ph.D. *Healthy Bones.*

And a statistic of the USA in the final decade of the old millennium stated that 90% of all bone fractures in 65+ year olds, were due to osteoporosis (weak bones), deficient in calcium due to upset body chemistry. An excess of sugar *can* mean that a sufficiency of calcium in diet, gets deposited in joints (as contribution to arthritis) and into the kidneys (as contribution to kidney stones), instead of maintaining the body's bones! Any, who have attended a Nancy Appleton lecture on the subject, will have received this message loud and clear. Bone upkeep through proper food to support the body chemistry, should be a lifelong process.

There was now a much greater emphasis on organic farming ... not so much the highly regulated 'cult pursuit' that it nearly became. The emphasis was now very much on soil condition. The successful fibrous and humic soils that had been achieved in the mixed farming systems of earlier decades, plus a *restored* trace chemical element balance, were now sought. Trace elements could be exhausted through intensive growing. 'Selenium' was now seen as a very important trace element, essential to arable farmland. (Soils in certain parts of the world contain this element in small proportion, and crops from those soils, accordingly also contain trace amounts. People who live in those areas and consume the crops, in turn have trace quantities of 'organic selenium' in their blood. It is protective, and cancer incidence is noticeably lower in those particular areas, which include the Eastern Mediterranean countries.) It is important that trace element balance is maintained in some way, where the same farmland is producing much the same crops year after year.

One *must* treat the soil with respect. It was another eminent North American Indian Chief who stated:

> *'We know that the white man does not understand our ways. One portion of the land is the same to him as the next, for he is a stranger who comes in the night and takes from the land whatever he needs ... His appetite will devour the earth and leave behind only a desert.'*
>
> Chief Seattle 1788 - 1866

Chief Seattle was aware that the white man could one day be faced with the problem of soil erosion through improper use!

Some parts of England and Europe had encountered problems of water shortage. This was partly due to increasing population with its attendant increased water usage and extravagant habits, and partly on account of over-efficient drainage systems. It had become the fashion to pipe vast volumes of water from urban and commercial areas, so that it had a fast passage to the rivers and straight back to the sea. A fast passage to the sea, meant that this portion of the rainfall no longer benefited the land in any way (and may also cause local flooding!).

One result of the spread of civilised communities, had been that always a larger proportion of water flowed straight back to the sea. It had become important to take account of this, and to see that more water was allowed to soak into the soil. This had benefited the landscape, and had topped up underground water levels. Today therefore, many more soak-away systems are being constructed to achieve this. New strategies with fresh water and its usage are being designed to make the most of the precious commodity before its return to the sea. Once salinated, it is of course no longer of value to agriculture or to the townships. Many of the industries using large volumes were now locating near river mouths. The river levels and underground reservoirs are being maintained, and it is all a part of a returning respect for the land.

Such serious matters are important where the health of nations is concerned, but there is more to life. There is the lighter side of living, which is just as well. At the turn of the millennium, the media had remarkable reviews, that looked back across a thousand years, or that dwelt upon the happenings of the last hundred years. Many had enjoyed the pop music of the last century; but to pick a *best list* had really been an impossible task. One can on such occasions, merely dip into as many memorable pieces as may come to mind. Along the way, tastes had changed so much! The media industries that utilise and support creative abilities had also changed. The best music might possibly be seen in retrospect as that which has withstood the test of time, which has for example, endured several decades of popularity. The merit of the particular piece might lie with the talent of the singer or its composer, the message, the poetry of the lyric, the impression of the tune and its instrumentation, or the emotive nature of the times could also play a part.

Some talented groups had created admirable styles, won wild popularity, perhaps without any one particular melody standing out from their repertoire as being undoubtedly *the best.* The Beatles had been like that, with *all* their work having been well received, and certainly well represented in the reviews. *'Yesterday'*, John Lennon/Paul McCartney, was a wonderful song. And John Lennon's *'Imagine'* contained bold words of unity, love and peace. Abba was a delightful frothy-with-candy-floss kind of a group. Many of their songs had appeal, not least: *'Thank You for the Music'*. In Bob Dylan's songs, there was an attractive philosophical content, and the answers to some of life's age-old problems could be seen in *'Blowin' in the Wind'*.

There was frequently a connection between the song and a film. In 1942, the film *'Holiday Inn'*, had featured a song by Irving Berlin entitled *'White Christmas'*. In 1961, the film *'Breakfast at Tiffany's'* had included *'Moon River'* written by Johnny Mercer and Henry Manciní. In 1969, the film *'Butch Cassidy and the Sundance Kid'* included a song by Hal David and Burt Bacharach called *'Rain Drops Keep Falling On My Head'*. One is so much indebted to the composers; but in memory, the song is so often linked with the singer or bandleader; examples being:

Bing Crosby... *'White Christmas'*.
Glen Miller... *'Moonlight Serenade'*.
Judy Garland... *'Over the Rainbow'*.
Bill Haley... *'Rock Around the Clock'*.
Louis Armstrong... *'What a Wonderful World'*.
Elvis Presley... *'Hound Dog'*.
Frank Sinatra... *'My Way'*.
Joe Loss... *'In the Mood'*.

The 50s decade was especially prolific, producing several of the songs already named. Well placed in the century reviews were: *'Unchained Melody'*, *'The Little Drummer Boy'*, *'When I Fall In Love'*, *'Heartbreak Hotel'*, *'Lay Down Your Arms'*, *'Raining In My Heart'*, *'Blueberry Hill'*, *'Only You'*, *'Blue Suede Shoes' and the Elvis number 'Don't Be Cruel'*. It was a wonderful decade for heart-warming creative melodies, and Dennis Potter was one TV playwright who later, dipped into them and re-presented helpings as part of soundtrack.

Scott Joplin was creating music in the very early decades and his catchy piano piece: *'The Entertainer'* was still being heard from time to time in the 90s and beyond! The piece just has a kind of perpetual quality about it. Other memorable early songs were *'Let Me Call You Sweetheart'* (1910) and *'Sweet Adeline'* (1903).

During the emotive years of World War II, lyrics that stayed in memory, for a time at least, were those that looked to survival of loved ones and that hoped for an end to it all. In memory, the songs were sometimes just as they had appeared in those days ... as lines on the music sheets ... the simply coloured covers of which, carry a nostalgia of their own. The war years had been a special time in music. A song entitled *'Silver Wings in the Moonlight'*, was a plea to the aircraft that it would bring 'him' home safely. And ... *'The White Cliffs of Dover'*, was about how things would be in tomorrow's *free* world. There would be love and laughter and peace. The war cast its shadow on such things. Those who retained the memory of it all, recalled that the nights were dark with night-time blackout, therefore the song *'When the Lights Go On Again'*. In 1940, *'A Nightingale Sang In Berkeley Square'* provided contrast imagery to the London blitz. The songs and their lines say much about the thoughts of those times, and of the psychology of our yesterdays. And it was Rodgers and Hammerstein who in 1945 gave us *'You'll Never Walk Alone'*.

As for Russia during those war-shadowed years, she shared much suffering and was then of course especially close to Western hearts, and '*Russian Rose'* was an especially moving lyric. It is valuable that the closeness between East and West should have been accounted in song. Without the memory of such lyrics, bad energies of later politics could the more easily spoil the bond.

The Irwin Dash Music Company's selection of waltz hits for that time, included *'The Last All Clear'*. But it was Marlene Dietrich who sang: *'Lili Marlene'* ... in both English and German; and both sounded superb. In those still lulls of the North African desert nights, there were moments when the war became transcended. All listened, regardless of whose radio ... whose language ... Magic moments in song, punctuated the tension of the desert war.

It was Vera Lynn who sang, and who continued to sing for more than fifty years *'We'll Meet Again'*. That one came from 1939 ... the first year of war. That the song continues, is a testimony to the singer, to the song, to the emotive nature of those times ... And to all that remains in memory.

There followed the years, in Germany, of the American Forces Network (AFN) radio stations, and Francis Craig's *'Near You'* was so popular that Roger Moffat played it on a record request programme three times in succession ... never been done before nor since! Then it died a death and was forgotten by most. Some tunes were like that. Stephen Foster's *'Beautiful Dreamer'*, is remembered for its melodic and delightful form. Stan Kenton formed his 'big band' and played *'Peanut Vendor'*. The quality clarinets of Benny Goodman ... *'Memories of You'* ... and of Acker Bilk ... *'Stranger on the Shore'* ... fell very easily on the ear, as did the rich bass voice of Paul Robeson ... *'Ol' Man River'* (1927).

John Denver delivered many important lyric-messages at a time when the world was under nuclear threat. No one at a John Denver concert could fail to be moved by his style of message, which sometimes came like a passionate plea from the newborn, to a world gone mad.

Perhaps we should ask ourselves: What *is* this musical expression? Is it not of a subtle nature? Clearly it arises out of a thought pattern. It might be described as a materialisation of thought form that emerges and 'touches' the people of the time. Songs have also been described as 'thoughts' that are sung out when normal speech becomes insufficient. Therefore, perhaps we should view enduring and impressionable song, as a valued and prized part of our evolution.

There were the many musical developments in early decades; the traditional jazz and *'St. Louis Blues'* (1914). Lovely numbers like *'My Blue Heaven'* (1927), *'Stardust'* (1929), *'As Time Goes By'* (1931), *'Smoke Gets in Your Eyes'* (1933), *'Winter Wonderland'* (1934), *'Summertime'* (1935) and *'Begin The Beguine'* (1935). There were tunes from the 'Twenties', re-popularised by the Pasadena Roof Orchestra ... *'You're the Cream in My Coffee'*, *'Tea for Two'* and many more. Some of *that* sheet music got put to bed when the time had seemed right. But they were strangely and unaccountably catchy tunes with simple, loving, gutsy lyrics; and they would just not stay quiet; and so, there came a time when they got dusted, re-worked, and played all over again, half a century later!

It may be true to say of the war years; that during World War I, the finer emotions of that time, were expressed more through war poetry, than through song lyric. Nevertheless, I recall a favourite of my grandmother's: *'There's a Long, Long Trail a-Winding to the Land of My Dreams.'* That song would have given a no doubt gentle and wistful comfort to so many mothers who, like my grandmother, had lost sons at the front. That front, the Somme ... the trenches ... wherever ... had then seemed such a long way off. It was ... just as another song suggested: *'It's A Long Way To Tipperary'*.

In later times, it was as if the world had become a smaller place. It felt as if it has shrunk, bringing us all closer together; and so much in a mere hundred years! First wireless telegraphy and telephone, followed by radio; then TV, computers and satellites, Fax and Internet ... and of course, the travel machines of air, land and sea. The world just seemed to contract, as technical development and our awareness expanded.

Awareness had its many aspects. The idea of 'quality' in foods became linked to 'natural' and 'unprocessed'. Adverse processing devalued food. 'Processed' became *almost* a dirty word, though not entirely so. People were now conscious of extent of modification and preferences in processing; and the market had responded to a more discerning and selective consumer. The more discerning attitude had extended to other things, including lottery systems. Lotteries still existed, but such gambling was now essentially a 'fun and flutter' pursuit, and was kept within reasonable bounds. No longer was there any link with the State, its taxation or directed charities. The systems, at the time of the millennium change, had run into big problems. Charity was now seen very clearly as a matter to be freely dealt with in accord with personal means and conscience. And of course, it would be wholly inappropriate for the conscience of the individual to be over-ruled by government. How could that be?

State moneys, are State moneys, while separately; charity moneys are charity moneys, and it would be simply wrong for the latter to be given, by hands other than those of the giver. There is a certain sanctity that accompanies the act of giving. Likewise, 'belief' should not be coerced by State. Conscience, charity and belief were and are ... all of a kind ... all of that subtle mind connection. None was ever a matter for the governing body, simply not the State's business. The rising awareness had found this important clarification.

The Earth vibration continued to rise. Refined perception embraced a deeper love, a sensitive compassion, a more far-sighted vision, and a better understanding of all things. But attendant with this, a main focus settled upon life itself; life in the spirit, within the material, yet bonded to the physical and entwined within it. Humankind of the 21st century was at last coming close to a better understanding of the *inner* subtlety of life; and sensitive to the *direction* in which its development was pointed ... the vital, necessary route of passage that all must eventually take. This direction is consistent with ... the increasing love, awareness, compassion, and the accumulating knowledge.

[I remember, in the distant past as a teenager coping with conscripted National Service, looking out on a confused world and thinking: *What is life?* My conclusion at that time was *Life makes no sense at all, unless there is a drift towards a greater perfection*. It was a simple, naive thought, but nonetheless it had the merit that it came from within. I realise now, that it was as much as I could handle at that time. The years and living have brought further understanding. The profit of the greater understanding is a part of the issue from the *mill of life*. And as the wind of change turns life's mill faster, we now confront more fortunate times of a wider awakening.]

The awareness had already accepted that 'we' ... the material 'we' on the material planet ... do not stand alone in the universe. How self-centred and utterly wrong had been that old, outmoded idea ... that we stand alone! It had eventually been incumbent upon us to accept with gladness, the help from other realms and from other galactic beings. All now knew the reality of those friendly UFOs, which had at last become the IFOs of the current media attention, whose emissaries were now welcomed in peace and with respect!

The true spiritual nature of creation was now perceived by most. The feeling of it had really been there all the time, but for too many it had been obsequiously obscured by all the inappropriate dogma of distorted religions and their state affiliations. Yet the teachings of Jesus and of the many Masters in their Earthly missions, had always centred upon the *truth* and the teachings of love. It had been distressing to some souls in spirit, that the delivered teachings should later have been 'cloaked' in such a fog of unclear presentation. It was of course, the confused and unknowing Earth-dwellers who were responsible for this. Some on Earth as well as many in spirit, had been surprised at the number of teaching missions that had been necessary, over the millennia, to bring us to our present circumstance. But now was a time of impending fruition. If awareness could be charted, then its steady upward graph must now be on a more significant slope, with the fuller realisation of what life *is*. Accordingly, now was a time for the living to be more strongly linked to inner feelings. And so there was good reason to rejoice.

Chapter XXXI

The Year 2,061

It was late evening. All was dim and indistinct in the garden. The only illumination was of the cold light that came to Earth from the many clusters of stars, away in the vaults of the night's dark distance. It seemed good to think of the twinkling mantle, as a vast chandelier of living crystal overhanging our physical domain. But up there, was an extra flush of brightness, as if some stray moonbeam had been left, cast off by the gracious Queen of Night at her passing.

A chill was in the air, and 'young' Alex wore a hat and warm coat with the collar pulled up. It was wise to wrap up well in the night air, for Alex, the youngest of the family of children who had shared growing up together, was now 97 years old; nonetheless, he still enjoyed a good mobility and well-reasoned thoughts. And to his family, he was still referred to on occasions, as 'young' Alex. It was good to be in the garden this night; and with hands thrust deep in pockets, he could lie back in his chair and enjoy this grand sight of the heavens. The thoughts trickled coherently: *'The comet was there alright. That was the flush! ... the comet that had passed this way so many times before ... and known to Earth-dwellers as 'Halley's' ... Earth's old celestial friend. And good heavens! ... Yes! ... This must be the fifth visit since Halley had addressed our friend up there, and first pondered the mechanics of its cometary motion. So much had happened on Earth since that time! It was worth coming out this night, just to look and nod acquaintance, and to reminisce. The fifth passage of the comet since then...'*

It had been a long time, and whilst dwelling upon this thought, the memory was triggered ... of another night when the stars had been as bright as this. Starlit nights are not always so spectacular. This has to do with conditions in the firmament ... moisture, haze, cloud; and the place of observation can make a difference ... and the eyes. That earlier time was well remembered. He had never forgotten it: *'Forget! Goodness ... no! It remains emblazoned on memory as fresh as if it were yesterday! Years back ... That night in Mexico, at Palenque, on the steps of the Mayan Sun Temple. The stars had on that occasion, been equally magnificent ... at least as bright ... brighter even! And to think, that had been almost a lifetime away. How lucky we humans are, that we can enjoy such an extreme of beauty by just looking up at a night sky! The price, on this particular night being ... merely to wrap up.'*

Now, here he was, watching *this* spectacular night sky, with its traveller passing through; while midst his favourite trees, in his own garden. He mused: *'Life was good ... had been good. His Earth life had been lived through challenging and on occasions, quite decidedly difficult times ... but then, there must be difficulties on the way, in order to build the spirit ... and that was never a disadvantage...'* Alex was well aware of the intricacies of the deeper raison d'être. That was all a part of the subtlety of growth. But he had travelled. Like a number born into the 'sixties' period, he had not welded himself rigidly to a single lengthy career. Those few work commitments that had become inevitable, he had managed to intersperse with travel. A penchant for getting about the planet had always been with him. Over the years, that desire had certainly been satisfied.

Alex had trekked through the rain forests of Malaysia and South America. He had visited the old Mayan shrines and townships of Mexico and Guatemala, staying long enough to pick up their messages. He had been down to Bolivia and Peru; there sat and dreamed his dreams at such wondrous locations as Machu Picchu, framed in an idyllic mountain space, and the old township of Tiahuanaco with its port of Puma Punku. *'To have sailed on the lake ... Titicaca ... as Viracocha himself would have done, and then to have trodden the same ground of a former grand civilisation, that was ... pre-Aztec ... pre-Inca ... pre-Olmec ... pre-Maya. The one ... the civilisation that had left the myth and legend of Viracocha and his great works. And the tales of the dual serpent energy that could hone and move the rock of mountains, as if it were but a glowing cube of feathers ... as light in weight and flecked as feathers and aglow with the transfused serpent energy ... summoned through the attenuated thought of innermost being. To have been there ... to that inspired place ... was somehow beyond words to describe...'*

There were many tales of the 'feathered serpent' and of a 'serpent energy' from the later cultures. They, the later cultures, knew something of the majestic rockwork and devotion. They *knew of* and had woven their legends to suit, but could not encompass the inner knowledge of it. *That* had remained with those who had built. The legends of the later ones still remain today. But of course, the sharper testimony to the building skills is now found in the standing monuments themselves, and their obvious rock technology, as it endures Earth's precession through the many equinoxes. Alex had seen the elegantly stacked stone units, each weighing hundreds of tons in their present ordinary gravitational condition. The structures had been built to last, the softer and more weatherable limestone often being sheathed by harder granite. They remain as monuments to be seen and marvelled at. Alex had seen and marvelled, and had been touched by the ancient presence.

'It was now accepted that such wonders of a past grand civilisation should be properly recognised and seen for what they are. The clear relationship to Egypt's more ancient constructions, before the time of its Pharaohs ... the same serpent energy and levitation to power the rock technology. And of course,' Alex reflected, *'serpent imagery was also accounted in the Bible. Moses had been commanded by God to throw down his staff; and it became the serpent. When told to seize it by the tail, it again became the staff.'*

The Egyptian myths had always held a fascination. It was in part their duality with more modern religious format, and in part the obvious references to an understanding of the 'energies'. His thoughts drifted on into that domain: *'On Earth, the followers of Horus were the forces of good, ever in conflict with Set the evil one, and those who did his bidding. It was Set and his conspirators who had killed Osiris the father of Horus, who was now in spirit and who continued close, to remain ever the good influence upon Horus. The wise Thoth also helped, and was able to guide Horus in becoming a winged sun-disc with twin serpents ... a great subtlety ... the powerful sun-and-serpent energy with the feathers symbolic of levitation! That is what the feather hieroglyph of the pyramid texts had meant! And the Great Pyramid, with its paramagnetic pink granite above the King's Chamber, would have collected more energy for levitation when its limestone cladding had been in place. But that is a digression ... To complete the myth ... It was always said that when on the Earth, good finally triumphs over evil, this will signal the second coming, and Osiris would return from spirit to once again be king...'*

He stopped and was silently within himself for a moment. Then resumed: *'The idea of a second coming was not confined to Ancient Egypt. And yes... Set and Satan even sound similar, and they would certainly be considered as doing the same job! The pharoahs of Egypt had received the rite of baptism and several temple frescos depict an infant baptism. The water used would be the summer floodwater of the Nile, seen as the moving and therefore 'living' water of life. The poured water was often represented as a stream of ankhs. The ankh ... the Egyptian symbol for 'life' ... sometimes called 'the key of life' ... and forerunner of the Christian cross; the cross being used in symbol form much later by Christians, from the time of Constantine.'*

The connections between more modern formal religions and that of ancient Egypt of course did not end there. His thoughts trickled on: *'That little word 'Amen' was used so regularly as a response by Christians, Jews and Muslims alike, and its meaning was 'so be it' or 'truly'. But its derivation would almost certainly have been the Egyptian 'Amun', the one and only, all-pervading God. What better word could there be to represent acknowledgement of truth? Suffice to name the one that is the essence of all that is. That Egypt under all pharoahs had recognised many gods had been a popular misconception. There were recognised exhalted ones who, in the days of Tutankhamun at least, were seen as having the elevated status of angels. They were thus exhalted and not seen as gods. But the one God of the entire cosmos was 'Amun' (to some he was 'Aten'). How could it be otherwise? All cultures having awareness and feeling for the spirit connection recognised the one source ... the one and only source.*

An evolution of awareness was apparent that some cared to see as a fusion between religions old and new.' He now viewed it from the perspective of the later teaching: *'The Christ teaching had been inspired and honed to suit the needs of a new millennium that we now, to mark that milestone in our spiritual development, choose to call the 1st century Anno Domini. There had been earlier teachings, through inspired ones returning to Earth; not least the one known in Egypt as Thoth, and the Greeks had named him 'Thrice-Great Hermes'. His words had been delivered around the time of another millennium 3,000 years earlier. He was exalted in Egypt and revered in Greece. It is likely that much of his written work was lost in the absurd burning of the Alexandrian library. Some of his words survive, written down in post hieroglyphic format in Greek, Latin and Coptic, some, including prophecies that are 20th century re-discoveries, amongst the invaluable Nag Hamâdi texts. And it was Thoth who has stated that a truly enlightened being has no opinions about God ... he is simply 'one' with God. We are sometimes, despite all, blessed with such good fortune...'*

He briefly summed it all up: *'The roots of the modern religions reach far back into prehistory. In Homer's day they partook of the communion cakes and wine in celebration of the Mysteries. Earlier, Thoth wrote of the oneness with God. And Mary has her link with the Earth Mother that became evident in the confrontation with Artemis at Ephesus. On Earth, the fundamental cosmic truth has been re-stated and re-stated so many times throughout history and prehistory. Each statement by a master returning to Earth became a religion. What became practised or written down was always a little out of focus in relation to the original teaching. The original cosmic message was of course always the same ... a teaching of love and peace and of oneness with the one God. There had been of course, different presentation to suit those of different time and culture. It had been a lengthy process. It all represented a progression in terms of acceptance of the spiritual essence that we already have within. But the God of creation and the message were cosmic and as such ... older than either Earth or Earth's populations.*

During the lifetime of Alex, there had come the fuller understanding of the stonework and of the use of energies, and a greater understanding of many things. Sometimes, *acceptance* was as good a word as *understanding.*

In the past, there had been times when fairly obvious facts, had simply not been 'accepted', on account of their going against tradition, or their being alien to established science. But the ever-rising awareness had somehow managed to unfix the wrong focus of a blinkered view. These matters all concern our interpretation and attitude towards the great civilisations of bygone millennia. Nowadays, much more could be both accepted as well as, in part at least, understood.

But the changes that Alex had seen in his own lifetime had been huge. There is a good sense of *spirit* that underlies *consciousness*, and as the two had grown closer together, it had become easier for old and trusted traditions, to be perceived as lacking. The old legal process, based on the work of Tribonian had eventually become so cluttered, that it had at last been drastically reworked and simplified. (And this indeed had been the original task of Tribonian himself in *his* day.) The emphasis had now become very much more on crime and misdemeanour *prevention* as opposed to its processing *after* the event. There had been too many 'open stable doors' inviting the young horses to go rampaging. Society had now re-shaped and many of those doors were now closed, and the young were encouraged into real and worthwhile interests. This was clearly a satisfactory advance.

Similar thinking had been applied to medication and hospitals. The emphasis was now on *prevention* in preference to cure, or attempted cure. This again, was much more satisfactory. Such changes were merely logical, and exemplified the rising awareness. But these things, although sufficiently necessary and interesting to warrant the mention, were really only the civilisation's 'superficia'. (The new word had, as ever, been devised to suit the needs of the times.) One might say that, society had its central core of *living*, and the superficia surrounded that centre. There had always been the possibility of more fundamental, more central-to-life, more strikingly obvious developments, and now, in better times, they were all just *happening*. And Alex considered himself fortunate that so much of interest had come about in *his* own lifetime.

Alex had lived through the changes in farming methods that had altered the English countryside. He had seen hedgerows vanish from cultivated areas. Wild corners and wetlands had become scarce. Colourful and scented clover fields had sadly disappeared with the demise of mixed farming. Pastures and hayfields had lost their rich abundance of flowers, and with that loss went beauty and the butterflies, (and diet became the more boring for the animals that grazed). Bird populations sadly diminished. In the

Hampshire farmland that he knew so well, lapwings, linnets and goldfinches no longer graced the scene with their subtle beauty of colour and form. Suddenly there were no thrushes. The continuous song of the skylark above the wheat fields was heard no more. And the artistic flight of swallows and martins became more rarely seen.

Melodious birdsong became much depleted, in part replaced by lower frequency sounds ... throbbing helicopters, the ever-present roar of distant traffic and a persistent gas-charged cannon that fired at intervals to scare pigeons from the freshly emerging rape crop. But those times had now passed. Farming ways had worked back again, towards a better countryside. The old ways were not exactly recaptured; life must go forward. But bird and butterfly populations had now revived and much beauty was again to be enjoyed. And despite over-use of insecticides, we still have the bumblebees. One must never underestimate the part played by bee populations, both the wild bee and the honeybee, in the planetary natural order. Their work and the pollination that accompanies it are vital for the system to survive in the form that we have come to know and cherish. They so deserve our respect!

The brief excursion into genetic modification of nature's excellence could so easily have led to new and difficult-to-redress disasters. It is impossible to stop cross-pollination from 'open' genetic test sites. Even the commercial data used in beekeeping, relates to a single hive site being sufficient for the foraging of a 6-acre orchard, and a fair working flight range to consider, should be 2,000 yards. The actual forays of the honeybee may quite easily exceed these recommended criteria on occasions, and what about wind? It is virtually impossible to have open field test sites that do not contribute to haphazard-cum-hapless cross-pollination.

How does gene implanting between different species affect disease transfer from one species to another? What is the genetic recipe for creating uncontrollable dominant weeds? How will insects respond and what effects will they in turn have on other agencies? What are the long-term effects of the new alien diet? And how will the economy survive if people boycott the derived foodstuffs? The questions from an aware society had inspired appropriate caution. How could the physical mind of mankind hope to match in a mere decade, what nature has been steadily and selectively evolving across the billions of years? Such an extravagant arrogance! The unknown risks had far outweighed the seeking of short-term profit. Alex turned his thoughts back to the new landscape: *'Restoration of rural England's richness, without loss of productivity, had been so worthwhile ... a triumph of analysis and revision; a triumph of coercion and caution. Beauty of form, colour and fragrance has such universal appeal. Its retrieval is widely and readily appreciated, and that process is therefore both a pleasure and an easy picture to describe.'*

But there were the 'new energies', now described in the teaching discs, that had not graced the pages of the old textbooks. He went on to reflect: *'They are of course, so much more difficult to describe in timeless terms, that is ... to describe to those of an earlier age. There is nothing much with which to compare. There is always this problem, when it comes to attempting to explain fundamental things that are new. (Those pioneers of the developing sciences, four centuries earlier, had been obliged to invent so many new words, and time had been required for their acceptance and familiarity in language.) Perhaps one might begin by saying that the new energies are a good deal more subtle than that of the familiar sunlight ... that is, the electromagnetic energy spectrum. Yes ... that would be an approach...'*

He smiled to himself and thought on: *'Electromagnetic wave energy is itself, more subtle than, say, the much more substantial 'sound wave' energy, but shares obvious attributes with it. Both* **light** *and* **sound** *exhibit: wavelength, a vibrational source, reflection from surfaces, penetration of certain materials, and a detectable pressure exerted when the wave is obstructed. These properties are common to both. The sound wave has displacement and compression components that can be measured. The light wave is the same, except that these same components are seen as magnetic and electric vectors. There is marked similarity between the two waveforms. But the light wave is so much more subtle. (More specifically,* **sound** *relates to a wave involving* **physical particles**, *while* **light** *relates to passage through the stuff of* **space continuum** *... which pervades both space and physical world alike. Quite simply, this is why we see displacement and compression in the* **light** *wave, as magnetic and electric effects. In the two waves, they are really the same effects, but the waves are in two dissimilar media, so that our perception of them is different.)'* He had argued the case in his mind, for light waves being of a more subtle nature than sound, and was then able to compare the 'new energies' and describe them as a step subtler even than light. In his meandering mind, he had set himself a problem in science communication and had solved it to his own satisfaction. He felt quite well pleased.

Alex continued his vigil of the heavens, and let his thoughts turn to aspects of the new energies: *'They were interesting enough, but the most amazing ... the most ... well ... the most far reaching development ... had happened so slowly, it was scarcely noticed and scarcely accounted by most. It was certainly not seen as any form of change. And ... well yes of course ... the development in question, does in itself involve ... a most subtle energy form.'*

Alex was well aware of the change, because he had lived so long, and also because he had such a wonderfully good memory. He could remember with clarity, how things had been in the latter 20th century. The change that he observed was to do with the human aura. In his youth, there was a small minority that had the aural sight; that is, a few who could see details of colour and form in the space, *surrounding* head and body. Those few would sometimes huff and puff and do exercise routines in order to enhance as best they could, their gift; for gift it was, because the vast majority, were at that time oblivious to aura-consciousness.

Even back in the 20th century, most had the *ability* to see a trace of aura, if they really took the trouble to carefully observe ... well, at least they could see a bright watery glow about the head, best observed against a neutral background. (It would help if the person moved a little in relation to that background.) It was usually possible to see the brightness around one's own fingers, whilst moving the hand slowly across a neutral background. But then, perhaps most just thought of that enveloping haze as *steam* or *reflected light* or some such aberration. Yet artists often depicted Buddha, Jesus, Mary, the Saints and the Prophets, with light, or halos about *their* heads. Clearly, this was how they were seen by some who had the gift.

The chair creaked a little, as Alex stretched and reached deeper into the warmth of his pockets; but his thoughts were with auras: *'unrecognised' is how they used to be. But not any more! During the course of sixty years or so, with the steadily increasing awareness, the auras had, as it were, come out into the open. Yes ... that's how he now thought of it. Perhaps it was that people were now more trusting, more open, less fearful ... certainly less fearful, now that the nature of life and its ongoingness were so much better understood and properly accepted.'* He reasoned: *'the new freedom had created a general feeling of ... 'wanting to come out into the open'. So, had the people, to a degree, willed it by their own power of thought? Yes, it might well have been self-projected by 'power of thought'.'* He smiled to himself as he then reflected: *'The colours were, in general, not at first noticed at all ... people just went about their business, with their bright hazy appendages that in a way, were the reverse of shadows. But then, as time went by, the colour detail slowly became more evident. Such a slow process it was, that it was not seen as a change. The auras, with their colours had of course, always been present as an essential part of our being. Only the seeing or recognition of them had ever been lacking. Now we had aura-consciousness!'*

Even without 'the sight', there were still many people back in past times who nonetheless 'sensed' how things were. Two people might have got along unaccountably well, despite being physically different and having unrelated interests. Another two, although of similar dispositions, might equally just not gel at all; for no reason that could be understood. The term 'sixth sense' had even been devised without really knowing what it meant. The sixth sense was now revealed! There had always been much more to humans than just the visible material aspect, and now this further (non-material) appendage was more clearly evident. Auras could be compatible or non-compatible. People wore their colours around their being, as well as in their clothing, with often matching effects. The streets and promenades had become the prettier for it. As for the trading domes (developed from the old out-of-town supermarkets), they were just a confusion of wispy and vague transparent tints on a busy day, swirling around with the shoppers. Virtually all shops were now located within the trading domes, the towns being essentially residential and with their amenities such as cafés, theatres, halls of music, and the disc libraries.

In keeping with these times, and with the genuine desire for openness, aura colours tended towards the nicer hues. Alex, like many others, had some considerable knowledge of what the colours mean, and he reflected in some detail upon this: *'Black clouds of hatred and dark deeds were simply not around these days. Black in the aura really signified the absence of any living colour, and deep red flashes against black, marked the turmoil of a vicious anger. Anything of this nature, would only be the merest fleeting thing in this world of the mid-21st century. Anger was unnecessary and just so illogical. Human nature still had its passing moods, but the behavioural absurdities were just so much better understood now, and in consequence were rapidly becoming 'old fashioned'.*

There was still some of the old muddy-green-brown colour of selfishness about; but of course, the 'muddy-green-browns' now knew about it, and were aware of their little foible ... and were making really honest efforts to 'get things right'. And, as for jealousy ... well there is bound to be some in the younger ones, when they are meeting their partners in life; getting 'in love' or 'out of love'; and so, there was a little of the dark green-brown with just a few red flashes accompanying. Thankfully, in these more uplifted times, the awful, heavy greys of depression and fear had virtually disappeared. There was not quite the same strength of motivation for such adverse qualities today.

There were so very many beautiful 'loving' rose auras about, some wonderfully tinged with lilac, showing love of a more spiritual character. The old expression: 'seeing the world through rose-tinted spectacles' connects well with the unselfish loving nature seen through a rose-tinted aura.' There had been some kind of a meeting during the day, and Alex had seen a group in town, who displayed a good measure of 'orange': *'They would have been ambitious business people as like as not, and together with ambition, there was often included a little pride. It had been clear from the way they talked, that they shared an obvious and likeable enthusiasm for their work. There were others displaying bright yellows and golds with subtle variations. These were, according to the precise shade, the intellectuals, philosophers, delvers into knowledge and the mathematicians.'* He recalled that in the more general scene, there had been many other colours: *'The greeny ones often showed an animated vitality, and a versatility of character and resourcefulness, and this could sometimes also equate to a deeply felt compassion. In Eastern cultures, green can sometimes be the colour used in mourning, but not as any symbol of sadness. Any symbolism would more likely be that of the journey to new life.*

There were so many different blues. The colour in general, identifies with developed spirituality. The really luminous lilac-blue, which may include sparkling gold stars, is extremely beautiful, and goes with a highly developed spirituality.' Here, Alex heaved a great sigh as he thought of such colours that he had seen, only on rare occasions. *'And the wonderful violet shades that go with the adept who scarcely belongs to this Earth plane at all, but really aspires to those higher realms. Darker blues accompany wisdom and saintliness. Then, right at the edge of violet and into ultra-violet is where the developed psychic ability is to be found.*

Auras are never composed of just the one colour. Individuals always have a mixture of qualities and associated colours. That is a part of the nature of life. And moods and respective colours are of course changing all the time. Each aura is a restless mixture of hues. Whenever there was a good gathering of people, it could be an enjoyably pretty sight; that is, just so long as one stopped to take account. It was still easy to overlook, on account of the sheer delicate transparency compared to physical matter.'

Alex's thoughts were wandering just a little. It was a part of his character these days. They alighted upon those occasions when one is able to observe a 'collective' change in colour: *'at a concert, you could 'see' the people's moods changing with the music. As the colours of the audience conformed in some moving part of the piece, there was a kind of 'oneness' ... a oneness of the shared experience that was felt as well as seen in colour. The 'feeling' of the shared experience had been quite a well-known phenomenon, even during his father's day. In the days of militarism, now difficult to envisage ... in the parachute drops of World War II, there were shared extreme feelings of fear, anxiety, relief and then the urgency for re-grouping. All would have shared similar aura colours to a degree. They would not have been seen, but as many had testified, such* ***feelings*** *in that situation had been strongly felt, and the 'sharing factor' had felt as a group-bond. Now, group-shared experiences could be openly seen as well as felt ... and the bonding between people that sometimes followed, was a visible attunement!*

A degree of aura conformity could also be seen at today's funerals. These were now much 'lighter' gatherings. There would always be some sadness in parting; but the parting was also now seen quite clearly as the journey that it is, and the journey would not be an unpleasant one.' It occurred to Alex as he reflected on funerals, that many of the older cultures had indeed seen these occasions as a journey for the departing spirit: '... *Now what had the Maya called it? ... The Wacah Chan ... the world tree ... Yes, that was it! That was their name for the path of that journey to the other-world. The path was the connecting tree. So now, here in this 21st century, we again were recognising the journey that all departing ones continue to take. So now we recognise the nature of our transition at death, the subtle energies, and how those subtle energies are also a part of ourselves.*

Yes ... one could see these qualities as extended parts of ourselves. There was also the telepathic principle.' Telepathy showed within daily life in curious little ways. He now thought back to his travels again: *'Indonesia ... the island of Bali. Now there was an interesting place! Why ... it must have been around the turn of the millennium or just before, for he had been a young man when he was there. Bali had become a popular centre for both tourism and trading. He remembered the buffet breakfasts at Bambang's restaurant in Kuta ... or was it Legian?'* Perhaps it was an irrational memory. But it was such a good breakfast at that place that he chose to dwell upon it: *'That breakfast! ... Unlimited fresh tropical fruits, toast and spicy dishes from the tureens, side orders of eggs, pancakes, jaffles, cold juice and a pot of Bali coffee ... and all for...'* He had long since forgotten how many thousand rupiahs it had cost, *'... in old UK currency, it had been equivalent to a mere 95p! Wonderful! Quite clearly, Bambang was not out to make a quick million from his customers. This had been a man who liked to see others having a good time. Neither could he have been taxed heavily by his government. That such excellent value could be enjoyed was most creditable to all that were concerned, and the memory of it, had remained with him ... a much-treasured memory. But the point was ... the waitress.'*

She was a sensitive soul, and Alex had been considering the filling for his jaffle ... a kind of toasted sandwich ... from the list on the menu, and finally he had thought ... *'egg, tomato and onion would be just perfect.'* She had stood attentive and repeated: *'egg, tomato and onion sir.'* It was not until she was walking off, that he realised, he had not actually spoken the words. He had merely thought them! Such were the little telepathic subtleties that now crept into conversations. It happened much more generally nowadays. But Bali, with its 'devotional' version of Hindu religion, its wholly organic agriculture and not *too* much Western influence; had always inspired a deep sensitivity. Through telepathy, Alex reasoned: *'People now must have a certain consciousness of the space around them. If one mind can have direct communion with another, then the space between must also be involved...'*

There had been many scientific experiments to prove the principle of telepathy, but Alex was well aware that the thought-connection was not just confined to humans. A connectedness permeated nature in its entirety. He had read of the experiments of Cleve Backster, conducted nearly a hundred years earlier. Backster had been an interrogation specialist with the CIA until he left to train policemen in use of the polygraph (lie detector). One day, he made the decision to place the two psychogalvanic-reflex electrodes on either side of a leaf of the office rubber plant. He then watered the plant and noted the absence of any response on the recording chart. It did not detect water uptake by the leaf. Knowing that humans under test, respond to *threat to well-being*, he next decided to strike a match and *burn* the leaf. In the instant of making that decision, and without him so much as moving, the recording pen swept upwards. The plant had sensed that it was under threat!

Backster had extended his experiments. He further explored the possibility of 'plant perception' by dropping brine shrimp into boiling water. Each time he repeated this, a peak on the polygraph chart, registered the plant's perception. He also worked with a potted philodendron. He himself showed it loving care. This time, he had his assistant cause stress in various ways that registered as peaks on the chart. Ultimately, the polygraph showed an agitated response whenever his assistant entered the room, and relaxed again if Backster came near. He went on to show that a variety fruit and vegetables and living cells exhibit sensitivity to other life forms in distress. Backster had reflected most seriously upon his findings. He gave up mowing the lawn. He had concluded that all life should be treated with respect, killing should always be accompanied by feelings of reluctance, despatching only that necessary for our survival. Earlier cultures had known this intuitively. He had proved the matter to his own satisfaction experimentally!

Alex now considered the obvious connectedness between all life ... all life forms ... through the space between:

'Concerning that space ... there was now some degree of understanding of this important subject. It was Einstein who had alone made the link between space and time and talked of a space-time continuum. Bohm and others had then forged the further step of linking all else to that continuum. The same universal 'space' that most in the 20th century had regarded as 'nothing', was now clearly no such thing ... or no

such 'nothing' if you like.' He chuckled to himself as he played with his own words.

'This realisation had been a key that had unlocked a door to major advances in what used to be called 'theoretical physics'. Earlier, the very few had braved their opinion that it follows from relativity theory plus the concept of 4-dimensional space-time, that **past, present and future are embodied within the space-time frame.** *This was scientific deduction that our future is to a large degree predetermined. Science had thus come to validate the principle of prophecy! And linear flowing time was an illusion of our Earthly perception! These facts had been hard for many to absorb.*

Space *had now become duly recognised as a fount of creation ... and source of all that is. The electron itself, is now seen, not so much as an elementary particle, but more as a contrived focus of Einstein's continuum; as indeed are all the primary entities of particle physics and of our physical perception. All are foci projecting out of space to collectively attract and excite our recognition.*

Again concerning space, a small number of scientists around the year 2000, had begun to view it in terms of a holographic-principled domain.' (A hologram is a contrived 3-dimensional picture. It is made by splitting and recombining a beam of laser light; whilst arranging for one split beam to pick up an image along its path. Instead of producing the 3-dimensional image right away, the hotchpotch of light may first be recorded on film as a kind of dotty image. Then, on shining an appropriate light through the film, the same solid-looking 3-dimensional picture again results. Space would appear to have a similar holographic-film-like quality; this underlying the physical world 'reality'.) Alex continued to reason, with the advantage of the knowledge of his own times: *'Space can be and is, acted upon by light, thought waves and by various subtle energies, to produce the perceived forms of our existence. The holographic principle had become a kind of 'model' for generating those forms from space; a model, in the sense of an 'imagined approximate device' to aid our further thought construction. But it was more than just an 'imagined' device; indeed, the principle had led to an actual healing system that worked through the holographic-repatterning-of-subconscious-shapes. The process followed 'body' interrogation by means of standard kinesiology, and it demonstrated the stark reality of biological dependence upon underlying energy configurations. It became clear to those concerned, that space has many properties that had not been accounted by the old 20th century science.*

This step together with a certain other matter, had led the way to 'science' understanding and accepting such things as telepathy, dowsing, healing, poltergeist encounters, mysticism and even 'Dreamtime' creation. That other matter that had contributed, was the development of the electromyograph, and its use to record the electrical activity of muscles. Valerie Hunt, a physical therapist and professor of kinesiology, had been the first to extend use of the machine to record the subtle aura energies. It was found that not only could the aura and changes within it, be recorded by the machine, but the presence of certain higher vibrations in the aura, related to psychic ability of the individual; and the contribution to our understanding did not stop there.

Those who are able to go into trance states, and to channel knowledge from spirit sources, were found to have a particular narrow range of still higher frequency vibrations. Scientists were thus able to map in detail, aura frequencies against the abilities of healers and trance mediums. This in turn had shed light on apparent healing miracles. The 'voices' from other realms, had for some years spoken of 'raised vibrations aiding the channel'. Now scientists were able to precisely measure these vibrations for themselves.

These had been very important steps along the way which had eventually led to the meeting point ... a triple point ... the meeting point of science, spiritualism/mysticism and that central essence from which formal religions had sprung.' Here he paused to just consider for a few moments. He saw it as such a hugely significant factor in humankind's advancement ... *'There had had to be a meeting, and that meeting time was right now, and the three quite different belief systems were so very well met. The process of 'scientificising' the data embraced by spiritualism and religious teachings, had been a process that had happened, little by little. Back in the 17th century, when Bruno had been burned for his science, who would have thought that science and religion could ever meet?'*

He thought of the old Papacy and the times of the dogmatic church: *'They were of the past ... no longer functioning as such. Had there been a Pope today, he would be feeling ... well ... redundant. That is not to discredit the* **proper** *strivings within the Christian Church or within any other religion. The process of change had been in part to expose ... to reveal ... make more readily recognisable ... the inner essence of the teaching that had always been. That was a spiritual movement in itself. Any 'cloaking' of that central essence was now, not only inappropriate, but was also* **seen** *to be inappropriate. As with an egg, the old doctrinal system had been merely, just a crude and crusty shell, encapsulating the precious prize within. The shell once broken, the rebirth and widespread understanding of the pure love teaching within, had quickly followed. The shell had been an unnecessary error. And yet, even the release of that error, perhaps had its own aspect of timeliness.*

The clear-sightedness of it had come with what was almost a feeling of relief. There had always been a trickle of really knotty questions addressed to the clergy of the past, for which the Church could simply find no satisfactory answers.' He considered for a moment before proceeding further ... *'questions like: 'Why has my baby been taken from me at 12 months?' The deep sadness of such times when the young are lost, will always remain ... it cannot possibly be otherwise. Emotion springs from the physical mind and will weigh heavily until its natural release. But there would be some who in their sadness, ask the reason? That is a separate matter. In the now-recognised ongoing nature of life, part in the physical, part in spirit; sometimes there would be a need ... of the soul ... for a brief time, of babyhood in the physical, followed by growing-up years in the realm of spirit. As for the parents, they might also have certain spiritual growth needs met by their experience of loss, and they would eventually be the stronger for it. The bonds would, in good measure, remain.* ***All life continues****. Life has both reason and structure. Such events are* ***not*** *punitive,* ***nor*** *are they spurious. They are meant ... and meant for growth of spirit ... growth of soul. We are always first and foremost, beings of spirit; we should not, whatever the circumstance, ever lose sight of that. Soul-progression is paramount in our existence. Life is the most precious thing, and in the terms of its spiritual value, is* ***never*** *wasted.'* In the light of present knowledge, and in accord with his own lifetime of learning, that was how Alex had come to see it.

It had all come about in a gentle way: *'Disintegration of the old dogma somehow seemed to happen without any real discredit to those in office. It simply became time for the old format of religious doctrine to drop away and for the vital inner essence ... its central flower ... to receive the light and unfold, to become an integral part of a more awakened life. It was like a re-birth. Spiritual growth, to that raised degree of maturity, had meant that the old-style religions were no longer needed. They had been* ***'planetary'*** *religions, and as such, their central teachings of love and peace had been (local) Earthly expressions of the infinite cosmic principle. And of course, the parables delivered by Jesus had always been seen as Earthly stories with their heavenly meaning. They had been honed to suit a humanity that was less aware.'*

He continued to reflect regarding those few enlightened ones who had actually voiced the idea of a beginning and an end to 'Religion' in their teachings. Just prior to the 20th century there had been Swami Vivekananda ... a much cherished favourite whom he had thoroughly read:

> *'Each soul is a star ... Religion began with the search after some of these stars that had passed beyond our horizon, and ended in finding them all in God, and ourselves in the same place.'*
>
> Swami Ananyananda. *Teachings of Swami Vivekananda.*

He now clearly understood the subtlety of the statement. Religion had been a search, and like all searches, it had now come to an end. The God within us all and within all else had at last been found ... identified ... acknowledged. The connectedness ... the oneness of it ... has been well expressed by Joel Goldsmith, a teacher and author who followed later. He refers to contacting the Source through meditation to be *one* with the spiritual mind of the universe ... this also being the mind of Buddha, of Jesus and every spiritual saint and seer. It is a part of his teaching that to be *one* with the source of one's own life is to be *one* with the universal Source.

The meeting point and triple point was also a bridge. Barely conscious of his movement, Alex, still with eyes on the heavens, eased further down within his warm coat, and rested his feet on a nearby log. In an entirely coincidental way, he too became a bridge, as he allowed his thoughts to amble through the events of recent decades. He thought much further back, to that point in history (which he had studied quite diligently in his more youthful days), when Constantine and his army had seen the message in the sky: 'CONQUER BY THIS'. *'Their battle shields had then been adorned with the 'chi-rho' ensignia that was later to become a Christian symbol. There are now those who would consider that, the sign in the sky, may have been generated from their own collective consciousness via the holographic principle of space. Whatever the generative principle involved ... after the battle, Milvian Bridge could be seen as a bridge between the old Roman pagan god system and the state-religion version of Christianity.*

But now there was an entirely new metaphoric bridge ... this time leading away from the old state-bonded and dogmatic religions that had remained with the planet for two thousand troublesome years! This long-awaited and necessary new bridge was at this time leading to a pure and simple understanding of life, and of the love that must be enmeshed with it. Life was now clearly seen as centred upon love and peace ... and that is all that there had ever been at the heart of the old religions. 'Love and peace'. They ... the old 'developed' religions ... were now left without further purpose ... obsolete, one might say. They had been imbued with too much complexity and clutter ... and this had quite simply got in the way of the message that they carried ... a message that was really so very simple. But ... most important ... despite all, it was never lost ... it was always there and there were always those who were able to seek it out.

The road to the new bridge had not been an easy one, and there were times when it looked as if mankind would fall by the wayside.' Alex felt a momentary sadness, as he considered how things might have evolved, in the absence of any guidance. *'Thankfully, help had been received from those other realms of which we are now well conscious ... from teaching missions, subtle and sometimes synchronistic guidance, raised vibrations, timely awareness, computer logic, unsealing of the Torah, the galactic ships and symbolic adornment of the wheat fields. The latter had awakened a deeper consciousness. Old prophecies had said there would be 'signs' in the troubled times. There had been the cornfield symbols. There had been the resurrection of the Ark, and then had come Chernobyl that translates to 'Wormwood'. And this had been accounted by St John in prophecy. These had been the most potent of signs.*

The conquests and wars of Islam and Christendom had surely been corruptions since they were alien to the teaching ... and yet not entirely so. At least, they too had been a part of John's Revelation and must accordingly be accepted as a 'necessary' part of our progression ... the progression of our past two millennia that he saw whilst in trance on Patmos.

A 'failed' outcome to the difficulties of the 20th century had been averted. As to the ongoing creation, there are Hindu Vedas that refer to the universe as 'God's Dream'. There are those who by reference to holographic space, would say that through interaction of our collective unconscious, we dream our own existence; or even that the dream is dreaming itself. But then God is the Divine Essence in all that is, so such distinctions simply do not matter. Suffice to be aware that the dream is God and is of God.'

It seemed to Alex, that the time and energy expended in attempting to define a 'Trinity of beings', at those early Church Councils, in the days of the Roman Empire; represented a strange digression from his present thought construction. But all that was in the past. God was now seen much more as the creative principle and not as an imagined effigy. Some words of his earlier reading came to mind: *'Something about God's creation being an infinite process ... a process in which order emerges from a primal chaos ... and God guides all through the workings of natural laws. That had been the gist of it.'* He considered that that had been a sound statement saying something of the nature of God, albeit seen at an entirely physical level.

What he now felt, was that his logical train of thought, was approaching the nub of where we currently stand: *'the most dedicated scientist might say that 'all' in the universe, is comprised of the 'formed' space and the 'unformed' space. Nothing else exists. Therefore space is all; and it follows that space and God are one...'* He then went on *'... but these are all just words that we pin to our perceptions. That such thoughts, can be expressed at all at this time, is surely illustrative that science, spiritualism and religion are now as one. If all that is, derives from space, and God is in all things, then perhaps in a strictly geographic sense, they would appear as if the same. But 'space' is a scientific notion honed out of an entirely material discipline, while 'God' comes from an ascetic domain of the non-material. A different meaning will therefore be ascribed to each word, the meanings albeit being flexible. Indeed, in the old 20th century thinking, the majority view was that 'space' is nothing, while 'God' is everything! It is the very substance of the scientific word that has now changed from being 'nothing' to being 'everything' ... A total reversal of definition! Currently, there is understandably some confusion of terms.*

'God' remains a perfectly acceptable term, just so long as we allow a rational meaning. The human form father figure had been an unreal but useful, childish notion, a stepping stone for some in past times. And the long road from 'unknowing' needed its stepping stones to the new levels of perception. Perhaps 'Divine Essence' and 'Creative Principle' now carry the imagery to convey more closely what we mean? And we must not forget

'love'. That too is apt description. All creation has evolved from the love-thought, with affinity and beauty of form running rife throughout.'

Alex was pleased by the construction of his thinking. It had gone in a somewhat roundabout way. But he was pleased with the clarity of the end result. It was good to have a strong feeling for the God ... the Divine Essence ... and to be a part of it all. In this lifetime, he had come to know the meaning of it ... of *life* ... that is.

His thoughts moved on to enter a reality that lies just beyond the physical Earth. He knew something of soul-structure ... not all, on account of the inability of a mere physical mind to encompass time's elusive fluidity. He knew the way in which past lives make up the soul. Many Earth lives were interspersed with periods of progression in spirit. Somehow, that ongoing collective that we know as 'soul', has a oneness that had been his source of intuition all this life, and of course it was his God-connection. He had felt the link strongly, especially in the quiet moments of his very early years; then again, with better understanding, in fuller maturity. That soul in spirit was his deeper reality, and very soon now, it would be his time to travel, to that unquenchable reality of his many pasts. With full memory re-awakened, how would he then see himself? Even now, his intuition re-assured that all would be well. After all, a traveller must always one day ... return home ... and experience the joy of glad reunion.

'Why, if the Soul can fling the Dust aside,
And Naked on the Air of Heaven ride,
Is't not a shame ... Is't not a shame for him
So long in this Clay suburb to abide!'
Omar Khayyám of Náishapúr *The Rubáiyát*

Author's notes: Before closing this work, there are just two further points that ought to be clarified:

1. I feel obliged to make the observation to the reader, that this book does not address the question: *Is it wise to, or should, spirit realms be accessed through mediumship?* And I would say that the answer to that question may well depend upon personal factors and upon the exigencies of the times; and so, it may well have a time-dependence. There are those who would maintain that the link with God *best* be accessed from *within* and all else connected with spirit, is simply unnecessary encumbrance. In the ordinary scheme of things, they may be right, or such belief may suit their present path. The point becomes clouded and of small importance, when one remembers that God has many, many helpers. One must not overlook the fact that there have been times with needs so great that the ordinary scheme of things is no longer seen to prevail. At such times, *extra*ordinary links with the spirit realms may form and may help us. In the latter 20th century, man came desperately close to destroying his physical presence upon this planet. It is my view that extraordinary events and communications have helped in no small way to avert that disaster, and that help continues. I believe that the latter 20th century, has been a time during which it has been appropriate for certain doorways to other realms, to open. This strategy however, whilst being of great benefit and guidance to physical man in times of his reckless and most careless folly, should not be *confused with* the inward direct link to God (which all spirit beings have, irrespective of their current realm).

2. Regarding the last two chapters, the appearance of the comet in the year 2,061 is a fair certainty. The electromyograph and holographic repatterning already in fact exist, and the scientific deduction that space-time holds past, present and future events, has already prompted TV discussion. (And Einstein in his day had suggested that the view of certain physicists, is that distinction between past, present and future, is illusion.) Apart from these items, the last two chapters contain my own speculation and ideas for building our future. I believe these to be ideas worthy of consideration, but I do not profess to be a seer and in any event, it does not seem right to attempt to map a firm future for physical humankind, other than that which is already encoded within the Torah. With this small proviso concerning 21st century detail, the book is essentially one of factual truth. I therefore close with three Latin words, the significance of which is explained in Appendix 1.

VERITAS SANCTUM SANCTOS.

Appendix I

6 April 1994: It was during the course of the evening that I made a second visit to Patricia for a psychic reading. It seems that, on this occasion, Ashenak, my Siberian guide and helper, at first appeared to her in silhouette on horseback and he identified himself; also my father, who quite took Patricia by surprise. She said to me: *'Would he smoke a pipe? ... And would he address you as 'George m' boy ... now listen...?'* I assured her that would be typical of my father, who had been a Hampshire farmer most of his life and had a quaint phrase or two in his repertoire. Both gentlemen then proceeded to advise on the 'belief' aspect of the book that I had been brooding upon, and to suggest some general guidelines that could be useful in its writing.

Firstly, the writing would not be rushed. The book would develop at its own pace, (and that has certainly been the way of it). Then there was the subject of 'evil'. It was explained to me in a very few words that there was a subtlety about it. It was a 'hidden thing' that I should not underestimate. I was instructed: *'the light unfolds'* just as *'the light unfolds spring flowers.'* The word: *'Proverbs'* came through, the significance of which I must confess escaped me for quite some time. In my notes there followed the instruction: *'Remember the words of Moses.'* The Ten Commandments, received by Moses, have to be seen as a major statement within the Christian faith, and 'love' is at the centre of the Commandments. They would surely be the words of Moses to remember. (At that time I had no knowledge at all of the encoded Torah; also words received by Moses. My knowledge of that was to come later!)

Then Patricia went to some length to make clear to me that she was being shown a wavy snake enclosed in a diamond-shaped box, its head at the top. I remembered this much later, when it came to writing about the 'serpent energy', and I referred back to my notes of this evening. And of course, the Bible story of the staff becoming a serpent also connects with Moses. The symbolism of the box connects well with the notion, that the serpent energy although real, is enclosed ... is not available to *this* civilisation. (There does seem to be evidence, that the serpent energy has been known to *previous* civilisations, and there may be the ancient 'staff god' connection with serpent energy.)

Other advice was more tangible ... *'Always use the guidelines you are shown ... Paths are made to be followed only if you wish'* ... And ***'this is the way of the wise:***

'Follow your feelings.' (Listen to the voice within. That is, take account of intuition, which has its source in spirit.)

'Don't rely on man's words.' (Use various sources of data. Use books, but cross-reference with inspired teachings, prophetic vision, spirit communication etc.)

'Fortunes are but dust.' (This may mean that profit in monetary terms should not be seen as the objective. The book is to be more a challenge and a crusade to spread the knowledge more widely. And this is certainly how I came to see it.)

'Don't forget your kindred spirit.' (Don't neglect your friends. In fact, it is truly amazing just how many friends began passing me splendid reference books that they thought might be useful; and each one seemed to arrive at the right moment! It really was quite uncanny the way this just happened during the five years of writing.)

Having moved on a few times in life, I at first felt confused as to who were my kindred spirit; whereupon Ashenak leaned forward to say: *'My kindred spirit are the wolves.'* (So he may have meant 'Minty' the cat that often sits on top of my computer when it is running!)

It was a good many months before I thought of following up *'Proverbs'* as the 'Book of Proverbs ... of Solomon-Ben-David, King of Israel'. On opening the book, I found I was looking at Proverbs 1, *6*:

> *'For the Lord is the giver of wisdom*
> *From His mouth come Knowledge and Thought;*
> *Salvation He stores for the upright;*
> *And shields those who walk in the truth...'*

It was a firm endorsement for the *'way of the wise'*. It seemed to give strength to the idea of spiritually sourced information. I was also given the three Latin words: 'VERITAS SANCTUM SANCTOS'. Again, it was some months later that I purchased an old, Latin dictionary and had a further look at my notes. The best translation I have been able to work out is:

TRUTH IS THE HOLY OF HOLIES.

It seemed a fitting way to conclude. But perhaps one should not overlook the fact that the keeping place, by instruction, for the encoded Torah, has always been beyond the veil of the synagogue, in the 'Holy of Holies'. Appropriately, that is the place where life's truth, as it is encoded, resides.

And that concluded the session, apart from Ashenak's parting gesture to Patricia. It appears that he likes to close with a poem:

'Farewell sweet May Queen
For you blossom like spring.
You entrance those around you
For the life that you bring.
God bless you.'

Then he kissed her hand, whereupon she shivered and for one fleeting moment felt a *really* cold chill.

Appendix II

24 May 1993 ... At the Royal Horticultural Halls, Victoria, London. It was the occasion of the Festival of Mind Body Spirit. Ann and I had decided to travel up to town and attend several of the lectures and workshops and to visit the commercial stands. This was the tenth festival in what had become an annual event. That this was so seemed in itself symptomatic of subtle inner change, long awaited in a culture strongly devoted to materialism.

Monday 24 May: I was at Michael Poynder's lecture, 'Pi in the Sky', which I thoroughly enjoyed and which filled in some useful gaps in my knowledge of dowsing and stone circles. Next it was the June Marsh Lazar workshop ... subject: *'Past Lives/Soul Mates'.* I felt especially drawn to this. You see I had been researching this book, on and off over the past 30 years or so, as a leisure activity. It was to be a factual account of where we are from and where we are heading, and it would span two million years. I wanted to get an authentic feel for the past life/reincarnation belief system, thinking at the time that it may provide a useful thread to toss into an already well-filled mixing pot of ideas.

So this was the situation: I found myself in a lecture hall with many others, happily engaged in a 'process', seeking past life regression. After a period of conditioning I was beginning to sense something. There were the mists of my mind ... clearing ... to reveal a scene, typical of a location around the shores of the Aegean in ancient times. There were dusty off-white buildings in hot summer, and as the scene came closer ... a white-robed figure. His hand extended; he held a scroll. He was handing me the scroll. It was closed. I saw no words, but somehow as if our minds momentarily came together, I knew that I *had* to include *the Greek connection* in the book. It was important that I should. And the wonderful look on that face! It conveyed love, approval and entrustment. I was being entrusted with the scroll; of that there was no doubt.

My recent work had dwelt upon the problem in the world, and the meaning of, the developing religions. More specifically, I was concerned with the change period from Earth Goddess to Christianity and the modern male-orientated, heavily dogmatised religions. Uncannily, intuitively, I just knew that the Greek connection applied here. But, in the writing, where should I pitch the timing? ... Homer? ... Aristotle? ... Plato? The white-robed figure of the 'process' had been of a most senior and learned status...

Wednesday 26 May am: At home, I continued reading *'Millennium' - David Maybury-Lewis*, a well-illustrated book of mostly tribal subject matter. But on turning the next page, there! ... in all its unexpected and synchronistic perfection, page 217, I found the festival of Eleusis accounted. The ancient Greek festival, a celebration of the goddess Demeter, rich with her Earth Goddess/harvest aspects, and a celebration of the 'mystery' of other-world and renewal; Aristotle himself being named as initiate!

[It was several months later, in the October, that Ann and I had the opportunity of visiting the west coast of what is now Turkey, and Assos where he had taught. That was another happy coincidence.]

Wednesday 26 May pm: Back to London and the festival. I attended a lecture entitled: *'Facing Unfinished Karma' - Roger Woolger.* It included a range of topics ... Do we have a collective karma? ... Visions of the new age ... Ancient prophecies of native people ... Political shadow. This was all very interesting. Then, midst the discourse, attention was drawn to a difficult time in ancient Greece. This was a period when Athens vied with Sparta, whose citizens followed Demeter. The Athenians followed Zeus and his 'power gods'. Sparta was suppressed, and the lecturer saw this as an influential *turning point* in world religion. The change was to be away from the Mother Goddess/Earth Goddess religion, centred on love and spirituality, to a masculine-headed religion based on power and soldiery. That was the Athenian style. Later, Christianity swept across Europe and became a state-bonded religion, carrying with it, soldiery, wars, conquest and the Crusades.

It transpired then, that this part of Roger Woolger's lecture clarified for me, that other side to the Greek connection. In Greece at the time of Aristotle, there were political factors that triggered the change from a 'Goddess' to a 'male orientated' religion and this change would exert its influence on the modern religions that were to follow. These modern religions would then reach into our present and our future, shaping and coercing the lives of so many.

Monday 31 May: This was our third and final day at the 10-day festival. A further Roger Woolger lecture and workshop *Finding the Goddess Within*, was an excellent follow-up and concerned seeing qualities of the six goddesses that spring from the Great Mother, in people of today's culture.

Fresh from the lively workshop and discussion, I felt quite a mental buzz. According to my reading on the subject of auras and energy fields, this should temporarily increase the *yellow* in my own aura. So this seemed a good time to put to test the aura camera in the exhibition hall. I sat whilst the instrument went to work. It produced on film quite a golden sunburst, and convinced me that it does a good job of aura-colour-simulation.

We rounded off our last day listening to Sir George Trevelyan ... *'The Human and Divine Adventure'*. It was heart warming to see this man of intellect in his mid-eighties, addressing such a New Age gathering. He spoke of the *power of poetry*, quoting a Gerard Manley Hopkins poem: *'God's Grandeur'*. He was clearly moved. It impressed him. And during the course of his lecture he quoted it in full ... three times! It impressed me too. I was later to realise that the poem contains the key word *'Smudge'* to make the title of this book, and in some measure expresses its dynamic. We have been here some two million years and the planet bears the scars to show. And we have most certainly left a sizeable *'smudge'* during this last century. But this will change as the *'morning'* of a new awakening dawns.

God's Grandeur

The world is charged with the grandeur of God.
It will flame out, like shining from shook foil;
It gathers to a greatness, like the ooze of oil
Crushed. Why do men then now not reck his rod?
Generations have trod, have trod, have trod;
And all is seared with trade; bleared, smeared with toil;
And wears man's smudge and shares man's smell: the soil
Is bare now, nor can foot feel, being shod.

And, for all this, nature is never spent;
There lives the dearest freshness deep down things;
And though the last lights off the black West went
Oh, morning, at the brown brink eastwards, springs -
Because the Holy Ghost over the bent
World broods with warm breast and with ah! bright wings.
Gerard Manley Hopkins 1877

It was just two weeks later that Ann's cousin Ken, a priest from Perth, Australia was over on one of his rare visits. I can picture him now, as he stood in our library at home, and ... out of the blue, looked up at the ceiling and began to recite a poem ... *'The world is charged with the grandeur of*

God...' I asked him why? ... He could not explain. It seems he just got the urge to say it!

I have recounted above in some detail about three days in May when preparations for the writing of this book were coming to a head. The curious synchronicities of this brief period are typical of several such periods that contributed to the writing. It may serve to illustrate some of the subtlety of synchronistic help from 'up there', that can sometimes be an influence in our lives.

Appendix III

Further Significant Events Around the Time of the New Millennium

In 1995 the Australian government set up the Canberra Commission on the elimination of nuclear weapons. Its findings, made known in 1996, indicated that immediate and determined efforts need to be made to rid the world of nuclear weapons; also that nuclear states should commit themselves to the elimination of such weaponry and agree to start negotiations to that end. The Commission was made up of politicians, ex-military and academic notaries.

On 8 July 1996 at the Peace Palace, The Hague, the World Court ruled the use and threat of nuclear weapons to be illegal. It went on to state unanimously that nuclear powers are obliged to pursue and bring to conclusion negotiations leading to all aspects of nuclear disarmament. (Response from the nations would not be immediate but the ruling now had its place in world consciousness.)

The Hague Appeal for Peace Conference of 1999 called for abolition of nuclear weapons, land mines and of all weapons incompatible with humanitarian law; also abolition of arms trade or reduction of it in compliance with the United Nations Charter. The resources so released should be used to eradicate poverty and preserve our environment.

In May 2,000, the United Nations reported that the five leading nuclear nations: Russia, U.S.A., China, France and Britain, had each agreed in principal to get rid of all nuclear arms.

There was also another peace move in May 2,000. Israel withdrew all her forces from South Lebanon.

On Earth, the changing consciousness clearly continued at this time, and although troubles remained, there were major events that thankfully kept us heading away from worldwide catastrophe. And our friends in spirit were also well aware of the pervasive changes that had begun and would continue.

On 10 March 1997, Salumet came through to us with a reassuring message:

~ '... *I wish to say this to you: that mankind in general upon this planet Earth, has reached an awareness which brings joy to those of us in my world who are striving ... who are striving to bring knowledge to this Earth.*

Surrounding this planet, there now prevails a stillness and peace, which you would not be aware of, but (which) brings much satisfaction to us. The stillness and peace, which over your next thousand-plus years, will pervade all of mankind to such an extent, that no longer will there be the fear and ... the distrust shall I say? ... over all things termed 'supernatural' ... They will become known and natural to mankind. Mankind will return to knowledge that belongs to them. Though I say to you, dear friends ... although you will not exist as you do now, in these times to come, I extend this knowledge to you in order that you carry it forward with you, to our side of life. Keep it with you. Use it wisely, and know that you have become part of it.'

On March 12th 2000 Pope John Paul II, during Mass at St. Peter's, Vatican City, asked forgiveness for sins committed by the Holy Roman, Catholic and Apostolic Church. It was made clear during the confessions and together with attendant Vatican statements that the sins referred to, related to past centuries. They included:

- intolerance for those on different pathways,
- the religious wars,
- violent acts against those who did not accept the teaching,
- violence and abuse during the Crusades,
- sins against the dignity of women,
- methods used by the Inquisition,
- the excommunications and persecutions.

It is reported that following the confessions, Pope John Paul repeated the words *'Never more'* five times in declaration that the Church would not commit such wrongs again.

The air needed to be cleared on these matters that had tarnished the structured and dogmatic version of the faith for so many centuries. It had been both a necessary and a difficult task. Now it was done, well done and seen-to-be-done. The media reported the expression of repentance as being a remarkable historical event. And what better time could there possibly be for this than the first Sunday of Lent in a new millennium?

Later in the month, Pope John Paul visited the Holy Land. At Jerusalem's Yad Vashem memorial he ceremonially rekindled the eternal flame that burns in memory of six million Jews who died in the holocaust. He expressed sorrow, saying that the Church was deeply saddened by hatred and acts of persecution against Jews by Christians in any time and place.

Appendix IV

Prayer and the Church

It is clear from the final paragraphs of Appendix III and other text that, throughout a chequered history, the formal Church has been in error in a number of ways. It would however be churlish to leave the matter there. The Church also has its good side and it would be improper to understate this, just as it is improper to be hostile and judgmental. Rank hostility is negative while debate and forgiveness offer ways forward. We all have our individual pathways and they all progress.

There have been occasions when our teacher Salumet has 'arranged' for others to come through and talk with us. On the evening of 13th March 2000, one named Edwin joined us. He and his colleagues normally work in the heavenly domain, receiving and blending prayers that proceed from our planet (A part of the detailed structure within spiritual domain). Needless to say, it was an interesting evening and there were many questions (all recorded as is our practise). The answer to one question that was put towards the end of the session may help to redress any unfair bias.

Q: *'Might I enquire how you regard the collective prayer in a church where all are speaking ... thinking together?'*

A: ~ *'Yes, it is difficult to give you one answer to this because with so many people being individual spirits, they are praying in different ways. You will have those who repeat words because it is words that they are used to saying. Those thoughts will not have great impact but there will be others within that congregation whose prayers and thoughts reach the targets that they are intended for.'*

Q: *'It very much comes down to the individual...'*

A: ~ *'Yes, I would suggest so ... yes. It is wrong, and I have heard it said that churches today ... it matters not what denomination ... that churches have no use for these masses of people uttering so many repetitive words. Do not dismiss it so lightly. Much good does come from such people ... those who are genuine, whether they know of their spiritual self or not ... because, after all, it is the spirit within which is at work. Do you understand this?'*

Q: *'I have always felt that the Church is an overt spiritual happening and it can set an individual on a particular course...'*

A: ~ *'Yes, you cannot dismiss out of hand all churches. Many of your great ... I believe you call them cathedrals ... and mosques ... all of these places, it matters not ... it is what is in the hearts of those people. It is the blending of spirit which counts. So* *again I would say this to you ... and I know this has been told to you many times ... do not judge others. Do not suppose that your prayers are any better than another human being's, because in judging thus, you are erroneous in your thinking.'*

I am very pleased to be able to add this late entry. It states in such concise and unquestionable terms the value that prayer may have when delivered up from the formal place of worship. And as has been stated in earlier text, its strength ... the power of prayer ... comes down to what is in the hearts of the people.

Appendix V

Subtleties of Vibration and Spirit

It was during the evening of 29th February 2000, about a year following the writing of the final chapter, that I was able to put a question to Salumet concerning the subtle coming together or union of physical vibration and spiritual vibration. Our teacher had spoken to us previously about the way vibration quickens as the spirit continues to progress in the realms beyond Earth. My scientific question and his clear answer may be seen to connect quite well with what I was attempting to say about how our improved perception might be in the mid-21st century.

Q: *'You talked to us recently about the quickening vibration in spirit and the way the vibration quickens until it is at one with source. It seems to me that there is a very striking parallel in the physical world. Our scientists can accelerate particles of matter and if a particle, such as an electron, is accelerated to approach the speed of light, it is said to approach infinite mass. I prefer to think of it as becoming one with its environment which would seem to be a route to infinite mass, and again the tiny particle we are told, can be regarded as a vibration. It seems that there is a very striking parallel between, shall I say, the edge of the physical world and the quickening vibration of spirit?'*

A: ~ *'I am not surprised by this question you have made. You of intellectual thinking would see this connection. Of course, when you are speaking of particles and mass and electrons and such, you are speaking of slightly slower vibration as compared to that in our world. I know you understand this, but the parallel is almost a perfect one ... not quite, but I can see the way of your thinking.'*

Q: *'It is almost, I would say* **almost,** *as if this edge of the physical is reaching out as a bridge to the spiritual world. It is probably quite wrong of me to think that, but I am tempted to see it as that...'*

A: ~ *'It is not a bridge. After all, the physical and the spiritual world* ***is*** *intertwined. Can you not see that there has to be the passing from one to the other? Therefore you might say that the higher vibration of your physical world is the lower vibration of the spiritual world. You must not try to separate the two. After all, all things within your planet, within the cosmos, belongs to spirit first and foremost. All vibration is spiritual in the sense that it is intertwined with all things material and physical. So, in your intelligent way of thinking, try to see these things as belonging to each other rather than trying to separate them, then you will have a greater understanding.'*

Q: *'Less of a bridge and more merging...'*

***A:* ~** *'Merging, not a bridge. That is the best way to put it to you. I feel these words will give you much to think of this time. I know you will come back to me and we will continue along these lines. Thank you for your question.'*

Appendix VI

On the Nature of Soul and Divinity

As time moves on, our teachings from Salumet more frequently turn to the nature of spirit and spiritual development. Sometimes we would learn a little of how things are 'structured' in those domains beyond our Earth. There have been occasions when I have put questions, rightly or wrongly, in an almost 'scientific' manner in an endeavour to get the physical mind to encompass the details about other realms. It is otherwise difficult for the underdeveloped physical mind to grasp ideas that simply have no physical basis. On 15 May 2,000 the following conversation took place and I make it a last minute inclusion in this work because it seems important and I feel it a privilege that we have such information:

Q: *'One of our failings is that we are not very good with the use of our own words. We get a little confused sometimes. It is good therefore if we can have definitions of words, and it would help me if we could begin by defining 'soul' ... which I think strictly is spirit or an entity in spirit and I believe a small part of that soul may be involved in Earth life ... physical life. The greater part of the soul will always be in spirit. Is that strictly correct for a start?'*

A: *~ 'Yes, there is much confusion in your world about the use of the words 'spirit' and 'soul'. Yes, let me clarify this for you. Yes, to clarify this for you, you are spirit. We come from the world of spirit ... That is words used because it simplifies what we have to do. But the spirit that is you here and now ... is but a tiny iota of the soul. This is where the confusion lies: many people feel that the soul is one entity within the human form.'*

Q: *'I think we sometimes refer to that part of the soul which is in spirit as the 'higher self'?'*

A: *~ 'That is part of the soul.'*

Q: *'The higher self would be the greater part of the soul?'*

A: *~ 'Not the greater part. Remember, I have told you that there are many parts to the soul and my dear friend, the diamond ... the facets of the diamond and then you will begin to understand ... the* ***facet*** *of the diamond is perhaps the higher self of the spirit that is here now. Do you understand? We are moving here into deep matters but I hope that will clarify it for you just a little. The spirit here within the human form is but one spark or one facet or one small piece ... choose your own phraseology ... but it is one small part of the whole.'*

Q: *'And that small part can have several Earth lives ... may reincarnate several times?'*

A: *~ 'Different facets, yes, yes.'*

Q: *'I just wanted to clarify that that same facet of soul could have several lives?'*

A: *~ 'Yes, yes, I understand. That one facet of the soul may return to your world many, many times. If the failure of the spirit in the human form ... fails in its mission, then it will return or accept that another facet of the soul needs to return in its place for a certain length of time.'*

Q: *'It could be either way?'*

A: *~ 'Yes, we are onto complex issues here.'*

Q: *'I think you also said (on a previous occasion) that more than one facet could have Earth life at the same time, but this would be very rare?'*

A: *~ 'Yes, it is not ... how should I say to you ... usual in the sense you would understand, but it happens, yes. But normally one facet of the soul returns to this planet at any one given time. Is that helpful to you? Are you happy with that explanation?'*

Q: *'Yes ... I was just wondering if the soul ... which is itself moving on ...'*

A: *~ 'Yes, I understand.'*

Q: *'I was just wondering if there was any further conglomeration of souls?*

A: *~ 'Yes. You must also understand that as I speak of soul, there are again many facets of soul which, as we move as energy, is also moving ... will join and expand and increase. And I think this is where you are falling down in trying to understand what happens to soul.* **It is not spirit returning to one soul in one time.** *There are many facets to the soul and the soul belongs to a much ... I use the expression: larger soul ... but it is actually a joining with Divine energy. These are difficult things to explain to you. The understanding is not there and will not be for some greater time, but try to imagine that the soul joins with the other moving Divine energy. It becomes a much larger issue.'*

Q: *'And you yourself would come to us from that ... that further domain?'*

A: *~ 'Part of me, yes. I am but one smaller issue from that Divine soul. It is difficult, is it not?'*

'But it does help to make it clearer for me. Thank you very much!'

A: *~ 'Yes ... I ... as I am speaking to you now through the human form ... am part of that Divinity which has come to your planet to help mankind expand its knowledge. I do not belong to the lower-integrated-smaller-version of what you call soul. No. It is something that we will speak about further on another occasion because it is a vast subject that I feel you are not quite ready for.'*

I was left with the feeling that our teacher had been extremely patient with my questioning for which I am most grateful. His answers provide a valuable picture of the complexity of soul. And it does not matter if that picture is hazy. It is difficult for those of us who live on the physical planet to fully grasp the details. But we each are an *iota* of soul that springs from that *lower-integrated-smaller-version* of soul system. (I think the scientific construct of words was probably for my benefit!) And this system is further integrated with the Divinity, whence come our teacher and other Masters.

Appendix VII

A Fond Farewell

Early in 1999, Leslie left Kingsclere for what he described as: '*... the so far unexplored and bewildering East Coast.*' There, although now physically frail, he would enjoy the company of his family. He kept in touch. There were letters and phone calls. Then as autumn approached, we learned that our dear friend of so many evenings together had passed to spirit. His family reported seeing a blue light.

The Kingsclere Monday meetings continue, now at Lilian's place. Salumet continues to come through to us and we have had the welcome news from the other side, that Leslie has been met and most well received. The sessions that we now have are mostly the teaching and spiritual knowledge, with questions to enhance our understanding.

On the evening of 17 January 2000, questions were invited and for my question, I returned yet again to 'power of thought'. We had been well instructed about the huge power that thought can have. I wanted to clarify that there are different categories of thought and some would carry no weight at all. The storywriter or actor, for example, would have no intention of projecting the words beyond their page or stage. The answer came clearly:

A: *~ 'Remember that although you are spirit, you are clothed in physical garb. You also have a brain that is within that physical garb. The power of thought that I speak of is the thought of the spirit.* ***That*** *is the power of thought. There is much thinking which is negligible within your lives. Of course there must be. It is when you come to the deep thought that comes from the spirit within ... there! lies the power of your thought. That is the power of thinking that you must be careful of because not only can it do good but you have the ability to affect many others also. You should be able to differentiate between the two and you have given a good example ... a good example of speaking about the writer and the actor upon the stage. These are everyday thoughts. Remember too in your dreamstate, many of your thoughts are flippant but many are spirit inspired ... Do not be afraid that every feeling, every thought is captured forever. That is not quite true and it is misunderstood by many, many people upon your Earth. Is this a little clearer for you?*

I say, my dear friends, that once more you become confused between what is spiritual and what is physical. I know it is difficult always to see yourselves as spiritual beings, but that is what you strive towards. If ever you are in doubt, go within. I have told you on many, many occasions, the answers to all things lies within you.'

Indeed, Salumet had spoken to us before ... of going within, of the difference between the *ego I* and the *Divine I am,* the voice of Divinity being always humble, gentle and loving ... of the *need* to go within ... where lies truth in abundance. It is a blessing that our Monday evenings continue and perhaps ... one never knows from one week to the next ... but perhaps there may be further news of our dear friend.

Salumet left us on this occasion with some particularly fine words of wisdom:

~'I say to you ... Seek only truth,
Seek only to help those in need,
Seek to shine forth to all those that you meet, but
I say to you ... Do it with humility and love that you all possess.
I leave you ... Encompassed as always within my love.'

Selected Bibliography

Part 1:

Richard Leakey and Roger Lewin, *Origins Reconsidered*, Little, Brown & Co., London, 1992.

Richard Leakey, *The Origin of Humankind*, Weidenfeld & Nicolson, London, 1994.

Robert Lawlor, *Voices of the First Day*, Inner Traditions International Ltd., Rochester, Vermont, 1991.

James G. Cowan, *The Aborigine Tradition*, Element Books Ltd., Shaftesbury, 1992.

Kilton Stewart, *Pygmies and Dream Giants*, The Scientific Book Club, London.

Dr Sonia M Zaide, *Philippine History and Government*, All-Nations Publishing Co. Inc., Quezon City, Philippines, 1998.

John Costello, *The Pacific War*, Collins, London, 1981.

Edwin P. Hoyt, *Japan's War The Great Pacific Conflict*, Hutchinson, London, 1986.

Winston Churchill, *The Second World War*, Cassell & Co. Ltd, London, 1950.

Gerhard L. Weinberg, *A World at Arms*, Cambridge University Press, 1994.

David Maybury-Lewis, *Millennium Tribal Wisdom and the Modern World*, Viking Penguin, New York, 1992.

Ronald Hutton, *The Shamans of Siberia*, The Isle of Avalon Press, Glastonbury, UK, 1993.

Kenneth Meadows, *The Medicine Way A Shamanic Path to Self-Mastery*, Element Books Ltd., Shaftesbury, 1990.

Linda Schele and David Freidel, *A Forest of Kings*, William Morrow & Co. Inc., New York, 1990.

Delia Goetz and Sylvanus G. Morley from translation of Adrián Recinos, *Popol Vuh The Sacred Book of the Ancient Quiché Maya*, University of Oklahoma Press, 1950.

Alma M. Reed, *The Ancient Past of Mexico*, Paul Hamlyn Ltd., London, 1966.

Adrian G. Gilbert & Maurice M. Cotterell, *The Mayan Prophecies*, Element Books Ltd, Shaftesbury, 1995.

Sandy Huff, *The Mayan Calendar Made Easy*, Sandy Huff, Safety Harbour, Florida, 1984.

Jack Schwarz, *Human Energy Systems*, Dutton, New York, 1980.

Dr. David Flores, *Psilocybe Caerulesens Murray, Variety Mazatecorum Initiating a Pathogenesia*, Toledo de Homeopatía de México.
Chris Griscom, *Time is an Illusion*, Simon & Schuster Inc., New York, 1988.

Part 2:

J. G. Frazer, *The Golden Bough*, Macmillan Publishers Ltd., London, 1987.
Robert Graves, *The White Goddess*, Faber & Faber, London, 1961.
Michael Jordan, *Gods of the Earth*, Bantam Press, London, 1992.
Ferrar Fenton, *The Holy Bible in Modern English*, Adam & Charles Black, London, 1938.
Homer, *The Odyssey*, Translated by A. T. Murray, Loeb Classical Library, Harvard/Heinemann, Cambridge, Mass./London, 1919.
Muhammad, *The Koran*, Translated from Arabic by J. M. Rodwell, Everyman's Library, London/Vermont, 1909.
David Fasold, *The Discovery of Noah's Ark*, Sidgwick & Jackson, London, 1990.
Henrietta McCall, *Mesopotamian Myths*, British Museum Publications Ltd., London, 1990.
N. K. Sandars, *The Epic of Gilgamesh*, Penguin Books, 1960.
George B. Quatman, revised Joseph B. Quatman, *House of Our Lady*, The American Society of Ephesus Inc., Lima, Ohio, 1991.
Desmond Seward, *The Dancing Sun. Journeys to the Miracle Shrines*, MacMillan, London, 1993.
Patrick Marnham, *Lourdes. A Modern Pilgrimage,* Heineman, London, 1980.
David Wallechinsky, Amy Wallace, Irving Wallace, *The Book of Predictions*, Elm Tree Books, London, 1981.
J. N. D. Kelly, *The Oxford Dictionary of Popes*, Oxford University Press, 1986.
Michael Walsh, *An Illustrated History of the Popes*, Marshall Cavendish Editions, London, 1980.
John Hogue, *The Last Pope*, Element Books Ltd, Shaftesbury, 1998.
C. W. Ceram, *Gods Graves & Scholars*, Victor Gollancz & Sidgwick & Jackson, London, 1952.
John Steinbeck, *Russian Journey*, 'Illustrated' magazine, May 1, 1948, Publ. Odham's Press Ltd., London.
Benjamin Wilson, *The Emphatic Diaglott* of what is commonly styled the New Testament, published by the International Bible Students Association and Watchtower Bible and Tract Society, New York, 1942.

Paramahansa Yogananda *Autobiography of a Yogi*, Self-Realization Fellowship, Los Angeles, 1998.
Robert Eisenman & Michael Wise, *The Dead Sea Scrolls Uncovered*, Element, Shaftesbury, 1992.
E. J. Brill, *The Gospel According to Thomas*, Translated by A. Guillaumont, H.-Ch. Puech, G. Quispel, W. Till and Yassah 'Abd Al Masïh, Leiden, Netherlands, 1976.
Henry C. Roberts, *The Complete Prophecies of Nostradamus*, (1947), Revised Lee Roberts Amsterdam & Harvey Amsterdam, HarperCollins Publishers Ltd, 1984.
Erika Cheetham, *The Prophecies of Nostradamus*, Corgi, London, 1982.
Erika Cheetham, *The Further Prophecies of Nostradamus 1985 and Beyond*, Corgi, London, 1985.
Alan Wykes, *Hitler*, Pan Ballantine, London, 1973.
Alan Bullock, *Hitler A Study in Tyranny*, Penguin Books, London, 1971.
François Genoud, Col. R. H. Stevens, H. R. Trevor-Roper, *The Testament of Adolf Hitler The Hitler-Bormann Documents*, Cassell, London, 1961.
Adolf Hitler, *Mein Kampf*, Translated by Ralph Manheim, Pimlico, London, 1984.
Philip Hanson Hiss & Hans Zinsser, *A Text Book of Bacteriology*, D. Appleton & Co., New York, 1912.
Clive Foss & Paul Magdalino, *Rome and Bysantium*, Elsevier-Phaidon, Oxford, 1977.
Stewart Perowne, *Caesars and Saints*, Hodder & Stoughton, London, 1962.
G. M. Durant, *Britain. Rome's Most Northerly Province*, Bell & Sons, London, 1969.
John Julius Norwich, *Bysantium. The Early Centuries*, Penguin Books, London, 1988.

Part 3:

Zoé Oldenbourg, *The Crusades*, Pantheon Books, New York, 1965.
Cynthia Sandys & Rosamond Lehmann, *The Awakening Letters*, Neville Spearman, Jersey, 1978.
James Jeans, *Physics and Philosophy*, Cambridge University Press, London, 1943.
Alma Smith Payne, *The Cleere Observer A Biography of Antoni van Leeuwenhoek*, MacMillan & Co. Ltd, London, 1970.

Chambers' Encyclopædia, W. & R. Chambers, London, 1860.
Gerald Messadié, *Great Modern Inventions*, Chambers, Edinburgh, 1991.
Gerald Messadié, *Great Inventions Through History*, Cambers, Edinberg, 1991.
Gerald Messadié, *Great Scientific Discoveries*, Chambers, Edinburgh, 1991.
Isaac Newton, *Principia Mathematica (1687)*, now available as *Mathematical Principles of Natural Philosophy*, in the series Great Books of the Western World, Encyclopædia Britannica, Chicago, 1990.
Rabindranath Tagore, *Gitanjali*, MacMillan, London, 1913.
Nigel Calder, *The Comet is Coming!*, British Broadcasting Corporation, London, 1980.
Brian Harpur, *The Official Halley's Comet Book*, Hodder & Stoughton, Sevenoaks, 1985.
J. G. Porter, *Catalogue of Cometary Orbits 1960*, British Astronomical Association, London, 1961.
L. J. Cheney, *A History of the Western World*, George Allen & Unwin Ltd, London, 1959.
H. A. L. Fisher, *A History of Europe,* Edward Arnold & Co, London, 1946.
Alexander Hellemans and Bryan Bunch, *The Timetables of Science*, Simon and Schuster, New York, 1988.
Bernard Grun, *Timetables of History*, Simon and Schuster, New York, 1979.
John Aubrey, *Brief Lives*, A modern English version edited by Richard Barber, The Boydell Press, Woodbridge 1982.
Daniel Defoe, *A Journal of the Plague Year*, J. M. Dent & Sons, London, 1936.
Christopher White, *Rembrandt*, Thames and Hudson, London, 1984.
Paul Zumthor, *Daily Life in Rembrandt's Holland*, translated by Simon Watson Taylor, Weidenfeld and Nicolson, London, 1962.
The Poetical Works of John Dryden, (With Memoir, Notes...), Frederick Warne & Co, London, 1893.
Swami Rama, *Living with the Himalayan Masters*, Himalayan International Institute of Yoga Science & Philosophy of the USA, Honesdale, Pennsylvania, 1980.
Margaret Cheney, *Tesla Man Out of Time*, Dorset Press, New York, 1989.
Derrik Mercer, Editor-in-chief, *Chronicle of the 20th Century*, Dorling Kindersley, London, 1995.

Part 4:

D. H. S. Nicholson and A. H. E. Lee, *The Oxford Book of English Mystical Verse*, Acropolis Books, Atlanta, Georgia, 1997, First published in England by Oxford University Press in 1917.
Graham Smith, *Death of a Rose Grower*, Cecil Woolf, London, 1985.
Judith Cook, *Who Killed Hilda Murrell?*, New English Library, Sevenoaks, Kent, 1985.
The Sunday Times Insight Team, Editors Robin Morgan, Brian Whitaker, *Rainbow Warrior*, Arrow Books Ltd, London, 1986.
Joan Ruddock, *CND Scrapbook*, MacDonald Optima, London 1987.
Albert Einstein, *The World As I See It*, Translation of *Mein Weltbild* by Alan Harris, John Lane the Bodley Head Ltd, 1935.
Bob Geldof, *Is That It?*, Macmillan Publishers Ltd, London, 1986.
A. Belyayev, Editor, *XX Century and Peace, November 1986 issue*, The Soviet Peace Committee, Moscow, 1986.
Pat Delgano & Colin Andrews, *Circular Evidence*, Bloomsbury, London, 1989.
Pat Delgano & Colin Andrews, *The Latest Evidence*, Bloomsbury, London, 1990.
Terence Meaden (Ed.), *Circles From the Sky*, Souvenir Press, London, 1991.
Alick Bartholemew, *Crop Circles Harbingers of World Change*, Gateway Books, Bath, 1991.
John Michell (Ed.), *Dowsing the Crop Circles*, Gothic Image, Glastonbury, 1991.
Beth Davis (Ed.), *Ciphers in the Crops*, Gateway Books, Bath, 1992.
Paul Devereux, *Earth Lights Revelation*, Blandford Press, London, 1989.
Hamish Miller & Paul Broadhurst, *The Sun and the Serpent*, Pendragon Press, Launceston, 1989.
Kathy Jones, *The Ancient British Goddess*, Ariadne, Glastonbury, 1991.
Michael Poynder, *Pi in the Sky*, Rider, London, 1992.
Paul Devereux & Ian Thomson, *The Ley Guide, The Mystery of Aligned Ancient Sites*, Empress, 1987.
Ferdinand Anton, *Ancient Peruvian Textiles*, Translated from *Altindianische Textilkunst aus Peru* by Michael Heron, Thames and Hudson, London, 1987.
Stephen W. Hawking, *A Brief History of Time*, Bantam Press, London, 1988.

Rev. G. Vale Owen, *The Highlands of Heaven*, The Greater World Christian Spiritualist Association, London, 1982.
Roger Woolger, *Other Lives Other Selves*, HarperCollins Publishers Ltd., London, 1999.
Stoker Hunt, *Ouija, The Most Dangerous Game*, Harper & Row, New York, 1985.
Linda Chard, *Dr Kahn: The Spirit Surgeon*, Elmore - Chard, London, 1992.
John G. Fuller, *Arigo: Surgeon of the Rusty Knife*, Hart-Davis, MacGibbon, London, 1975.
Anthony Borgia, *Life in the World Unseen*, Psychic Press, London, 1985.
Leslie Bone NFSH, *Conversations with 'Salumet'. Transcripts of conversations in which a highly evolved spirit communicator answers questions on a wide variety of subjects affecting our lives.* Unpublished mss.
Antonia Fraser, *Mary Queen of Scots*, Weidenfeld & Nicolson, London, 1985.
Vincent Cronin, *Catherine, Empress of All the Russias*, The Harvill Press, London, 1978.
Lynne McTaggart, *What Doctors Don't Tell You*, Thorsons, London, 1996.
Nancy Appleton, *Healthy Bones*, Avery Publishing Group, New York, 1991.
John Davidson, *The Web of Life*, The C. W. Daniel Co, Saffron Walden, 1988.
Renée Weber, *Dialogues with Scientists and Sages*, Ankana Penguin, 1986.
John Colville, *The Fringes of Power Downing Street Diaries 1939-1955*, Hodder and Stoughton, London, 1985.
Graham Hancock, *Fingerprints of the Gods*, William Heinemann, London, 1995.
Lewis Spence, *The Illustrated Guide to Egyptian Mythology*, Studio, London, 1996.
Ahmed Osman, *Out of Egypt*, Century, London, 1998.
Timothy Freke & Peter Gandy, *The Hermetica*, Piatkus, London, 1997.
Paul Davis & John Gribbin, *The Matter Myth*, Viking Penguin, London, 1991.
Eric J. Lerner, *The Big Bang Never Happened*, Simon & Schuster, London, 1992.
Ervin Laszlo, *The Creative Cosmos*, Floris Books, Edinburgh, 1993.
Michael Talbot, *The Holographic Universe*, Grafton Books, London, 1991.
Lyall Watson, *Supernature*, Book Club Associates, London, 1974.
Published by the President, Advaita Ashrama, Mayavati, Pithoragarh, Himalayas, India, *The Teachings of Swami Vivekananda, 1981.*

Joel S. Goldsmith, *A Parenthesis in Eternity*, Harper & Row, New York, 1986.
Michael Drosnin, *The Bible Code*, Weidenfeld & Nicolson, London, 1997.
Jeffrey Satinover, *The Truth Behind The Bible Code*, Sidgwick & Jackson, London, 1997.